The Law of Impaired Driving

and Related Implied Consent Offenses in North Carolina

2014

Shea Riggsbee Denning

UNC
SCHOOL OF GOVERNMENT

Printed in the United States of America

21 20 19 18 17 2 3 4 5 6

ISBN 978-1-56011-757-5

Contents

Chapter 2

Implied Consent Offenses

Chapter 4

Motions and Motions Procedures in Implied Consent Cases

Chapter 5

Sentencing under G.S. 20-179

Tables

Preface

This book builds upon the foundation of an earlier publication by my colleagues, the late Ben F. Loeb, Jr. and James C. Drennan, *Motor Vehicle Law and The Law of Impaired Driving in North Carolina.* It is not, however, a new edition of that work, as this book focuses exclusively on the law of impaired driving and related implied consent offenses. This book does not cover other rules of the road, driver's license law, or motor vehicle liability insurance—topics that were addressed in Loeb and Drennan's earlier work.

My colleagues James Drennan, Robert Farb, and James Markham helped with the book by reading chapters and providing substantive feedback. The book is better as a result. Matt Osborne of the Administrative Office of the Courts also took time out of his busy schedule to read draft chapters. I'm grateful for his keen eye and his deep understanding of the law governing civil license revocations and vehicle forfeitures. Christopher Tyner performed a detailed cite-check of the entire book, and Melissa Twomey edited the work. Both of them improved the work technically and substantively. I welcome comments about this publication's scope, organization, or content. Comments may be sent to me at denning@sog.unc.edu.

This book is dedicated to my colleague and mentor James "Jim" Drennan, who retired this year after spending forty years on the faculty of the School of Government. I work in just one of the many legal fields that Jim covered during his time here. Jim's intellect and knowledge are vast, and I am lucky that he has shared so much of what he knows about motor vehicle law with me. What I appreciate even more, however, is the opportunity to observe a true role model. Jim's interactions with everyone—clients, colleagues, friends, and strangers—reflected the ideals of integrity, kindness, and humility. Jim has led and continues to lead a balanced, engaged, and meaningful life, and I am honored to travel in his wake.

Shea Riggsbee Denning
Chapel Hill
November 2014

Chapter 1

Implied Consent Laws: Theory and Procedure

Chapter 1

Implied Consent Laws: Theory and Procedure

I. Introduction

Driving while impaired and several related criminal offenses involving the consumption of alcohol or other impairing substances are categorized under the North Carolina General Statutes (hereinafter G.S.) as implied consent offenses. When a person is charged with or arrested for an implied consent offense, the officer may require the person to undergo chemical testing for purposes of detecting the presence of alcohol and other impairing substances and measuring their concentration. If a person refuses to submit to such testing, the person's license may be administratively revoked and the refusal may be considered as substantive evidence of his or her guilt of the underlying criminal charges. This chapter reviews the statutory scheme governing the chemical analysis of a person's breath or other bodily fluids in an implied consent case as well as the legal theory of implied consent.

II. Implied Consent Testing

The following offenses are categorized as implied consent offenses:[1]

- Impaired driving (G.S. 20-138.1)
- Impaired driving in a commercial vehicle (G.S. 20-138.2)
- Habitual impaired driving (G.S. 20-138.5)
- Death by vehicle or serious injury by vehicle (G.S. 20-141.4)
- First- or second-degree murder (G.S. 14-17) or involuntary manslaughter (G.S. 14-18) when based on impaired driving
- Driving by a person less than 21 years old after consuming alcohol or drugs (G.S. 20-138.3)
- Violating no-alcohol condition of limited driving privilege (G.S. 20-179.3(j))
- Impaired instruction (G.S. 20-12.1)
- Operating commercial motor vehicle after consuming alcohol (G.S. 20-138.2A)

---

1. *See* Chapter 20, Sections 16.2(a1) and 4.01(24a) of the North Carolina General Statutes (hereinafter G.S.).

- Operating school bus, school activity bus, child care vehicle, ambulance or other EMS vehicle, firefighting vehicle, or law enforcement vehicle after consuming alcohol (G.S. 20-138.2B)
- Transporting an open container of alcohol (G.S. 20-138.7(a))
- Driving in violation of restriction requiring ignition interlock (G.S. 20-17.8(f))

When a person is arrested for an implied consent offense, or if criminal process has been issued, including a citation, a law enforcement officer who has reasonable grounds to believe that the person charged has committed the offense may require that person to undergo chemical analysis.[2] The officer is authorized to transport the accused to any location within North Carolina for the purposes of administering one or more chemical analyses.[3]

North Carolina law defines "chemical analysis" as a test or tests of the breath, blood, or other bodily fluid or substance of a person performed in compliance with statutory requirements to determine the person's blood alcohol level or the presence of an impairing substance.[4] The concentration of alcohol in a person is expressed either as grams of alcohol per 100 milliliters of blood or as grams of alcohol per 210 liters of breath.[5] The results of a defendant's alcohol concentration determined by a chemical analysis are reported to the hundredths, with any result between hundredths reported to the next-lower hundredth.[6]

While any competent evidence of a defendant's alcohol concentration that is lawfully obtained may be introduced in a defendant's trial on implied consent charges,[7] the State enjoys several advantages when it seeks to admit the results of a chemical analysis performed pursuant to G.S. 20-139.1. First, such results are deemed admissible by statute[8] without the need for further evidence as to the scientific reliability of the instrument used or the validity of the underlying scientific principles.[9] Second, the results of a chemical analysis are "deemed sufficient evidence to prove a person's alcohol concentration."[10] This means that, in the context of a case in which the defendant's alcohol concentration as reported by a chemical analysis is 0.08 or more, the introduction of the results of the chemical analysis satisfies the State's burden to present prima facie evidence of impairment.[11]

---

2. G.S. 20-16.2(a).

3. *Id.* § 20-38.3(2).

4. *Id.* § 20-4.01(3a).

5. *Id.* § 20-4.01(1b). The alcohol concentration for breath tests is based on an assumption that a breath alcohol concentration of 0.10 grams per 210 liters of breath is equivalent to a blood alcohol concentration of 0.10 percent, or, in other words, a 2,100 to 1 blood-breath ratio. *See* State v. Cothran, 120 N.C. App. 633, 635 (1995).

6. G.S. 20-4.01(1b).

7. *See id.* § 20-139.1(a); *see also* State v. Davis, 142 N.C. App. 81, 87 (2001) (holding that results of blood and urine tests obtained pursuant to search warrant issued after defendant refused blood test were properly admitted at defendant's impaired driving trial, as "the General Assembly does not limit the admissibility of competent evidence lawfully obtained").

8. G.S. 20-139.1(a), (b).

9. *See* State v. Powell, 279 N.C. 608 (1971); State v. George, 77 N.C. App. 470 (1985).

10. *See* G.S. 20-138.1(a)(2) ("The results of a chemical analysis shall be deemed sufficient evidence to prove a person's alcohol concentration.").

11. *See* State v. Narron, 193 N.C. App. 76, 84 (2008) (construing G.S. 20-138.1(a)(2) as providing that the results of a chemical analysis constitute prima facie evidence of the defendant's alcohol concentration, thereby authorizing the jury to find that the report adequately proves the defendant's alcohol concentration).

A. Implied Consent Rights

Before any type of chemical analysis is administered, a person charged with an implied consent offense must be taken before a chemical analyst authorized to administer a test of the person's breath or a law enforcement officer authorized to administer a chemical analysis of the breath.[12] The term "chemical analyst" is defined as a person granted a permit by the Department of Health and Human Services (DHHS) under G.S. 20-139.1 to perform such analyses.[13] The chemical analyst must first inform the person charged as to, and provide that person with notice in writing of, the following rights:

(1) You have been charged with an implied-consent offense. Under the implied-consent law, you can refuse any test, but your drivers [sic] license will be revoked for one year and could be revoked for a longer period of time under certain circumstances, and an officer can compel you to be tested under other laws.
(2) [Repealed, 2006]
(3) The test results, or the fact of your refusal, will be admissible in evidence at trial.
(4) Your driving privilege will be revoked immediately for at least 30 days if you refuse any test or if the test result is 0.08 or more, 0.04 or more if you were driving a commercial vehicle, or 0.01 or more if you are under the age of 21.
(5) After you are released, you may seek your own test in addition to this test.
(6) You may call an attorney for advice and select a witness to view the testing procedures remaining after the witness arrives, but the testing may not be delayed for these purposes longer than 30 minutes from the time you are notified of these rights. You must take the test at the end of 30 minutes even if you have not contacted an attorney or your witness has not arrived.[14]

These rights are printed on a form created by DHHS.[15] There is a place on the form for the signature of the person charged. Normally, the notice of rights is read to and a copy handed to a defendant, who then signs the form. Sometimes, however, handing the form to a defendant for his or her signature is not possible due to the defendant's condition. One such circumstance arose in *State v. Lovett*,[16] a case in which the defendant's hands were strapped down in the emergency room and needles for intravenous fluids were in both arms. The chemical analyst in *Lovett* placed the written rights form with defendant's emergency room chart. The North Carolina Court of Appeals determined that this "was tantamount to 'giving' defendant notice in writing."[17] Noting that "[i]n light of the treatment defendant

---

12. G.S. 20-16.2(a).

13. *Id.* § 20-4.01(3b). The requirements for obtaining a permit to perform an analysis of a person's breath to determine his or her alcohol concentration are set forth in Title 10A of the North Carolina Administrative Code (hereinafter N.C.A.C.), Subchapter 41B, Section .0301. For purposes of determining whether the person performing the analysis had a current permit, the court or administrative agency "shall take judicial notice" of the lists of persons possessing permits. G.S. 20-139.1(b), (c).

14. G.S. 20-16.2(a). The North Carolina Supreme Court in *State v. Howren*, 312 N.C. 454 (1984), held that the administration of a chemical analysis to determine if a driver is impaired by an impairing substance is not a critical stage of the prosecution; thus, the defendant has no Sixth Amendment right to have counsel present before deciding whether to take or refuse a breath test and is not entitled more than the thirty minutes provided in G.S. 20-16.2 to secure a lawyer.

15. The form is designated DHHS 4081.

16. 119 N.C. App. 689 (1995).

17. *Id.* at 693.

was receiving for his injuries, there was effectively no other means by which the notice could have been given to him," the court determined that the defendant clearly was informed of his rights.[18]

The State does not have to prove that the defendant read the notice of rights form,[19] nor, apparently, that he or she understood the rights.[20] The court of appeals in *State v. Carpenter*[21] determined that a chemical analyst fully complied with the advisement requirements in G.S. 20-16.2(a) by orally advising the defendant of his implied consent rights and placing the required information in writing before the defendant, who had an opportunity to read the information.[22] Were the rule otherwise, the court explained, "any belligerent or uncooperative defendant" could defeat evidence of test results "by merely refusing to read the information that was placed before him."[23]

If a law enforcement officer has reasonable grounds to believe that a person has committed an implied consent offense, and the person is unconscious or otherwise in a condition that makes the person incapable of refusing the test, the officer may direct the taking of a blood sample or the administration of any other type of chemical analysis that may be effectively performed.[24] There is no statutory requirement that the chemical analyst inform such a person of the implied consent rights in G.S. 20-16.2(a) or that the person be asked to submit to the analysis pursuant to G.S. 20-16.2(c).[25]

B. Administering a Chemical Analysis

The law enforcement officer or the chemical analyst designates the type of test or tests to be administered, that is, a test of blood, breath, or urine.[26] The officer or chemical analyst then asks the person to submit to the designated type of chemical analysis.[27] If the person charged "willfully refuses to submit

---

18. *Id.*

19. State v. Carpenter, 34 N.C. App. 742 (1977).

20. G.S. 20-16.2 is designed "to provide scientific evidence of intoxication not only for the purpose of convicting the guilty and removing them from the public highways for the safety of others, but also to protect the innocent by eliminating mistakes from objective observation such as a driver who has the odor of alcohol on his breath when in fact his consumption is little or those who appear to be intoxicated but actually suffer from some unrelated cause." Seders v. Powell, 298 N.C. 453, 464–65 (1979). The warnings "ensure[] civil cooperation in providing scientific evidence and avoid[] incidents of violence in testing by force." *Id.* at 465. Given that notice is provided to secure submission to a chemical analysis rather than to procure a knowing, voluntary, and intelligent waiver of rights, the statutory purposes arguably are met when the person submits to testing, regardless of whether the person knew of the right to refuse testing. *See* Yokoyama v. Comm'r of Pub. Safety, 356 N.W.2d 830, 831 (Minn. Ct. App. 1984) (rejecting the argument of a petitioner who "willingly blew into the testing machine" that he had a statutory right to have the implied consent advisory read to him in Japanese and finding that he "understood he was being asked to take the test," which was the only understanding required); Martinez v. Peterson, 322 N.W.2d 386, 388 (Neb. 1982) (citations omitted) (holding that person is required to understand only that he or she has been asked to take a test and that "[t]here is no defense to refusal that [the person] does not understand the consequences of refusal or is not able to make a reasonable judgment as to what course of action to take"); *cf.* Sermons v. Peters, 51 N.C. App. 147, 150 (1981) (explaining that officers had no duty to explain the statutory rights relative to the granting of a limited driving privilege, as "[w]hether or not the petitioner would have taken the breathalyzer test had he been aware of the law is irrelevant").

21. 34 N.C. App. 742 (1977).

22. *Id.* at 744.

23. *Id.*

24. G.S. 20-16.2(b).

25. *Id.*

26. *Id.* § 20-16.2(c). Tests of urine are the only type of test of "other bodily fluid[s] or substances[s]" (*see id.* § 20-4.01(3a)) currently conducted pursuant to the implied consent procedures.

27. *Id.* § 20-16.2(c).

to that chemical analysis, none may be given under [G.S. 20-16.2]."[28] The refusal does not, however, preclude testing pursuant to other applicable procedures of law,[29] such as pursuant to a search warrant or the exigency exception to the search warrant requirement of the Fourth Amendment to the United States Constitution.[30]

1. Breath Tests

Chemical analyses are most frequently obtained through utilization of a breath-testing instrument.[31] DHHS approves breath-testing instruments on the basis of results of evaluations by the department's Forensic Tests for Alcohol Branch.[32] The breath-testing instrument currently authorized and used is the Intoximeter, Model Intox EC/IR II.[33] The operational procedures for the instrument are prescribed by statute and administrative regulation.[34] The person being tested must be observed to ensure that he or she has not ingested alcohol or other fluids or regurgitated, vomited, eaten, or smoked in the fifteen minutes before the collection of a breath specimen.[35] At least two sequential breath samples must be tested.[36] The results of the chemical analysis of all breath samples is admissible in evidence in any court or administrative hearing if the test results from any two consecutively collected breath samples do not differ from each other by an alcohol concentration of more than 0.02.[37] Only the lower of the two test results of the consecutively administered tests may be used to prove a particular alcohol

---

28. *Id.*

29. *Id.*; *see also* State v. Davis, 142 N.C. App. 81, 87 (2001) (holding that results of blood and urine tests obtained pursuant to search warrant issued after defendant refused blood test were properly admitted at defendant's impaired driving trial, as "the General Assembly does not limit the admissibility of competent evidence lawfully obtained").

30. *See* G.S. 20-139.1(d1) (providing that if a person refuses to submit to a test, a law enforcement officer with probable cause may, without a court order, compel the person to provide blood or urine for analysis if the officer reasonably believes that the delay necessary to obtain a court order would result in the dissipation of the percentage of alcohol in the person's blood or urine) *and* State v. Fletcher, 202 N.C. App. 107 (2010) (finding exigent circumstances warranting blood draw and upholding G.S. 20-139.1 as constitutional); *see also* Missouri v. McNeely, 133 S. Ct. 1552 (2013) (plurality opinion) (holding that in impaired driving investigations, the natural dissipation of alcohol in the bloodstream does not constitute an exigency in every case sufficient to justify conducting a blood test over a defendant's objection without a warrant); Schmerber v. California, 384 U.S. 757 (1966) (concluding that an officer's warrantless taking of the defendant's blood incident to his arrest for driving while impaired was constitutional under the Fourth Amendment where the officer reasonably believed he was confronted with an emergency in which the delay necessary to obtain a warrant threatened the dissipation of alcohol in the defendant's blood and where the blood was taken in a hospital environment according to accepted medical practices); State v. Steimel, 921 A.2d 378 (N.H. 2007) (upholding as constitutional warrantless blood draw to detect drugs incident to defendant's arrest for aggravated driving while intoxicated and refusing to distinguish between metabolization of alcohol and controlled drugs for purposes of applying the Fourth Amendment's exigency exception); People v. Ritchie, 181 Cal. Rptr. 773 (Cal. Ct. App. 1982) (upholding as constitutional warrantless blood draw to detect drugs incident to defendant's arrest for driving under the influence of drugs).

31. *See* 10A N.C.A.C. 41B, § .0101(2); *see also* G.S. 20-139.1 (chemical analysis of the breath administered pursuant to the implied consent law is admissible in court if it is performed in accordance with DHHS rules and the person performing the analysis had a current permit issued by DHHS authorizing him or her to perform a breath test using the type of instrument employed).

32. 10A N.C.A.C. 41B, § .0313.

33. *Id.* § .0322.

34. G.S. 20-139.1; 10A N.C.A.C. 41B, § .0322.

35. 10A N.C.A.C. 41B, § .0101(6).

36. G.S. 20-139.1(b3).

37. *Id.*; *see also* 10A N.C.A.C. 41B, § .0322 (directing the collection of two breath samples and providing that if the alcohol concentrations differ by more than 0.02, a third or fourth breath sample shall be collected).

concentration.[38] A person's refusal to give the sequential breath samples necessary to constitute a valid chemical analysis amounts to a refusal to submit to testing under G.S. 20-16.2(c).[39] A person's refusal to give the second or subsequent breath sample renders the result of the first breath sample, or the result of the sample providing the lowest alcohol concentration if more than one breath sample is provided, admissible in any judicial or administrative hearing for any relevant purpose.[40]

DHHS is required to perform preventative maintenance on breath-testing instruments used for chemical analysis.[41] A court or administrative agency "shall take judicial notice" of the Department's preventative maintenance records.[42] Breath test results are inadmissible if a defendant objects to their introduction and demonstrates that preventative maintenance procedures required by DHHS regulations had not been performed within the time limits required by those regulations.[43] Regulations for the breath-testing instrument currently in use, the Intoximeter, Model Intox EC/IR II, require that preventative maintenance be performed at least once every four months.[44] These instruments, unlike their predecessors, use ethanol gas canisters to provide a control sample for testing, rather than an alcoholic breath simulator.[45] Ethanol gas canisters must be changed before their expiration date.[46] A signed original of the preventive maintenance record must be kept on file for at least three years.[47]

2. Refusal

A person's willful refusal to submit to a chemical analysis may, depending on other factors, result in the revocation of his or her driver's license for a period of twelve months—in addition to resulting in the immediate civil revocation of his or her driver's license for a period of at least thirty days.[48] A refusal is "'the declination of a request or demand, or the omission to comply with some requirement of law, as the result of a positive intention to disobey.'"[49] A willful refusal occurs when a person (1) is aware that he or she has a choice to take or refuse a test, (2) is aware of the time limit within which he or she must take the test, and (3) voluntarily elects not to take the test or knowingly permits the prescribed thirty-minute time limit to expire before electing to take the test.[50] In essence, a willful refusal is a refusal that occurs after the defendant is advised of his or her implied consent rights and is asked to submit to a chemical analysis.[51]

---

38. G.S. 20-139.1(b3).
39. *Id.*
40. *Id.*
41. *Id.* § 20-139.1(b2).
42. *Id.*
43. *Id.*
44. 10A N.C.A.C. 41B, § .0323.
45. It is possible to use alcoholic breath simulator solution with these instruments, though that is not done in practice.
46. 10A N.C.A.C. 41B, § .0323.
47. *Id.*
48. G.S. 20-16.2(d); -16.5.
49. Joyner v. Garrett, 279 N.C. 226, 233 (1971) (quoting BLACK'S LAW DICTIONARY (4th ed. 1951)).
50. Etheridge v. Peters, 301 N.C. 76, 81 (1980).
51. *See, e.g.*, Rice v. Peters, 48 N.C. App. 697, 700–01 (1980) (holding that purpose of refusal-revocation statute is "fulfilled when the petitioner is given the option to submit or refuse to submit to a breathalyzer test and his decision is made after having been advised of his rights in a manner provided by the statute").

3. Blood or Urine Tests

At a law enforcement officer's discretion, a person may be asked to submit to a chemical analysis of his or her blood or urine in addition to or in lieu of a chemical analysis of his or her breath.[52] If a subsequent chemical analysis is requested, the person must again be advised of the implied consent rights under G.S. 20-16.2(a).[53] When a law enforcement officer specifies a blood or urine test as the type of chemical analysis to be conducted, a physician, registered nurse, emergency medical technician, or other qualified person must withdraw the blood sample or obtain the urine sample.[54] If the person withdrawing the blood requests written confirmation of the officer's request, the officer must furnish that request before the blood is drawn.[55] A medical provider may refuse to draw blood "if it reasonably appears that the procedure cannot be performed without endangering the safety of the person collecting the sample or the safety of the person from whom the sample is being collected."[56] An officer may request written justification for a medical provider's refusal to withdraw blood pursuant to his or her request. If the officer does so, the medical provider must provide the written justification at the time of the refusal.[57] A person's willful refusal to submit to a blood or urine test constitutes a willful refusal to submit to testing under G.S. 20-16.2.[58]

To qualify as a "chemical analysis," and thus to be admissible under G.S. 20-139.1(a), (c1), blood and urine specimens procured under the state's implied consent laws must be analyzed by an analyst who has a DHHS permit. Most of these analyses are blood analyses and are performed at the North Carolina State Crime laboratory. There are, however, other laboratories in the state that are approved by DHHS to conduct chemical analyses. Among them is the Charlotte-Mecklenburg Police Department Laboratory.[59] The results must be certified by the analyst who performed the testing.[60]

A person charged with any of the death or serious injury by vehicle offenses codified in G.S. 20-141.4[61] must be requested to provide a blood sample in addition to or in lieu of a chemical analysis of his

---

52. G.S. 20-139.1(b5).

53. *Id.*; *See* State v. Williams, ___ N.C. App. ___, 759 S.E.2d 350 (2014) (holding that the trial court did not err in suppressing the result of a chemical blood test administered to a defendant who was not re-advised of his implied consent rights after being so advised and refusing a breath test).

54. G.S. 20-139.1(c) (applicable when officer seeks withdrawal of blood from a consenting defendant or from a defendant who is unconscious or otherwise incapable of refusal; likely also applicable to withdrawal of blood in implied consent case pursuant to search warrant); (d2) (applicable to nonconsensual warrantless blood draws).

55. *Id.* §§ 20-139.1(c), (d2).

56. *Id.* § 20-139.1(c).

57. *Id.* It is unclear whether a medical provider who refuses to withdraw blood upon an officer's request pursuant to G.S. 20-139.1(c) has committed a crime. The most likely criminal charge is resisting, delaying, or obstructing an officer in violation of G.S. 14-233. For an analysis of whether a medical provider's refusal to assist an officer in light of this statutory duty amounts to resisting, delaying, or obstructing an officer, see Shea Denning, *The Requirement that Medical Providers Withdraw Blood in Implied Consent Cases*, N.C. Crim. L., UNC Sch. of Gov't Blog (Nov. 20, 2012), http://nccriminallaw.sog.unc.edu/?p=3975.

58. G.S. 20-139.1(b5).

59. *Id.* § 20-139.1(c1).

60. *Id.*

61. With the exception of the offense of misdemeanor death by vehicle, all of the offenses codified in G.S. 20-141.4 contain, as an element, impaired driving in violation of G.S. 20-138.1 or G.S. 20-138.2 (impaired driving in a commercial vehicle). Misdemeanor death by vehicle, in contrast, consists of (1) unintentionally causing the death of another person (2) while engaged in the operation of any state law or local ordinance applying to the operation or use of a vehicle or to the regulation of traffic—other than G.S. 20-138.1—that (3) proximately causes the death. G.S. 20-141.4(a2). Notwithstanding its lack of relationship to alcohol-related offenses, misdemeanor death by vehicle also is classified as an implied consent offense.

or her breath—unless the breath sample shows an alcohol concentration of 0.08 or more.[62] As with other defendants, such persons must again be advised of their implied consent rights before being asked to submit to a chemical analysis of their blood. If a person charged with death or serious injury by vehicle willfully refuses to provide a blood sample, then a law enforcement officer with probable cause to believe that the offense involved impaired driving or was an alcohol-related implied consent offense must seek a warrant to obtain a blood sample.[63]

4. Alcohol Screening Tests

A law enforcement officer may require a driver to submit to an alcohol screening test within a relevant time after driving if the officer has (1) reasonable grounds to believe that the driver had consumed alcohol and has committed a moving traffic violation or been involved in an accident or collision or (2) an articulable and reasonable suspicion that the driver has committed an implied consent offense and the driver has been lawfully stopped or "lawfully encountered by the officer in the course" of his duties.[64]

DHHS approves alcohol screening devices and adopts regulations governing the manner of their use.[65] To be valid, alcohol screening tests must be conducted in accordance with applicable regulations.[66] Even then, the results of such tests are of limited evidentiary value. A law enforcement officer may use the fact that a driver showed a positive or negative result on an alcohol screening test in determining if there are reasonable grounds (in other words, probable cause) for determining that the driver committed an implied consent offense or that the driver had consumed alcohol and the driver had in his or her body previously consumed alcohol.[67] The result may not be used to prove a particular alcohol concentration.[68] (And given that a result is positive at an alcohol concentration as low as 0.01, a positive result on an alcohol screening test, without more, does not establish reasonable grounds to believe that a person is impaired.[69]) Similarly, the fact that a result was positive or negative, but not the actual result, is admissible in court or may be used by an administrative agency in determining reasonable grounds for the determinations referenced above.[70] Negative results on an alcohol screening test may be used in factually appropriate cases by the officer, a court, or an administrative agency in determining whether a person's alleged impairment is caused by an impairing substance other than alcohol.[71]

---

62. This requirement, which is codified in the "subsequent test[]" provisions of G.S. 20-139.1(b5), appears to apply only if the law enforcement officer initially exercises his or her discretion under G.S. 20-16.2(a) to obtain a chemical analysis of the person.

63. G.S. 20-139.1(b5) (further providing that the failure to obtain a blood sample shall not be grounds for the dismissal of a charge). *See supra* note 30 for a further discussion of these statutory provisions as they relate to the Fourth Amendment's prohibition on unreasonable searches.

64. G.S. 20-16.3(a). The statute specifies that requiring a driver to submit to an alcohol screening test in accordance with its provisions does not, by itself, constitute an arrest.

65. *Id.* § 20-16.3(b).

66. *Id.* § 20-16.3(c); *but see* State v. Rogers, 124 N.C. App. 364, 370 (1996) (determining that the fact that the law enforcement officer failed to administer a second alcohol screening test as required by G.S. 20-16.3(b) did not prevent the results from being used by the officer to form probable cause).

67. G.S. 20-16.3(d).

68. *Id.*

69. *See* Shea Denning, *You Can't Tell Just from the Smell*, N.C. Crim. L., UNC Sch. of Gov't Blog (Aug. 10, 2009), http://nccriminallaw.sog.unc.edu/?p=606.

70. *Id.*

71. *Id.*

A different rule governs the use of alcohol screening test evidence to establish a violation of the various statutes[72] that prohibit driving while consuming alcohol or while alcohol remains in the person's body.[73] In such cases, the results of an alcohol screening test or the driver's refusal to submit to an alcohol screening test may be used by a law enforcement officer, a court, or an administrative agency in determining if alcohol was present in the driver's body.[74] Thus, not only are the numerical results admissible in such cases, but they also may be used to establish the underlying offense—not simply whether the arrest or charge was supported by probable cause.

5. Pre-Arrest Testing

Although normally a person submits to chemical analysis only after he or she is arrested or charged with an implied consent offense, or both, a person who is stopped or questioned by a law enforcement officer who is investigating whether that person may have committed an implied consent offense may request that a chemical analysis be administered before any arrest or other charge is made.[75] Upon such a request, the officer must afford the person the opportunity to have a chemical analysis of his or her breath, if available, in accordance with the procedures required by G.S. 20-139.1(b).[76] The notice of rights required before administration of a pre-charge test is prescribed by statute and differs from the notice provided in a case in which the person already has been charged with an implied consent offense.[77] It does not include the right to call an attorney for advice or select a witness to view testing procedures, nor does it provide for a delay in testing for these purposes.[78] A pre-charge chemical analysis, like one administered after a defendant is charged, can give rise to a civil license revocation under G.S. 20-16.5.[79]

6. Affidavit and Revocation Report

In an implied consent case in which a defendant is asked to submit to a chemical analysis, the law enforcement officer and the chemical analyst (who may be the same person) complete a form created by the Administrative Office of the Courts called AOC-CVR-1A (Affidavit and Revocation Report)[80] averring that the implied consent testing procedures have been followed. The affidavit, which in certain cases serves also as a revocation report, typically is sworn and subscribed before a magistrate at the charged person's initial appearance.

After completing all investigatory and other specified procedures, crash reports, and chemical analyses, a law enforcement officer must take the person charged before a judicial official for an initial appearance.[81]

---

72. G.S. 20-138.2A (prohibiting the operation of a commercial vehicle while consuming alcohol or while alcohol remains in the person's body); -138.2B (prohibiting the operation of a school bus, school activity bus, child care vehicle, ambulance or other emergency medical services vehicle, firefighting vehicle, or a law enforcement vehicle while consuming alcohol or while alcohol remains in the person's body); -138.3 (prohibiting driving by person less than 21 years of age while consuming alcohol or while alcohol remains in the person's body).

73. *Id.* §§ 20-138.2A(b2); -138.2B(b2); -138.3(b2).

74. *Id.*

75. *Id.* § 20-16.2(i).

76. *Id.*

77. *Id.*

78. *Id.*

79. *Id.* § 20-16.5(b1).

80. The form is available on the website for the Administrative Office of the Courts at www.nccourts.org/Forms/Documents/1049.pdf.

81. G.S. 20-38.3(5).

III. Theory of Implied Consent

As previously noted, G.S. 20-16.2(a) provides that "[a]ny person who drives a vehicle on a highway or public vehicular area hereby gives consent to a chemical analysis if charged with an implied-consent offense" and that "[a]ny law enforcement officer with reasonable grounds to believe that the person charged has committed the implied-consent offense may obtain a chemical analysis of the person." Before any chemical analysis is administered, the person must be advised orally and in writing of his or her implied consent rights. Among those rights is a warning: "Under the implied-consent law, you can refuse any test, but your drivers [sic] license will be revoked for one year and could be revoked for a longer period of time under certain circumstances, and an officer can compel you to be tested under other laws."[82] Suspects also are advised that "[t]he test results, or the fact of your refusal, will be admissible in evidence at trial."[83] An exception to the requirement that these warnings be given applies if the person is unconscious or otherwise incapable of refusal. If a person willfully refuses to submit to the chemical analysis requested by the officer, none may be given under the provisions of G.S. 20-16.2, but the refusal does not prohibit testing under other applicable procedures of law, such as compelled blood testing pursuant to a search warrant.

A. Implied Consent Testing and the Fourth Amendment

The Fourth Amendment to the United States Constitution, applicable to the states by the Fourteenth Amendment,[84] prohibits unreasonable searches and seizures by government actors.[85] What is reasonable under the Fourth Amendment "depends on the context within which a search takes place."[86] Determining the standard of reasonableness "governing any specific class of searches requires 'balancing the need to search against the invasion which the search entails.'"[87] "On one side of the balance are . . . the individual's legitimate expectations of privacy and personal security; on the other, the government's need for effective methods to deal with breaches of public order."[88] The Fourth Amendment's reasonableness requirement does not apply to all interactions government actors have with people or property.[89] Instead, it applies only to searches and seizures.[90] Government actors conduct a search when they infringe on a person's expectation of privacy that society recognizes as reasonable or legitimate.[91]

Courts have long recognized that the "'compelled intrusio[n] into the body for blood to be analyzed for alcohol content'" is a Fourth Amendment search.[92] The physical intrusion necessary to obtain blood, which involves penetrating beneath the skin, infringes a person's reasonable

82. *Id.* § 20-16.2(a)(1).
83. *Id.* § 20-16.2(a)(3).
84. Mapp v. Ohio, 367 U.S. 643 (1961).
85. U.S. Const. amend. IV.
86. New Jersey v. T.L.O., 469 U.S. 325, 337 (1985).
87. *Id.* (quoting Camara v. Mun. Court, 387 U.S. 523, 536–37 (1967)).
88. *Id.*
89. *See* Robert L. Farb, Arrest, Search, and Investigation in North Carolina 174 (UNC School of Government, 4th ed. 2011) (hereinafter *Arrest, Search, and Investigation*).
90. Fourth Amendment seizures are not discussed here. The law of search and seizure is thoroughly treated in Farb, *Arrest, Search, and Investigation*, *supra* note 89, ch. 3.
91. *Id.* at 174; *see also T.L.O.*, 469 U.S. at 338.
92. Skinner v. Ry. Labor Executives' Ass'n, 489 U.S. 602, 616 (1989) (quoting Schmerber v. California, 384 U.S. 757, 767–68 (1966)).

expectation of privacy.[93] Moreover, the "ensuing chemical analysis of the sample to obtain physiological data" further invades a person's privacy interests.[94]

The sort of breath testing performed pursuant to the State's implied consent laws, which requires the person to produce aveolar or deep lung breath, "implicates similar concerns about bodily integrity."[95] For this reason, a compelled breath test likewise constitutes a search under the Fourth Amendment.[96] A compulsory urine test in an implied consent case implicates the Fourth Amendment as well.[97] Though the testing of urine does not require a surgical intrusion into the body, the chemical analysis of urine, like that of blood, can reveal "a host of private medical facts about [a person]."[98] Furthermore, the process of collecting a urine sample entails the government's incursion into an area in which a person has a reasonable expectation of privacy.[99]

Because each type of test conducted pursuant to the State's implied consent laws implicates privacy interests protected by the Fourth Amendment, to be lawful, each must satisfy the reasonableness requirement of the Fourth Amendment. The traditional Fourth Amendment standard of reasonableness for a government search requires that the search be carried out based on probable cause pursuant to a warrant.[100] There are, however, several exceptions to the probable cause or the warrant requirement, or to both, including exceptions for searches incident to arrest (exceptions to both), searches carried out pursuant to a person's consent (exceptions to both), searches carried out pursuant to special governmental needs (sometimes exceptions to both), and searches carried out in exigent circumstances (warrant exception).[101]

While the United States Supreme Court has not analyzed the reasonableness of searches carried out under implied consent laws in circumstances in which a person acquiesces to the test,[102] many state courts have considered the constitutionality of testing carried out pursuant to their implied consent laws—laws that exist in every state.[103] Implied consent statutes typically require that a law enforcement officer have probable cause to believe that the driver is under the influence of alcohol

93. *Id.* at 616.

94. *Id.*

95. *Id.* at 617.

96. *Id.*

97. *Id.*

98. *Id.*

99. *Id.* (noting that " '[t]here are few activities in our society more personal or private than the passing of urine.' ") (quoting Nat'l Treasury Emps. Union v. Von Raab, 816 F.2d 170, 175 (5th Cir. 1987)).

100. State v. Cook, 306 N.C. 132 (1982).

101. Craig M. Bradley, *Two Models of the Fourth Amendment*, 83 MICH. L. REV. 1468, 1473–74 (1985) (listing exceptions, noting that they are "neither few nor well-delineated," and arguing that reasonableness should be governing analysis, rendering the warrant requirement less important).

102. The United States Supreme Court has considered the reasonableness of compelled testing in implied consent cases in which a person refuses to be tested, holding that compulsory blood testing over a defendant's objection may be carried out based on probable cause but without a warrant when, under the circumstances, the time necessary to obtain a warrant threatens the dissipation of alcohol in the person's body. Schmerber v. California, 384 U.S. 757 (1966). The Court's holding regarding nonconsensual, warrantless blood draws is discussed *infra* in section III.B.1).

103. *See* Missouri v. McNeely, 133 S. Ct. 1552, 1566 (2013) (plurality opinion) (stating that "all 50 States have adopted implied consent laws that require motorists, as a condition of operating a motor vehicle within the State, to consent to BAC [blood-alcohol content] testing if they are arrested or otherwise detained on suspicion of a drunk-driving offense"); *see also* Kenneth J. Melilli, *The Consequences of Refusing Consent to a Search or Seizure: The Unfortunate Constitutionalization of an Evidentiary Issue*, 75 S. CAL. L. REV. 901, 920 n.84 (2002) (citing Matthew J. Dougherty, *Casenote, Hays v. City of Jacksonville*, 518 So. 2d 892 (Ala. Crim. App. 1987), 19 CUMB. L. REV. 177, 177 & n.3 (1988)) (citing implied consent statutes in effect in 1988 for "all fifty states and the District of Columbia")).

or has committed an alcohol-related offense before the officer may conduct a chemical test[104] since, "in the criminal context, the reasonableness of a search under the Fourth Amendment is measured with a " 'probable cause' yardstick."[105]

State courts have determined on various grounds that chemical testing carried out pursuant to implied consent statutes satisfies the reasonableness requirement of the Fourth Amendment. Courts have held that (1) "the bodily intrusion the motorist is being asked to allow, in return for retaining the license to drive, is a minimal one," and the State has a "compelling need to get intoxicated drivers off the highways,"[106] (2) breath testing is the type of nonintrusive search that may be carried out incident to arrest,[107] (3) the warrant requirement is excused by the exigencies created by the evanescent

---

104. *See* Elizabeth F. Rubin, *Trying to Be Reasonable About Drunk Driving: Individualized Suspicion and the Fourth Amendment*, 62 U. Cin. L. Rev. 1105, 1106–07 (1994) (citing Ga. Code Ann. § 40-5-55 (Michie 1992) (tests authorized after arrest and with "reasonable grounds"); Iowa Code § 321J.6 (1991) (tests authorized on "reasonable grounds" and additional condition such as arrest, injury, or death); Minn. Stat. § 169.123 (1992) (tests authorized with "probable cause" and additional condition such as arrest, property damage, injury, or death); Mont. Code Ann. § 61-8-402 (1992) (tests authorized on "reasonable grounds" and after arrest); N.D. Cent. Code § 39-20-14 (1991) (tests authorized on officer's "opinion" of alcohol use); Vt. Stat. Ann. tit. 23, § 1202 (1991) (tests authorized on "reasonable grounds"); Wash. Rev. Code § 46.20.308 (1991) (tests authorized on "reasonable grounds")). Georgia, Illinois, Mississippi, and Pennsylvania enacted implied consent statutes that authorized chemical testing of any driver involved in (Georgia, Mississippi, Pennsylvania) or at fault for (Illinois) an automobile accident involving death or, in some cases, serious injury, even if the officer did not have probable cause that the driver was under the influence of alcohol. Ga. Code Ann. § 40-5-55(a) (Michie 1992); 625 Ill. Comp. Stat. Ann. 5/11-501.6 (Smith-Hurd 1992); 75 Pa. Cons. Stat. § 1547(a)(2) (1992); Miss. Code Ann. § 63-11-8(1) (1996). Supreme courts in those states held that those statutory provisions violated the Fourth Amendment. *See* Cooper v. State, 587 S.E.2d 605 (Ga. 2003); King v. Ryan, 607 N.E.2d 154 (Ill. 1992); McDuff v. State, 763 So. 2d 850 (Miss. 2000); Commonwealth v. Kohl, 615 A.2d 308 (Pa. 1992). *Compare* State v. Blank, 90 P.3d 156 (Alaska 2004) (construing similar state statute to be constitutional in context of warrantless searches for breath or blood in accident cases when probable cause to search exists); State v. Roche, 681 A.2d 472, 474 (Me. 1996) (upholding similar state statute which required a showing of probable cause only when admission of the test result was sought at trial rather than before testing; holding that the justification for suspicionless testing of drivers involved in fatal accidents is linked to the gravity of the accident as well as the "evanescent nature of evidence of intoxication and the deterrent effect on drunk driving of immediate investigations of fatal accidents"). One of the offenses deemed an implied consent offense under North Carolina law, misdemeanor death by vehicle, is an offense unrelated to alcohol consumption. *See* G.S. 20-16.2(a1) (defining "implied-consent offense" to include a violation of G.S. 20-141.4(a2)); 20-141.4(a2) (defining misdemeanor death by vehicle as unintentionally causing the death of another person while engaged in the violation of a state law or local ordinance applying to the operation or use of a vehicle or to the regulation of traffic, other than impaired driving, and the commission of the law or ordinance violation is the proximate cause of death).

105. Cooper v. State, 587 S.E.2d 605, 609 (Ga. 2003) (quoting Adams v. State, 498 S.E.2d 268, 271 (Ga. 1998)).

106. State v. Wintlend, 655 N.W.2d 745, 751 (Wis. Ct. App. 2002); *see also* South Dakota v. Neville, 459 U.S. 553, 563, 558 (1983) (characterizing a "simple blood-alcohol test" as "safe, painless, and commonplace" and noting the "well documented" "carnage caused by drunk drivers"); Mackey v. Montrym, 443 U.S. 1, 15 (1979) (finding that Massachusetts' compelling interest in highway safety justifies the summary suspension of a person's license for refusing a breath test; noting, in response to petitioner's claim that he requested to take the test after his initial refusal, that the state "must have the authority, if it is to protect people from drunken drivers, to require that the breath-analysis test record the alcoholic content of the bloodstream at the earliest possible moment.").

107. *See* United States v. Reid, 929 F.2d 990 (4th Cir. 1991) (finding breath tests permissible under the exigency and search incident to arrest exceptions to the Fourth Amendment's warrant requirement); Burnett v. Municipality of Anchorage, 806 F.2d 1447, 1450 (9th Cir. 1986) (concluding that a breath test following an arrest for impaired driving "is an appropriate and reasonable search incident to arrest" that arrestees "have no constitutional right to refuse"); Wing v. State, 268 P.3d 1105, 1110 (Alaska Ct. App. 2012) ("[T]he statutory scheme that requires a DUI arrestee to take a chemical breath test is a valid search incident to arrest under

nature of alcohol;[108] and (4) by driving on a road within the state, a person has given his or her consent to evidentiary testing.[109] North Carolina's appellate courts have never expressly considered whether chemical testing pursuant to the state's implied consent statutes satisfies the reasonableness requirement of the Fourth Amendment. Instead, the state's appellate courts have relied upon the legal theory of implied consent in upholding such testing as lawful. In *Seders v. Powell*,[110] the state supreme court explained that "anyone who accepts the privilege of driving upon our highways has already consented to the use of the breathalyzer test and has no constitutional right to consult a lawyer to void that consent." The court later reaffirmed that principle in a criminal case, *State v. Howren*,[111] and has characterized the right to refuse as a matter of legislative grace, not a constitutional right.[112]

In his treatise on the Fourth Amendment, Professor Wayne LaFave eschews this consent justification on the basis that "[c]onsent 'in any meaningful sense' cannot be said to exist merely because a person (a) knows that an official intrusion into his privacy is contemplated if he does a certain thing, and then (b) proceeds to do that thing."[113] "Were it otherwise," LaFave continues, "the police could utilize the implied consent theory to subject everyone on the streets after 11 p.m. to a search merely by making public announcements in the press, radio and television that such searches would be undertaken."[114]

LaFave suggests that the better approach is to ask whether the search meets the reasonableness requirement of the Fourth Amendment, "an inquiry in which it will . . . be relevant that advance notice was given of the circumstances" in which a search might occur. He explains:

> If the answer to that question is no, a statute may not produce a contrary result via the fiction of implied consent. As one court aptly put it: " 'To hold that the legislature could

---

either theory of DUI [the "under the influence" theory and the "blood alcohol level" theory] when there is independent evidence to charge the arrestee with driving under the influence."); Commonwealth v. Anderl, 477 A.2d 1356, 1364 (Pa. Super. Ct. 1984) (citations omitted) ("warrantless seizure of appellant's alcohol-laden breath is valid either as a search incident to arrest . . . or a search necessitated by exigent circumstances, i.e., the evanescent nature of alcohol in the appellee's blood stream").

108. *See Reid*, 929 F.2d 990 (finding breath tests permissible under the exigency and search incident to arrest exceptions to the Fourth Amendment's warrant requirement); *Anderl*, 477 A.2d at 1364 (citations omitted) ("warrantless seizure of appellant's alcohol-laden breath is valid either as a search incident to arrest . . . or a search necessitated by exigent circumstances, i.e., the evanescent nature of alcohol in the appellee's blood stream").

109. State v. Diaz, 160 P.3d 739 (Idaho 2007).

110. 298 N.C. 453, 462 (1979).

111. 312 N.C. 454 (1984).

112. *Id.* at 456; *Accord* South Dakota v. Neville, 459 U.S. 553, 560 n.10, 565 (1983) (person has no constitutional right to refuse to take a blood-alcohol test; instead, right to refuse blood-alcohol test is a matter of grace bestowed by the legislature); *see also* People v. Harris, 170 Cal. Rptr. 3d 729, 735 (Cal. App. Dep't Super. Ct. 2014) (citations omitted) (certified for partial publication) (concluding that "motorists freely consent for Fourth Amendment purposes to chemical testing in accordance with the terms of the implied consent law, in exchange for the privilege of using the roads").

113. 4 Wayne R. LaFave, Search and Seizure: A Treatise on the Fourth Amendment 164–65 (5th ed. 2012).

114. *Id.* Other commentators share LaFave's skepticism. *See* Comment, *The Theory and Practice of Implied Consent in Colorado*, 47 U. Colo. L. Rev. 723, 762 (1976) (stating that "the state can use [the threat of license revocation] only under the same circumstances that it can use force; viz, if the search would have been a reliable one, done pursuant to a lawful arrest, in a reasonable, medically approved manner, where the arresting officer had probable cause to believe that the licensee was indeed intoxicated"); *see also* D. Bernard Zaleha, *Alaska's Criminalization of Refusal to Take a Breath Test: Is It a Permissible Warrantless Search Under the Fourth Amendment*, 5 Alaska L. Rev. 263, 289 (1988); Penn Lerblance, *Implied Consent to Intoxication Tests: A Flawed Concept*, 53 St. John's L. Rev. 39, 63–64 (1978).

> nonetheless pass laws stating that a person 'impliedly' consents to search under certain circumstances where a search would otherwise be unlawful would be to condone an unconstitutional bypassing of the Fourth Amendment.' "[115]

Adoption of LaFave's suggested approach would require courts to extend the reasonableness analysis applied to so-called "special needs" searches, intrusions justified by purposes divorced from the state's general interest in law enforcement, to searches in implied consent cases.[116] If North Carolina's courts were to apply this analysis, searches carried out pursuant to the state's implied consent laws might be deemed reasonable under this framework in light of (1) the government's compelling interest in eliminating the threat impaired drivers pose to public safety, (2) the safe, relatively painless, and commonplace methods of testing employed, (3) the requirement of probable cause to believe the person committed an alcohol-related offense,[117] and (4) the advance notice provided by the implied consent statutes themselves.[118]

B. Statutory Right to Refuse

Given that a person has no constitutional right to refuse an implied consent test, one might question why implied consent statutes, such as North Carolina's, incorporate a statutory right of refusal. Indeed, Professor Jack Weinstein, writing about implied consent a year after New York's enactment of the first state statute requiring drivers to consent to a chemical test for intoxication, noted the paradox in providing that "although the driver has constructively consented to take the test, when the chips are down and he is actually apprehended he may renege on his imputed promise and refuse."[119] Professor Weinstein recognized the "practical merit" of coupling free choice with mandatory consent, stating that freedom to refuse "prevents the unseemly struggle likely to arise when an intoxicated driver refuses to do what the police insist he is bound to do,"[120] while implied consent in advance avoids "the need for explicit consent from a heavily intoxicated person" or from someone rendered dazed or unconscious in a crash.[121]

Thirty years ago, one writer argued that impaired driving prosecutions would be facilitated by scrapping the notion of implied consent and resorting to compulsory testing, arguing that "[a]lthough

---

115. 4 LaFave, cited in full *supra* note 113, at 165.

116. *See* New Jersey v. T.L.O., 469 U.S. 325, 351 (1985) (Blackmun, J., concurring in judgment) ("Only in those exceptional circumstances in which special needs, beyond the normal need for law enforcement, make the warrant and probable-cause requirement impracticable, is a court entitled to substitute its balancing of interests for that of the Framers.").

117. This justification does not apply to implied consent testing carried out when probable cause exists for no other implied consent offense than misdemeanor death by vehicle. See *supra* note 100.

118. *Cf.* State v. Yong Shik Won, 332 P.3d 661, 681 (Haw. Ct. App. 2014) (concluding that "[i]n balancing the government's interest against the individual's privacy interest . . . obtaining a driver's breath test under the procedures set forth in the implied consent statute is reasonable and does not violate the Fourth Amendment").

119. Jack B. Weinstein, *Statute Compelling Submission to a Chemical Test for Intoxication*, 45 J. Crim. L., Criminology, & Police Sci. 541, 543 (1954–55).

120. *Id.*; *see also* South Dakota v. Neville, 459 U.S. 553, 559 (1983) (noting that South Dakota permits suspects to refuse a blood-alcohol test "to avoid violent confrontations").

121. *Weinstein*, 45 J. Crim. L., Criminology, & Police Sci. at 545. Professor Weinstein wrote that these practical concerns were not, however, the impetus for the choice/consent dichotomy. Instead, the drafters viewed the coupling of implied consent with the ability to refuse as a method for avoiding any question about a driver's constitutional right to refuse to take the test: By accepting the privilege to drive, a person waives any constitutional right to refuse the search. Weinstein acknowledged doubts about whether, in actuality, this "indirect approach using a theory of conditions" avoids the need for constitutional analysis. *Id.* at 545.

implied consent developed as a means of facilitating the use of chemical evidence, the statutes currently constitute the primary barriers to the use of that evidence in as many as forty-five percent of potential DWI prosecutions."[122]

1. Compelled Testing after Refusal

When a person charged with an implied consent offense refuses to participate in or acquiesce to the type of testing requested by a law enforcement officer, the person may nevertheless be compelled to provide a sample of his or her blood for analysis. Indeed, the implied consent notice set forth in G.S. 20-16.2(a)(1) informs a person that he or she may refuse any test, but an officer can compel testing under other laws. Any such compulsory test must comport with the Fourth Amendment.

The United States Supreme Court first considered the Fourth Amendment restrictions on the withdrawal of blood from an impaired driving suspect over his objection in *Schmerber v. California*.[123] The defendant in *Schmerber* was injured in an automobile accident and was taken to the hospital, where he subsequently was arrested for driving under the influence of alcohol. A police officer then ordered a blood test over the defendant's objection. After explaining that the warrant requirement applied generally to searches that intrude into the human body, the Court concluded that the warrantless blood draw was permissible because the officer might reasonably have believed that he was confronted with an emergency in which the delay necessary to obtain a warrant threatened the destruction of evidence, given the natural dissipation of alcohol from a person's blood. The Court noted that "[p]articularly in a case such as this, where time had to be taken to bring the accused to a hospital and to investigate the scene of the accident, there was no time to seek out a magistrate and secure a warrant."[124] In the decades following *Schmerber*, a split of authority developed among state courts regarding whether the dissipation of alcohol alone provided a sufficient exigency to excuse the Fourth Amendment's warrant requirement in any impaired driving case or whether special facts of exigency beyond the evanescence of alcohol were required.[125] North Carolina's courts appeared to require a showing of facts beyond the evanescence of alcohol to establish exigent circumstances,[126] while courts in other jurisdictions considered the dissipation of alcohol sufficient to excuse the warrant requirement.[127]

---

122. Phillip T. Bruns, *Driving While Intoxicated and the Right to Counsel: The Case Against Implied Consent*, 58 TEX. L. REV. 935 (1980). Bruns further contended that "implied consent procedures produce disparities in the treatment of drunk drivers, to the advantage of those who are aware of the benefits of refusing chemical testing. If these adverse consequences are not necessary to avoid the potential evils of physical coercion in administering the tests, then states have no reason for retaining them." *Id.* at 959.

123. 384 U.S. 757 (1966).

124. *Id.* at 770–71.

125. *See, e.g.*, State v. Netland, 762 N.W.2d 202, 214 (Minn. 2009).

126. *See* State v. Fletcher, 202 N.C. App. 107 (2010) (evaluating the reasonableness of an officer's belief that the delay associated with obtaining a warrant would result in the dissipation of the percentage of alcohol in the defendant's blood in light of the two to three hours that the officer testified the process would require, and concluding that sufficient exigency existed). *Accord* United States v. Chapel, 55 F.3d 1416 (9th Cir. 1995); State v. Johnson, 744 N.W.2d 340 (Iowa 2008); State v. Rodriguez, 156 P.3d 771 (Utah 2007).

127. *See, e.g., Netland*, 762 N.W.2d at 214 (footnote omitted) (holding that the criminal test-refusal statute does not violate the Fourth Amendment "because under the exigency exception, no warrant is necessary to secure a blood-alcohol test where there is probable cause to suspect a crime in which chemical impairment is an element of the offense"). *Accord* State v. Machuca, 227 P.3d 729, 736 (Or. 2010); State v. Bohling, 494 N.W.2d 399 (Wis. 1993).

The United States Supreme Court resolved the split among state courts in 2013, holding in *Missouri v. McNeely*[128] that in impaired driving investigations, the natural dissipation of alcohol in the bloodstream does not constitute an exigency in every case sufficient to justify conducting a blood test without a warrant over a defendant's objection. In so holding, the high court rejected the state's call for a categorical rule authorizing nonconsensual warrantless blood draws whenever an officer has probable cause to believe a person has been driving while impaired based solely on the evanescent nature of alcohol. Thus, while the natural dissipation of alcohol in the blood may support a finding of exigency in a specific case in which a defendant refuses to acquiesce to a request for chemical testing, it does not do so categorically. Whether a nonconsensual warrantless blood test of a drunk-driving suspect is reasonable must be determined case by case based on the totality of the circumstances.[129]

The North Carolina Court of Appeals in *State v. Fletcher*,[130] a case decided before *McNeely*, employed the totality of the circumstances analysis later approved by the United States Supreme Court in considering whether exigent circumstances existed to support the nonconsensual, warrantless withdrawal of the defendant's blood in an impaired driving case. The *Fletcher* court considered not only the dissipation of alcohol, but also the distance to the magistrate's office and the time required to obtain a warrant on a Saturday night.[131] The court in *Fletcher* concluded that an exigency existed based on a potential delay of two to three hours.[132] Because the U.S. Supreme Court in *McNeely* rejected only the per se rule advocated by the state and did not define what length of delay would constitute an exigency, *McNeely* sheds no light on whether a delay of the sort projected in *Fletcher* is a "significant" delay that "negatively affect[s] the probative value of the results,"[133] though that seems a likely conclusion.

Fletcher also upheld as constitutional G.S. 20-139.1(d1), which states: "If a person refuses to submit to any test or tests pursuant to this section, any law enforcement officer with probable cause may, without a court order, compel the person to provide blood or urine samples for analysis if the officer reasonably believes that the delay necessary to obtain a court order, under the circumstances, would result in the dissipation of the percentage of alcohol in the person's blood or urine." The court held that the statute required "both probable cause and an officer's reasonable belief that a delay in testing would result in dissipation of the person's blood alcohol content," noting that "[i]n effect, our legislature has codified what constitutes exigent circumstances with respect to DWI's."[134] Given that *Fletcher* itself required more than dissipation to support an exigency, perhaps G.S. 20-139.1(d1), as interpreted in *Fletcher* and because of its "under the circumstances" clause, is constitutional. On the other hand, if the statute is read to authorize warrantless blood draws based on the dissipation of alcohol alone, it clearly violates the standard[135] announced in *McNeely*.

---

128. 133 S. Ct. 1552 (2013).

129. *Id.* at 1568. The Court noted that exigent circumstances may exist when there is no accident. *Id.* The procedures for obtaining a warrant and the availability of a magistrate may affect whether there is time to obtain a warrant and thus may establish an exigency.

130. 202 N.C. App. 107 (2010).

131. *Id.* at 111.

132. *Id.* at 110–111.

133. *McNeely*, 133 S. Ct. at 1561.

134. *Fletcher*, 202 N.C. App. at 113 (referencing G.S. 20-139.1(d1)).

135. *See* Orin Kerr, *Missouri v. McNeely and Exigent Circumstances to Conduct Blood Tests for Drunk Driving Cases*, The Volokh Conspiracy (group blog produced primarily by law professors), www.volokh.com/2013/04/17/missouri-v-mcneely-and-exigent-circumstances-to-conduct-blood-tests-for-drunk-driving-cases/ (Apr. 17, 2013) (noting Court's adoption of a standard rather than a bright-line rule).

In its first published opinion post-*McNeely* considering whether a warrantless nonconsensual blood draw was lawful, the state court of appeals in *State v. Dahlquist*[136] determined that the four to five hours that the arresting officer estimated would have elapsed had he first traveled to the intake center at the jail to obtain a search warrant and then taken the defendant to the hospital for a blood draw constituted an exigency sufficient to excuse the Fourth Amendment's warrant requirement.[137] Thus, the *Dahlquist* court held that the trial court properly denied the defendant's motion to suppress, as the warrantless withdrawal of the defendant's blood at a nearby hospital over his objection was lawful. The holding in *Dahlquist* was unsurprising, as it was presaged by *Fletcher*[138] and by *McNeely* itself. Dicta in the opinion indicates, however, that the court might evaluate the totality of the circumstances differently in future cases.[139] After determining that the facts in the case gave rise to an exigency that supported a warrantless search, the *Dahlquist* court suggested that law enforcement officers consider amending their post-arrest procedures in two respects. First, the court suggested that where the technology is available, officers should testify in support of search warrants by videoconference as authorized by G.S. 15A-245. Second, the court recommended that officers call magistrates' offices and hospitals to obtain current information about wait times rather than estimating wait times based on past experience.

The North Carolina Court of Appeals subsequently held in *State v. Granger*[140] that exigent circumstances justified the warrantless withdrawal of the defendant's blood about an hour and a half after he drove when it would have taken an additional forty minutes to obtain a warrant and it was impractical for the lone investigating officer to leave the defendant unattended in the hospital.

2. Missouri v. McNeely and the Theory of Implied Consent

McNeely considered the reasonableness of the withdrawal of a suspect's blood over his or her objection—not the extraction and testing of blood pursuant to a suspect's acquiescence under a state's implied consent laws. Because the standard announced in *McNeely* applies only when a person refuses a request for the withdrawal of blood, its holding did not bar states from procuring blood samples without a warrant pursuant to their implied consent laws.[141] Indeed, the *McNeely* plurality appeared to equate implied consent with actual consent by referring to consequences when a motorist "withdraws consent."[142]

Yet *McNeely*'s holding that there was no per se exigency in every impaired driving case authorizing the warrantless withdrawal of blood challenged one of the rationales relied upon as rendering lawful warrantless implied consent searches. As noted earlier, some courts had reasoned that searches carried out pursuant to implied consent statutes were lawful because they were searches that law enforcement

---

136. ___ N.C. App. ___, 752 S.E.2d 665 (2013).

137. Shea Denning, *Four hour delay to obtain search warrant an exigency, at least for now,* N.C. Crim. L., UNC Sch. of Gov't Blog (Dec. 4, 2013), http://nccriminallaw.sog.unc.edu/?p=4556.

138. 202 N.C. App. 107.

139. *Dahlquist,* ___ N.C. App. at ___, 752 S.E.2d at 668–69.

140. ___ N.C. App. ___, 761 S.E.2d 923 (2014). For further discussion of *Granger,* see Shea Denning, *State v. Granger Adds to State's Missouri v. McNeely Jurisprudence,* N.C. Crim. L., UNC Sch. of Gov't Blog (July 21, 2014), http://nccriminallaw.sog.unc.edu/?p=4856.

141. See *supra* section B.1; *see also McNeely,* 133 S. Ct. at 1566 (citing implied consent laws requiring motorists to consent to blood-alcohol content (BAC) testing as among the legal tools states have to enforce drunk-driving laws and to secure BAC evidence without undertaking warrantless nonconsensual blood draws).

142. *See* 133 S. Ct. at 1566.

officers could have compelled in any event without the need for consent or a warrant.[143] In light of the *McNeely* Court's clarification that law enforcement officers cannot compel such searches in every implied consent case, that particular rationale for implied consent laws rests on shaky ground.

Recent litigation from other states indicates that this post-*McNeely* concern about the analytical framework for implied consent statutes is not just academic. Defendants have argued that *McNeely* requires more than a totality of the circumstances review of non-consensual warrantless blood draws. They contend that it also requires a court to consider whether so-called "consensual" blood draws, carried out without a warrant pursuant to a state's implied consent laws, are constitutional. In other words, they contend that *McNeely* requires reconsideration of the long-accepted theory of implied consent. Two state supreme courts have undertaken that analysis.

a. *State v. Butler*

The Supreme Court of Arizona, sitting en banc, considered in *State v. Butler*[144] whether a juvenile's consent to implied consent testing under state law was involuntary so as to require the suppression of evidence. The court held that independent of the state's implied consent law, the Fourth Amendment requires an arrestee's consent to be voluntary to justify a warrantless blood draw.[145] If the arrestee is a juvenile, the youth's age and a parent's presence are relevant factors in assessing whether consent was voluntary.[146] The court found sufficient evidence to support a juvenile court's finding that the juvenile's consent in *Butler* was not voluntary, noting, among other facts, the juvenile's age, the fact that no parent was present, that the juvenile was detained for about two hours, and that the juvenile was informed that he was required to submit to the test.[147]

One justice wrote a concurring opinion noting, perhaps presciently, that the opinion "might well engender dubious involuntariness claims and related suppression hearings aimed at excluding evidence derived from chemical testing of impaired drivers whose express consent was ostensibly voluntary and valid under Arizona's implied consent law."[148] The concurring justice opined that the "safest course of action for law enforcement might simply be to obtain search warrants . . . for obtaining blood samples in DUI investigations[,] . . . . [as] that default approach, although arguably diluting the effectiveness of the implied consent law, and not constitutionally required under *McNeely* (which neither involved nor discounted consent as a valid exception to the Fourth Amendment's warrant requirement), would certainly comport with the Fourth Amendment and alleviate many potential, foreseeable problems in this area."[149]

b. *State v. Brooks*

The Minnesota Supreme Court in *State v. Brooks*[150] likewise considered the voluntariness of a defendant's consent to the warrantless withdrawal of his blood and the collection of his urine pursuant to the state's implied consent laws. While the Minnesota court in *Brooks*[151] undertook the same examination as the Arizona court in *Butler*,[152] it reached a different conclusion as to voluntariness.

---

143. See *supra* section III.A.
144. 302 P.3d 609 (Ariz. 2013).
145. *Id.* at 613.
146. *Id.*
147. *Id.* at 613–14.
148. *Id.* at 617 (Pelander, J., concurring).
149. *Id.* (statutory citations omitted).
150. 838 N.W.2d 563 (Minn. 2013).
151. *Id.*
152. 302 P.3d 609.

The defendant in *Brooks* was arrested for impaired driving three times within a six-month period.[153] Each time, he was read Minnesota's implied consent advisory, which informs drivers that Minnesota's law requires them to take a chemical test, that refusing to take a test is a crime, and that drivers have the right to talk to a lawyer before deciding whether to take a test.[154] The defendant also was advised of his right to consult an attorney, a right that he exercised in each instance before submitting to testing.[155]

The defendant moved at trial to suppress evidence of the tests, arguing that the state was required to obtain a warrant before conducting these searches, as there was no exigency and no voluntary consent. The defendant pointed out that he agreed to chemical testing only after the police told him that refusal to do so was a crime. He contended that his consent was therefore not voluntary but instead was coerced.

In analyzing the defendant's claim, the Minnesota Supreme Court invoked the reasoning of the United States Supreme Court in *South Dakota v. Neville*.[156] *Neville* held that a defendant's refusal to submit to a blood-alcohol test pursuant to an officer's lawful request was not an action protected by the Fifth Amendment privilege against self-incrimination; thus, evidence regarding a suspect's refusal to submit to chemical testing was admissible.[157] Central to *Neville*'s analysis was its determination that no impermissible coercion was involved when the suspect refused testing.[158] *Neville* explained that since the "offer of taking a blood-alcohol test is clearly legitimate, the action becomes no less legitimate when the State offers a second option of refusing the test, with the attendant penalties for making that choice."[159]

Brooks reasoned that, notwithstanding Neville's examination of coercion within the context of the Fifth Amendment, the question before the *Neville* Court was "whether the existence of a consequence for refusing to take a chemical test rendered the driver's choice involuntary."[160] *Neville*'s conclusion that the consequences attendant to a refusal did not amount to impermissible coercion led the *Brooks* court to conclude that "a driver's decision to agree to take a test is not coerced simply because Minnesota has attached the penalty of making it a crime to refuse the test."[161]

Brooks distinguished the defendant's consent from that the United States Supreme Court deemed involuntary in *Bumper v. North Carolina*.[162] In *Bumper*, the police sought to justify the search of a house based on the owner's consent, contending that she consented after police told her they had a warrant.[163] The Court held that this sort of submission to authority was not consent.[164] *Brooks* distinguished *Bumper* on the basis that Minnesota law afforded a suspect the absolute right to refuse chemical testing.[165] *Brooks* further held that the defendant's arrest did not render his consent coerced, as he was not confronted with repeated police questioning, nor was he asked to consent after

---

153. 838 N.W.2d at 565–66.
154. *Id.*
155. *Id.*
156. *Id.* at 570 (citing South Dakota v. Neville, 459 U.S. 553 (1983)).
157. 459 U.S. at 563–64.
158. *Id.*
159. *Id.* at 563.
160. *Brooks*, 838 N.W.2d at 570.
161. *Id.* (footnote omitted).
162. 391 U.S. 543 (1968).
163. *Id.* at 546–47.
164. *Id.* at 548.
165. *Brooks*, 838 N.W.2d at 571.

having spent days in custody.[166] The defendant's consultation with an attorney reinforced the court's conclusion that his consent was not illegally coerced.[167] The court clarified that it did not "hold that [the defendant] consented because Minnesota law provides that anybody who drives in Minnesota consents . . . to a chemical test."[168] Instead, it determined that the defendant consented based on a totality of the circumstances.

3. Limitations of Consent-Based Justification

Thus, neither *Butler*[169] nor *Brooks*[170] relied upon implied consent as vitiating Fourth Amendment concerns. It is unclear whether, if asked to reconsider its analysis, the North Carolina Supreme Court would depart from its previously expressed view that "anyone who accepts the privilege of driving upon our highways has already consented to [chemical testing for alcohol] and has no constitutional right to consult a lawyer to void that consent."[171]

If, however, consent is the sole justification for allowing testing under implied consent laws, then states may procure—upon threat of license revocation, use of the refusal as evidence, and, in some cases, criminal prosecution—a suspect's acquiescence to a search that, were the person to refuse, would only be lawful if carried out pursuant to a warrant or if exigent circumstances existed. Though the Minnesota Supreme Court in *Brooks*[172] attempted to distinguish *Bumper v. North Carolina*,[173] *Brooks*' analysis of consent doesn't materially differ from that rejected by the *Bumper* court. In essence, *Brooks* reasons that the suspect consented to a search that would have been lawful with a warrant. The fiction of advance, implied consent (which both *Brooks*[174] and *Butler*[175] rejected) is even more problematic for the reasons noted above in section III.A.[176]

The second problem with evaluating the voluntariness of a suspect's consent is a practical one. Persons requested to submit to implied consent testing are thought to be impaired to varying degrees. Determining whether an individual was so impaired as to render his or her consent not free and voluntary could prove difficult and would, at a minimum, require case-by-case evaluation by officers. As noted earlier, one of the advantages of a statute purporting to imply consent in

---

166. *Id.*

167. *Id.*

168. *Id.* at 572 (internal quotation marks, citations omitted). Justice Stras concurred in the court's judgment for reasons that diverged sharply from the majority's analysis. The concurrence called the majority's conclusion that the defendant's consent was voluntary mistaken, noting that "[i]t is hard to imagine how [the defendant's] consent could have been voluntary when he was advised that refusal to consent to a search is a crime." *Id.* at 573–74 (citations omitted). Justice Stras would have affirmed the decision below to admit the evidence based on *Davis v. United States*, 131 S. Ct. 2419 (2011), which held that searches conducted in objectively reasonable reliance on binding appellate precedent are not subject to the exclusionary rule. *Brooks*, 838 N.W.2d at 574. Stras noted that the police gathered the samples from the defendant in accordance with *State v. Netland*, 762 N.W.2d 202, 214 (Minn. 2009), which approved of the warrantless collection of blood-alcohol evidence based solely on the evanescent nature of alcohol in the bloodstream, a holding abrogated by *McNeely*. *Brooks*, 838 N.W.2d at 576. "Netland was wrongly decided," Stras wrote, "[b]ut that was our mistake, not a mistake by law-enforcement officials." *Id.* at 576.

169. 302 P.3d 609 (Ariz. 2013).

170. 838 N.W.2d 563.

171. *Seders v. Powell*, 298 N.C. 453, 462 (1979).

172. 838 N.W.2d 563 (Minn. 2013).

173. 391 U.S. 543 (1968).

174. 838 N.W.2d 563.

175. 302 P.3d 609.

176. *But see* People v. Harris, 170 Cal. Rptr. 3d 729 (Cal. App. Dep't Super. Ct. 2014) (determing that a suspect's cooperation with the implied consent law constitutes Fourth Amendment consent).

advance is avoiding "the need for explicit consent from a heavily intoxicated person or one dazed—or indeed unconscious—from a crash."[177] Thus, a voluntariness standard would appear to require, notwithstanding a statutory provision to the contrary,[178] that a warrant be obtained before chemical testing of an unconscious suspect could be performed.

If free and voluntary consent is the test, the concurring justice in *Butler* likely is correct that the safest course of action for the police is to procure a warrant in advance of every blood draw.

4. Fifth Amendment and Refusals

The Fifth Amendment to the United States Constitution, made applicable to the states by the Fourteenth Amendment, provides that no person "shall be compelled in any criminal case to be a witness against himself." North Carolina's implied consent laws, like those in other states, provide that a person's refusal to submit to a chemical analysis or to perform field sobriety tests is admissible in any criminal, civil, or administrative action against the person.[179] The United States Supreme Court in *South Dakota v. Neville*[180] held that a defendant's refusal to submit to a blood-alcohol test pursuant to a law enforcement officer's lawful request is not an act protected by the privilege against self-incrimination.[181] The Court explained that the values behind the Fifth Amendment are not hindered when the state offers a suspect the choice of submitting to the blood-alcohol test or having his or her refusal used against him or her, as the "simple blood-alcohol test is so safe, painless, and commonplace . . . that the state could legitimately compel the suspect, against his will, to accede to the test."[182] Given "that the offer of taking a blood-alcohol test is clearly legitimate, the action becomes no less legitimate when the State offers a second option of refusing the test, with the attendant penalties for making that choice."[183] Thus, the *Neville* court concluded that suppression of the defendant's statement that "I'm too drunk, I won't pass the test," was not required by the U.S. Constitution. North Carolina's courts have likewise concluded that the admission into evidence of a defendant's refusal to submit to a chemical analysis does not violate the North Carolina Constitution.[184]

---

177. *See* Jack B. Weinstein, *Statute Compelling Submission to a Chemical Test for Intoxication*, 45 J. Crim. L., Criminology, & Police Sci. 541, 543 (1954–55).

178. *See* G.S. 20-16.2(b) (providing that an unconscious person may be tested without notification of rights or request).

179. *Id.* § 20-139.1(f).

180. 459 U.S. 553 (1983).

181. *Id.*; *see also* State v. Flannery, 31 N.C. App. 617 (1976) (admission of evidence of defendant's refusal did not infringe right against self-incrimination).

182. *Neville*, 459 U.S. at 563 (citations omitted).

183. *Id.*

184. State v. Jones, 63 N.C. App. 411, 419–20 (1983).

Chapter 2

Implied Consent Offenses

Chapter 2

Implied Consent Offenses

This chapter sets forth the elements of and the punishment and license revocation for each of the twelve implied consent offenses identified in chapter 1.

I. Driving While Impaired

A. Elements

Driving while impaired under G.S. 20-138.1 is the most commonly charged implied consent offense.[1] A person commits this offense if he or she

(1) drives
(2) a vehicle
(3) while impaired
(4) on a street, highway, or public vehicular area.

Each of these elements is discussed in further detail below.

1. Drive

The term "driver" is defined in G.S. 20-4.01(7) as being synonymous with the term "operator," defined in G.S. 20.4.01(25). Cognates of both words (such as drive, driving, operate, operating) also share the same meaning. An operator is "[a] person in actual physical control of a vehicle which is in motion or which has the engine running."[2]

A defendant's purpose for taking actual physical control of a car is not relevant to consideration of whether he or she was driving.[3] Thus, in the criminal prosecution of defendants for offenses of which driving is an element, there is no requirement that the State establish that the vehicle was in motion with the defendant behind the wheel or that the defendant started the car for purposes of driving it.[4] In *State v. Fields,*[5] for example, a law enforcement officer came upon a vehicle sitting in the right

1. There were 51,131 charges for this misdemeanor offense in 2013 (statistics from N.C. Administrative Office of the Courts, on file with author).
2. G.S. 20-4.01(25).
3. State v. Fields, 77 N.C. App. 404 (1985).
4. *Id.*
5. *Id.*

hand lane of the road. The vehicle was motionless and the defendant was seated behind the wheel. The vehicle's owner was seated on the passenger side. Both the defendant and the passenger testified at trial that the passenger had been driving and stopped the vehicle on the street so that they could use the bathroom. The defendant got back into the driver's seat of the car and started it because he was cold. The court found that this constituted sufficient evidence of driving in the prosecution of defendant for the offense of driving while impaired.

Driving can be established by circumstantial as well as direct evidence. In *State v. Dula*,[6] the court found sufficient evidence to justify the inference that the defendant was driving where the driver of another car saw black tire marks on the highway, dust in the air, and a car, with its headlights on, lying on its top in a field near the highway. The driver of the other car stopped at the scene and found the defendant in the overturned car, the doors of which were closed and the windows rolled up. He did not see anyone else in the area. The investigating officer saw tire marks leading from the black marks on the highway across the highway shoulder and into the field where the overturned car was located. The officer could not open the car doors. Testimony from a witness for the defendant that the witness was driving the car and fled the scene did not render the State's evidence insufficient.

Likewise, in *State v. Riddle*,[7] the court found circumstantial evidence of driving sufficient to warrant submission of the case to the jury where the defendant was seen getting out of the car immediately after the collision and no one else was seen in or near the car. The defendant said that his friend had been driving and left the scene of the accident, running through the woods. A witness and law enforcement officers checked the woods and discovered no evidence to support the defendant's claim. The defendant in *Riddle* claimed that the driver of the car left through the driver's side door, but an investigating law enforcement officer was unable to open the door because of the damage it sustained during the collision. When the wrecker driver arrived, the defendant pulled the keys to the car out of his pocket and handed them to the wrecker driver.[8]

The court reached a different conclusion in *State v. Ray*,[9] finding insufficient evidence to support the impaired driving charge where the only evidence that the defendant was driving was that he was sitting "halfway [in] the front seat."[10] In *Ray*, an officer responded to an accident call and saw the defendant seated in a car that had hit two parked cars. There was no evidence that the car had been operated recently or that the motor was running.

2. Vehicle

The term "vehicle" is defined in G.S. 20-4.01(49) as "[e]very device in, upon, or by which any person or property is or may be transported or drawn upon a highway, excepting devices moved by human power or used exclusively upon fixed rails or tracks." There are several exceptions to this general definition. First, despite the exclusion from the definition for devices moved by human power, bicycles are

---

6. 77 N.C. App. 473 (1985).

7. 56 N.C. App. 701 (1982).

8. *See also* State v. Mack, 81 N.C. App. 578, 579, 583 (1986) (defendant's admission that he fell asleep driving and "ran over there to the fence," combined with officer's observation of the defendant's car sitting on top of a chain link fence approximately forty-five feet from the road with the headlights on, the "key in the ignition, the warm hood, the defendant asleep in the driver's seat, and the near-empty bottle of Canadian Mist on the floorboard" were "sufficient to allow a reasonable jury to infer that defendant drove the vehicle on a public street").

9. 54 N.C. App. 473 (1981).

10. *Id.* at 475.

deemed vehicles for purposes of G.S. Chapter 20.[11] Second, several other devices that would satisfy the general definition are excepted, and thus are not vehicles for purposes of Chapter 20, including G.S. 20-138.1. The term "vehicle" does not include certain devices used as a means of transportation by a person with a mobility impairment. To qualify for the exception, the device must be "designed for and intended to be used as a means of transportation for a person with a mobility impairment, or who uses the device for mobility enhancement, [be] suitable for use both inside and outside a building, including on sidewalks, and [be] limited by design to 15 miles per hour when the device is being operated by a person with a mobility impairment, or who uses the device for mobility enhancement."[12] The court of appeals in *State v. Crow*[13] rejected an argument by the defendant, a healthy 25-year-old man who had no mobility impairment, that the motorized scooter he was driving was not a "vehicle" in that it was a device used for mobility enhancement. The scooter the defendant was driving "was powered by an electric motor and was likened at trial to a skateboard with handlebars on the front."[14] It had two wheels, six to eight inches in diameter, that were arranged in tandem. The court held that the device did not qualify for the mobility impairment exception, explaining that the legislature's addition in 2001 of the term "mobility enhancement" to the sentence concerning "mobility impairment" "was a technical change that did not substantively expand the existing mobility impairment exception to the term 'vehicle.' "[15] Thus, the court concluded that the defendant's use of the scooter solely for "recreational purposes," did not except the device from the definition of vehicle.[16]

Electric personal assistive mobility devices also are excluded from the definition of vehicle.[17] These are self-balancing, non-tandem, two-wheeled devices that are designed to transport one person and have a propulsion system that limits their maximum speed to 15 miles per hour or less.[18] The "Segway Human Transporter"[19] is an example of such a device. The court in *Crow* concluded that the defendant's scooter did not qualify for this exception, as it was not self-balancing and its wheels were arranged in tandem.[20]

Horses are not vehicles for purposes of the impaired driving statute, G.S. 20-138.1,[21] though they apparently may be considered vehicles for other Chapter 20 offenses.[22]

---

11. G.S. 20-4.01(49) further provides that "every rider of a bicycle upon a highway shall be subject to the provisions of this Chapter applicable to the driver of a vehicle except those which by their nature can have no application."

12. *Id.* § 20-4.01(49).

13. 175 N.C. App. 119 (2009).

14. *Id.* at 121.

15. *Id.* at 124.

16. *Id.*

17. G.S. 4.01(49).

18. *Id.* § 20-4.01(7a).

19. *Crow*, 175 N.C. App. at 124.

20. *Id.* The court also rejected the defendant's argument that electric scooters should be excepted from the definition of "vehicle" since "in light of the express exception for bicycles and electric personal assistive mobility devices, an average person might infer that small, lightweight, low-speed devices such as scooters would also fall outside the reach of the statute." *Id.* at 126. The court explained that while it was "wary of requiring the legislature to be overly specific in drafting exceptions to the statute," the General Assembly had deliberately defined "a small number of very specific exceptions," to G.S. 20-138.1. *Id.* The court concluded that "the absence of a motorized scooter from the list of exceptions is indicative of the General Assembly's intent to include such devices in the statutory definition of vehicle." *Id.* at 126 (citations omitted).

21. G.S. 20-138.1(e).

22. In *State v. Dellinger*, 73 N.C. App. 685 (1985), the court upheld the defendant's conviction for impaired driving based upon his riding of a horse on a street with an alcohol concentration of 0.18. The court reasoned that G.S. 20-171 renders traffic laws applicable to persons riding an animal or driving an animal pulling a

3. Street, Highway, or Public Vehicular Area

The third element of driving while impaired is that a person must drive on a street, highway, or public vehicular area.

a. Street, Highway

G.S. 20-4.01(13) defines the term "highway" as "[t]he entire width between property or right-of-way lines of every way or place of whatever nature, when any part thereof is open to the use of the public as a matter or right for the purposes of vehicular traffic." The provision further specifies that "[t]he terms 'highway' and 'street' and their cognates are synonymous."[23] There is no requirement that the street be part of the state highway system.[24]

b. Public Vehicular Area

"Public vehicular areas" (or PVAs) are defined to include four broad types of areas: (1) areas "used by the public for vehicular traffic at any time," (2) beach areas used by the public for vehicular traffic, (3) roads used by vehicular traffic within or leading to a gated or non-gated subdivision or community, whether or not the subdivision or community roads have been offered for dedication to the public, and (4) portions of private property used by vehicular traffic and designated by the private property owner as a public vehicular area in accordance with G.S. 20-219.4.[25] G.S. 20-4.01(32)a. sets forth several illustrative examples of areas satisfying the first type. Thus, public vehicular areas include drives, driveways, roads, roadways, streets, alleys, or parking lots upon the grounds or premises of any of the following:

1. Any public or private hospital, college, university, school, orphanage, church, or any of the institutions, parks or other facilities maintained and supported by the State of North Carolina or any of its subdivisions.
2. Any service station, drive-in theater, supermarket, store, restaurant, or office building, or any other business, residential, or municipal establishment providing parking space whether the business establishment is open or closed.
3. Any property owned by the United States and subject to the jurisdiction of the State of North Carolina.

---

vehicle on a highway. The legislature defined the term "vehicle" in broad terms in G.S. 20-4.01(49). This broad definition reflects the legislature's intent that horses are vehicles within the meaning of G.S. 20-138.1, the statute prohibiting impaired driving. Whatever the view of the legislature pre-*Dellinger*, that body acted a few years later to express its then-current determination that a person *should not* be convicted of impaired driving for riding a horse (or a bicycle or lawnmower) while impaired. 1989 N.C. Sess. Laws, ch. 711 enacted G.S. 20-138.1(e) excepting the aforementioned conveyances from the definition of "vehicle" as that term is used in the DWI statute. In 2006, the legislature removed the bicycle and lawnmower exceptions. S.L. 2006-253.

23. G.S. 20-4.01(13); *see also id.* § 20-4.01(46) (providing that the "terms 'highway' and 'street' and their cognates are synonymous").

24. *Cf.* State v. Hopper, 205 N.C. App. 175 (2010) (rejecting defendant's argument that the provisions of G.S. 20-129 requiring lighted headlamps and rear lamps during certain conditions did not apply because the street on which he was driving was not part of the state highway system; concluding that officer's testimony that the street on which the defendant drove was within an apartment complex owned by the City of Winston-Salem that the officer was assigned to patrol and that there were parking spots on the street with cars parked in them at the time of the stop was sufficient to support the trial court's finding that the defendant was traveling on a street "open to the use of the public as a matter of right for the purposes of vehicular traffic" per G.S. 20-4.01(13)).

25. G.S. 20-4.01(32).

North Carolina's appellate courts have adopted a broad view of the term "public vehicular area," noting on several occasions that their interpretation accords with the legislature's desire to protect people in parking lots from the dangers posed by those who drive while impaired.[26] The court of appeals has deemed the following locations to be public vehicular areas:

- the parking lot of a car wash, notwithstanding a town ordinance prohibiting parking on the premises unless the facilities were being used[27]
- a privately maintained paved road in a privately owned mobile home park[28]
- a wheelchair ramp in the parking lot of a hotel[29]
- an area of a public park occasionally used for public parking[30]
- the parking lot of a private nightclub[31]

4. While Impaired

The offense of impaired driving under G.S. 20-138.1 is a single offense that may be proven in one of three ways:[32] (1) by showing that the defendant was under the influence of an impairing substance; (2) by showing the presence of an alcohol concentration of 0.08 or more; or (3) by showing the presence of a Schedule I controlled substance. In many cases, more than one theory of impairment may be proven. The State is not required to elect a single theory, nor must it specify its theory in the charging instrument. All impairment theories for which sufficient evidence exists may be presented to the fact finder. If the case is being heard by a jury, the judge is not required to instruct the jury to indicate which theory or theories it relied upon,[33] and the fact that jurors may have relied upon different theories of impairment in finding a defendant guilty does not render the verdict nonunanimous.[34]

a. Under the Influence of an Impairing Substance

A person is "under the influence of an impairing substance" when his or her physical or mental faculties are appreciably impaired by an impairing substance.[35] This theory of impairment frequently is referred to as "appreciable impairment." An impairing substance is (1) alcohol, (2) a controlled

---

26. *See* State v. Robinette, 124 N.C. App. 212 (1996); State v. Turner, 117 N.C. App. 457 (1994); State v. Mabe, 85 N.C. App. 500 (1987); State v. Carawan, 80 N.C. App. 151 (1986).

27. *Robinette*, 124 N.C. App. 212.

28. *Turner*, 117 N.C. App. 457.

29. *Mabe*, 85 N.C. App. 500.

30. *Carawan*, 80 N.C. App. 151.

31. State v. Snyder, 343 N.C. 61 (1996). The definition of a public vehicular area at the time of the offense in *Snyder* was significantly narrower than the current one and consisted of areas "generally open to and used by the public for vehicular traffic," including parking lots upon the grounds of a business establishment "providing parking space for customers, patrons, *or* the public." *Id.* at 67 (referencing former G.S. 20-4.01(32)). *Snyder* explained that "even if an establishment is cloaked in the robe of being a private club, it is still a 'business establishment providing parking space for its customers, patrons, *or* the public' and cannot escape liability simply because a membership fee is required." *Id.* at 69. *See also* Shea Denning, *Private Clubs and Public Vehicular Areas*, N.C. Crim. L., UNC Sch. of Gov't Blog (Dec. 11, 2012), http://nccriminallaw.sog.unc.edu/?p=4002 (explaining that in most circumstances the parking lots of private social clubs qualify as public vehicular areas).

32. *See* State v. Oliver, 343 N.C. 202 (1996) (describing impaired driving under former G.S. 20-138.1 as a single offense that may be proven in one of two ways).

33. *Oliver*, 343 N.C. at 215; State v. Garvick, 98 N.C. App. 556, 567 (1990).

34. *Oliver*, 343 N.C. at 215.

35. G.S. 20-4.01(48b).

substance under G.S. Chapter 90, (3) any drug or psychoactive substance capable of impairing a person's physical or mental faculties, or (4) any combination of these substances.[36]

(i) Alcohol

Alcohol is defined as any substance containing any form of alcohol, including ethanol, methanol, propanol, and isopropanol.[37]

(ii) Controlled Substance under G.S. Chapter 90

Article 5 of G.S. Chapter 90 categorizes numerous controlled substances into Schedules I through VI.[38]

(iii) Drug

The term "drug" is not defined in G.S. Chapter 20, but it is defined in G.S. Chapter 90 as follows:

> . . . a. substances recognized in the official United States Pharmacopoeia, official Homeopathic Pharmacopoeia of the United States, or official National Formulary, or any supplement to any of them; b. substances intended for use in the diagnosis, cure, mitigation, treatment, or prevention of disease in man or other animals; c. substances (other than food) intended to affect the structure or any function of the body of man or other animals; and d. substances intended for use as a component of any article specified in a, b, or c of this subdivision; but [the term "drug"] does not include devices or their components, parts, or accessories.[39]

Thus, prescription as well as illicit drugs may qualify as impairing substances, as may over-the-counter medications and other psychoactive substances like inhalants, depending upon their potential effect on the body. The fact that a person is legally entitled to use a particular drug is not a defense to a charge of impaired driving,[40] though it may be a mitigating factor at sentencing.[41]

The model jury instructions direct the judge to determine whether a particular substance is an impairing substance and to so instruct the jury.[42] The state's appellate courts have not considered whether an instruction from a judge that a particular substance is an impairing substance is proper or whether it improperly permits the judge to resolve a material fact. In most circumstances, the instruction likely is proper. For example, a judge's instruction to the jury that "alcohol" or "a controlled substance under Chapter 90" is an impairing substance would not invade the province of the jury. That sort of instruction simply defines the term "impairing substance." Likewise, an instruction that "a drug or psychoactive substance capable of impairing a person's physical or mental faculties is an impairing substance" is not objectionable. Furthermore, there would appear to be no problem with a judge instructing the jury that any of the specific substances listed in Chapter 90 is an impairing substance. Thus, the judge could properly inform the jury that a substance such as cocaine, alprazolam (Xanax), or zolpidem (Ambien) is an impairing substance.[43] In some drugged driving cases,

---

36. *Id.* § 20-4.01(14a).
37. *Id.* § 20-4.01(1a).
38. *See* G.S. 90-89 (Schedule I); 90-90 (Schedule II); 90-91 (Schedule III); 90-92 (Schedule IV); 90-93 (Schedule V); 90-94 (Schedule VI).
39. *Id.* § 90-87(12).
40. *Id.* § 20-138.1(b).
41. *Id.* § 20-179(e)(5).
42. N.C. Pattern Jury Instructions—Crim. 270.00 (Replacement June 2011) (suggesting that the judge instruct the jury in such cases that "((Name substance involved) is an impairing substance").
43. *See* G.S. 90-90(1)c.; 90-92(a)(1)a.; 90-92(a)(1).

however, the substance that a defendant is alleged to have consumed is *not* a controlled substance under Chapter 90. The State may contend, for example, that a defendant is impaired from inhalants or from prescription medication that is not a scheduled controlled substance. In this circumstance, it arguably is improper for the judge to instruct the jury that the specified drug (such as, for example, sertraline (Zoloft)) is a controlled substance.[44]

b. Proving Appreciable Impairment

Neither a chemical analysis nor a field sobriety test is required to establish appreciable impairment. A chemical analysis that reveals an alcohol concentration below the per se threshold does not create a presumption that a person is not appreciably impaired.[45] Substantial evidence of impairment may exist to prove appreciable impairment even when a person's alcohol concentration does not reach the per se threshold.[46]

(i) Opinion Testimony

North Carolina's courts have long held that a lay witness who has personally observed a person may express an opinion as to whether the person was impaired by an impairing substance.[47] Though officers frequently base such opinions in part upon their training and experience regarding the physical manifestations of having consumed alcohol or some other impairing substance in addition to their personal observations, courts have considered such opinions to be those of a lay rather than an expert witness.[48]

During trial in an impaired driving prosecution, an exchange similar to the following often occurs.

Prosecutor: Did you form an opinion, satisfactory to yourself, that the defendant had consumed a sufficient amount of some impairing substance so as to appreciably impair his mental or physical faculties or both?

Arresting Officer: Yes, I did.

Prosecutor: What was that opinion?

---

44. There is at least one other circumstance in which our state appellate courts have permitted judges to instruct the jury as to its determination on a material fact. In *State v. Torain*, 316 N.C. 111 (1986), the state supreme court determined that the trial court did not err in instructing the jury in a first-degree rape trial that "a utility knife is a dangerous or deadly weapon." *Id.* at 116. The court relied on earlier opinions stating that when "the alleged deadly weapon and the manner of its use are of such character as to admit of but one conclusion, the question as to whether or not it is deadly . . . *is one of law, and the Court must take the responsibility of so declaring*." *Id.* at 119 (internal citations, quotation marks omitted) (emphasis in original). Even were this reasoning to be applied in the drugged driving context, however, it likely would authorize no more than instructing the jury that a specific substance scheduled under Chapter 90 is an impairing substance. Those substances are *per se* impairing in much the same way that certain weapons are *per se* deadly. The judge still must leave to the jury the determination of whether other types of "drugs or psychoactive substances" are impairing substances. *Cf.* Jessica Smith, North Carolina Crimes 120–21 (7th ed. 2012) (distinguishing circumstances involving weapons that "are deadly by their very nature" from those in which the jury must be permitted to decide whether the weapon is deadly).

45. State v. Sigmon, 74 N.C. App. 479, 482 (1985) (officer's observation of defendant's driving, odor of alcohol, and inability to perform certain sobriety tests was substantial evidence of impairment regardless of 0.06 breath test result).

46. *Id.*

47. *See* State v. Lindley, 286 N.C. 255 (1974).

48. *See id.*

Arresting Officer: It was my opinion that the defendant had consumed a sufficient quantity of an impairing substance so that his/her mental and physical faculties were both appreciably impaired.

Prosecutor: Did you have an opinion as to what the impairing substance was?

Arresting Officer: I believed it to be some type of alcohol [drug] [psychoactive substance].

This line of questioning is both proper and prevalent. Perhaps because this line of questioning is so common and the answers so typically uniform, defendants sometimes argue that the State's evidence is insufficient as matter of law if an officer does not testify as to his or her opinion that the defendant was "appreciably impaired" by an "impairing substance." Such opinion testimony is not, however, essential to proving the elements of impaired driving, even under the appreciable impairment theory.

Instead, an officer's testimony regarding his or her observations, which might include faulty driving; an odor of alcohol; red, glassy eyes; poor performance on field sobriety tests; and slurred speech, among other observations, often is legally sufficient, without the opinion based on those perceptions, to prove impairment. Thus, while the arresting officer's opinion often will be helpful to the jury or finder of fact,[49] it is not essential to the State's case.

(ii) Proving Impairment by Drugs

Proving impairment by an impairing substance other than alcohol can be more challenging for the State than proving impairment from alcohol. No particular form of evidence is required, and there is no requirement that the State prove the specific drug or impairing substance that the defendant consumed.[50] There are several ways in which the State may seek to prove impairment in such cases.

(A) Drug Recognition Expert Combined with Chemical Analysis

In the State's ideal case, it would elicit testimony from an officer certified as a Drug Recognition Expert (DRE)[51] regarding the defendant's impairment and its cause,[52] along with testimony from a chemical

---

49. *See* State v. Adkerson, 90 N.C. App. 333, 338 (1988).

50. *See* State v. Lindley, 286 N.C. 255 (1974) (State established prima facie case based in part on patrol officer's testimony that the defendant was under the influence of "some drug"); State v. Cousins, 152 N.C. App. 478 (2002) (unpublished) (evidence of defendant's poor performance on field sobriety tests, his refusal to submit to a blood test, and his admission to taking Lortab, a painkiller, were sufficient to show that he was impaired and that his impairment was caused by an impairing substance; the State was not required to produce expert testimony on the impairing effects of Lortab or as to whether defendant's condition was consistent with someone who had taken Lortab). In a jury trial in which the State's proof fails to identify a particular impairing substance, the court arguably should instruct the jury on the definition of "impairing substance" but should refrain from identifying any particular substance for which the State has failed to establish a prima facie case. See *supra* note 44.

51. DREs are trained to administer a twelve-step protocol designed to determine whether a person is impaired by drugs, and, if so, what category of drug (central nervous system depressant, central nervous system stimulant, hallucinogen, dissociative anesthetic, narcotic analgesic, inhalant, or cannabis) caused the impairment. *See* Shea Denning, *Expert Testimony Regarding Impairment*, N.C. Crim. L., UNC Sch. of Gov't Blog (June 9, 2010), http://nccriminallaw.sog.unc.edu/?p=1335; *see also* Shea Denning, *Daubert and Expert Testimony of Impairment*, N.C. Crim. L., UNC Sch. of Gov't Blog (July 1, 2014), http://nccriminallaw.sog.unc.edu/?p=4834 (analyzing admission of DRE testimony under amended N.C. R. Evid. 702).

52. *See* N.C. R. Evid. 702(a1)(2) (providing that a certified DRE may give expert testimony on the issue of whether a person was under the influence of one or more impairing substances and on the category of such impairing substance or substances).

analyst corroborating the DRE's conclusions.[53] In many cases, however, no DRE will be available to examine the defendant. The results of a chemical analysis, standing alone, may be inconclusive. The analysis may not reveal how recently the substance was ingested or the level of concentration of a particular drug. In addition, the chemical analyst may lack the necessary expertise to testify about the impairing effects of a particular substance. Fortunately for the State, it can establish impairment by drugs in a less ironclad way.

(B) Opinion Testimony from Experienced Officer

The North Carolina Supreme Court held in *State v. Lindley*[54] that the trial court in an impaired driving case properly allowed a patrol officer with five years' experience to testify that in his opinion the defendant was under the influence of some drug. The officer in *Lindley* stopped the defendant for erratic driving. When the defendant got out of his car, the officer saw that he was unsteady on his feet, the pupils of his eyes were contracted nearly to pinpoints, and there was a white substance on his lips. Two passengers in the car were in the same condition. The officer smelled no alcohol on the defendant, who subsequently performed poorly on dexterity tests and appeared to be in a mental stupor. The officer asked the defendant if he had diabetes, had physical defects, was sick, limped, had been injured, had recently seen a doctor or dentist, or had taken any medication. The defendant answered no to all of these questions. Based on these responses, the officer ruled out other causes of the defendant's condition and concluded that he was under the influence of a drug. The state supreme court held that the officer was competent to express that opinion as he was "better qualified than the jury to draw inferences and conclusions from what he saw and heard."[55] The court also held that the State's evidence, which consisted solely of the officer's testimony, was sufficient to establish a prima facie case.

(C) Defendant's Admission Corroborated by Expert Testimony

State v. Highsmith[56] illustrates another manner in which the State might establish impairment by drugs. After an officer stopped the defendant in *Highsmith* for erratic driving, the defendant said he was on the way home from the dentist and had taken a pain medication known as Floricet. The officer testified that the defendant's movements were sluggish and his speech was slurred but that he did not smell alcohol. At trial, the officer testified to his observations and the defendant's statements. The State also elicited testimony from an expert in pharmaceuticals, who testified that Floricet was an impairing substance and that a healthcare professional should have warned the defendant of its effects. The North Carolina Court of Appeals held that this evidence was sufficient to establish that the defendant drove while under the influence of an impairing substance.

c. Per Se Impairment

G.S. 20-138.1(a)(2) prohibits a person from driving a vehicle upon a highway, street, or public vehicular area after having consumed sufficient alcohol that the person has, at any relevant time after the driving, an alcohol concentration of 0.08 or more. This type of impairment generally is referred to as *per se*

---

53. The final step in the DRE evaluation protocol is to obtain a blood or urine specimen, which is sent to a laboratory for chemical analysis. *See* State of North Carolina, Forensic Tests for Alcohol Branch, Division of Public Health, Department of Health and Human Services, North Carolina Drug Evaluation & Classification (DEC) Program, "The 12 Steps of the Drug Evaluation Process," www.ncdistrictattorney.org/dwi/dre/dre_info_app.pdf, at 4.

54. 286 N.C. 255 (1974).

55. *Id.* at 259.

56. 173 N.C. App. 600 (2005).

impairment. An outwardly sober person is impaired under this theory if his or her alcohol concentration reaches or exceeds the threshold level. G.S. 20-138.1(a)(2) further provides that "[t]he results of a chemical analysis shall be deemed sufficient evidence to prove a person's alcohol concentration."

(i) Alcohol Concentration

A person's alcohol concentration may be expressed either as grams of alcohol per 100 milliliters of blood or grams of alcohol per 210 liters of breath.[57] These formulas are based on the average ratio that the concentration of alcohol in an individual's blood bears to that in his or her breath: 2,100 to 1. The court of appeals in *State v. Cothran*[58] held that it is immaterial that this formulation is based only on an average blood to breath ratio and that breath test results based on this formula may thus overstate (in the case of an individual with a lower blood to breath ratio) or understate (in the case of an individual with a higher ratio) the person's blood-alcohol concentration.[59] The defendant in *Cothran* sought to introduce testimony from a chemist that the defendant's blood to breath ratio was 1,722 to 1, which meant that his breath test result was 18 percent higher than his blood-alcohol concentration. The appellate court upheld the trial court's exclusion of this testimony, explaining that the legislature adopted a breath-alcohol concentration per se offense as an alternative method of committing the offense of impaired driving. Thus, the court deemed irrelevant the relationship of a particular defendant's breath-alcohol concentration to his or her blood-alcohol concentration.

(ii) Relevant Time after Driving

Every state and the District of Columbia prohibits driving with an alcohol concentration of 0.08 or more, though state laws vary regarding whether to establish a violation of the per se impaired driving law an alcohol concentration of 0.08 or more must exist at the time of driving[60] or, instead, at the time of testing.[61] Some of the states that base the per se offense on the time of driving presume, subject to rebuttal by the defendant, that a 0.08 result from a chemical test performed within a designated time period after the driving establishes that the person drove with an alcohol concentration of 0.08. Some states have a hybrid system, prohibiting driving with a 0.08 alcohol concentration at the time of driving or within a specified time period after driving.[62]

These distinctions in the time of measurement can be significant given that a person's alcohol concentration, which depends upon the rate at which alcohol is absorbed into the bloodstream and at which it is eliminated from the body, changes over time. Alcohol absorption rates vary depending upon many individual factors, including gender,[63] whether a person consumes food with alcohol,[64] whether a person is a heavy or light drinker,[65] the concentration of the alcohol[66] in the beverage,

---

57. G.S. 20-4.01(1b).

58. 120 N.C. App. 633 (1995).

59. *Id.* at 635.

60. *See, e.g.*, ALA. CODE § 32-5A-191; ARK. CODE ANN. § 5-65-103; CAL. VEH. CODE § 23152(b); FLA. STAT. § 316.193; IOWA CODE § 321J.2; IND. CODE § 9-30-5-1; VA. CODE ANN. § 18.2-266.

61. *See, e.g.*, ARIZ. REV. STAT. ANN. § 28-1381; D.C. CODE § 50-2206.01.

62. *See, e.g.*, COLO. REV. STAT. § 42-4-1301; GA. CODE ANN. § 40-6-391.

63. Martin S. Mumenthaler et al., *Gender Differences in Moderate Drinking Effects*, 23 ALCOHOL RESEARCH 55 (1999), http://pubs.niaaa.nih.gov/publications/arh23-1/55-64.pdf.

64. J. B. Saunders & A. Paton, *Alcohol in the Body*, 283 BRIT. MED. J. 1380, 1380 (1981), www.ncbi.nlm.nih.gov/pmc/articles/PMC1507801/pdf/bmjcred00686-0036.pdf.

65. Neil R. Wright & Douglas Cameron, *The Influence of Habitual Alcohol Intake on Breath-Alcohol Concentrations Following Prolonged Drinking*, 33 ALCOHOL & ALCOHOLISM 495, 497–99 (1998), http://alcalc.oxfordjournals.org/content/33/5/495.full.pdf.

66. Saunders & Paton, *supra* note 64, at 1380.

and even whether the beverage is mixed with regular or diet soda.[67] On an empty stomach, alcohol concentration peaks about an hour after consumption,[68] depending on the amount drunk. Alcohol is removed from the blood at a rate of about 15mg per 100ml per hour, though this rate likewise varies.[69]

In a state that measures its per se impaired driving violations based on a person's alcohol concentration at the time of driving, a defendant might successfully argue that he or she consumed a large quantity of an alcoholic beverage just before being stopped by police and that the alcohol had not been absorbed into his or her body at the time of the driving. Termed the "big gulp," or delayed absorption, defense, this argument gave rise to 2004 amendments to Alaska's impaired driving laws, which now provide that a person is guilty of impaired driving if a chemical test conducted within four hours of driving detects an alcohol concentration of at least 0.08, regardless of the person's alcohol concentration at the time of driving.[70]

North Carolina neither requires the State to prove a defendant's alcohol concentration at the time of driving nor sets a specific hourly limit in which a chemical analysis must be performed. Instead, G.S. 20-138.1(a)(2) provides that a person commits the offense of impaired driving by driving after having consumed sufficient alcohol such that he or she has, at any relevant time after the driving, an alcohol concentration of 0.08 or more. A "relevant time after . . . driving" is defined as "[a]ny time after the driving in which the driver still has in his body alcohol consumed before or during the driving."[71] As the state supreme court explained in *State v. Rose*,[72] "[a] person whose blood-alcohol concentration, as a result of alcohol consumed before or during driving, was at some time after driving 0.10 or greater must have had some amount of alcohol in his system at the time he drove. The legislature has decreed that this amount, whatever it might have been, is enough to constitute an offense."[73] Thus, the big gulp defense is no defense at all to a charge of impaired driving based upon an alcohol concentration of 0.08 or more in North Carolina.

To prove impaired driving based upon a per se alcohol concentration, the State must demonstrate that at least 0.08 of the defendant's alcohol concentration was based on alcohol consumed before or during the driving. Such proof is made more complicated when there is evidence that the defendant consumed alcohol after driving. In *State v. Ferrell*,[74] the court of appeals rejected the defendant's argument that breath test results were inadmissible given the defendant's admission that he drank several big swallows from a Jack Daniels bottle given to him by the person who picked him up after the accident where defendant also admitted that he had consumed three beers before the accident. The court, however, granted the defendant a new trial based on the prosecutor's improper questioning of the defendant regarding his failure to testify in district court as part of the State's effort to establish that the defendant fabricated his post-accident drinking after learning that it was a defense to the impaired driving charge. In *State v. Mumford*,[75] the court likewise held that the State's evidence was

---

67. Keng-Liang Wu et al., *Artificially Sweetened Versus Regular Mixers Increase Gastric Emptying and Alcohol Absorption*, 119 Am. J. Med. 802, 803 (2006), www.sciencedirect.com/science/article/pii/S0002934306001823#.

68. Alex Paton, *Alcohol in the Body Clinical Review*, 330 Brit. Med. J. 85, 86 (2005), www.bmj.com/content/330/7482/85.pdf%2Bhtml.

69. Saunders & Paton, *supra* note 64, at 1381.

70. *See* Valentine v. State, 215 P.3d 319 (Alaska 2009).

71. G.S. 20-4.01(33a).

72. 312 N.C. 441 (1984).

73. *Id.* at 447. The per se threshold was reduced from 0.10 to 0.08 for offenses committed on or after October 1, 1993. 1993 Sess. Laws, ch. 285.

74. 75 N.C. App. 156 (1985).

75. 201 N.C. App. 594, *rev'd in part on other grounds by* 364 N.C. 394 (2010).

sufficient for a reasonable juror to conclude that the defendant was impaired at the time of the incident where a breath test administered three hours after the accident revealed a blood-alcohol concentration of 0.09 and defendant admitted to drinking one 32-ounce beer, having a few swallows of another beer, and drinking a shot of liquor in the hours before the accident, despite the defendant's contention that his alcohol concentration resulted from his drinking of part of a beer after the accident.[76]

(iii) Results Shall Be Deemed Sufficient

As noted earlier, G.S. 20-138.1(a)(2) provides that "[t]he results of a chemical analysis shall be deemed sufficient evidence to prove a person's alcohol concentration."[77] The court of appeals in *State v. Narron*[78] upheld the provision as constitutional, explaining that it did not establish a mandatory presumption that compels the jury or fact finder to find that the results of a chemical analysis accurately reflect a defendant's alcohol concentration. Instead, the provision sets forth the prima facie standard for proof of impairment under the per se prong of G.S. 20-138.1. Thus, the "results of a chemical analysis are sufficient evidence to submit the issue of a defendant's alcohol concentration to the factfinder," who "may find [them to be] adequate proof."[79]

(iv) Per Se Impairment Sufficient as a Matter of Law

One argument made with some frequency by defendants prosecuted under the per se impairment theory is that the defendant showed no outward signs of impairment. That is, he or she drove well and satisfactorily performed field sobriety tests. This, the defendant argues, casts doubt on the veracity of the alcohol concentration results reported from the chemical analysis. This sort of argument is proper and supported in law. Determining whether the evidence establishes the defendant's guilt beyond a reasonable doubt unquestionably is the province of the finder of fact.[80] Moreover, "[t]he State's introduction of evidence supporting the statutory elements in a per se criminal statute does not endow the evidence with infallibility."[81]

There's a variant on this argument, however, that is not supported in law. Defendants sometimes argue that the State's evidence is insufficient as a matter of law to establish impaired driving under the per se prong unless, in addition to proving the defendant's alcohol concentration, the State also proves that the defendant was appreciably impaired. This argument may be a hold-over from the statutory scheme that preceded the Safe Roads Act of 1983, which defined a per se violation of the impaired driving laws as a lesser-included offense of driving under the influence and under which the results of a chemical test yielding a result of 0.10 or more created a presumption that the person was under the influence.[82] Whatever its origins, this argument reflects a misunderstanding of the impairment

---

76. *See also* State v. George, 77 N.C. App. 470 (1985) (evidence was sufficient for conviction where defendant testified that he drank additional alcohol subsequent to driving; a test taken three hours and forty-five minutes after the driving was admissible, and jury could consider delay in determining the weight afforded to the test results).

77. G.S. 20-138.1(a)(2). This provision was added by S.L. 2006-253, effective for offenses committed on or after December 1, 2006.

78. 193 N.C. App. 76 (2008).

79. *Id.* at 81, 84.

80. *See, e.g.,* State v. Finch, 244 P.3d 673, 679 (Kan. 2011) (stating that proof of the elements of a per se criminal statute will not compel conviction as a matter of law, as "[t]he defense may still attack the State's proof and attempt to discredit its witnesses, their machines, and their methods during the State's case-in-chief or later" and "[t]he jury may finally agree that reasonable doubt prevents a conviction").

81. *Id.*

82. *See* G.S. 20-138 (Cum. Supp. 1981); 20-139.1 (Cum. Supp. 1981); State v. Shuping, 312 N.C. 421 (1984).

element of impaired driving as a single element that may be proved in any one of three ways.[83] As the court of appeals clarified in *State v. Arrington*,[84] "it is not necessary for the State to prove that the defendant was appreciably impaired, uncooperative, or driving in an unsafe manner in order to prove that defendant is guilty of a violation of [G.S. 20-138.1(a2)]. To prove guilt, the State need only show that defendant had an alcohol concentration of .08 or more . . . ."[85]

(v) Margin of Error

Another argument sometimes made by defendants is that the "margin of error" for the breath-testing instrument renders the State's proof of per se impairment based on a breath-alcohol concentration of 0.08 unreliable. The argument generally points to one of two sources for the margin of error. First, administrative regulations deem a breath-testing instrument to be accurate if the control sample used to verify instrument accuracy before the defendant's test measures at the expected result of 0.08 or 0.01 less than the expected result.[86] Second, G.S. 20-139.1(b3) deems admissible results of a chemical analysis consisting of "two consecutively collected breath samples [that] do not differ from each other by an alcohol concentration greater than 0.02" and provides that "[o]nly the lower of the two . . . can be used to prove a particular alcohol concentration."[87] Under the first basis, the margin of error is 0.01 (though any such variance engenders a lower alcohol concentration result than actually is present); under the second, the margin of error is 0.02. While alleged unreliability based upon a margin of error, like other questions about the reliability of a reported alcohol concentration result, is fair game for the fact-finder's consideration,[88] an alleged margin of error does not render the State's evidence of impairment insufficient as a matter of law.[89]

(vi) Proving Per Se Impairment with a Chemical Analysis

The usual way for the State to establish that a person drove while impaired under the per se prong of G.S. 20-138.1 is to introduce the results of a chemical analysis demonstrating that the person had an alcohol concentration of 0.08 or more at any relevant time after the driving. Not only are the results of a chemical analysis "deemed sufficient evidence to prove a person's alcohol concentration," but they also may be admitted at trial without the foundation required for similar types of scientific evidence.[90] Not just any test of a person's breath, blood, or bodily fluid, however, constitutes a "chemical analysis."[91] To qualify, the test must be performed in accordance with G.S. 20-139.1.

---

83. *See* State v. Coker, 312 N.C. 432, 440 (1984); *Narron*, 193 N.C. App. at 79.

84. 215 N.C. App. 161 (2011).

85. *Id.* at 165.

86. *See* Title 10A of the North Carolina Administrative Code (hereinafter N.C.A.C.), Subchapter 41B, Section .0101.

87. G.S. 20-139.1(b3).

88. *See, e.g.*, State v. Finch, 244 P.3d 673, 679 (Kan. 2011).

89. *See* State v. Shuping, 312 N.C. 421, 430 (1984) (rejecting defendant's challenge to the sufficiency of the evidence based on an alleged margin of error and characterizing the 0.01 deviation allowance below the expected reading as "a safeguard to insure that when the actual test is subsequently run, any possible error during actual testing is in favor of defendant"); *Arrington*, 215 N.C. App. at 164 (rejecting defendant's contention that since his reported alcohol concentration of 0.08, the result from both breath tests, was the lowest for which he could be convicted of a per se violation, the "margin of error of the [instrument] should be taken into account to undermine the State's case against him"; determining that the testing satisfied statutory requirements, was reliable, and accurately identified the defendant's level of impairment).

90. G.S. 20-139.1 (quoted language from *id.* § 20-138.1(a)(2)).

91. *Id.* § 20-4.01(3a).

A breath test "administered pursuant to the implied-consent law" and performed in accordance with rules of the Department of Health and Human Services (DHHS) by a person with a current DHHS permit for the type of instrument employed is an admissible chemical analysis.[92] In addition, the results of a chemical analysis of blood or urine reported by the North Carolina State Crime Laboratory; the Charlotte, N.C., Police Department Laboratory; or any other laboratory approved for chemical analysis by DHHS, including a hospital laboratory, are admissible without further identification.[93]

(A) Confrontation Clause and Notice and Demand

The Sixth Amendment to the United States Constitution, made applicable to the states via the Fourteenth Amendment,[94] provides, in a portion of its text known as the Confrontation Clause, that "[i]n all criminal prosecutions, the accused shall enjoy the right . . . to be confronted with the witnesses against him."[95] The United States Supreme Court in *Ohio v. Roberts*[96] interpreted the right as allowing the admission of an unavailable witness's statement against a criminal defendant if the statement bore "adequate 'indicia of reliability.'"[97] To meet that test, evidence had to either fall within a "firmly rooted hearsay exception" or bear "particularized guarantees of trustworthiness."[98]

The Supreme Court overruled *Roberts* in the landmark case of *Crawford v. Washington,*[99] in which it rejected the view that the application of the confrontation right to out-of-court statements depended on the "vagaries of the rules of evidence" or "amorphous notions of 'reliability.'"[100] Instead, the Court reasoned that the protection applied to those who "bear testimony"[101] against an accused and requires that reliability be assessed "by testing in the crucible of cross-examination."[102] *Crawford* held that the Confrontation Clause bars the admission of testimonial hearsay statements against the defendant unless the witness who made the statements testifies at trial or the witness is unavailable and the defendant had a prior opportunity to cross-examine the witness.[103] *Crawford* declared the statements at issue in that case—statements made in response to formal police interrogation—to be testimonial but "le[ft] for another day . . . a comprehensive definition of 'testimonial.'"[104]

It was thus unclear for several years post-*Crawford* whether the affidavits issued by chemical analysts in implied consent cases were testimonial for purposes of the Confrontation Clause. Indeed, the North Carolina Supreme Court concluded in *State v. Heinricy*[105] that they were not, reasoning that such affidavits were limited to "objective analysis of the evidence and routine chain of custody information."[106] Though noting that such affidavits were prepared with the understanding that their

---

92. *Id.* § 20-139.1(b).
93. *Id.* § 20-139.1(c1).
94. Pointer v. Texas, 380 U.S. 400, 403 (1965).
95. U.S. Const. amend. VI.
96. 448 U.S. 56 (1980).
97. *Id.* at 66.
98. *Id.* (footnote omitted).
99. 541 U.S. 36 (2004).
100. *Id.* at 61.
101. *Id.* at 51 (citation omitted).
102. *Id.* at 61.
103. *Id.* at 53–54.
104. *Id.* at 68 (footnote omitted).
105. 183 N.C. App. 585 (2007), *overruled by Melendez-Diaz v. Massachusetts*, 557 U.S. 305 (2009).
106. *Id.* at 591.

use in court was probable, the court characterized the analysts as "ha[ving] no interest in the outcome of the trial."[107] Post-*Crawford*, the General Statutes continued to permit the admission in an implied consent trial of affidavits prepared by chemical analysts without requiring the analyst to testify as a witness.[108]

But five years after *Crawford*, the U.S. Supreme Court held in *Melendez-Diaz v. Massachusetts*[109] that certified forensic analyses prepared for purposes of prosecution by employees of a state crime lab were testimonial statements within the meaning of *Crawford*. The Court further held that a defendant's ability to subpoena analysts—a right then afforded by North Carolina's implied consent statutes—did not obviate the prosecution's duty to present at trial the witnesses whose statements it sought to introduce.[110] The Court signaled its approval, however, of notice and demand statutes that "require the prosecution to provide notice to the defendant of its intent to use an analyst's report as evidence at trial, after which the defendant is given a period of time in which he may object to the admission of the evidence absent the analyst's appearance live at trial."[111] The North Carolina legislature responded to the ruling by amending G.S. 20-139.1 to incorporate notice and demand provisions, which are discussed below.

(1) Chemical Analysis of Breath in District Court

In a hearing in trial in district court, the State may introduce a chemical analyst's affidavit reporting information related to the administration of a breath test or the collection of blood or urine samples for analysis without calling the analyst as a witness at trial if it provides proper notice to a defendant and the defendant fails to file a timely written objection.[112] To avail itself of this provision, the State must (1) notify the defendant at least fifteen business days before the proceeding at which the affidavit would be used of its intention to introduce the affidavit and (2) provide a copy of the affidavit to the defendant. To prevent the introduction of the affidavit without an appearance from the chemical analyst, the defendant must, at least five business days before the proceeding at which the affidavit would be used, file a written notification with the court, with a copy provided to the State, stating that the defendant objects to the introduction of the affidavit into evidence.[113] A properly executed affidavit from a chemical analyst is admissible in evidence without further authentication and without the testimony of the analyst in any hearing or trial in district court with respect to: (1) the alcohol concentrations or the presence or absence of an impairing substance; (2) the time of the collection of the blood, breath, and/or bodily fluid for testing; (3) the type of chemical analysis administered and the procedures followed; (4) the type and status of any permit issued by DHHS that the analyst held when he or she performed the chemical analysis; and (5), if the chemical analysis is performed on a breath-testing instrument for which regulations require preventative maintenance, the date the

---

107. *Id.*

108. G.S. 20-139.1(c1) (2008) (rendering affidavit reporting results of a chemical analysis of blood or urine by an approved laboratory admissible in any court); 20-139.1(e1) (2008) (rendering affidavit by chemical analyst admissible in district court without testimony from analyst unless defendant subpoenaed analyst); *see also* State v. Smith, 312 N.C. 361 (1984) (determining pre-*Crawford* that a defendant's right to confrontation was not violated by the procedure that permitted the affidavit of an analyst who did not testify at trial to be introduced into evidence in district court).

109. 557 U.S. 305 (2009).

110. *Id.* at 324.

111. *Id.* at 326 (citations omitted).

112. G.S. 20-139.1(e1).

113. *Id.* § 20-139.1(e2).

most recent preventative maintenance procedures were performed as shown on the maintenance records for the instrument.

(2) Chemical Analysis of Blood or Urine in District or Superior Court

The State may introduce the certified results of a chemical analysis of blood or urine without further authentication and without the testimony of the analyst in cases tried in district and superior court and in adjudicatory hearings in juvenile court if (1) the State (a) notifies the defendant at least fifteen business days before the proceeding at which the evidence would be used of its intention to introduce the report into evidence and (b) provides a copy of the report to the defendant; and (2) the defendant fails to file a written objection with the court, with a copy provided to the State, at least five business days before the proceeding at which the report would be used stating that he or she objects to the introduction of the report.[114] If the defendant timely files a written objection, the admissibility of the report is determined by the appropriate rules of evidence.

(a) Remote Testimony

The General Assembly enacted in 2014 a provision allowing an analyst, with the defendant's acquiescence, to testify remotely regarding the results of a chemical analysis of the defendant's blood or urine.[115] To utilize this provision, the State must provide (1) notice to the defendant at least fifteen business days before the proceeding at which the evidence would be used that it intends to introduce the evidence using remote testimony and (2) a copy of the analyst's report to the defendant at least fifteen business days before the proceeding.[116] If the defendant fails to object to the remote testimony by filing a written objection with the court at least five business days before the proceeding at which the testimony will be presented, the analyst may testify remotely.[117] The method used for remote testimony must allow the trier of fact and all parties to observe the demeanor of the analyst as the analyst testifies in a similar manner as if the analyst were testifying in person.[118] The court must ensure that the defendant has a full and fair opportunity to examine and cross-examine the analyst.[119] While the statutory provisions for remote testimony became effective September 1, 2014, the legislative act further provided that its provisions did not obligate the Administrative Office of the Courts or the State Crime Laboratory to incur expenses related to remote testimony absent an appropriation of funds for this purpose.[120] Given that no such funds have yet been appropriated, no analysts were testifying remotely as of the date of this publication.

(3) Chemical Analysis of Blood or Urine in Administrative Hearings

Certified results of a chemical analysis may be introduced in an administrative hearing before the North Carolina Division of Motor Vehicles (NC DMV) without the testimony of the analyst, regardless of whether the State notifies the defendant in advance of its intent to introduce such results. The protections of the Confrontation Clause apply only to criminal prosecutions, and thus are not implicated in administrative license hearings conducted by NC DMV.

(B) Proving Per Se Impairment Without a Chemical Analysis

The State is not limited to proving a defendant's alcohol concentration by means of a chemical analysis performed in accordance with G.S. 20-139.1. Instead, the State also may prove a defendant's alcohol concentration by introducing the results of other reliable tests showing the presence of a controlled

114. *Id.* § 20-139.1(c1).
115. S.L. 2014-119, sec. 8.(b).
116. G.S. 20-139.1(c5).
117. *Id.*
118. *Id.*
119. *Id.*
120. S.L. 2014-119, secs. 8.(b), (c).

substance.[121] One circumstance in which the State might rely upon a test that is not a chemical analysis occurs when a defendant is hospitalized after an incident of suspected impaired driving and his or her blood or urine is analyzed for purposes of medical treatment. In such a case, testing is performed pursuant to hospital laboratory procedures rather than the procedures required by G.S. 20-139.1. In *State v. Drdak*,[122] the state supreme court determined that the trial court did not err by denying the defendant's motion to suppress blood test results from a hospital laboratory proffered by the State at the defendant's trial on impaired driving charges to prove his alcohol concentration. The court characterized the defendant's contention that the blood test results were inadmissible because the test was not performed in accordance with the procedures set forth in G.S. 20-16.2 and 20-139.1 as "fl[ying] squarely in the face of the plain reading of [G.S.20-139.1(a)],"[123] which states that "[t]his section does not limit the introduction of other competent evidence as to a person's alcohol concentration or results of other tests showing the presence of an impairing substance, including other chemical tests."[124]

Of course, results of tests performed outside the scope of implied consent laws are not afforded the presumptive admissibility of chemical analyses satisfying the requirements of G.S. 20-139.1. Instead, the State must provide a proper foundation for the introduction of such results, which may require that the State demonstrate their reliability.[125]

The *Drdak* court determined that the State established a proper foundation for introduction of hospital blood test results by showing, among other facts, that "the hospital's blood alcohol test was performed less than an hour after the defendant's car crashed into the tree, that an experienced phlebotomist withdrew the blood sample under routine procedure pursuant to the doctor's orders, and that a trained laboratory technician analyzed the blood sample using a Dupont Automatic Clinical Analyzer which was capable of testing either whole blood or serum."[126] The court of appeals in *State v. Mac Cardwell*[127] likewise concluded that the trial court, in denying the defendant's motion to suppress evidence of hospital blood test results in an impaired driving trial, did not abuse its discretion in determining that the Dupont ACA Star Analyzer ("Analyzer") used by the hospital to measure the defendant's alcohol concentration was a "reliable scientific method of proof."[128] The *Mac Cardwell* court further noted that the trial court properly allowed the defendant to present evidence to the jury attacking the reliability of the Analyzer and the defendant's results.[129]

Hospital laboratories sometimes calculate a patient's plasma-alcohol concentration rather than the alcohol concentration in whole blood. To prove a specific alcohol concentration based on such results, the State must provide testimony from an expert capable of converting the results to grams of alcohol per 100 milliliters of blood in order to prove that the defendant had a specific alcohol concentration.[130]

---

121. G.S. 20-139.1(a).

122. 330 N.C. 587 (1992).

123. *Id.* at 592.

124. G.S. 20-139.1(a).

125. Hospital records are business records for purposes of the business records hearsay exception in North Carolina Rule of Evidence 803(6). Yet, as described below, North Carolina's appellate courts have indicated that some greater foundational showing may be required to support the introduction of a defendant's alcohol concentration as contained in such records. That mode of analysis comports with a trend of distinguishing among opinions in business records. *See generally* Imwinkelreid et al., 1 COURTROOM CRIMINAL EVIDENCE § 1220 (5th ed. 2011).

126. 330 N.C. at 592.

127. 133 N.C. App. 496 (1999).

128. *Id.* at 506.

129. *Id.* at 507.

130. *See* G.S. 20-4.01(1b) (requiring that the concentration of alcohol be expressed either as "a. Grams of alcohol per 100 milliliters of blood; or b. Grams of alcohol per 210 liters of breath").

The *Mac Cardwell* court held that the trial court did not abuse its discretion in finding the conversion ratio of 1 to 1.18 utilized by a forensic chemist at the State Bureau of Investigation laboratory reliable.[131] As it had with respect to the test results, the court noted the propriety of permitting the defendant to present evidence attacking the conversion ratio used by the State.[132]

(C) Retrograde Extrapolation

Retrograde extrapolation is a methodology used to estimate a person's alcohol concentration at some earlier point in time based upon a later reported alcohol concentration.[133] The calculation of a person's earlier alcohol concentration is based upon the time that elapsed between the specified earlier event (such as a vehicle crash) and the time of the chemical analysis and the average rate of elimination of alcohol from a person's blood. North Carolina's appellate courts have, on numerous occasions, recognized retrograde extrapolation as a reliable method of proving a person's alcohol concentration and have allowed qualified experts to testify about alcohol concentration results derived from such calculations.[134]

---

131. *Mac Cardwell,* 133 N.C. App. at 506–07.

132. *Id.* at 507.

133. *See generally* Justin Noval & Edward J. Imwinkelried, *Retrograde Extrapolation of Blood Alcohol Concentration,* 50 Crim. L. Bull., no. 1, art. 7 (Winter 2014) (describing the technique of retrograde extrapolation).

134. *See, e.g.,* State v. Green, 209 N.C. App. 669 (2011); State v. Taylor, 165 N.C. App. 750 (2004); State v. Davis, 142 N.C. App. 81 (2001); State v. Catoe, 78 N.C. App. 167 (1985); *but see* State v. Davis, 208 N.C. App. 26 (2010) (holding that expert testimony as to the defendant's blood-alcohol concentration at the time of the crash was improper and prejudicial, where that testimony was founded solely on the fact that an officer who talked to the defendant more than ten hours after the accident smelled alcohol on her breath).

Courts in other states have viewed retrograde extrapolation testimony with skepticism. The Texas Court of Criminal Appeals in *Mata v. Texas,* 46 S.W.3d 902 (Tex. Crim. App. 2001) (en banc), summarized its view of the limitations of retrograde extrapolation as follows:

> Initially, we recognize that even those who believe retrograde extrapolation is a reliable technique have utilized it only if certain factors are known, such as the length of the drinking spree, the time of the last drink, and the person's weight. . . . In addition, there appears to be general disagreement on some of the fundamental aspects of the theory, such as the accuracy of Widmark's formulas, . . . whether a standard elimination rate can be reliably applied to a given subject, . . . and the effect that food in the stomach has on alcohol absorption. . . . Nevertheless, given the studies, other concepts seem indisputable, including that multiple tests will increase the ability to plot a subject's BAC [blood-alcohol concentration] curve, a test nearer in time to the time of the alleged offense increases the ability to determine the subject's offense-time BAC, and the more personal information known about the subject increases the reliability of an extrapolation. . . .

We believe that the science of retrograde extrapolation can be reliable in a given case. The expert's ability to apply the science and explain it with clarity to the court is a paramount consideration. In addition, the expert must demonstrate some understanding of the difficulties associated with a retrograde extrapolation. He must demonstrate an awareness of the subtleties of the science and the risks inherent in any extrapolation. Finally, he must be able to clearly and consistently apply the science.

Id. at 915–16 (footnotes omitted). *See also* Burns v. State, 298 S.W.3d 697, 702 (Tex. App. 2009) (trial court abused its discretion by admitting retrograde extrapolation testimony where expert "admitted he knew none of the factors required by *Mata*"; such testimony was unreliable); State v. Dist. Ct. (Armstrong), 267 P.3d 777, 783 (Nev. 2011) (citing *Mata* favorably and finding that, while retrograde extrapolation evidence was relevant, the trial court did not abuse its discretion by precluding such evidence where significant personal characteristics of defendant were unknown to expert). *But see* Bigon v. State, 252 S.W.3d 360, 368 (Tex. Crim. App. 2008) (trial court did not abuse its discretion by admitting retrograde extrapolation testimony where expert clearly explained the underlying theory and explained the specific methodologies utilized as required by *Mata*; fact that two tests were administered diminished the importance of expert's lack of knowledge of defendant's personal characteristics); Kennedy v. State, 264 S.W.3d 372, 381 (Tex. App. 2008) (same); United States v. Tsosie, 791 F. Supp. 2d 1099, 1113 (D.N.M. 2011) (trial court did not abuse its discretion by admitting

As a general matter, the admissibility of retrograde extrapolation evidence tends to turn on traditional evidentiary analyses related to expert testimony rather than on jurisdiction-specific views of the reliability of retrograde extrapolation as a scientific technique in the abstract.[135] In determining the admissibility of such evidence courts tend to consider an expert's qualifications,[136] the particular methods employed in a given case,[137] and a jurisdiction's statutory scheme[138] rather than the soundness of retrograde extrapolation as a scientific theory.[139]

---

retrograde extrapolation testimony where expert used assumptions favorable to defendant to account for certain unknown personal factors); People v. Ikerman, 973 N.E.2d 1008, 1019 (Ill. App. Ct. 2012) (retrograde extrapolation evidence admissible through testimony of qualified expert; no mention of personal factors).

See also United States v. DuBois, 645 F.2d 642, 644, 645 (8th Cir. 1981) (evaluating sufficiency of the evidence, "emphasiz[ing] that this was a criminal trial," and finding expert's extrapolation based on a test taken two and one-half hours after the accident and after the undisputed consumption of an unknown amount of beer subsequent to the accident insufficient to establish intoxication at time of accident); *Cf.* Weinstein v. Siemens, No. 2:07-CV-15000, 2010 WL 4825205 (E.D. Mich. Nov. 22, 2010) (finding retrograde extrapolation testimony from expert with Ph.D. in toxicology admissible to prove driver's alcohol concentration at the time of accident where expert relied on three consecutive blood draws to determine the driver's rate of elimination and applied that rate in his extrapolation analysis to conclude that driver's alcohol concentration was in the range of 0.36 to 0.39, depending upon whether his alcohol concentration was increasing or decreasing). *See generally* A.W. Jones, "Disposition and Fate of Ethanol in the Body," in Medical-Legal Aspects of Alcohol 95 (James C. Garriott ed., 4th ed. 2003) ("Requests to back extrapolate [blood-alcohol concentration] from time of sampling to time of driving are common in DUI litigation although this is a dubious practice with many variables to consider.").

135. *See generally* Noval & Imwinkelried, *supra* note 133 (asserting that "[e]ven if the courts are generally receptive to retrograde extrapolation testimony, post-*Daubert* the testimony should be admitted only if the scientific theory underlying such testimony is empirically valid").

136. *Compare* People v. Barham, 788 N.E.2d 297, 308–09 (Ill. App. Ct. 2003) (state failed to lay proper foundation for expert testimony regarding rate at which alcohol is eliminated from the human system where there was no evidence of the expert's relevant education, training, or experience), *with Ikerman*, 973 N.E.2d at 1019 (retrograde extrapolation evidence admissible through testimony of qualified expert).

137. *Compare Davis*, 208 N.C. App. 26 (finding retrograde extrapolation based on a "smell test" which lacked independent verification, had never been submitted to peer review, and had never been previously utilized by the expert to be an insufficiently reliable method of proof), *with Green*, 209 N.C. App. at 680 (finding retrograde extrapolation testimony based on the results of a test performed with an Intoxilyzer 5000 to be admissible).

138. *Compare* State v. Day, 176 P.3d 1091, 1098 (N.M. 2008) (retrograde extrapolation admissible to prove defendant's blood-alcohol concentration (BAC) at the time of driving), *with* People v. Emery, 812 P.2d 665, 667 (Colo. App. 1990) (retrograde extrapolation evidence should not have been admitted because it was irrelevant where test results were statutorily deemed to relate back to the offense by virtue of "within a reasonable time [of the offense]" language), State v. Tischio, 527 A.2d 388, 395 (N.J. 1987) (legislative intent precluded defendant's extrapolation evidence meant to show a lower BAC at the time of driving than at the time of testing; a reliable breathalyzer test administered within a reasonable time after driving which reported a BAC exceeding statutory limit was sufficient to prove the offense notwithstanding the fact that a strict reading of statute suggested that crime was in the nature of an "at the time of driving" offense), *and* State v. Daniel, 979 P.2d 103, 105 (Idaho 1999) (statute explicitly prohibiting prosecution where test shows BAC less than 0.10 (now 0.08) precluded extrapolation evidence; statute meant to incentivize submission to testing and allowing extrapolation would eliminate incentive); *see also* Noval and Imwinkelried, *supra* note 133 (indentifying "weaknesses in the popular method of applying the retrograde extrapolation technique" and suggesting improvements for more accurate results).

139. *But see* State v. Burgess, 5 A.3d 911, 916 (Vt. 2010) (noting that "Vermont courts have accepted evidence regarding retrograde extrapolation for a number of decades" and determining that trial court "went too far in holding that the test results . . . were unreliable as a matter of law").

d. Schedule I Controlled Substance

The third way in which a person may be deemed impaired is if there is any amount of a Schedule I controlled substance or its metabolites in his or her blood or urine. Schedule I controlled substances are listed in G.S. 90-89, a provision of the Controlled Substances Act.[140] This schedule includes specified opiates, opium derivatives, hallucinogenic substances, central nervous system depressants, and stimulants. Some of the more commonly known substances included on this schedule are heroin,[141] lysergic acid diethylamide (LSD), [142] and MDMA (ecstasy).[143] Cocaine is a Schedule II,[144] not a Schedule I, controlled substance. Hydrocodone and oxycodone likewise are Schedule II rather than Schedule I controlled substances.[145] Thus, the presence of cocaine, hydrocodone, oxycodone, or the metabolites of any of these substances in a person's blood or urine does not establish per se impairment pursuant to G.S. 20-138.1(a)(3). The State may, however, establish that a person was appreciably impaired by a controlled substance not included on Schedule I.[146]

B. Pleading Requirements

A pleading charging misdemeanor impaired driving in violation of G.S. 20-138.1 "is sufficient if it states the time and place of the alleged offense in the usual form and charges that the defendant drove a vehicle on a highway or public vehicular area while subject to an impairing substance."[147] The State is not required to allege the specific hour and minute that the offense occurred.[148] Nor must the State allege the theory of impairment under which the defendant is charged.[149] A defendant who feels he or she may be surprised at trial by the pleadings' lack of specificity may request a bill of particulars.[150]

Moreover, while the State must provide the defendant with notice of any aggravating sentencing factor it intends to use for an impaired driving conviction appealed to superior court, no such notice requirement applies in district court.[151]

---

140. G.S. Chapter 90, Article 5.
141. G.S. 90-89(2)j.
142. *Id.* § 90-89(3)m.
143. *Id.* § 90-89(3)c.
144. *Id.* § 90-90(1)d.
145. *Id.* § 90-90(1).
146. *See, e.g.*, State v. Norton, 213 N.C. App. 75, 80 (2011) (evidence that the defendant drove recklessly and that he consumed alcohol and cocaine was sufficient to establish his guilt on charges of driving while impaired).
147. G.S. 20-138.1(c).
148. State v. Friend, 219 N.C. App. 338 (2012).
149. State v. Coker, 312 N.C. 432, 434 (1984).
150. *Id.* at 437.
151. G.S. 20-179(a1)(1). *See infra* chapter 5 for a detailed discussion of this requirement. The notice provisions of G.S. 20-179(a1)(1) were crafted to protect a defendant's Sixth Amendment right to be informed of the charges against him or her—as contrasted with a defendant's Sixth Amendment right to confront witnesses.

For a thorough analysis of the impetus for imposing similar notice requirements upon the State in structured sentencing cases post-*Blakely v. Washington*, see Jessica Smith, *North Carolina Sentencing after* Blakely v. Washington *and the* Blakely *Bill* (UNC School of Government, Sept. 2005) (hereinafter *Blakely Bill*), 10–13, www.sog.unc.edu/sites/www.sog.unc.edu/files/Blakely%20Update.pdf.

It is well settled that all of the constitutional protections that apply in superior court need not be afforded a defendant at the first level of a two-tier trial system. *See* Ludwig v. Massachusetts, 427 U.S. 618 (1976) (defendant's Fourteenth Amendment right to jury trial not violated by bench trial at first tier of two-tier system where defendant had right to trial by jury at second tier). Thus, there is some questions as to whether *Blakely v. Washington*, 530 U.S. 466 (2000), applies to non-Structured Sentencing Act misdemeanors tried in district court. The issue has been stated this way:

C. Aiding and Abetting

A defendant may be convicted of impaired driving in violation of G.S. 20-138.1 under the common law concept of aiding and abetting. A defendant aids and abets impaired driving when he or she knowingly advises, instigates, encourages, or aids another person to drive while impaired and his or her actions cause or contribute to the commission of the crime.[152]

One situation clearly covered by the aiding and abetting theory is that in which a person knowingly gives control of his or her vehicle to an impaired person who then drives the vehicle on a street, highway, or public vehicular area while the owner rides along as a passenger.[153]

> One view is that *Blakely* is not simply a ruling on the constitutional right to a jury trial, but also rests on rights (such as notice and proof beyond a reasonable doubt) that flow from a sentence that exceeds the statutory maximum as defined in the ruling. Therefore, requirements of a criminal pleading providing notice (either by specific allegations or a statutory short-form pleading) and proof beyond a reasonable doubt apply . . . in district court . . . just as they apply in superior court—except that a district court judge, not a jury, decides whether these factors have been proved beyond a reasonable doubt. . . .
>
> Another view is that *Blakely* rests squarely on the constitutional right to a jury trial. The United States Supreme Court ruled in *Ludwig v. Massachusetts*, 427 U.S. 618 (1976), that there is no federal constitutional right to a jury trial at the first level of a state's trial de novo system. If *Blakely* is based solely on the protection of that right, then it apparently does not apply to the first level of a system, such as North Carolina's, where jury trials are provided only on de novo appeal.

See Smith, *Blakely Bill*, at 28.

As Smith discusses in the article cited above, the North Carolina Supreme Court held in *State v. Speight*, 359 N.C. 602 (2005), *vacated and remanded*, 548 U.S. 923 (2006) (remanding case for reconsideration in light of *Washington v. Recuenco*, 548 U.S. 212 (2006) (reversing lower court's determination that *Blakely* violations could never be harmless)), that grossly aggravating and aggravating factors in an impaired driving case need not be alleged in an indictment. However, the state supreme court in *State v. Hunt*, 357 N.C. 257 (2003), recognized that the Sixth Amendment imposes a notice requirement on the State. In *Hunt*, the short-form murder indictment combined with an exclusive statutory list of aggravating circumstances was held to provide sufficient notice. G.S. 20-138.1(c) provides for a short-form criminal pleading for impaired driving, though as previously noted, G.S. 20-179(a1)(1) requires additional pleadings in superior court. *Hunt* can be read to suggest that in district court this short-form pleading combined with the exclusive list of grossly aggravating factors in G.S. 20-179(c) provides sufficient notice as to grossly aggravating factors. The same argument could be made regarding the aggravating factors in G.S. 20-179(d), with the exception of the catch-all aggravating factor in G.S. 20-179(d)(9). *Hunt* might be read to suggest that some sort of additional notice would be required for this factor, if, in fact, *Blakely* applies in district court. However, given that this catch-all aggravating factor must be based on conduct that occurs during the same transaction or occurrence as the impaired driving offense, it may be sufficiently circumscribed so as to place the defendant on notice. *Contrast* G.S. 15A-1340.16(d)(20) (listing as a catch-all "[a]ny other aggravating factor reasonably related to the purposes of sentencing").

152. *See* State v. Goode, 350 N.C. 247, 260 (1999).

153. *See* State v. Gibbs, 227 N.C. 677, 678 (1947) (citations omitted) ("When an owner places his motor vehicle in the hands of an intoxicated driver, sits by his side, and permits him, without protest, to operate the vehicle on a public highway, while in a state of intoxication, he is as guilty as the man at the wheel."); State v. Whitaker, 43 N.C. App. 600, 605 (1979) (citations omitted) ("[W]e hold that when a death results from the operation of a motor vehicle by an intoxicated person not the owner of that vehicle, the owner who is present in the vehicle and who with his knowledge and consent permits the intoxicated driver to operate the vehicle, is as guilty as the intoxicated driver."); *see also* Story v. United States, 16 F.2d 342, 344 (D.C. Cir. 1926) (owner of and passenger in vehicle convicted as aider and abettor where impaired passenger asked defendant for and was given permission to drive); State v. Satern, 516 N.W.2d 839, 840 (Iowa 1994) (owner of and passenger in vehicle convicted as an accomplice where he "turned over" the driving to a person who was impaired); State v. Stratton, 591 A.2d 246, 248 (Me. 1991) (owner of and passenger in vehicle convicted as an accomplice where he asked his impaired employee to drive because employee was "soberer"); State v. Lemacks, 996 S.W.2d 166, 172 (Tenn. 1999) (owner of and passenger in vehicle convicted as an accomplice where evidence uncertain if

It is somewhat less clear whether a person may be convicted of aiding and abetting impaired driving if he or she knowingly gives control of his or her vehicle to a person who is impaired, but does not himself/herself accompany the driver. No North Carolina appellate court cases consider this circumstance, though it seems likely that such conduct would support a conviction for aiding and abetting DWI. The vehicle owner's presence in the car in the aiding and abetting cases previously cited[154] was probative of his or her consent to the driving as well as his or her knowledge of the driver's impairment. Yet a vehicle owner who hands over his or her keys to an impaired driver but does not himself/herself ride along has provided the same degree of assistance and appears no less culpable than the owner who elects to accompany the driver. Indeed, the Court of Appeals of Georgia concluded in *Guzman v. State*[155] that the owner of a vehicle who was neither the driver nor a passenger in the car aided and abetted driving under the influence where he gave beer and his car keys to the 14-year-old driver.

A person may not be convicted of aiding and abetting impaired driving based on nothing more than his or her failure to stop from driving a person he or she knows to be impaired.[156] The North Carolina Court of Appeals considered such a claim in *Smith v. Winn-Dixie Charlotte, Inc.*[157] *Smith* was a civil action in which the plaintiff, who was injured when a 17-year-old impaired driver struck her vehicle, alleged negligence by the grocery store who sold beer to the driver's underage friend and negligence per se by the driver's friends whom she contended aided and abetted the underage driver in violating G.S. 20-138.1.

The record in *Smith* established that the driver's friends drank with him on the evening of the accident and that they saw the driver consume six beers in a short period of time. They did not attempt to stop him from driving his own car afterwards. The court of appeals determined, for purposes of the defendant-friends' motions for summary judgment, that this evidence was not sufficient to establish that the friends aided and abetted the driver in committing the offense of driving while impaired. The court noted the lack of evidence that the friends intended to aid the driver or that they communicated any such intent. Moreover, the court stated that even assuming the friends knew or should have known the driver was impaired, they had no duty to prevent him from getting into his car and attempting to drive.

The Supreme Court of Vermont wrestled with more difficult facts in *State v. Millette*.[158] There, the evidence established that the defendant and his friend left a night club in the early morning hours after a day and night of drinking. The defendant, whose car was parked in the parking lot, suggested to his friend that they pull the car behind the night club and sleep. The defendant's friend removed the keys from the defendant's pocket and said he would drive the defendant home. The friend wrecked the car on the way home and was killed. The court concluded that these facts failed to establish that the defendant aided and abetted driving while impaired, noting that cases predicated on this theory of criminal liability rested on "more active participation" by the defendant than was present in *Millette*.[159]

---

he was driving but where, in any event, he gave keys to impaired co-defendant); Williams v. State, 352 S.W.2d 230, 230 (Tenn. 1961) (owner of and passenger in vehicle convicted as aider and abettor where he had no valid license and had impaired friend drive).

154. See *supra* note 153.

155. 586 S.E.2d 59 (Ga. Ct. App. 2003).

156. *See* State v. Sanders, 288 N.C. 285, 290 (1975) (citations omitted) ("The mere presence of the defendant at the scene of the crime, even though he is in sympathy with the criminal act and does nothing to prevent its commission, does not make him guilty of the offense.")

157. 142 N.C. App. 255, 264 (2001).

158. 795 A.2d 1182 (Vt. 2002).

159. *Id.* at 1184.

D. Punishment

Impaired driving and several related offenses are sentenced under G.S. 20-179, which sets forth six levels of punishment. The applicable level is determined by the finding and weighing of statutorily enumerated aggravating and mitigating factors. Aggravated Level One is the most serious level, punishable by up to three years' imprisonment. Level Five is the least serious level and is punishable by no more than sixty days' imprisonment. A person convicted of impaired driving under G.S. 20-138.1 under the common law concept of aiding and abetting is subject to Level Five punishment.[160] The procedures for sentencing, sentencing factors, the punishment permitted at each level, and mandatory conditions of probation under G.S. 20-179 are discussed at length in chapter 5.

E. License Revocation

Clerks of court are required to send to the North Carolina Division of Motor Vehicles (NC DMV) a record of "[a] conviction of a violation of law regulating the operation of a vehicle."[161] Thus, a conviction for impaired driving under G.S. 20-138.1 triggers this reporting requirement. Upon receiving a record of a driver's conviction for impaired driving under G.S. 20-138.1, NC DMV must "forthwith" revoke the person's driver's license.[162] A person convicted of impaired driving and sentenced at Aggravated Level One, which requires a finding of three or more grossly aggravating factors, is subject to a permanent revocation.[163] Though such revocations are termed "permanent," there are circumstances under which NC DMV may conditionally restore the person's driver's license after it has been revoked for at least twenty-four months.[164] The revocation period for a defendant convicted of impaired driving under G.S. 20-138.1 and sentenced at Level One, Two, Three, Four, or Five varies, depending upon whether the person previously has been convicted of an offense involving impaired driving and when that prior offense occurred. The driver's license of a person who has no such prior convictions will be revoked for one year upon his or her conviction of impaired driving under G.S. 20-138.1.[165] The driver's license of a person who has been convicted of another offense involving impaired driving that occurred within three years before the date of the offense for which his or her license is being revoked will be revoked for four years.[166] A person who has two or more previous convictions for impaired driving for offenses that occurred within five years of the date of the offense for which his or her license is being revoked is subject to a permanent revocation.[167]

NC DMV may only revoke a person's license upon *final conviction* of a qualifying offense.[168] For a conviction to be final, not only must the person be adjudged guilty, but a judgment also must be entered from which the defendant may exercise his or her right to appeal. Impaired driving convictions in district court from which a defendant has given notice of appeal to superior court are not final for purposes of imposing a license revocation, just as they are not final for purposes of sentencing. Thus, while a defendant's conviction in district court for DWI is the triggering event for a

160. G.S. 20-179(f1).
161. *Id.* § 20-24(b)(1).
162. *Id.* § 20-17(a)(2).
163. *Id.* § 20-19(e).
164. *Id.* § 20-19(e2); *see also id.* § 20-19(e1) (permitting conditional restoration after at least three years).
165. *Id.* § 20-19(c1).
166. *Id.* § 20-19(d). NC DMV may conditionally restore the person's license after it has been revoked for at least two years if the person satisfies certain conditions.
167. *Id.* § 20-19(e).
168. *See id.* § 20-4.01(4a) (defining conviction as "a final conviction").

license revocation based upon that conviction, it is not always the date on which the post-conviction revocation period begins.

A defendant may render the post-conviction revocation period immediately applicable by surrendering at sentencing his or her driver's license to the clerk of court.[169] When this occurs, the clerk provides the defendant with form DL-53, which serves as the defendant's receipt for the surrender of his or her license and calls for the defendant's signature acknowledging that his or her license is suspended as of that date. The clerk then either destroys the license or forwards it to NC DMV. The DL-53 is transmitted to NC DMV and the date of receipt noted on that form is recorded as the beginning date for the post-conviction revocation in the person's driving record.

When a defendant does not surrender his or her license at sentencing, the post-conviction revocation is not immediately effective. Instead, NC DMV imposes the revocation after it is notified by the clerk of the conviction. After receiving notice, NC DMV sends the driver a letter notifying him or her that the revocation becomes effective on 12:01 a.m. on the eleventh day after the notification. This ten-day notice period is not explicitly required by statute, but corresponds to the ten-day period for filing a notice of appeal to superior court for trial de novo, thus ensuring that NC DMV does not impose a collateral licensure consequence for a district court conviction that is not yet final.

Thus, it is the clerk's provision of notice to NC DMV or the defendant's surrender of his or her license to the clerk at sentencing—rather than the date of conviction or sentencing—that marks the inception of the revocation period resulting from a conviction for DWI.

There is an exception to the mandatory revocation rule for circumstances in which NC DMV does not receive a record of a defendant's conviction until more than a year after it is entered.[170] In such a case, NC DMV may, but is not required to, substitute a period of probation for all or part of the revocation required.

II. Habitual Impaired Driving

A person commits the offense of habitual impaired driving if he or she

(1) drives while impaired as defined in G.S. 20-138.1, and
(2) has been convicted of three or more offenses involving impaired driving as defined in G.S. 20-4.01(24a) within ten years of the date of this offense.[171]

Habitual impaired driving is a separate offense from impaired driving under G.S. 20-138.1 and is not enhanced punishment for that offense.[172] Impaired driving under G.S. 20-138.1 is a lesser-included offense of habitual impaired driving.

A. Offenses Involving Impaired Driving

The following are offenses involving impaired driving:

- Impaired driving under G.S. 20-138.1
- Habitual impaired driving under G.S. 20-138.5
- Impaired driving in a commercial vehicle under G.S. 20-138.2

169. *See id.* § 20-24(a).
170. *Id.* § 20-24(b1).
171. *Id.* § 20-138.5.
172. State v. Priddy, 115 N.C. App. 547 (1994).

- Death or serious injury by vehicle under G.S. 20-141.4 based on impaired driving
- Murder under G.S. 14-17 based on impaired driving
- Involuntary manslaughter under G.S. 14-18 based on impaired driving
- Substantially similar offenses committed in another jurisdiction

B. Prior Convictions

1. Defined

The term "conviction" is defined in G.S. 20-4.01(4a) as "[a] conviction for an offense committed in North Carolina or another state." The term "state" is defined as "[a] state, territory, or possession of the United States, District of Columbia, Commonwealth of Puerto Rico, a province of Canada, or the Sovereign Nation of the Eastern Band of the Cherokee Indians."[173]

2. Time of Conviction

Unlike the habitual felon statute,[174] the violent habitual felon statute,[175] and the habitual misdemeanor assault statute,[176] the habitual impaired driving statute does not explicitly state that the underlying impaired driving offense must occur *after* the convictions for other qualifying impaired driving convictions. Nevertheless, reading G.S. 20-138.5 to require that the instant impaired driving offense occur after the predicate convictions arguably is the most straightforward interpretation of the statute. The court of appeals' characterization of the legislature's intent in cases challenging the constitutionality and scope of G.S. 20-138.5 supports this view. In *State v. Bradley*,[177] for example, the court stated that "[th]e habitual impaired driving statute is intended to provide an increased sentence for someone convicted of a fourth impaired driving offense, with the previous three offenses occurring within seven years of the fourth offense."[178] And, in *State v. Vardiman*,[179] the court stated that "[p]rior convictions of driving while impaired are the elements of the offense of habitual impaired driving,

---

173. G.S. 20-4.01(45). Thus, conviction in a Canadian court of an offense substantially similar to any of the North Carolina offenses deemed to involve impaired driving within ten years of the instant offense meets the statutory requirements for a qualifying prior conviction. These statutory provisions may not, however, end the inquiry in all cases. Though no North Carolina court has considered the issue, case law from other states indicates that reliance at sentencing upon a Canadian conviction obtained without affording the defendant certain rights guaranteed by the U.S. Constitution may be impermissible. *See, e.g.,* State v. Payne, 69 P.3d 889, 893 (Wash. Ct. App. 2003) (concluding that trial court properly refused to consider at sentencing a Canadian conviction for which the defendant had no right to trial by jury); State v. Roberts, 14 P.3d 713, 745 (Wash. 2001) (holding that Canadian convictions were properly admitted at defendant's capital sentencing proceeding as the convictions "appear, from the well developed record, to be reliable, to have afforded [defendant] counsel, and to be free of any facial constitutional defects" and because defendant "offered no specific reasons why the Canadian convictions were constitutionally defective or unreliable"); State v. Williams, 706 A.2d 795, 798 (N.J. Super. Ct. App. Div. 1998) (holding that "absent a showing of fundamental unfairness surrounding the prior foreign conviction, its use [in sentencing] is presumed to be appropriate where the conviction occurs in a jurisdiction that has a judicial system that affords protections similar to our own" and noting that the trial judge "found that the Canadian system offers the accused a trial where he is represented by counsel, and if convicted, has the opportunity to appeal").

174. G.S. 14-7.1.

175. *Id.* § 14-7.7.

176. *Id.* § 14-33.2.

177. 181 N.C. App. 557 (2007).

178. *Id.* at 559.

179. 146 N.C. App. 381 (2001).

but the statute 'does not impose punishment for [these] previous crimes, [it] imposes an enhanced punishment' for the latest offense."[180]

There is no requirement that each of the qualifying prior convictions for an offense involving impaired driving occur consecutively to one another as there is, for example, in the habitual felon law.[181] Thus, qualifying prior convictions may occur on the same date.

The State may prove the existence of a prior conviction in several ways,[182] including through the introduction of printouts of records of prior convictions maintained on the Administrative Office of the Courts computer database.[183]

C. Indictment

Because habitual impaired driving is a felony offense predicated upon the commission of a lesser offense by a person who has qualifying prior convictions, special rules for charging the offense by indictment or information apply.

An indictment or information charging habitual impaired driving must allege the prior convictions in (1) a separate count of the indictment or information charging the substantive offense or (2) a separate indictment or information.[184] The defendant must be arraigned upon the separate indictment or the count alleging the prior convictions during the superior court trial before the close of the State's case and in the jury's absence.[185] If the defendant admits the prior convictions, this element is satisfied and proof of the convictions and jury instructions about this element are not permitted.[186] (The State is not prohibited from introducing proof of prior convictions when otherwise permitted under the rules of evidence.)[187] If the defendant denies the prior convictions or a particular conviction, then the State has the burden of proving the conviction(s) before the jury.[188] The defendant has the burden of proving that a conviction was obtained in violation of the right to counsel[189] and may not collaterally attack a conviction on grounds other than a right-to-counsel violation.[190]

---

180. *Id.* at 385 (citations omitted); *see also* State v. Smith, 139 N.C. App. 209, 213 (2000) (stating that "[b]oth the habitual misdemeanor assault statute and the habitual impaired driving statute declare that a person 'commits the offense' if that person currently commits specified acts and has been convicted of a specified number of similar offenses in the past").

181. G.S. 14-7.1.

182. *See, e.g., id.* § 8-35.2 (providing that certified copies of records contained in the criminal index or similar records maintained by the clerk of superior court are admissible as prima facie evidence of prior convictions of the person named in the records if the original documents have been destroyed pursuant to law); 15A-1340.14(f) (providing that prior conviction may be proved by (1) stipulation of the parties, (2) an original or copy of the court record of the prior conviction, (3) a copy of records maintained by the Division of Criminal Information, the Division of Motor Vehicles, or of the Administrative Office of the Courts, or (4) any other method found by the court to be reliable); 15A-924(d) (providing that a certified transcript of the record of a prior conviction is sufficient evidence of a prior conviction).

183. State v. Ellis, 130 N.C. App. 596, 598 (1998) (finding a certified AOC computer printout was properly admitted under G.S. 15A-1340.14(f)).

184. G.S. 15A-928; *see also* Jeffrey B. Welty, Arrest Warrant and Indictment Forms § G.S. 20-138.5 (6th ed. 2010) (setting forth sample charging language).

185. G.S. 15A-928(c).

186. *Id.* § 15A-928(c)(1).

187. *Id.* § 15A-928(c)(2).

188. *Id.*

189. *Id.* § 15A-980.

190. Custis v. United States, 511 U.S. 485 (1994); State v. Stafford, 114 N.C. App. 101 (1994); State v. Muscia, 115 N.C. App. 498 (1994).

D. Conviction

Defendants frequently are charged with and convicted of both habitual impaired driving and misdemeanor impaired driving in a single trial based on a single incident of impaired driving. When this occurs, the defendant may not be punished for both offenses. Instead, the trial court must arrest judgment for the misdemeanor impaired driving conviction.

Habitual impaired driving, unlike habitual felon, is not a status. Instead, it is a substantive offense.[191] Misdemeanor impaired driving is an element of habitual impaired driving, and thus it is a lesser-included offense of habitual impaired driving. The U.S. Constitution's Double Jeopardy Clause does not prohibit multiple punishments for offenses when one is included within the other under the "same elements" test established by the U.S. Supreme Court in *Blockburger v. United States*[192] if both are tried at the same time and if the legislature specifically authorizes cumulative punishment for both offenses.[193] Thus, even if the elements of two crimes are the same, a defendant may in a single trial be convicted of and punished for both crimes if it is found that the legislature intended for multiple punishments to apply.[194] And, while the U.S. Supreme Court in *Missouri v. Hunter*[195] referred to specific authorization for cumulative punishment, the North Carolina Supreme Court has found such authorization in the absence of an explicit statutory rule by examining legislative and judicial history and by inferring that inaction from the legislature constitutes "acquiesce[nce]" as to the conviction and punishment of both crimes in a single trial.[196]

Given that G.S. 20-138.5 elevates conduct that otherwise would be a misdemeanor to felony status, it seems quite unlikely that the legislature intended for both felony and misdemeanor punishment to be imposed for a single act of driving while impaired.[197] Indeed, there is no indication in the legislation that multiple punishments are authorized. Accordingly, the court of appeals in *State v. Haith*[198] held in an unpublished opinion that the trial court "should have arrested defendant's conviction of driving while impaired" upon sentencing the defendant for habitual driving while impaired and remanded the case for arrest of judgment.[199]

E. Sentencing

Habitual impaired driving is a Class F felony.[200] A person convicted of habitual impaired driving must be sentenced to "a minimum active term of not less than 12 months of imprisonment, which shall not be suspended."[201] A sentence for habitual impaired driving must run consecutively with, and commence at the expiration of, any sentence being served.[202]

---

191. *See* State v. Vardiman, 146 N.C. App. 381, 385 (2001).
192. 284 U.S. 299 (1932).
193. *See* Missouri v. Hunter, 459 U.S. 359 (1983).
194. *See* State v. Gardner, 315 N.C. 444 (1986).
195. 459 U.S. 359 (1983).
196. *Gardner*, 315 N.C. at 462.
197. *See, e.g.*, State v. Vardiman, 146 N.C. App. 381, 385 (2001) (characterizing habitual DWI as imposing "an enhanced punishment" for the latest DWI offense) (internal quotations omitted).
198. 158 N.C. App. 745 (2003) (unpublished); *see also* State v. Heath, 175 N.C. App. 795 (2006) (unpublished) (noting, without analysis, that defendant was sentenced for habitual impaired driving and that judgment was arrested for misdemeanor impaired driving).
199. *Haith*, 158 N.C. App. 745, No. COA-02-1316, 2003 WL 21499297, at *4.
200. G.S. 20-138.5(b).
201. *Id.*
202. *Id.*

Habitual impaired driving, unlike misdemeanor impaired driving, is sentenced pursuant to the Structured Sentencing Act.[203] A detailed discussion of the provisions of that act is beyond the scope of this publication. It bears mentioning, however, that in determining the prior record level of a defendant sentenced for habitual impaired driving,[204] the court may not consider or assign points for the prior impaired driving convictions that were used to establish the felony offense of habitual impaired driving.[205]

Another question that arises frequently in connection with sentencing for habitual impaired driving under G.S. 20-138.5(b) is whether any portion of the sentence may be suspended. As previously noted, the statute provides for a minimum active term of at least 12 months "which shall not be suspended." On occasion, judges impose a sentence of longer than 12 months (for example, a sentence of 15 to 27 months), suspended, with an intermediate condition of special probation (that is, a split sentence) requiring an active term of 12 months in custody. Such sentences arguably are illegal.[206]

The dispute arises over whether G.S. 20-138.5(b) should be construed to mean that habitual DWI sentences cannot be suspended at all or whether the statute merely requires that at least 12 months of the sentence not be suspended. The former interpretation is, in the view of the author, the better one. First, it is the more straightforward reading of the statute. Second, that interpretation avoids a conflict with G.S. 15A-1351(a), which ordinarily would cap the active portion of a split sentence at one-fourth the maximum sentence imposed (which, for a 15–27 month sentence, would be 6.75 months). Moreover, the other reading of the law is inconsistent with the nature of special probation. The entirety of a split sentence is "suspended," not just the part served outside the jail or prison. The period of imprisonment is a condition of probation, not a residual "unsuspended" portion of an active sentence. Thus, the command in G.S. 20-138.5(b) that habitual DWI sentences "shall not be suspended" most reasonably can be read to require active punishment.

A panel of the state Court of Appeals thought otherwise in *State v. Groce*, an unpublished opinion.[207] In that case the court upheld a 12-month split sentence for a habitual DWI, reasoning that G.S. 20-138.5 and G.S. 15A-1351 *are* in conflict, and thus the later-enacted statute—which happens to be G.S. 20-138.5—should control. In addition, the court relied upon the statutory construction principle that the specific controls the general, concluding therefore that G.S. 20-138.5 ought to control a habitual impaired driving sentence.

F. License Revocation

A conviction for habitual impaired driving results in the permanent revocation of a person's driver's license.[208] Notwithstanding the "permanent" revocation, the North Carolina Division of Motor Vehicles (NC DMV) may restore the driver's license of a person permanently revoked for conviction of habitual impaired driving after it has been revoked for at least ten years following the completion of the person's sentence—if the person satisfies three additional conditions.[209] First, the person must provide NC DMV with satisfactory proof that, in the ten years immediately preceding the person's

---

203. G.S. Chapter 15A, Article 81B.
204. *See* G.S. 15A-1340.14.
205. State v. Gentry, 135 N.C. App. 107 (1999).
206. Jamie Markham and Shea Denning, *Split Sentences for Habitual DWI?* N.C. Crim. L., UNC Sch. of Gov't Blog (May 19, 2009), http://nccriminallaw.sog.unc.edu/?p=365.
207. 187 N.C. App. 510 (2007) (unpublished).
208. G.S. 20-138.5(d).
209. *Id.* § 20-19(e4).

application for a restored license, the person has not been convicted in North Carolina or in any other state or federal court of a motor vehicle offense, an alcohol beverage control law offense, a drug law offense, or any other criminal offense.[210] Second, the person must provide NC DMV with satisfactory proof that he or she is not currently a user of alcohol, is not unlawfully using any controlled substance, or is not an excessive user of prescription drugs.[211] Third, the person must submit to NC DMV proof that he or she has notified his/her insurance agent or company that he/she is seeking the restoration and is financially responsible.[212] An exception to this last requirement applies in certain circumstances. A person who owns no registered motor vehicles of his or her own and who drives only fleet vehicles owned by others that are insured under commercial motor vehicle liability insurance policies is not required to submit proof of financial responsibility.[213]

G. Vehicle Seizure and Forfeiture

Because habitual impaired driving is an offense involving impaired driving, motor vehicles driven in the commission of this offense are subject to seizure and forfeiture in certain circumstances. The seizure and forfeiture of motor vehicles in impaired driving cases pursuant to G.S. 20-28.2 and G.S. 20-28.3 is discussed in chapter 7. Vehicle seizure and forfeiture is mentioned separately here because G.S. 20-138.5(e) also addresses forfeiture. That subsection provides that in applying the forfeiture procedure set out in G.S. 20-28.2, which allows a motor vehicle to be permanently released to an "innocent owner," an owner or lienholder is considered an innocent party if (1) the owner or lienholder did not know and had no reason to know that the defendant had been convicted within the previous seven years of three or more offenses involving impaired driving or (2) the defendant drove the motor vehicle without the consent of the owner or lienholder.[214]

III. Homicide, Death, and Serious Injury by Vehicle

A. Homicide Generally

First-degree murder, second-degree murder, and involuntary manslaughter, if the offense involved impaired driving, all are defined as implied consent offenses.[215] While first-degree murder is so defined, first-degree murder requires intent to kill or intent to commit one or more of the underlying felonies delineated in the state's murder statute.[216] Culpable negligence, the intent required for commission of the misdemeanor offense of impaired driving and related felony offenses predicated upon impaired driving, is insufficient as a matter of law to satisfy the *mens rea* requirement for first-degree murder.[217] Thus, first-degree murder is not discussed herein.[218] The remaining homicide offenses are discussed in further detail below.

---

210. *Id.*
211. *Id.*
212. *Id.* § 20-19(k).
213. *Id.* If this exception to the financial responsibility requirements applies, the person must sign a written certificate to that effect. *Id.*
214. *Id.* § 20-138.5(e).
215. *Id.* § 20-16.2(a1); 20-4.01(24a).
216. State v. Jones, 353 N.C. 159, 166 (2000).
217. *Id.* at 172.
218. For a thorough treatment of this offense, *see* Smith, North Carolina Crimes, *supra* note 44, at 83–90.

B. Second-Degree Murder

1. Elements

The elements of second-degree murder are

(1) killing
(2) another human being
(3) with malice.[219]

Sufficient evidence of malice exists to establish second-degree murder where the defendant's acts show cruelty, recklessness of consequences, or a mind that disregards social duty and is deliberately bent on mischief or where those acts manifest a total disregard for human life.[220] The State need not show that the defendant intended to kill in order to establish malice for second-degree murder, but may instead, in cases involving impaired driving resulting in death, meet its burden by showing that the defendant "had the intent to perform the act of driving in such a reckless manner as reflects knowledge that injury or death would likely result, thus evidencing depravity of mind."[221]

The Supreme Court of North Carolina in *State v. Rich*[222] distinguished impaired driving and death cases involving malice (and thereby supporting murder charges) from those involving culpable negligence (supporting a conviction for manslaughter, but not murder) this way:

> [T]he difference between the type of malice at issue in [this second-degree murder case] and culpable negligence is the degree of recklessness that would support a finding of each.... Standing alone, culpable negligence supports the submission of involuntary manslaughter.... But when that negligence is accompanied by an act which imports danger to another [and] is done so recklessly or wantonly as to manifest depravity of mind and disregard of human life, then it is sufficient to support a second-degree murder charge.[223]

In *Rich*, for example, the court found sufficient evidence of malice to support a second-degree murder charge where the State demonstrated that the defendant "drove his vehicle at a high rate of speed while impaired, on the wrong side of the road, in a no-passing zone and in violation of right-of-way rules."[224]

---

219. State v. McAllister, 138 N.C. App. 252, 256 (2000); *see also* G.S. 14-17.
220. State v. Rich, 351 N.C. 386 (2000); State v. Wilkerson, 295 N.C. 559 (1978).
221. *Rich*, 351 N.C. at 395.
222. 351 N.C. 386.
223. *Id.* at 395–96 (citations, internal quotation marks omitted).
224. *Id.* at 395. *See also* State v. Westbrook, 175 N.C. App. 128, 135 (2005) (finding sufficient evidence of malice where, in addition to driving while impaired, "the State's evidence tended to show that Defendant was speeding, traveling seventy-five to eighty miles per hour in a forty-five miles per hour speed zone, crossing the center lane, traveling in a lane in the opposite direction, and running a red light without attempting to brake or stop").

The United States Court of Appeals for the Fourth Circuit in *United States v. Fleming*, 739 F.2d 945, 948 (4th Cir. 1984) (emphasis in original), distinguished impaired driving and death cases involving malice from those involving culpable negligence this way:

> In the vast majority of vehicular homicides, the accused has not exhibited such wanton and reckless disregard for human life as to indicate the presence of malice on his part. In the present case, however, the facts show a deviation from established standards of regard for life and the safety of others that is markedly different in degree from that found in most vehicular homicides. In the average drunk driving homicide, there is no proof that the driver has acted while intoxicated with the purpose of wantonly and intentionally putting the lives of others in danger.

The following are examples of evidence deemed sufficient by North Carolina's appellate courts to establish malice in impaired driving cases resulting in the death of someone other than the driver:

- Driving by the defendant with a revoked license and having previously been convicted of impaired driving[225]
- Driving with a blood-alcohol concentration measuring 0.113 three hours after the accident and driving into the victim's lane of travel after having previously been convicted of driving after consuming by a person under 21 and while facing pending charges of driving while impaired and driving while license revoked[226]
- Driving while substantially impaired after prior convictions for driving while impaired, driving with a revoked license, and using false license tags along with an inspection sticker obtained by lying to inspection personnel[227]
- After fighting with a bar proprietor, driving away and passing a car in a no passing zone, striking a motorcycle, and driving through a red light into an intersection at 60 miles per hour, crashing into a car and killing all three of its occupants.[228]

2. Sentencing

Second-degree murder based upon commission of an inherently dangerous act performed in a reckless and wanton manner, such as impaired driving, is punished as a Class B2 felony.[229] The maximum term of imprisonment for a Class B2 felony sentenced in the aggravated range for the highest prior record level exceeds 40 years.[230]

3. License Revocation

No provision of the license revocation laws sets forth a license revocation specifically applicable to drivers convicted of second-degree murder resulting from the operation of a motor vehicle. Given the sentence length associated with such convictions, the existence of such a revocation may, in any event, be of little consequence. Nevertheless, it appears that persons convicted of second-degree murder premised upon impaired driving are subject to the revocation set forth in G.S. 20-17(a)(3) for conviction of a felony in the commission of which a motor vehicle is used.[231] The revocation period under this provision is one year.[232]

> Rather, his driving abilities were so impaired that he recklessly put others in danger simply by being on the road and attempting to do the things that any driver would do. In the present case, however, danger did not arise only by defendant's determining to drive while drunk. Rather, in addition to being intoxicated while driving, defendant drove in a manner that could be taken to indicate depraved disregard of human life, *particularly* in light of the fact that because he was drunk his reckless behavior was all the more dangerous.

225. *See* State v. Armstrong, 203 N.C. App. 399, 405 (2010); State v. McAllister, 138 N.C. App. 252, 260 (2000).

226. *See* State v. Gray, 137 N.C. App. 345, 351–52 (2000).

227. *See* State v. McBride, 109 N.C. App. 64, 68 (1993).

228. *See* State v. Snyder, 311 N.C. 391, 392–94 (1984).

229. G.S. 14-17(b)(1).

230. *Id.* § 15A-1340.17(c) (providing for minimum sentence at prior record level VI punished in the aggravated range of 393 months); 15A-1340.17(e1) (setting maximum term as 120 percent of the minimum term, rounded to the next highest month, plus 12 additional months).

231. *Id.* § 20-17(a)(3) (requiring NC DMV to revoke the license of any driver upon receiving a record of the driver's conviction for any felony in the commission of which a motor vehicle is used).

232. *Id.* § 20-19(c) (providing that when no specific period of suspension is provided, the period is one year).

C. Involuntary Manslaughter

1. Elements

Involuntary manslaughter is a common law offense.[233] A person commits the offense of involuntary manslaughter if he or she

(1) kills
(2) another person
(3)(a) by an unlawful act that does not amount to a felony and is not ordinarily dangerous to life or (b) by a culpably negligent act or omission.[234]

Because the act of driving while impaired violates a safety statute designed for the protection of human life and limb, it amounts to culpable negligence as a matter of law.[235] Thus, driving while impaired and proximately (but unintentionally) causing the death of another is involuntary manslaughter.[236]

Proximate cause is a cause "(1) [that], in a natural and continuous sequence and unbroken by any new and independent cause, produces an injury; (2) without which the injury would not have occurred; and (3) from which a person of ordinary prudence could have reasonably foreseen that such a result, or some similar injurious result, was probable."[237] Proximate cause need not have been the sole, the last, or the nearest cause of death.[238]

2. Sentencing

Involuntary manslaughter is a Class F felony sentenced under the Structured Sentencing Act.

Driving while impaired and proximately causing the death of another constitutes both involuntary manslaughter and felony death by vehicle. A person convicted of both offenses based on a single death in a single incident may be sentenced only for felony death by vehicle, the more serious offense.[239]

3. License Revocation

A conviction of manslaughter resulting from the operation of a motor vehicle results in a one-year revocation of a person's driver's license.[240]

D. Death by Vehicle

Several death by vehicle offenses are codified in G.S. 20-141.4: felony death by vehicle, aggravated felony death by vehicle, repeat felony death by vehicle, and misdemeanor death by vehicle. Each of these offenses is discussed in further detail below.

---

233. SMITH, NORTH CAROLINA CRIMES, *supra* note 44, at 99.

234. *Id.*

235. *See* State v. Davis, 198 N.C. App. 443, 446 (2009).

236. SMITH, NORTH CAROLINA CRIMES, *supra* note 44, at 100 (stating that "[f]or involuntary manslaughter, as with all homicides, the defendant's act must proximately cause the victim's death").

237. State v. Pierce, 216 N.C. App. 377, 383 (2011).

238. SMITH, NORTH CAROLINA CRIMES, *supra* note 44, at 100; *see also* State v. Leonard, 213 N.C. App. 526 (2011) (explaining in connection with defendant's conviction for felony serious injury by vehicle that even if his attempt to elude arrest was a cause of the victim's serious injury, his driving under the influence could also be—and substantial evidence established that it was—a proximate cause).

239. *See* State v. Lopez, 363 N.C. 535, 536 (2009) (explaining that "[b]ecause involuntary manslaughter is a lesser-included offense of felony death by vehicle, the [defendant's] involuntary manslaughter conviction merged into the conviction of felony death by vehicle").

240. G.S. 20-17(a)(1); 20-19(c).

1. Felony Death by Vehicle

a. Elements

A person commits the offense of felony death by vehicle if he or she

(1) unintentionally causes the death of another person
(2) while engaged in the offense of (a) impaired driving under G.S. 20-138.1 or (b) impaired driving in a commercial vehicle under G.S. 20-138.2, and
(3) commission of the impaired driving offense is the proximate cause of death.[241]

b. Sentencing

Felony death by vehicle is a Class D felony, punished under the Structured Sentencing Act.[242] That act requires that sentences for Class D felonies, regardless of the defendant's prior record level, consist of active punishment.[243] "Active punishment" is defined as a sentence in a criminal case that requires an offender to serve a sentence of imprisonment and that is not suspended.[244] An exception to this rule applies for defendants convicted of felony death by vehicle who are prior record Level I offenders.[245] Such offenders may be sentenced to intermediate punishment, which means that their sentences may be suspended so long as a term of supervised probation is imposed.[246]

The conduct constituting felony death by vehicle also may constitute a more serious felony offense, such as second-degree murder (a Class B2 felony), or a less serious felony offense, such as assault with a deadly weapon with intent to inflict serious injury (a Class E felony). The classification of felony death by vehicle as a Class D offense in G.S. 20-141.4(b) applies "[u]nless the conduct is covered under some other provision of law providing greater punishment."[247] Thus, when a defendant is punished for a more serious offense based on the same conduct for which he or she is convicted of felony death by vehicle, he or she may not also be punished for felony death by vehicle.[248]

In addition, G.S. 20-141.4(c), captioned "No Double Prosecutions," provides that "[n]o person who has been placed in jeopardy upon a charge of death by vehicle may be prosecuted for the offense of manslaughter arising out of the same death; and no person who has been placed in jeopardy upon a charge of manslaughter may be prosecuted for death by vehicle arising out of the same death." Read literally, the "may be prosecuted" language appears to prohibit the State from pursuing charges of death by vehicle and manslaughter in the same proceeding. However, the court of appeals in *State v. Elmore* rejected that interpretation, holding that the legislature's intent was to bar the *sentencing* of a defendant for both involuntary manslaughter and felony death by vehicle arising out of the same

---

241. *Id.* § 20-141.4(a1). The meaning of proximate cause is discussed in connection with the offense of involuntary manslaughter, above.

242. *Id.* § 20-141.4(b)(2).

243. *Id.* § 15A-1340.17.

244. *Id.* § 15A-1340.11(1).

245. An offender is prior record Level I if he or she has no more than one point assigned for prior convictions. *Id.* § 15A-1340.14(c)(1).

246. *Id.* § 15A-1340.11(6). The defendant's sentence also may include drug treatment court, special probation, and one or more of the community and intermediate probation conditions set forth in G.S. 15A-1343(a1).

247. *Id.* § 20-141.4(b).

248. State v. Davis, 364 N.C. 297 (2010).

death.[249] Simultaneous *prosecution* of a defendant for both offenses in a single trial is permissible, though the defendant may be convicted of only one of the offenses.[250]

c. License Revocation

Upon receiving a record that a driver has been convicted of felony death by vehicle, the North Carolina Division of Motor Vehicles (NC DMV) must permanently revoke the person's driver's license.[251] Notwithstanding the characterization of the revocation as permanent, NC DMV may conditionally restore the person's driver's license after it has been revoked for at least five years if the person proves that (1) in the five years preceding his or her application for a restored license, he or she has not been convicted of a motor vehicle offense, an alcohol beverage control law offense, a drug law offense, or any criminal offense involving the consumption of alcohol or drugs and (2) he or she is not currently an excessive user of alcohol or drugs.[252]

2. Aggravated Felony Death by Vehicle

a. Elements

A person commits aggravated felony death by vehicle if he or she

(1) unintentionally causes serious injury to another person
(2) while engaged in the offense of (a) impaired driving under G.S. 20-138.1 or (b) impaired driving in a commercial vehicle under G.S. 20-138.2 and
(3) the commission of the impaired driving offense is the proximate cause of death and
(4) the person has a previous conviction involving impaired driving within seven years of the date of the offense.[253]

Thus, aggravated felony death by vehicle consists of the commission of felony death by vehicle by a person with a qualifying prior conviction involving impaired driving. Offenses involving impaired driving are defined in G.S. 20-4.01(24a) as any of the following offenses:

- Impaired driving under G.S. 20-138.1
- Habitual impaired driving under G.S. 20-138.5
- Impaired driving in commercial vehicle under G.S. 20-138.2
- Any offense under G.S. 20-141.4 (felony and misdemeanor death by vehicle and serious injury by vehicle) based on impaired driving
- First- or second-degree murder under G.S. 14-17 based on impaired driving
- Involuntary manslaughter under G.S. 14-18 based on impaired driving
- Substantially similar offenses committed in another state or jurisdiction

---

249. State v. Elmore, ___ N.C. App. ___, 736 S.E.2d 568, 570 (2012), *review denied*, 366 N.C. 562 (2013).

250. State v. Davis, 198 N.C. App. 443, 452 (2009) (concluding that under G.S. 20-141.4(c), "a defendant may not be sentenced for both involuntary manslaughter and felony death by vehicle arising out of the same death" and remanding for resentencing by the trial court with instructions to vacate the defendant's conviction of either involuntary manslaughter or felony death by vehicle).

251. G.S. 20-17(a)(9); 20-19(i).

252. *Id.* § 20-19(i).

253. *Id.* § 20-141.4(a5).

b. Sentencing

Aggravated felony death by vehicle is a Class D felony punished under the Structured Sentencing Act.[254] Notwithstanding provisions of the Structured Sentencing Act that permit sentencing in the presumptive range of punishment in any case[255] and that permit a sentence in the aggravated range only if aggravating factors are present and the court determines they are sufficient to outweigh any mitigating factors,[256] G.S. 20-141.4(b)(1a) requires the court to sentence a defendant convicted of aggravated felony death by vehicle in the aggravated range of punishment that corresponds to the defendant's prior record level.

As with all offenses in G.S. 20-141.4, a person may not be sentenced for aggravated felony death by vehicle if the conduct is covered under some other provision of law providing for greater punishment.[257]

c. License Revocation

Upon receiving a record that a driver has been convicted of aggravated felony death by vehicle, the North Carolina Division of Motor Vehicles (NC DMV) must permanently revoke the person's driver's license.[258] Notwithstanding the characterization of the revocation as permanent, NC DMV may conditionally restore the person's driver's license after it has been revoked for at least five years if the person proves that (1) in the five years preceding his or her application for a restored license, he or she has not been convicted of a motor vehicle offense, an alcohol beverage control law offense, a drug law offense, or any criminal offense involving the consumption of alcohol or drugs and (2) he or she is not currently an excessive user of alcohol or drugs.[259]

3. Repeat Felony Death by Vehicle

a. Elements

A person commits repeat felony death by vehicle if he or she

(1) commits felony death by vehicle or aggravated felony death by vehicle and
(2) has a previous conviction for felony death by vehicle, aggravated felony death by vehicle, or murder based on the unintentional death of another person while engaged in impaired driving.[260]

b. Sentencing

Repeat felony death by vehicle is a Class B2 felony. Thus, it is punished the same as second-degree murder premised upon impaired driving.[261]

---

254. *Id.* § 20-141.4(b)(1a).

255. *See id.* § 15A-1340.17(c)(2) (setting forth a presumptive range of minimum sentence duration that applies when sentence is neither aggravated nor mitigated; providing that any minimum term of imprisonment in presumptive range is permitted unless court finds pursuant to G.S. 15A-1340.16 that an aggravated or mitigated sentence is appropriate).

256. *Id.* § 15A-1340.16(b).

257. *Id.* § 20-141.4(b) (providing that "[u]nless the conduct is covered under some other provision of law providing greater punishment, the following classifications apply to the offenses set forth in this section . . . .").

258. *Id.* § 20-17(a)(9); 20-19(i).

259. *Id.* § 20-19(i).

260. *Id.* § 20-141.4(a6).

261. *See id.* § 14-17(b)(1).

c. License Revocation

Upon receiving a record that a driver has been convicted of repeat felony death by vehicle, NC DMV must permanently revoke the person's driver's license.[262] Notwithstanding the characterization of the revocation as permanent, NC DMV may conditionally restore the person's driver's license after it has been revoked for at least five years if the person proves that (1) in the five years preceding his or her application for a restored license, he or she has not been convicted of a motor vehicle offense, an alcohol beverage control law offense, a drug law offense, or any criminal offense involving the consumption of alcohol or drugs and (2) he or she is not currently an excessive user of alcohol or drugs.[263]

4. Misdemeanor Death by Vehicle

a. Elements

Misdemeanor death by vehicle is defined in G.S. 20-141.4(a2) as

(1) unintentionally causing the death of another person
(2) while violating a state law or local ordinance applying to the operation or use of a vehicle or to the regulation of traffic—other than impaired driving under G.S. 20-138.1—where
(3) the commission of the offense is the proximate cause of the death.[264]

For offenses committed on or after December 1, 2011, misdemeanor death by vehicle is an implied consent offense, rendering it subject to implied consent testing procedures.

b. Sentencing

Misdemeanor death by vehicle is a Class A1 misdemeanor and is sentenced pursuant to provisions of the Structured Sentencing Act. Class A1 misdemeanors may be punished by up to 150 days imprisonment, depending on the defendant's prior record of convictions.[265]

c. License Revocation

Upon receiving a record that a driver has been convicted of misdemeanor death by vehicle, the North Carolina Division of Motor Vehicles must revoke the person's driver's license for one year.[266]

5. Felony Serious Injury by Vehicle

a. Elements

A person commits the offense of felony serious injury by vehicle if

(1) the person unintentionally causes serious injury to another person;
(2) the person was engaged in the offense of impaired driving under G.S. 20-138.1 or G.S. 20-138.2, and

---

262. *Id.* § 20-17(a)(9); 20-19(i).
263. *Id.* § 20-19(i).
264. G.S. 20-141.4(a2) broadly defines the types of traffic violations that can satisfy the second element of the misdemeanor death by vehicle offense. It is doubtful, however, whether the violation of traffic laws that do not involve or affect the method in which a defendant operates a vehicle can satisfy the second prong of the statute or whether, even if it does, it can ever properly be considered the proximate cause of a death resulting from the defendant's driving. *See* Shea Denning, *Qualifying Predicate Traffic Violations for Purposes of Misdemeanor Death by Vehicle*, N.C. CRIM. L., UNC SCH. OF GOV'T BLOG (Jan. 26, 2012), http://nccriminallaw.sog.unc.edu/?p=3243.
265. G.S. 15A-1340.23.
266. *Id.* § 20-17(a)(9); 20-19(c).

(3) the commission of the impaired driving offense is the proximate cause of the serious injury.[267]

(i) Serious Injury

The term "serious injury," is not defined by statute. In the assault context, the state supreme court has stated that serious injury is injury that is serious but falls short of causing death and has characterized "[f]urther definition" of the term as "neither wise nor desirable."[268] The courts have identified several relevant factors for purposes of assault prosecutions that may guide the determination of whether serious injury has been inflicted for purposes of G.S. 20-141.4. Those factors include, but are not limited to, pain and suffering, loss of blood, hospitalization, and time lost from work.[269] Any one of the factors is sufficient by itself to constitute substantial evidence of serious injury.[270] Thus, whether a serious injury has been inflicted depends upon the facts of each case[271] and is generally for the jury to decide under appropriate instructions.[272]

(ii) Proximate Cause

Proximate cause is a cause "(1) [that], in a natural and continuous sequence and unbroken by any new and independent cause, produces an injury; (2) without which the injury would not have occurred; and (3) from which a person of ordinary prudence could have reasonably foreseen that such a result, or some similar injurious result, was probable."[273] Proximate cause need not have been the sole, the last, or the nearest, cause of death.[274]

---

267. *Id.* § 20-141.4(a3).

268. State v. Jones, 258 N.C. 89, 91 (1962).

269. State v. McLean, 211 N.C. App. 321, 325 (2011).

270. *Id.* (citing State v. Bagley, 183 N.C. App. 514, 526 (2007) (citations omitted) ("Substantial evidence of a serious injury that is sufficient to survive a motion to dismiss includes, but is not limited to, evidence of 'hospitalization, pain, blood loss, and time lost at work.' "); State v. Joyner, 295 N.C. 55, 65 (1978) ("Evidence that the victim was hospitalized is not necessary for the proof of serious injury.")).

271. *See* State v. Ferguson, 261 N.C. 558, 559 (1964) (finding sufficient evidence to submit element of serious injury to the jury based upon evidence that the defendant, in a pickup truck, rammed the back of an automobile driven by the victim, causing him to suffer a whiplash injury that prevented the victim from turning his head without pain and "caus[ing] pains to run down his back into the back of his legs," injuries for which the victim was not hospitalized); State v. Field, 75 N.C. App. 647 (1985) (court ruled on constitutionality of judge determining grossly aggravating factor, finding it constitutional, a holding since overruled by *Blakely v. Washington*, 542 U.S. 296 (2004); judge found serious injury based on (1) injury to one person consisting of a severe cut to the head requiring twenty-nine stitches and fractures of the knee that required surgery and (2) injury to another person consisting of a blow to the head and a broken nose, requiring surgery and a skin graft to cover a hole in the membrane).

272. *See* State v. James, 321 N.C. 676 (1988) (stating general standard and finding evidence that defendant shot victim with a rifle and that victim was hospitalized as a result of injuries received during the assault sufficient to go to the jury on the element of "serious injury"); *see also McLean*, 211 N.C. App. at 326–27 (holding that trial judge's failure to give North Carolina Pattern Jury Instruction—Crim. 120.12, defining "serious injury" as an injury that "causes great pain and suffering," was not error as the appellate courts have chosen not to narrowly define "serious injury" in the context of assaults).

273. State v. Pierce, 216 N.C. App. 377, 383 (2011) (citation omitted).

274. Smith, North Carolina Crimes, *supra* note 44, at 100; *see also* State v. Leonard, 213 N.C. App. 526 (2011) (explaining in connection with defendant's conviction for felony serious injury by vehicle that even if his attempt to elude arrest was a cause of the victim's serious injury, his driving under the influence could also be—and substantial evidence established that it was—a proximate cause).

b. Sentencing

Felony serious injury by vehicle is a Class F felony. As with other offenses defined in G.S. 20-141.4, a trial court may not impose a sentence for felony serious injury by vehicle when a defendant is convicted of a more serious crime based on the same conduct.[275] Thus, if a defendant is convicted of assault with a deadly weapon inflicting serious injury, a Class E felony,[276] based on an incident of impaired driving that seriously injured another, he or she may not also be punished for felony serious injury by vehicle.[277]

c. License Revocation

Upon receiving a record that a person has been convicted of felony serious injury by vehicle, the North Carolina Division of Motor Vehicles (NC DMV) must revoke the person's driver's license for four years.[278] NC DMV may conditionally restore the person's license after it has been revoked for at least two years if the person proves that (1) he or she has not during the period of the revocation been convicted of a motor vehicle offense, an alcoholic beverage control law offense, a drug law offense, or any other criminal offense involving the possession or consumption of alcohol or drugs and (2) he or she is not currently an excessive user of alcohol, drugs, or prescription drugs or is not unlawfully using any controlled substance. The person may voluntarily submit to continuous alcohol monitoring under an approved system[279] to prove his or her abstinence from alcohol during a period of revocation immediately prior to the restoration consideration. NC DMV must accept monitoring periods of 120 days or longer as evidence of abstinence if it receives sufficient documentation that the person abstained from alcohol use during the monitoring period.

6. Aggravated Felony Serious Injury by Vehicle

a. Elements

A person commits the offense of aggravated felony serious injury by vehicle if he or she

(1) unintentionally causes serious injury to another person
(2) while engaged in the offense of impaired driving under G.S. 20-138.1 or impaired driving in a commercial vehicle under G.S. 20-138.2 and
(3) the commission of the impaired driving offense is the proximate cause of the serious injury and
(4) the person has a previous conviction involving impaired driving within seven years of the date of the instant offense.

---

275. *See* G.S. 20-141.4(b); State v. Davis, 364 N.C. 297, 305 (2010).

276. G.S. 14-32(b); *see Davis*, 364 N.C. at 303 (citations omitted) (noting that "it has long been the law in North Carolina that common law homicide and assault offenses apply to deaths and injuries caused by impaired driving").

277. *Davis*, 364 N.C. at 305.

278. G.S. 20-17(a)(9); 20-19(d).

279. G.S. 15A-1343.3 requires the Division of Adult Correction of the Department of Public Safety to establish regulations for continuous alcohol monitoring systems that are authorized for use by the courts as evidence that an offender on probation has abstained from the use of alcohol for a specified period of time. A "continuous alcohol monitoring system" is defined as "a device that is worn by a person that can detect, monitor, record, and report the amount of alcohol within the wearer's system over a continuous 24-hour daily basis." G.S. 15A-1343.3(a).

Thus, aggravated felony serious injury by vehicle occurs when a person who has a previous conviction involving impaired driving commits the offense of felony serious injury by vehicle within seven years of the earlier conviction.

The first three elements of this offense are discussed above in connection with the offense of felony serious injury by vehicle.[280] The last element requires that the person have a previous conviction for an offense involving impaired driving. This also is an element of aggravated felony death by vehicle and is discussed above in connection with that offense.[281]

b. Sentencing

Aggravated felony serious injury by vehicle is a Class E felony. As with other offenses set forth in G.S. 20-141.4, this punishment applies unless the conduct is covered under some other provision of law providing for greater punishment and the defendant is convicted of that greater offense.[282]

c. License Revocation

Upon receiving a record that a driver has been convicted of aggravated felony serious injury by vehicle, the North Carolina Division of Motor Vehicles (NC DMV) must permanently revoke the person's driver's license.[283] Notwithstanding the characterization of the revocation as permanent, NC DMV may conditionally restore the person's driver's license after it has been revoked for at least three years if the person proves that (1) in the three years preceding his or her application for a restored license, he or she has not been convicted of a motor vehicle offense, an alcohol beverage control law offense, a drug law offense, or any criminal offense involving the consumption of alcohol or drugs and (2) he or she is not currently an excessive user of alcohol or drugs.[284] The person may voluntarily submit to continuous alcohol monitoring under an approved system[285] to prove his or her abstinence from alcohol during a period of revocation immediately prior to the restoration consideration.[286] NC DMV must accept monitoring periods of 120 days or longer as evidence of abstinence if it receives sufficient documentation that the person abstained from alcohol use during the monitoring period.[287]

---

280. See the text beginning at note 267, *supra*.
281. See the text beginning at note 253, *supra*.
282. G.S. 20-141.4(b); *see Davis*, 364 N.C. at 305–06.
283. G.S. 20-17(a)(9); 20-19(e).
284. *Id.* § 20-19(e1).
285. G.S. 15A-1343.3 requires the Division of Adult Correction of the Department of Public Safety to establish regulations for continuous alcohol monitoring systems that are authorized for use by the courts as evidence that an offender on probation has abstained from the use of alcohol for a specified period of time. A "continuous alcohol monitoring system" is defined as "a device that is worn by a person that can detect, monitor, record, and report the amount of alcohol within the wearer's system over a continuous 24-hour daily basis." *Id.* § 15A-1343.3(a).
286. *Id.* § 20-19(e2).
287. *Id.*

IV. Impaired Driving in a Commercial Motor Vehicle

A. Elements

A person commits the offense of impaired driving in a commercial motor vehicle if he or she

(1) drives a commercial motor vehicle
(2) upon any highway, street, or public vehicular area
(3)(a) while under the influence of an impairing substance or (b) after having consumed sufficient alcohol that he or she has, at any relevant time after the driving, an alcohol concentration of 0.04 or more or (c) with any amount of a Schedule I controlled substance or its metabolites in his or her blood or urine.[288]

The offense of impaired driving in a commercial motor vehicle set forth in G.S. 20-138.2 differs from impaired driving in violation of G.S. 20-138.1 in two respects. First, the offense may only be committed in a commercial motor vehicle. Second, the threshold alcohol concentration that establishes a per se violation of G.S. 20-138.2 is a 0.04 rather than the 0.08 required for a per se violation of G.S. 20-138.1. These additional elements are discussed in further detail below.

1. Commercial Motor Vehicle

The term "commercial motor vehicle" is defined in G.S. 20-4.01(3d) as any of the following vehicles that are designed or used to transport passengers or property:

(1) A Class A motor vehicle[289] that has a combined gross vehicle weight rating (GVWR)[290] of at least 26,001 pounds and includes as part of the combination a towed unit that has a GVWR of at least 10,001 pounds
(2) A Class B motor vehicle. Either of the following is a Class B motor vehicle:
  (a) A single motor vehicle that has a GVWR of at least 26,001 pounds or
  (b) A combination of motor vehicles that includes as part of the combination a towing unit that has a GVWR of at least 26,001 pounds and a towed unit that has a GVWR of less than 10,001 pounds[291]
(3) A Class C motor vehicle that meets either of the following descriptions:
  (a) Is designed to transport sixteen or more passengers, including the driver
  (b) Is transporting hazardous materials and is required to be placarded in accordance with Title 49, Part 172, Subpart F of the Code of Federal Regulations.

---

288. *Id.* § 20-138.2.
289. A "Class A Motor Vehicle" is defined in G.S. 20-4.01(2a) as "[a] combination of motor vehicles that meets either of the following descriptions:

a. Has a combined GVWR [gross vehicle weight rating] of at least 26,001 pounds and includes as part of the combination a towed unit that has a GVWR of at least 10,001 pounds.

b. Has a combined GVWR of less than 26,001 pounds and includes as part of the combination a towed unit that has a GVWR of at least 10,001 pounds.

290. A vehicle's GVWR is the maximum loaded weight a vehicle is capable of safely hauling, as specified by its manufacturer. G.S. 20-4.01(12f). The GVWR of a combination vehicle is the GVWR of the power unit plus the GVWR of the towed unit or units. *Id.* When a law enforcement officer determines that a vehicle has been structurally altered from the manufacturer's original design to increase its hauling capacity, the GVWR of the vehicle for enforcement purposes is the greater of the license weight or the total weight of the vehicle or combination of vehicles. *Id.*
291. *Id.* at § 20-4.01(2b).

A motor vehicle that satisfies the definition above is a commercial motor vehicle even when it is operated for private, non-commercial purposes.[292] In addition, the GVWR of a two-part combination vehicle (such as a tractor trailer) is controlling for purposes of determining whether one of the vehicle's integral parts (such as the tractor portion) is a commercial motor vehicle.[293]

The State may establish a vehicle's GVWR in several ways.[294] It may elicit the opinion of a person who observed the vehicle. It may offer proof of the GVWR affixed to the vehicle, the registered or declared weight shown on North Carolina Division of Motor Vehicles (NC DMV) records, the GVWR as determined from the vehicle identification number, the listed gross weight publications from the manufacturer of the vehicle, or any other description or evidence.[295]

2. Alcohol Concentration of 0.04 or More

The State may prove the impairment element of impaired driving in a commercial vehicle by demonstrating that the person was appreciably impaired, that the person had any amount of a Schedule I controlled substance or its metabolites in his or her blood or urine, or that he or she had an alcohol concentration of 0.04 or more. Note that the threshold alcohol concentration is considerably lower than the 0.08 required for per se impairment in a noncommercial vehicle. Like G.S. 20-138.1, G.S. 20-138.2(a)(2) provides that "[t]he results of a chemical analysis shall be deemed sufficient evidence to prove a person's alcohol concentration."

G.S. 20-138.2(a1) specifically authorizes a person who has submitted to a chemical analysis of a blood sample pursuant to G.S. 20-139.1(d) to use the results in rebuttal as evidence that the person did not have, at a relevant time after the driving, an alcohol concentration of 0.04 or more.

As with impaired driving under G.S. 20-138.1, the fact that a person is legally entitled to use alcohol or a drug is not a defense to a charge of driving a commercial motor vehicle while impaired.[296]

3. Relationship to Impaired Driving under G.S. 20-138.1

Driving a commercial motor vehicle while impaired in violation of G.S. 20-138.2 appears to be a separate and distinct offense from driving while impaired in violation of G.S. 20-138.1, and not a lesser-included offense. The general rule in North Carolina for determining whether certain crimes are separate and distinct offenses is based on *Blockburger v. United States*[297] and requires that, to be separate offenses, each must include an element not common to the other.[298] Proof that only one of the crimes requires proof of an additional element, in contrast, establishes that one offense is a lesser-included offense of the other.[299]

Driving while impaired in violation of G.S. 20-138.1 requires proof of impairment, which may be established by demonstrating that the defendant had an alcohol concentration of 0.08 or more.

---

292. *See* State v. Jones, 140 N.C. App. 691, 698 (2000) (emphasis in original) (rejecting defendant's argument that the motor vehicle he was driving was not a commercial motor vehicle because he was driving it for its private use at the time he was stopped; noting that G.S. 20-4.01(3d) "specifies that a vehicle is a 'commercial motor vehicle' if the vehicle is '*designed or used* to transport passengers or property' and meets other requirements").

293. *Jones*, 140 N.C. App. at 698 (determining that the "defendant did not change the nature of the vehicle or what it was designed or used to transport" or its GVWR "[b]y simply detaching the trailer portion of [the] tractor-trailer").

294. G.S. 20-138.2(a2).

295. *Id.*

296. *Id.* § 20-138.2(b).

297. 284 U.S. 299 (1932).

298. State v. Strohauer, 84 N.C. App. 68, 72–73 (1987).

299. *Id.*

Driving a commercial vehicle while impaired also requires proof of impairment, but it may be established by demonstrating that the defendant had an alcohol concentration of 0.04 or more. In addition, driving while impaired in a commercial motor vehicle requires proof that the defendant drove a commercial motor vehicle, whereas driving while impaired in violation of G.S. 20-138.1 requires proof that the defendant drove a vehicle. While all commercial motor vehicles are included within the broader category of vehicles that may be driven in violation of G.S. 20-138.1, the threshold per se alcohol concentration for driving a commercial motor vehicle while impaired does not satisfy G.S. 20-138.1's per se threshold of 0.08 or more.

B. Sentencing

Impaired driving in a commercial vehicle, like impaired driving under G.S. 20-138.1, is a misdemeanor sentenced under G.S. 20-179, which sets forth six levels of punishment. The applicable level is determined by the finding and weighing of statutorily enumerated aggravating and mitigating factors. Aggravated Level One is the most serious level, punishable by up to 3 years' imprisonment. Level Five is the least serious level, and is punishable by no more than 60 days imprisonment. The procedures for sentencing, sentencing factors, the punishment permitted at each level, and mandatory conditions of probation under G.S. 20-179 are discussed at length in chapter 5.

As discussed in the previous section, impaired driving in a commercial vehicle does not appear to be a lesser-included offense of impaired driving under G.S. 20-138.1. Thus, a person may be convicted of and sentenced for both offenses arising from a single incident of driving. However, if a person is convicted under G.S. 20-138.2 and G.S. 20-138.1 based on a single incident, the aggregate punishment imposed may not exceed the maximum punishment applicable to the offense involving impaired driving under G.S. 20-138.1.[300]

C. License Revocation

NC DMV must revoke the license of a driver convicted of impaired driving in a commercial vehicle under G.S. 20-138.2 if the driver's alcohol concentration level was 0.06 or higher.[301] Otherwise, the bare fact of a conviction under G.S. 20-138.2 does not trigger revocation of a defendant's license. For purposes of the statutory provision requiring revocation based on a 0.06 or higher result, G.S. 20-17(a)(2)b. provides that a driver's alcohol concentration result, as obtained by a chemical analysis, is conclusive and is not subject to modification by any party, with or without approval by the court.

A person convicted of driving a commercial vehicle while impaired is disqualified from driving a commercial motor vehicle for a year.[302]

---

300. G.S. 20-138.2(e). It is not clear whether the applicable maximum is 3 years (the outright maximum sentence for the most serious level of impaired driving under G.S. 20-179) or the applicable maximum for the applicable level of DWI. The latter interpretation better accords with a defendant's constitutional—and statutory—right to have his or her sentence elevated only by factors found by a jury (in superior court) beyond a reasonable doubt. Blakely v. Washington, 542 U.S. 296 (2004); G.S. 20-179(c), (d).

301. G.S. 20-17(a)(2)b.

302. *Id.* § 20-17.4(a)(2). Other implied consent offense convictions likewise disqualify persons from driving commercial motor vehicles. *See id.* § 20-17.4. The statutory regime governing the operation of commercial motor vehicles is not discussed in this chapter or elsewhere in this book, other than in the brief mention above.

V. Open Container Offenses

G.S. 20-138.7 sets forth two types of open container offenses. The first is a misdemeanor offense that may be committed only by the driver of a motor vehicle. The second is an infraction that may be committed by any person, driver or passenger, in a motor vehicle.[303]

A. Misdemeanor Offense: G.S. 20-138.7(a)

1. Elements

G.S. 20-138.7(a) makes it a crime to

(1) drive
(2) a motor vehicle
(3) on a highway or the right-of-way of a highway
(4) while there is an alcoholic beverage in the passenger area in other than the unopened manufacturer's original container and
(5) while the driver is consuming alcohol or while alcohol remains in the driver's body.

The term "motor vehicle" is separately defined for purposes of G.S. 20-138.7. For offenses committed on or after October 1, 2013, "motor vehicle" means any vehicle driven or drawn by mechanical power and manufactured primarily for use on public highways, including mopeds.[304] For earlier offenses, the term "motor vehicle" included only those types of motor vehicles that were required to be registered under North Carolina law, regardless of whether or where the vehicle was registered.[305]

An alcoholic beverage is any beverage containing at least one-half of one percent (0.5%) alcohol by volume, including malt beverages, unfortified wine, fortified wine, spirituous liquor, and mixed beverages.[306]

If the seal on a container of alcoholic beverages has been broken, it is considered opened.[307] This rule applies even if the lid to the original container has been reapplied. A glass or cup containing an alcoholic beverage also is an open container as that term is defined by G.S. 20-138.7(f).

The passenger area of a motor vehicle means the area designed to seat the driver and passengers and any area within the reach of a seated driver or passenger, including the glove compartment. The area of the trunk or the area behind the last upright back seat of a station wagon, hatchback, or similar vehicle is not considered part of the passenger area.[308]

---

303. G.S. 18B-401(a) also prescribes an open container offense, rendering it unlawful "to transport fortified wine or spirituous liquor in the passenger area of a motor vehicle in other than the manufacturer's unopened original container" or "for a person who is driving a motor vehicle on a highway or public vehicular area to consume in the passenger area of that vehicle any malt beverage or unfortified wine." Violation of either provision is Class 3 misdemeanor, see G.S. 18B-401(a), but is not an implied consent offense.

304. S.L. 2013-348.

305. Mopeds formerly were excluded from registration requirements. Beginning July 1, 2015, mopeds must be registered S.L. 2014-114.

306. G.S. 20-138.7(f) (adopting definition of alcoholic beverage in G.S. 18B-101(4)).

307. *Id.*

308. *Id.*

2. Alcohol Screening Tests

An alcohol screening test may be administered to a driver suspected of violating G.S. 20-138.7(a).[309] The test must be performed on an approved device and in accordance with applicable regulations.[310] The results of the alcohol screening test or the driver's refusal to submit to it may be used by a law enforcement officer, a court, or an administrative agency in determining if alcohol was present in the driver's body.

The odor of an alcoholic beverage on the breath of the driver is insufficient evidence to prove beyond a reasonable doubt that alcohol was remaining in the driver's body unless the driver was offered an alcohol screening test or chemical analysis and refused to provide the required samples of breath or blood for analysis.[311]

3. Sentencing

A first offense under G.S. 20-138.7(a) is a Class 3 misdemeanor. A second or subsequent offense is a Class 2 misdemeanor.

A violation of G.S. 20-138.7(a) is not a lesser-included offense of impaired driving under G.S. 20-138.1. Nevertheless, special punishment rules apply to a person convicted of violating G.S. 20-138.7(a) and convicted of an offense involving impaired driving arising out of the same transaction. The punishment imposed may not exceed the maximum applicable to the offense involving impaired driving, and any minimum applicable punishment must be imposed.[312]

A violation of G.S. 20-138.7(a) is considered a moving violation by the North Carolina Division of Motor Vehicles (NC DMV) for purposes of assessing points for convictions under G.S. 20-16(c).

4. License Revocation

A first conviction of transporting an open container in violation of G.S. 20-138.7 does not trigger a license revocation. However, upon receiving a record of a second conviction for this offense, NC DMV must revoke the person's license for six months.[313] Upon receiving a record for a third or subsequent conviction under G.S. 20-138.7(a), NC DMV must impose a one-year revocation.[314]

B. Infraction: G.S. 20-138.7(a1)

1. Elements

A person violates G.S. 20-138.7(a1) when he or she

(1)(a) possesses an alcoholic beverage other than in the unopened manufacturer's original container or (b) consumes an alcoholic beverage

(2) in the passenger area of motor vehicle

(3) while the motor vehicle is on a highway or the right-of-way of a highway.

Only the person who possesses or consumes an alcoholic beverage in violation of G.S. 20-138.7(a1) may be charged with a violation of that provision.

---

309. *Id.* § 20-138.7(d).

310. *Id. See also* 10 N.C.A.C. 41B, §§ .0501–.0503 (setting forth regulations for alcohol screening tests and listing approved devices).

311. G.S. 20-138.7(d).

312. *Id.* § 20-138.7(e).

313. *Id.* § 20-17(a)(12); 20-19(g1).

314. *Id.* § 20-17(a)(8); 20-19(g1).

2. Sentencing

Violation of G.S. 20-138.7(a1) is an infraction, punishable by a maximum fine of $100,[315] and is not considered a moving violation for purposes of the assessment of driver's license points under G.S. 20-16(c).

3. Implied Consent Offense Procedures

Though G.S. 20-138.7(b) provides that an offense under G.S. 20-138.7 "is an alcohol-related offense subject to the implied-consent provisions of G.S. 20-16.2," and it is clear that a violation of G.S. 20-138.7(a)—a misdemeanor—is an implied consent offense, it is not clear whether the implied consent laws apply to persons charged with a violation of G.S. 20-138.7(a1)—an infraction. While an officer who has probable cause to believe that a person has committed an infraction may detain the person for a reasonable period to issue and serve a citation, a person may not be arrested for committing an infraction. A law enforcement officer may, in certain limited circumstances, require a person charged with an infraction who is not a resident of North Carolina to accompany him or her to a judicial official's office for purposes of allowing a judicial official to determine if an appearance bond is necessary.[316] Perhaps a similar rationale would allow a law enforcement officer to require a person charged with a violation of G.S. 20-138.7(a1) to accompany the officer to a facility where a chemical test could be performed. If so, then the restriction on the period for which a law enforcement officer may detain a person for purposes of issuing and serving a citation would appear to have very little meaning in the context of violations of G.S. 20-138.7(a1), since chemical testing involves a much lengthier detention.

4. License Revocation

The same license revocation provisions that apply to the misdemeanor open container violation under G.S. 20-138.7(a1) apply to infractions under G.S. 20-138.7(a).[317] Thus, there is no revocation for a first conviction. The revocation period for a second conviction is six months, and a one-year revocation follows a third or subsequent conviction.[318]

VI. Impaired Instruction

A. Elements

G.S. 20-12.1 makes it unlawful for a person to

(1) serve as a supervising driver under G.S. 20-7(l) or G.S. 20-11 or as an approved instructor under G.S. 20-7(m)

(2)(a) while under the influence of an impairing substance or (b) after having consumed sufficient alcohol to have, at any relevant time after the driving, an alcohol concentration of 0.08 or more.

An offense under G.S. 20-12.1 is an implied consent offense.

A supervising driver under G.S. 20-7(l) is a person who is licensed to drive the motor vehicle being driven and who is seated beside the holder of a learner's permit of the type issued to a person

315. *Id.* § 20-176(b).
316. *Id.* § 15A-1113(c).
317. *Id.* § 20-17(a)(12); 20-19(g1); see the text beginning at footnote 313, *supra*.
318. *Id.* § 20-17(a)(12); 20-19(g1).

at least 18 years old. The following persons may serve as a supervising driver under G.S. 20-11: a parent, grandparent, or guardian of the holder of a limited learner's permit or provisional license or a responsible person approved by the parent or guardian or by the North Carolina Division of Motor Vehicles (NC DMV).[319] A supervising driver must have been licensed for at least five years and must currently be licensed.[320]

An approved instructor under G.S. 20-7(m) supervises a person with a restricted instruction permit. A restricted instruction permit may be issued for a school year or for a lesser period to any applicant who is (1) less than 18 years old and is enrolled in a driver's education program or (2) seeking certification under G.S. 20-218 as a school bus driver.

B. Sentencing

A violation of G.S. 20-12.1 is a Class 2 misdemeanor,[321] punished pursuant to the Structured Sentencing Act.[322]

C. License Revocation

NC DMV is authorized to suspend the driver's license of a person convicted of impaired instruction under G.S. 20.12.1.[323] The period of the suspension is for the time period deemed by NC DMV to be "best for public safety," but it may not exceed six months.[324]

VII. Zero-Tolerance Offenses: Driving after Consuming by Person under 21, Driving School Bus/Child Care Vehicle after Consuming; Driving Commercial Motor Vehicle after Consuming

A. Generally

Several statutes prohibit driving by certain persons or the driving of certain vehicles while consuming alcohol or while alcohol remains in the driver's body. These offenses commonly are referred to as *zero-tolerance offenses*, pursuant to the notion that the law tolerates no measurable alcohol concentration by drivers subject to these provisions.

Each of these offenses is an implied consent offense. None is classified as an offense involving impaired driving.

As with other implied consent offenses, an alcohol screening test may be administered to a driver suspected of violating any of the zero-tolerance offenses discussed below.[325] However, in this context, law enforcement officers and others may rely on the numerical results of the test rather than whether the results are positive or negative.[326] The test results or the driver's refusal to submit to the test may

---

319. *Id.* § 20-11(k).
320. *Id.* § 20-11(k).
321. *Id.* § 20-35(a).
322. *Id.* § 15A-1340.20.
323. *Id.* § 20-16(a)(8).
324. *Id.* § 20-19(a).
325. *Id.* § 20-138.3(b2).
326. *Compare* G.S. 20-138.2A(b2), 20-138.2B(b2), and 20-138.3(b2) (permitting use of the results of an alcohol screening test) *with* G.S. 20-16.3(d) (permitting law enforcement officers and others to use "a positive or negative result on an alcohol screening test, but not the actual alcohol concentration result").

be used by a law enforcement officer, a court, or an administrative agency in determining if alcohol was present in the driver's body. To be valid, the testing device used must be one approved by the Department of Health and Human Services (DHHS)[327] and the screening test must be carried out pursuant to DHHS regulations governing the manner and use of such a device.[328]

The odor of an alcoholic beverage on the breath of a driver generally is not sufficient evidence, by itself, to prove beyond a reasonable doubt that alcohol was remaining in the driver's body in violation of any of the zero-tolerance offenses discussed below.[329] An exception to this general rule applies when a driver refuses to submit to an alcohol screening test or a chemical analysis. When a driver is offered testing and refuses to provide all required samples of breath or blood for analysis, the odor of an alcoholic beverage on his or her breath is sufficient evidence to establish that alcohol was remaining in his or her body at the time of the driving.

B. Driving after Consuming by Person under 21

1. Elements

G.S. 20-138.3 makes it unlawful for a person

(1) less than 21 years of age
(2) to drive a motor vehicle
(3) on a highway or public vehicular area
(4)(a) while consuming alcohol
(b) at any time while he or she has remaining in his or her body any alcohol previously consumed or
(c) at any time while he or she has remaining in his or her body any previously consumed controlled substance, unless the controlled substance was lawfully obtained and taken in therapeutically appropriate amounts.

2. Sentencing

Driving by a person under the age of 21 after consuming alcohol or a controlled substance in violation of G.S. 20-138.3 is a Class 2 misdemeanor. This offense is not a lesser-included offense of driving while impaired in violation of G.S. 20-138.1, but certain punishment limitations apply when a person is convicted of violating G.S. 20-138.3 and of an offense involving impaired driving that arose out of the same transaction. In this circumstance, the aggregate punishment imposed may not exceed the maximum applicable to the offense involving impaired driving, and any applicable minimum punishment must be imposed.[330]

3. License Revocation

The North Carolina Division of Motor Vehicles must revoke the license of a person convicted of violating G.S. 20-138.3 upon receiving notice of the conviction.[331] The period of revocation is one year, and the revocation runs concurrently with any other revocations. The statute requiring revocation, G.S. 20-13.2, is somewhat misleadingly captioned "Grounds for revoking provisional license," though

327. Approved devices are listed in 10A N.C.A.C. 41B, § .0503.
328. G.S. 20-138.3(b2). 10A N.C.A.C. 41B, § .0502(b) sets forth the procedure for administering an alcohol screening test.
329. *See* G.S. 20-138.3(b1); 20-138.2A(b1); 20-138.2B(b1).
330. *Id.* § 20-138.3(c).
331. *Id.* § 20-13.2(a).

its license revocation provisions apply to persons under 21, rather than exclusively to provisional license-holders, all of whom are under 18.[332] The incongruous reference resulted from the General Assembly's failure to amend the title of G.S. 20-13.2, which formerly applied only to provisional licensees, when it raised from 18 to 21 the age below which a person is prohibited from driving after consuming.[333]

A person whose license is revoked *solely* for conviction of the offense of driving by a person under 21 after consuming alcohol or drugs in violation of G.S. 138.3 is eligible for a limited driving privilege if the person is 18, 19, or 20 years old on the date of the offense, has not previously been convicted of a violation of G.S. 20-138.3, and meets other eligibility requirements set forth in G.S. 20-179.3.[334]

C. Operating a Commercial Vehicle after Consuming Alcohol

1. Elements

A person violates G.S. 20-138.2A if he or she

(1) drives
(2) a commercial motor vehicle
(3) on any street, highway, or public vehicular area
(4) while consuming alcohol or while alcohol remains in his or her body.

The terms "drive," "street," "highway," "public vehicular area," and "alcohol" are defined earlier in this chapter, in connection with the discussion of impaired driving in violation of G.S. 20-138.1. The term "commercial motor vehicle" also is discussed earlier in this chapter, in connection with the offense of impaired driving in a commercial motor vehicle in violation of G.S. 20-138.2. For purposes of driving a commercial motor vehicle after consuming in violation of G.S. 20-138.2A, however, a slightly different definition of commercial motor vehicle applies. G.S. 20-138.2A applies only to the following types of commercial motor vehicles:

(1) Class A motor vehicles that have a combined gross vehicle weight rating (GVWR) of at least 26,001 pounds and include as part of the combination a towed unit that has a GVWR of at least 10,001 pounds and
(2) Class B motor vehicles.[335]

Thus, the statute prohibiting driving a commercial motor vehicle after consuming alcohol does not apply to the driving of Class C motor vehicles that are designed to transport sixteen or more passengers or that are transporting hazardous materials and are required, by federal regulations, to be placarded.[336]

---

332. *Id.* § 20-4.01(31a); 20-11.
333. *See* S.L. 1995-506.
334. *See* G.S. 20-138.3(d). A person convicted of impaired driving based upon the same conduct is ineligible for a limited driving privilege under this provision because his or her license also will be revoked pursuant to G.S. 20-17(a)(2).
335. *Id.* § 20-138.2A(a) (prohibiting driving a commercial vehicle, as defined in G.S. 20-4.01(3d)a. and b., after consuming alcohol, omitting any reference to commercial motor vehicles under G.S. 20-4.01(3d)c.)
336. *Id.* § 20-4.01(3d)c.

2. Sentencing

A violation of G.S. 20-138.2A(a) is a Class 3 misdemeanor and is punishable solely by a penalty of $100.[337] A second or subsequent violation is a misdemeanor punishable under G.S. 20-179. The provisions of that sentencing scheme are discussed in chapter 5. A conviction for violating G.S. 20-138.2A is a second or subsequent conviction if at the time of the current offense the person has a previous conviction under the statute that occurred in the seven years preceding the date of the current offense.[338] Driving a commercial motor vehicle after consuming is a lesser-included offense of impaired driving in a commercial vehicle under G.S. 20-138.2.[339]

3. License Revocation

Upon receiving notice that a person has been convicted of a second or subsequent offense of driving a commercial vehicle after consuming under G.S. 20-138.2A, the North Carolina Division of Motor Vehicles must revoke the person's license for a period of one year.[340] Second or subsequent convictions are defined for license revocation purposes as they are for sentencing purposes.[341] Thus, a conviction under G.S. 20-138.2A is a second or subsequent conviction requiring license revocation if, within seven years preceding the date of the current offense, the person was convicted under G.S. 20-138.2A.

D. Driving School Bus Vehicle/Child Care Vehicle/Ambulance/EMS Vehicle/ Firefighting Vehicle/Law Enforcement Vehicle after Consuming

1. Elements

A person commits a violation of G.S. 20-138.2B if he or she

(1) drives
(2) a school bus, school activity bus, child care vehicle, ambulance, other emergency medical services vehicle, firefighting vehicle, or law enforcement vehicle.
(3) upon any highway, street, or public vehicular area
(4) while consuming alcohol or while alcohol remains in his or her body.

The terms "drive," "highway," "street," "public vehicular area," and "alcohol" are defined in the section of this chapter describing impaired driving in violation of G.S. 20-138.1.[342]

A school bus is a vehicle whose primary purpose is to transport school students over an established route to and from school for the regularly scheduled school day and that

(1) is equipped with alternately flashing red lights on the front and rear and a mechanical stop signal,
(2) is painted primarily yellow below the roofline, and
(3) bears the plainly visible words "School Bus" on the front and rear.[343]

The term "school bus" includes a public, private, or parochial vehicle that meets this description.[344]

---

337. *Id.* § 20-138.2A(c).
338. *Id.* § 20-138.2A(d).
339. *Id.* § 20-138.2(c).
340. *Id.* § 20-17(a)(13); 20-19(c).
341. *Id.* § 20-17(a)(13).
342. See *supra* section I.
343. G.S. 20-4.01(27)d4.
344. *Id.*

A school activity bus is a vehicle, generally painted a different color from a school bus, whose primary purpose is to transport school students and others to or from a place for participation in an event other than regular classroom work.[345] The term includes a public, private, or parochial vehicle that meets this description.[346]

A child care vehicle is a vehicle that is under the direction and control of a child care facility[347] and is "driven by an owner, employee, or agent of the child care facility for the primary purpose of transporting children to and from the child care facility, or to and from a place for participation in an event or activity in connection with the child care facility."[348] This provision does not apply to law enforcement officers acting in the course of, and within the scope of, their duties.[349]

2. Alcohol Screening Test

As with other implied consent offenses, an alcohol screening test may be administered to a driver suspected of violating G.S. 20-138.2B.[350] However, in this context, law enforcement officers and others may rely on the numerical results of the test rather than whether the results are positive or negative.[351] The test results or the driver's refusal to submit to the test may be used by a law enforcement officer, a court, or an administrative agency in determining if alcohol was present in the driver's body. To be valid, the testing device used must be one approved by the Department of Health and Human Services (DHHS)[352] and the screening test must be carried out pursuant to DHHS regulations governing the manner and use of such a device.[353]

The odor of an alcoholic beverage on the breath of a driver generally is not sufficient evidence, by itself, to prove beyond a reasonable doubt that alcohol was remaining in the driver's body in violation of G.S. 20-138.2B.[354] An exception to this general rule applies when a driver refuses to submit to an alcohol screening test or a chemical analysis. When a driver is offered testing and refuses to provide all required samples of breath or blood for analysis, the odor of an alcoholic beverage on his or her breath is sufficient evidence to establish that alcohol was remaining in his or her body at the time of the driving.

3. Sentencing

A violation of G.S. 20-138.2B(a) is a Class 3 misdemeanor. Notwithstanding provisions in the Structured Sentencing Act setting punishment limits and requirements for misdemeanor offenses, a first-time violation of G.S. 20-138.2B is punishable solely by a fine of $100.[355] A second or subsequent violation of G.S. 20-138.2B is a misdemeanor punishable under G.S. 20-179, the statute prescribing

345. *Id.* § 20-4.01(27)d3.

346. *Id.*

347. The term "child care facility" is defined in G.S. 110-86(3) as including "child care centers, family child care homes, and any other child care arrangement not excluded by G.S. 110-86(2), that provides child care, regardless of the time of day, wherever operated, and whether or not operated for profit."

348. G.S. 20-4.01(27)c1.

349. *Id.* § 20-138.2B(a).

350. *Id.* § 20-138.2B(b2).

351. *Compare* G.S. 20-138.2B(b2) (permitting use of the results of an alcohol screening test) *with* G.S. 20-16.3(d) (permitting law enforcement officers and others to use "a positive or negative result on an alcohol screening test, but not the actual alcohol concentration result").

352. Approved devices are listed in 10A N.C.A.C. 41B, § .0503.

353. G.S. 20-138.2B(b2). 10A N.C.A.C. 41B, § .0502(b) sets forth the procedure for administering an alcohol screening test.

354. G.S. 20-138.2B(b1).

355. *Id.* § 20-138.2B(c).

the punishment for impaired driving under G.S. 20-138.1. A conviction for violating G.S. 20-138.2B is a second or subsequent conviction if at the time of the current offense the person has a previous conviction under G.S. 20-138.2B, and the previous conviction occurred in the seven years immediately preceding the date of the current offense.[356] Those provisions are discussed in detail in chapter 5. G.S. 20-138.2B(c) provides that a violation of G.S. 20-138.2B is a lesser-included offense of impaired driving of a commercial motor vehicle, even though one may violate the statute without driving a commercial motor vehicle.[357]

4. License Revocation

Upon receiving notice that a person has been convicted of violating G.S. 20-138.2B, the North Carolina Division of Motor Vehicles must revoke the person's license for a period of one year.[358]

VIII. Driving While License Revoked

This section discusses two implied consent offenses that are types of driving while license revoked. The first is violating a no-alcohol condition of a limited driving privilege.[359] The second is driving in violation of a restriction requiring ignition interlock.[360]

A. Violation of a No-Alcohol Condition of a Limited Driving Privilege

A limited driving privilege is a judgment issued by a court that authorizes a person with a revoked driver's license to drive for essential and enumerated purposes. The eligibility requirements and restrictions for limited driving privileges associated with implied consent offenses are discussed in detail in chapter 6. Limited driving privileges issued to persons whose licenses are revoked upon conviction for impaired driving under G.S. 20-138.1 are issued pursuant to G.S. 20-179.3. All such limited driving privileges must include, in addition to other restrictions, a restriction that the driver not consume alcohol while driving or drive at any time while he or she has remaining in his or her body any alcohol or controlled substance previously consumed, unless the controlled substance was lawfully obtained and taken in therapeutically appropriate amounts.[361] A holder of a limited driving privilege who violates any of its restrictions commits the offense of driving while license revoked under G.S. 20-28(a).[362] If a law enforcement officer has reasonable grounds to believe that the holder of a limited driving privilege has consumed alcohol while driving or has driven while he or she has remaining in his or her body any alcohol previously consumed, the suspected offense of driving while license revoked is an alcohol-related offense subject to the implied consent provisions of G.S. 20-16.2.

An alcohol screening test may be administered to a person suspected of violating G.S. 20-179.3, and the results of the test or the driver's refusal to submit to testing may be used by a law enforcement officer, a court, or an administrative agency in determining if alcohol was present in the driver's

356. *Id.* § 20-138.2B(d).
357. *Id.* § 20-138.2B(c).
358. *Id.* § 20-17(a)(14); 20-19(c).
359. *Id.* § 20-179.3(j).
360. *Id.* § 20-17.8(f).
361. *Id.* § 20-179.3(h).
362. *Id.* § 20-179.3(j).

body. The alcohol screening test must be performed on an approved device and carried out pursuant to Department of Health and Human Services regulations.[363]

1. Sentencing

A person charged with driving while license revoked based on the violation of a no-alcohol condition of a limited driving privilege is subject to punishment as provided in G.S. 20-28.[364] Driving while license revoked is a Class 1 misdemeanor if the person's license was originally revoked for an impaired driving revocation.[365] Sentencing is governed by the Structured Sentencing Act.[366] If the person's license was originally revoked for an impaired driving revocation, the court may order as a condition of probation that the person abstain from alcohol consumption and verify compliance by use of an approved continuous alcohol monitoring system for a minimum period of 90 days.[367]

2. License Revocation

Upon conviction of driving while license revoked, a person's license must be revoked for an additional period of one year for the first offense, two years for the second offense, and permanently for the third or subsequent offense.[368]

B. Driving in Violation of a Restriction Requiring Ignition Interlock

Certain people convicted of impaired driving under G.S. 20-138.1 are required, as a condition of having their license restored, to equip any motor vehicle they drive for a designated time thereafter with an approved, functioning ignition interlock system.[369] Ignition interlock systems are devices wired to a car's ignition system that require a driver to submit a sample of his or her breath before turning on the engine in a vehicle and to provide additional breath samples at intervals thereafter. If the alcohol concentration of a breath sample submitted before turning on the car's ignition exceeds the permissible limit (in some cases 0.00, in others 0.04), the car's ignition will be temporarily disabled. If the results of a breath sample submitted during driving reveal an impermissible alcohol concentration, some other consequence ensues, such as the activation of a siren, and the driver is warned to cease operation of the vehicle. Drivers subject to an ignition interlock restriction are required to report at a designated interval to an ignition interlock facility so that the provider may check the installed interlock device and download information electronically recorded by the device. The ignition interlock provider prepares reports based on the information downloaded from the device. If the report includes an alcohol concentration violation, it is forwarded to the Driver's License Section of the North Carolina Division of Motor Vehicles (NC DMV).

The requirement to install ignition interlock carries with it several restrictions, including requirements that the person operate only a vehicle equipped with ignition interlock, that the person

---

363. *Id.* § 20-179.3(j).

364. *Id.* § 20-179.3(j). The person also is subject to license revocation as provided in G.S. 20-28(a).

365. S.L. 2013-360, sec. 18B.14(f) (amending G.S. 20-28(a) to provide, for offenses committed on or after December 1, 2013, that driving while license revoked is a Class 3 misdemeanor unless the person's license was originally revoked for an impaired driving revocation, in which case the offense is a Class 1 misdemeanor).

366. *See* G.S. 15A-1340.10.

367. *See id.* § 20-28(a). A continuous alcohol monitoring system is "a device worn by a person that can detect, monitor, record, and report the amount of alcohol within the wearer's system over a continuous 24-hour daily basis." *Id.* § 15A-1343.3(a).

368. *Id.* § 20-28(a).

369. *See id.* § 20-17.8(b).

personally activate the ignition interlock system before driving the vehicle, that the person install ignition interlock on all of the vehicles he or she owns,[370] and that the person not violate the alcohol concentration restriction imposed. A person who violates any ignition interlock restriction imposed as a condition of license restoration commits the offense of driving while license revoked under G.S. 20-28(a).[371]

If a law enforcement officer has reasonable grounds to believe that a person subject to an ignition interlock restriction under G.S. 20-17.8[372] has consumed alcohol while driving or has driven while he or she has remaining in his or her body any alcohol previously consumed, the suspected offense of driving while license revoked is an alcohol-related offense subject to the implied consent provisions of G.S. 20-16.2.

An alcohol concentration report from the ignition interlock system is not admissible as evidence of driving while license revoked unless the person operated a vehicle when the ignition interlock system indicated an alcohol concentration in violation of the restriction imposed.[373] Thus, an ignition interlock report for a restricted driver of an alcohol concentration of 0.02 is inadmissible in the prosecution of the person for driving while license revoked for violating an ignition interlock restriction if the person was prohibited from driving with an alcohol concentration of 0.04 or more. Such a report would be admissible, however, if the person was subject to a restriction that he or she not drive with an alcohol concentration of greater than 0.00.

1. Sentencing

A person convicted of driving while license revoked based on the violation of an ignition interlock restriction is subject to punishment as provided in G.S. 20-28.[374] Driving while license revoked is a Class 1 misdemeanor if the person's license was originally revoked for an impaired driving revocation.[375] Sentencing is governed by the Structured Sentencing Act.[376] If the person's license was originally revoked for an impaired driving revocation, the court may order as a condition of probation

370. S.L. 2013-348 (S 659), effective for offenses committed on or after October 1, 2013, amended G.S. 20-17.8 (restoration of a license after certain driving while impaired convictions; ignition interlock) to prohibit NC DMV from issuing a license to a person subject to the statute until presented with proof of the installation of an ignition interlock system in all registered vehicles owned by the person. Formerly, a person was not required to install ignition interlock on a vehicle he or she owned if NC DMV determined that another member of the person's family relied on the vehicle and the vehicle was not in the possession of the person subject to the ignition interlock requirement. This exception applied, for example, when the college-age child of a parent convicted of impaired driving and subject to ignition interlock drove a vehicle owned by the parent while residing in a different location from the parent. Amended G.S. 20-17.8(c1) requires that NC DMV determine whether a waiver of the ignition interlock requirement is appropriate under the family-member exception on a case-by-case basis following an assessment of financial hardship to the person subject to the restriction. S.L. 2013-348 also deleted the last sentence of G.S. 20-17.8(f), which required a court, on finding that the aforementioned family-member exception to ignition interlock applied, to find the person not guilty of driving while license revoked for violating the conditions under G.S. 20-17.8(c1).

371. G.S. 20-17.8(f).

372. *Id.*

373. *Id.* § 20-17.8(f).

374. *Id.* The person also is subject to license revocation as provided in G.S. 20-28(a). License revocations are discussed in detail in chapter 6.

375. S.L. 2013-360, sec. 18B.14(f) (amending G.S. 20-28(a) to provide, for offenses committed on or after December 1, 2013, that driving while license revoked is a Class 3 misdemeanor unless the person's license was originally revoked for an impaired driving revocation, in which case the offense is a Class 1 misdemeanor).

376. *See* G.S. 15A-1340.10.

that the person abstain from alcohol consumption and verify compliance by use of an approved continuous alcohol monitoring system for a minimum period of 90 days.[377]

2. License Revocation

Upon conviction of driving while license revoked, a person's license must be revoked for an additional period of one year for the first offense, two years for the second offense, and permanently for the third or subsequent offense.[378]

---

377. *See id.* § 20-28(a).
378. *Id.*

Chapter 3

Initial Appearances, Confinement, and Access to Witnesses

Chapter 3

Initial Appearances, Confinement, and Access to Witnesses

I. Introduction

When a defendant is arrested for a criminal offense, he or she must be taken before a judicial official without unnecessary delay for an *initial appearance*.[1] The procedures set forth in Article 24 of Chapter 15A of the North Carolina General Statutes (hereinafter G.S.) govern initial appearances in implied consent cases[2] just as they do in other criminal cases, except where those procedures are modified by the implied consent offense procedures set forth in Article 2D of G.S. Chapter 20. The implied consent offense procedures permit a magistrate—the judicial official who typically presides over an initial appearance—to hold an initial appearance at any place within the county and require, "to the extent practicable," that a magistrate "be available at locations other than the courthouse when it will expedite the initial appearance."[3] As in all cases, the magistrate must determine whether the charges are supported by probable cause and must impose conditions of pretrial release. To determine whether there is probable cause to believe a person charged with an implied consent offense is

1. Section 15A-501(2) of the North Carolina General Statutes (hereinafter G.S.); *see also id.* § 20-38.3(5) (requiring that a law enforcement officer take a person arrested for an implied consent offense before a judicial official for an initial appearance after completing all investigatory and other specified procedures, crash reports, and chemical analyses).

2. The following offenses are categorized as implied consent offenses:

1. Impaired driving (G.S. 20-138.1)
2. Impaired driving in a commercial vehicle (G.S. 20-138.2)
3. Habitual impaired driving (G.S. 20-138.5)
4. Death by vehicle or serious injury by vehicle (G.S. 20-141.4)
5. First- or second-degree murder (G.S. 14-17) or involuntary manslaughter (G.S. 14-18) when based on impaired driving
6. Driving by a person less than 21 years old after consuming alcohol or drugs (G.S. 20-138.3)
7. Violating no-alcohol condition of limited driving privilege (G.S. 20-179.3(j))
8. Impaired instruction (G.S. 20-12.1)
9. Operating commercial motor vehicle after consuming alcohol (G.S. 20-138.2A)
10. Operating school bus, school activity bus, or child care vehicle after consuming alcohol (G.S. 20-138.2B)
11. Transporting an open container of alcohol (G.S. 20-138.7(a))
12. Certain violations of restriction requiring ignition interlock (G.S. 20-17.8(f))

3. G.S. 20-38.4(a)(1).

impaired, a magistrate may review all alcohol screening tests[4] and chemical analyses and may receive testimony from any law enforcement officer concerning impairment and the circumstances of the arrest.[5] The magistrate also may observe the person arrested.[6]

Several additional requirements beyond those that apply to initial appearances in criminal cases generally apply to initial appearances for implied consent offenses.[7] For example, the judicial official who conducts the proceeding, typically a magistrate, may be required to revoke the defendant's driver's license, order that a vehicle driven by the defendant be seized and impounded, consider whether the defendant should be detained because his or her impairment poses a danger to others, and inform the defendant of the procedure for having witnesses appear at the jail to observe his or her condition or perform additional chemical analyses. The law and procedures governing the imposition of a civil license revocation at a defendant's initial appearance, a requirement that an impaired driver be detained because of his or her impairment, and a requirement that a defendant be informed of procedures for contacting witnesses are discussed in this chapter. This chapter also discusses the North Carolina Supreme Court's determination in *State v. Knoll*[8] that impaired driving charges must be dismissed when a defendant establishes a substantial statutory violation of his or her right to pretrial release that is prejudicial. The seizure of motor vehicles driven by certain defendants charged with offenses involving impaired driving is discussed in chapter 8.

II. Civil License Revocations

State law requires the immediate civil revocation of driver's licenses of certain persons charged with implied consent offenses.[9] When the results of a chemical analysis or a report indicating a willful refusal to submit to a chemical analysis are available at the time of the initial appearance, the law enforcement officer and chemical analyst must execute a revocation report before the magistrate.[10] The magistrate must, after completing any other proceedings involving the person, determine whether there is probable cause to believe that the conditions requiring civil license revocation are met.[11]

---

4. A valid alcohol screening test must be performed with an approved portable breath-testing device, such as an ALCO-SENSOR. G.S. 20-16.3(b), (c); Title 10A, Subchapter 41B, Sections .0501–.0503 of the North Carolina Administrative Code (hereinafter N.C.A.C.). A law enforcement officer may use "[t]he fact that a driver showed a positive or negative result on an alcohol screening test, but not the actual alcohol concentration result," in determining probable cause for an implied consent offense. G.S. 20-16.3(d). An officer also may use a driver's refusal to submit to an alcohol screening test in determining probable cause. *Id.*

A different rule governs the use of alcohol screening tests in cases in which a defendant is charged with driving by a person less than 21 years old after consuming alcohol. *See* G.S. 20-138.3(b2). In such cases, a law enforcement officer, court, or administrative agency may use the results of an alcohol screening test to determine whether alcohol was present in the driver's body. *Id.* Thus not only may the results of the test be used in such cases, but reliance on the results also is not limited to determining probable cause.

5. G.S. 20-38.4(a)(2).

6. *Id.*

7. See *supra* note 2 (listing implied consent offenses).

8. 322 N.C. 535 (1988).

9. G.S. 20-16.5.

10. *Id.* §§ 20-16.5(c), (d).

11. *Id.* § 20-16.5(e).

A. Conditions Requiring Civil License Revocation

> A person's driver's license is subject to civil revocation under G.S. 20-16.5 if each of the following four conditions is satisfied:
>
> 1. A law enforcement officer has reasonable grounds to believe that the person has committed an implied consent offense.
> 2. The person is charged with an implied consent offense.
> 3. The law enforcement officer and the chemical analyst comply with the procedures of G.S. 20-16.2 and -139.1 in requiring the person to submit to or in procuring a chemical analysis.
> 4. The person
>   a. willfully refuses to submit to the chemical analysis,[12]
>   b. has an alcohol concentration of 0.08 or more within a relevant time after the driving,[13]
>   c. has an alcohol concentration of 0.04 or more at any relevant time after the driving of a commercial motor vehicle, or
>   d. has any alcohol concentration at any relevant time after the driving and the person is under 21 years of age.

Although normally a person submits to chemical analysis only after he or she is arrested and charged with an implied consent offense, a person who is stopped or questioned by a law enforcement officer who is investigating whether that person may have committed an implied consent offense may request that a chemical analysis be administered before any arrest or other charge is made.[14] Upon such a request, the officer must "afford the person the opportunity to have a chemical analysis of his or her breath, if available, in accordance with the procedures required by G.S. 20-139.1(b)."[15] The notice of rights required prior to administration of a precharge test is prescribed by statute and differs slightly from the notice provided in a case in which the person already has been charged with

---

12. A refusal is " 'the declination of a request or demand, or the omission to comply with some requirement of law, as the result of a positive intention to disobey.' " Joyner v. Garrett, 279 N.C. 226, 233 (1971) (quoting Black's Law Dictionary (4th ed. 1951)). A *willful* refusal occurs when a person (1) is aware that he or she has a choice to take or refuse a test, (2) is aware of the time limit within which he or she must take the test, and (3) voluntarily elects not to take the test or knowingly permits the prescribed thirty-minute time limit to expire before electing to take the test. Etheridge v. Peters, 301 N.C. 76, 81 (1980). In essence, a willful refusal is a refusal that occurs after the defendant is advised of his or her implied consent rights and is asked to submit to a chemical analysis. *See, e.g.*, Rice v. Peters, 48 N.C. App. 697, 700–01 (1980) (holding that purpose of refusal-revocation statute is "fulfilled when the petitioner is given the option to submit or refuse to submit to a breathalyzer test and his decision is made after having been advised of his rights in a manner provided by the statute").

13. While a person may commit the offense of driving while impaired by driving a vehicle while impaired by drugs, no civil license revocation may be issued based upon impairment by drugs.

14. G.S. 20-16.2(i).

15. *Id.*

an implied consent offense.[16] A precharge chemical analysis can give rise to a license revocation if the following conditions are satisfied:[17]

1. The person requested a precharge chemical analysis pursuant to G.S. 20-16.2(i) and
2. The person has
   a. an alcohol concentration of 0.08 or more at any relevant time after driving,
   b. an alcohol concentration of 0.04 or more at any relevant time after driving a commercial vehicle, or
   c. any alcohol concentration at any relevant time after driving and the person is under 21 years of age, and
3. The person is charged with an implied consent offense.

1. Driving in Violation of an Alcohol Restriction that Is Not an Implied Consent Offense

When a person's license is restored after having been revoked as a result of the person's conviction for being under the age of 21 and driving after consuming alcohol or drugs, for impaired driving, or for another offense involving impaired driving specified in G.S. 20-19, the license is restored with the restriction that the person not operate a motor vehicle while having an alcohol concentration of 0.04 or more, or, in the case of a second or subsequent restoration or conviction of certain specified offenses involving impaired driving, greater than 0.00.[18] A person seeking to have his or her license restored "must agree to submit to a chemical analysis in accordance with G.S. 20-16.2 at the request of a law enforcement officer who has reasonable grounds to believe that the person is operating a motor vehicle on a highway or public vehicular area in violation of the restriction [set out in the General Statutes]."[19] The person must also agree to be transported by the officer to the place where the chemical analysis is to be administered.[20]

Questions frequently arise regarding whether a person who drives in violation of such a restriction is subject to a civil license revocation based merely on the violation of the alcohol restriction. The usual answer is no. Driving in violation of an alcohol restriction imposed as a condition of a license restoration pursuant to G.S. 20-19(c3) is *not* an implied consent offense, so the conditions for civil license revocation are not met based merely on violating such a restriction.[21] That said, there may be instances in which there is probable cause to believe that a person with an alcohol restriction has, in addition to violating the conditions of a restricted license, also committed an implied consent offense. In such a case, if the other conditions for civil license revocation exist, the civil revocation must be issued.

One reason for the confusion may be that in addition to its use in the civil revocation context, form AOC-CVR-1A, Affidavit and Revocation Report of Law Enforcement Officer/Chemical Analyst,[22] also is used to report violations of alcohol concentration restrictions to the North Carolina Division of Motor Vehicles (NC DMV). When a person's driver's license has an alcohol concentration restriction and the results of a chemical analysis establish a violation of that restriction, or when a law

---

16. *Id.*
17. *Id.* § 20-16.5(b1).
18. *Id.* § 20-19(c3).
19. *Id.*
20. *Id.*
21. *See* Letter from Roy Cooper, North Carolina Attorney General, to Members of the Criminal Justice Community (June 4, 2001) (on file with author).
22. Available on the N.C. Administrative Office of the Courts' website at www.nccourts.org/Forms/Documents/1049.pdf.

enforcement officer has reasonable grounds to believe that the person has violated another provision of the restriction, the law enforcement officer must execute an affidavit regarding the violation and "immediately mail" it to the NC DMV.[23]

2. Driving in Violation of Ignition Interlock Restriction

Certain persons convicted of impaired driving may have their licenses restored only in conjunction with an ignition interlock restriction.[24] A person whose license is revoked as a result of a conviction of impaired driving pursuant to G.S. 20-138.1 who had (1) an alcohol concentration level of 0.15 or higher, (2) a prior conviction for an offense involving impaired driving, that offense having occurred within seven years immediately preceding the date of the offense for which the person's license is revoked, or (3) who was sentenced at Aggravated Level One pursuant to G.S. 20-179(f3) may have his or her license restored only with an ignition interlock restriction.[25] This requires that a person operate only a vehicle that is equipped with a functioning ignition interlock system.[26] The person must personally activate the ignition interlock system before driving the vehicle.[27] An alcohol concentration restriction of 0.04 or 0.00 also applies, with the level dependent on the circumstances of the conviction giving rise to the ignition interlock requirement.[28]

A person who violates an ignition interlock restriction commits the offense of driving while license revoked (DWLR) under G.S. 20-28(a) and "is subject to punishment and license revocation as provided in that section."[29] If a law enforcement officer has reasonable grounds to believe that a person subject to an ignition interlock restriction has consumed alcohol while driving or has driven while any previously consumed alcohol remains in his or her body, the suspected offense of DWLR is "an alcohol-related offense subject to the implied-consent provisions of G.S. 20-16.2."[30]

Thus, certain violations of ignition interlock restrictions constitute implied consent offenses. If a person is charged with such an offense and the other requirements of G.S. 20-16.5 are satisfied, the magistrate must order the person's driver's license civilly revoked under G.S. 20-16.5.

The person's license also will be suspended pursuant to G.S. 20-17.8(f), which provides that when a person subject to an ignition interlock restriction is charged with DWLR based on a violation of the ignition interlock restrictions set forth in G.S. 20-17.8(b)[31] and the judicial official finds probable

---

23. G.S. 20-16.2(c1).
24. *Id.* § 20-17.8.
25. G.S. 20-17.8(l) sets forth a medical exception to the ignition interlock requirement for people subject to the requirement solely because of an alcohol concentration of 0.15 or higher who establish that they are not capable of personally activating the ignition interlock system.
26. *Id.* § 20-17.8(b)(1).
27. *Id.* § 20-17.8(b)(2).
28. *Id.* § 20-17.8(b)(3).
29. *Id.* § 20-17.8(f). Most violations of G.S. 20-28(a) committed before December 1, 2013, were Class 1 misdemeanors. The law changed, however, for offenses committed on or after December 1, 2013. *See* S.L. 2013-360, Section 18B.14(f) (amending G.S. 20-28(a)); *see also* Shea Denning, *A New Kind of DWLR*, N.C. CRIM. L., UNC SCH. OF GOV'T BLOG (Dec. 10, 2013), http://nccriminallaw.sog.unc.edu/?p=4565. Now, a person who (1) drives (2) a motor vehicle (3) on a street or highway (4) while his or her license has been revoked by the State of North Carolina (4) knowing that his or her license is revoked commits a Class 3 misdemeanor. If, however, the person's license is revoked for impaired driving, the person is guilty of a Class 1 misdemeanor. A person who drives in violation of an ignition interlock requirement is not, at the time he or she drives, revoked for impaired driving; thus, it appears that this sort of violation, if committed on or after December 1, 2013, is a Class 3 misdemeanor.
30. G.S. 20-17.8(f).
31. These restrictions are that the person (1) operate only a vehicle equipped with interlock, (2) personally activate the ignition interlock before driving, and (3) comply with the alcohol concentration restrictions.

cause for the charge, the person's license is suspended pending the resolution of the case. The judicial official must require the person to surrender the license and inform the person that he or she is not entitled to drive until the case is resolved.[32]

B. Affidavit and Revocation Report (AOC-CVR-1A)

In implied consent cases in which the law enforcement officer and a chemical analyst determine that the conditions requiring an immediate civil license revocation exist, the law enforcement officer and chemical analyst (who may be the same person) must execute an AOC-CVR-1A, Affidavit and Revocation Report of Law Enforcement Officer/Chemical Analyst.[33] This duty also applies when the law enforcement officer and chemical analyst have all of the information supporting the issuance of a civil license revocation save a report from a laboratory regarding the analysis of the person's blood. This report is a sworn statement by a law enforcement officer and chemical analyst containing facts indicating that the conditions requiring a civil license revocation are met and reporting whether the person has a pending offense for which the person's license has been or is revoked under the civil revocation statute.[34]

A law enforcement officer must ensure that the AOC-CVR-1A is "expeditiously filed" with the appropriate judicial official.[35] If no revocation report has previously been filed and the results of the chemical analysis or the report indicating the defendant's willful refusal to submit to a chemical analysis are available, the law enforcement officer must file the report with the judicial official conducting the initial appearance on the underlying criminal charge—typically a magistrate.[36] If no report previously has been filed, and a judicial official is conducting any other proceeding relating to the underlying criminal charge at which the person is present, then the report must be filed with that judicial official.[37] If neither of these two provisions is applicable at the time the report must be filed, then the report must be filed with the clerk of court in the county in which the underlying criminal charge was brought.[38]

---

32. G.S. 20-17.8(f). This type of revocation typically is ordered on form AOC-CR-341, Order to Surrender License or Limited Driving Privilege. This form is available on the N.C. Administrative Office of the Courts' website at www.nccourts.org/Forms/Documents/132.pdf.

33. This form is available on the N.C. Administrative Office of the Courts' website at www.nccourts.org/Forms/Documents/1049.pdf. *See* G.S. 20-16.5(c). The charging officer may also perform the work of the chemical analyst—the person authorized to conduct chemical analyses of the breath—if the officer has a current permit issued by the Department of Health and Human Services authorizing the officer to perform a breath test using the type of instrument employed. *Id.* § 20-139.1(b1).

34. G.S. 20-16.5(a)(4). If the charging officer and the chemical analyst are different people, the officer will complete the pertinent part of one AOC-CVR-1A (paragraphs 1–5), and the chemical analyst will complete the remaining portions (paragraphs 6–14) of a separate AOC-CVR-1A. If one chemical analyst analyzes a person's blood and another chemical analyst informs a person of his or her rights and responsibilities under G.S. 20-16.2, the affidavit and report must include the statements of both analysts. The officer also must state in the last block of paragraph 4 of the AOC-CVR-1A whether the person has a pending offense for which the person's license has been or is revoked under G.S. 20-16.5, as this will affect the length of the revocation period.

35. G.S. 20-16.5(c).

36. *Id.* § 20-16.5(d)(1).

37. *Id.* § 20-16.5(d)(2).

38. *Id.* § 20-16.5(d)(3).

C. Procedure if Report Filed at Initial Appearance

When an affidavit and revocation report is filed with a magistrate at a person's initial appearance, G.S. 20-16.5(e) instructs the magistrate to first complete all other proceedings involving the person and then to determine whether there is probable cause to believe that the conditions requiring civil license revocation are satisfied.[39] If the magistrate determines that the requirements are met, the magistrate must enter an order revoking the defendant's license for the requisite period, unless the exception for revoked licenses, described below, applies.[40] The revocation begins at the time the order is issued.[41]

1. Exception for Revoked Licenses

If the magistrate finds that the person whose license is subject to civil revocation has a currently revoked driver's license, no limited driving privilege, and will not become eligible for restoration of his or her license or a limited driving privilege during the period of civil revocation, the magistrate is not required to issue the civil revocation order.[42] If this exception applies and the revocation order is not issued, the magistrate must file in the records of the civil proceeding a copy of any documentary evidence and set out in writing all other evidence on which he or she relied in making that determination.[43]

2. Revocation Order (AOC-CVR-2)

Revocation orders by magistrates are entered on form AOC-CVR-2, titled Revocation Order When Person Present.[44] The magistrate must make findings as to whether the defendant (a) willfully refused to submit to a chemical analysis, (b) had an alcohol concentration of 0.08 or more at any relevant time after driving, (c) had an alcohol concentration of 0.04 or more at any relevant time after the driving of a commercial motor vehicle, or (d) had any alcohol concentration at any relevant time after the driving and, at the time of the offense, was under 21 years of age. If the defendant has been charged with an offense for which his or her license had been or is revoked pursuant to G.S. 20-16.5 and that offense is pending, the magistrate must make a finding to that effect.

In rendering his or her order, the magistrate must indicate whether the revocation is in effect for (1) at least thirty days from the date the order is entered, (2) at least thirty days from the date the defendant surrenders his or her driver's license to the court or demonstrates that he or she is not currently licensed to drive, or (3) the date the defendant surrenders his or her driver's license to the court or demonstrates that he or she is not currently licensed to drive and indefinitely until a final judgment, including appeals, has been entered for the current offense and for all pending offenses for which his or her driver's license had been or is revoked under G.S. 20-16.5. In no event may the period of revocation be shorter than thirty days.[45]

---

39. *Id.* § 20-16.5(e).

40. A person's license is subject to immediate civil revocation if the aforementioned statutory requirements are met—even if the person was driving a vehicle for which no license was required, such as a moped, bicycle, or lawn mower.

41. G.S. 20-16.5(e).

42. *Id.* § 20-16.5(n).

43. *Id.*

44. This form is available on the N.C. Administrative Office of the Courts' website at www.nccourts.org/Forms/Documents/194.pdf.

45. G.S. 20-16.5(e).

The magistrate must give the defendant a copy of the revocation order. Although G.S. 20-16.5 does not require that the magistrate orally notify the defendant of the revocation period, a magistrate should, in the interest of securing compliance with the revocation, inform the defendant that his or her license is revoked for at least thirty days. If the revocation is indefinite because of a pending implied consent charge,[46] the magistrate should inform the defendant that his or her license is revoked for at least thirty days and that it remains revoked indefinitely, until a final judgment is entered for the current offense and all pending offenses for which his or her license had been or is revoked under G.S. 20-16.5. The magistrate must state in the order and personally inform the defendant that he or she may request a hearing to contest the validity of the revocation order and that his or her license remains revoked pending that hearing.[47]

3. Surrender of Driver's License

Upon entering a revocation order, the magistrate must order the person to surrender his or her license and, if necessary, may order a law enforcement officer to seize the license.[48] Licenses issued by jurisdictions other than North Carolina are covered by the surrender provisions and must, like North Carolina driver's licenses, be surrendered to the magistrate.[49]

A person may surrender the license by turning over to a court or a law enforcement officer his or her most recent, valid driver's license or learner's permit or a limited driving privilege issued by a North Carolina court.[50] In July 2008, the North Carolina Division of Motor Vehicles (NC DMV) launched a central system for issuing licenses.[51] Under this system, a person who applies to renew his or her driver's license does not receive a newly minted license from the local NC DMV office.[52] Instead, the person receives a temporary driving certificate valid for twenty days.[53] In the interim, the person's driver's license is produced at a central location and then mailed to the applicant.[54] When a magistrate orders a civil license revocation for a person who has a temporary driving certificate rather than a renewed license, the magistrate should require the driver to surrender the temporary certificate. The magistrate should further instruct the person that upon receiving his or her renewed license in the mail, he or she must immediately surrender it to the office of the clerk for superior court for the remainder of the revocation period.

4. Affidavit of No License or Lost License (AOC-CVR-8)

A person who is validly licensed but unable to locate his or her license may surrender the license by filing an affidavit with the clerk.[55] The form affidavit is denominated AOC-CVR-8 (Affidavit—No License).[56] A person who is not licensed to drive in North Carolina and thus has no license from North Carolina or elsewhere may complete the AOC-CVR-8 and submit the affidavit to either the

---

46. *See id.*
47. *Id.*
48. *Id.*
49. *Id.* § 20-16.5(a)(5).
50. *Id.*
51. *See id.* § 20-7(f)(5).
52. *Id.*
53. *Id.*
54. *Id.*
55. *Id.* § 20-16.5(a)(5).
56. This form is available on the N.C. Administrative Office of the Courts' website at www.nccourts.org/Forms/Documents/200.pdf.

magistrate or the clerk.[57] A person also may demonstrate to the magistrate that he or she is not licensed by producing appropriate identification that the magistrate can check against NC DMV records. If a person submits form AOC-CVR-8 to establish that he or she does not have a license or otherwise demonstrates to the magistrate that he or she has no license, the magistrate must make the appropriate findings on AOC-CVR-2.[58]

When an affidavit and revocation report is submitted to a magistrate at an initial appearance, a driver who has lost his or her license often returns an affidavit of lost license, completed on form AOC-CVR-8, to the magistrate rather than the clerk. While there is no explicit statutory authorization for the practice, magistrates typically accept such filings on the clerk's behalf and note the surrender of the license in the supplemental findings section of the revocation order.

5. Driver's License Pick-Up Order

If a person does not surrender his or her license or demonstrate that he or she is not licensed within five working days of the effective date of the revocation order, the clerk of court must issue a pick-up order.[59] Pick-up orders are issued on form AOC-CVR-4.[60] The pick-up order must be issued to a member of a local law enforcement agency if the arresting law enforcement officer was employed by the agency at the time of the charge and the person charged resides in or is present in the agency's territorial jurisdiction.[61] G.S. 20-16.5(e) provides that in all other cases, the pick-up order must be issued to an NC DMV officer or inspector—positions that no longer exist within NC DMV. As a result, pick-up orders that are not issued to a member of a local law enforcement agency are issued to the State Highway Patrol.

6. Revocation Period

A civil license revocation ordered by a magistrate begins at the time the revocation order is issued and continues until the person's license has been surrendered for the minimum revocation period and the person has paid the applicable costs.[62] Revocations under G.S. 20-16.5 are never shorter than thirty days from the date the person surrenders the license. The revocation period may be longer, depending on whether the person timely surrenders his or her license and whether the person has another pending offense for which the license is or was revoked under G.S. 20-16.5.

If the person surrenders his or her license at the time of revocation and has no pending offenses for which the license was or is revoked under G.S. 20-16.5, the magistrate must state that the revocation is in effect for at least thirty days from the date of the order. If the person does not surrender his or her license at the time of the revocation but has no pending offenses for which the license was revoked, the magistrate must state that the revocation is in effect for at least thirty days from the date the defendant surrenders his or her driver's license to the court or demonstrates that he or she is not currently licensed to drive. Regardless of when the minimum revocation period begins, revocation orders issued by a magistrate are effective when they are issued.[63]

---

57. G.S. 20-16.5(e).
58. See *supra* note 44.
59. G.S. 20-16.5(e).
60. This form, aptly named the Drivers License Pick-Up Order, is available on the N.C. Administrative Office of the Courts' website at www.nccourts.org/Forms/Documents/197.pdf.
61. G.S. 20-16.5(e).
62. *Id.*
63. *Id.*

For a person who at the time of the new offense has a pending implied consent charge for which his or her license was or is civilly revoked, the new civil revocation is indefinite and lasts until a final judgment (including all appeals) has been entered for the current offense and all pending implied consent offenses. In no event may the revocation period be shorter than thirty days. This indefinite revocation period applies regardless of whether the *civil revocation* in the earlier case was in place at the time of the instant offense; the key is whether the prior implied consent charge itself is still pending.

D. Procedure if Report Filed with Clerk of Court When the Person Is Not Present

When a clerk receives a properly executed revocation report under G.S. 20-16.5(d)(3) and the person named in the revocation report is not present before the clerk, the clerk must determine whether there is probable cause to believe that each of the conditions of G.S. 20-16.5(b) has been met.[64] A "properly executed report" filed with the clerk always consists of more than one affidavit. The law enforcement officer who arrested the defendant must submit a sworn statement, as must the chemical analyst who advised the person of his or her implied consent rights. If the arresting officer also is the chemical analyst, these statements will be contained on a single AOC-CVR-1A.[65] In addition, the chemical analyst who analyzed the sample of the person's blood or urine also must submit an affidavit directly to the clerk.[66]

If the clerk determines that there is probable cause for each of the conditions in G.S. 20-16.5(b), the clerk must send the person charged a revocation order by first class mail.[67] Revocation orders issued by the clerk become effective on the fourth day after they are mailed.[68] These orders are entered on form AOC-CVR-3.[69] The order must direct the person to surrender his or her license to the clerk or to appear before the clerk and demonstrate that he or she is not currently licensed on or before the date the order becomes effective.[70] The order also must inform the person of the time and effective date of the revocation and of its duration; that the person has the right pursuant to G.S. 20-16.5(g) to request a hearing to contest the revocation; and that the revocation remains in effect pending the hearing. If the person does not surrender his or her license to the clerk or appear before the clerk to demonstrate that he or she is not currently licensed within five working days of the effective date of the order, the clerk must immediately issue a pick-up order.[71] Pick-up orders must inform the person of the right to a hearing to contest the revocation pursuant to G.S. 20-16.5(g) and that the revocation remains in effect pending the hearing.[72] Driver's license pick-up orders are issued on form AOC-CVR-4, which satisfies these requirements.[73] After serving a pick-up order, an officer must return the order to the court indicating the date on which it was served or that he or she was unable to serve the

---

64. *Id.* § 20-16.5(f).
65. See *supra* note 33.
66. G.S. 20-16.5(f).
67. *Id.*
68. Since the civil license revocation is a civil action, see G.S. 20-13.3(g), the civil counting rules of G.S. 1A-1, Rule 6(a) apply. Pursuant to Rule 6(a), the four days are calculated beginning with the day following the date of mailing.
69. This form, Revocation Order When Person Not Present, is available on the N.C. Administrative Office of the Courts' website at http://www.nccourts.org/Forms/Documents/196.pdf.
70. G.S. 20-16.5(f).
71. *Id.* See *supra* section II.C.5.
72. *Id.* Form AOC-CVR-4 satisfies these requirements.
73. See *supra* note 60.

order. If the license was surrendered, the officer serving the order must deposit the license with the clerk within three days of the surrender.

A revocation ordered by the clerk pursuant to G.S. 20-16.5(f) begins on the date specified in the order and continues until the person's license has been revoked for the minimum period and he or she has paid the applicable costs.

1. Minimum Period of Thirty or Forty-Five Days

If the person has no pending offenses for which his or her license had been or is revoked under G.S. 20-16.5, the minimum period of revocation is either thirty or forty-five days, depending upon whether the person surrenders his or her driver's license in a timely manner.[74] If the person surrenders his or her driver's license within five working days from the effective date of the revocation order, the minimum revocation period is thirty days.[75] Similarly, the minimum revocation period is thirty days if the person appears before the clerk within five working days of the effective date of the order and demonstrates that he or she is not licensed to drive.[76] If neither of these events occurs within five working days of the effective date of the revocation order, the clerk must issue a pick-up order, and the minimum revocation period becomes forty-five days.[77] Pick-up orders issued in these circumstances must be issued and served in the same manner as those issued and served following a revocation order issued by a magistrate.[78]

A minimum revocation period of forty-five days runs from the time that (a) the person's driver's license is picked up by a law enforcement officer after service of a pick-up order; (b) the person demonstrates to a law enforcement officer who has a pick-up order for his or her license that he or she is not currently licensed; (c) the person's driver's license is surrendered to the court if the surrender occurs more than five working days after the effective date of the revocation order; or (d) the person appears before the clerk to demonstrate that he or she is not currently licensed, if the person appears more than five working days after the effective date of the revocation order.[79]

2. Revocation Period if Pending Offense

Just as with revocation orders issued by a magistrate, if, at the time of the current offense, the person charged has one or more pending offenses for which his or her license had been or is revoked under G.S. 20-16.5, the revocation remains in effect until a final judgment, including all appeals, has been entered for the current offense and for all pending offenses.[80] The period of revocation for the current offense may never be less than the applicable minimum period of revocation of thirty or forty-five days calculated in accordance with the rules cited in the previous section.[81]

E. Multiple Offenses

A person may be charged with more than one implied consent offense arising from a single event. For example, as a result of one episode of driving while impaired a person may be charged under G.S. 20-138.1 as well as under G.S. 20-138.3 if the driver is less than 21 years old. Both of these offenses

---

74. G.S. 20-16.5(f).
75. *Id.*
76. *Id.*
77. *Id.*
78. *Id.*
79. *Id.*
80. *Id.*
81. *Id.*

are implied consent offenses that, when combined with other requisite factors, require a civil license revocation. The statutes are silent regarding whether two civil license revocations should be issued in such circumstances. The better practice in the view of this author is that when a defendant is charged with more than one offense requiring a civil license revocation based on conduct arising from a single occurrence, only one civil license revocation should be issued.

F. Contesting a License Revocation (AOC-CVR-5)

As previously mentioned, a person whose license is revoked under G.S. 20-16.5 may request a hearing to contest the validity of the revocation. The request must be in writing and may be made at the time of the person's initial appearance or within ten days of the effective date of the revocation.[82] The appropriate form for this situation is AOC-CVR-5.[83] The request must be made to the clerk or to a magistrate designated by the clerk and must specify the grounds upon which the revocation is challenged.[84] The ensuing hearing must be limited to the grounds specified in that request.[85]

The person may specifically request that the hearing be conducted by a district court judge.[86] If the person does not make that request, the hearing must be conducted by a magistrate assigned by the chief district court judge to conduct such hearings.[87] The General Statutes are silent on the matter, but in order to ensure meaningful and impartial review, the hearing contesting revocation should be held by a magistrate other than the magistrate who entered the initial revocation order. If the person does request that a district court judge hold the hearing, it must be conducted within the district court district by a district court judge assigned to conduct such hearings.[88] The revocation remains in effect pending the hearing.[89] The hearing must be held within three working days following the request if the hearing is before a magistrate or within five working days if before a district court judge.[90] If the hearing is not held and completed by a magistrate within three working days or by a district court judge within five working days of the written request, the judicial official must enter an order rescinding the revocation, unless the person contesting the revocation contributed to the delay.[91] If the person requesting the hearing fails to appear at the hearing or at any rescheduled hearing after having been property notified, he or she forfeits the right to a hearing.[92]

A witness may submit evidence via affidavit at the hearing unless the witness is subpoenaed.[93] Any person who appears and testifies is subject to questioning by the judicial official conducting the hearing, and the judicial official may adjourn the hearing to seek additional evidence if he or she deems necessary.[94] If the hearing is adjourned, it must be reconvened and the matter resolved within the applicable time limit (three working days if held by the magistrate, five working days if held by a

---

82. *Id.* § 20-16.5(g).
83. This form, titled Request for Hearing to Contest License Revocation, is available on the N.C. Administrative Office of the Courts' website at http://www.nccourts.org/Forms/Documents/199.pdf.
84. G.S. 20-16.5(g).
85. *Id.*
86. *Id.*
87. *Id.*
88. *Id.*
89. *Id.*
90. *Id.*
91. *Id.*
92. *Id.*
93. *Id.*
94. *Id.*

district court judge).[95] The person contesting the validity of the revocation may, but is not required to, testify on his or her own behalf.[96] Unless contested by the person requesting the hearing, statements in the revocation report may be accepted as true by the judicial official.[97] If any relevant condition under G.S. 20-16.5(b) is contested, the judicial official must find by the greater weight of the evidence that the condition was met in order to sustain the revocation.[98] At the end of the hearing, the judicial official must enter an order on side two of form AOC-CVR-5 sustaining or rescinding the revocation. The decision of the judicial official is final and may not be appealed.[99]A defendant who satisfies certain conditions may be granted a limited driving privilege that authorizes driving during a period of civil license revocation under G.S. 20-16.5. The eligibility requirements and parameters for such a privilege are discussed in chapter 6.

G. Return of License

After the applicable period of revocation has passed, or if a magistrate or judge orders the revocation rescinded, the person whose license was revoked may apply to the clerk for return of the surrendered license. The clerk generally keeps surrendered licenses rather than mailing them to the North Carolina Division of Motor Vehicles (NC DMV). An exception applies if the person's license is revoked pursuant to G.S. 20-16.5 and under another section of G.S. Chapter 20. In such cases, the clerk must surrender the license to the NC DMV if the G.S. 20-16.5 revocation can end before the other revocation.[100] The $100 in costs[101] still must be paid before the G.S. 20-16.5 civil revocation may be terminated, even after the other revocation ends.[102]

Unless the clerk finds that the person charged is not eligible to use the surrendered license, the clerk must return a person's license if (1) the applicable period of revocation has passed and the person has paid the $100 in costs or (2) the magistrate or judge has rescinded the revocation.[103] If the

---

95. *Id.*
96. *Id.*
97. *Id.*
98. *Id.*
99. *Id.*
100. An exception applies for out-of-state licenses revoked because the driver refused to submit to a chemical analysis. When a person refuses to submit to a chemical analysis, the person's license is revoked by the NC DMV for twelve months, unless the person requests a hearing on the matter and the NC DMV concludes that certain statutory requirements are not met. G.S. 20-16.2(d). Upon refusal to test by a nonresident and out-of-state license holder, the NC DMV may revoke only the person's privilege to drive in North Carolina—not the person's privilege to drive in his or her home state. *See* G.S. 20-16.2(f) (providing for notice to other states of revocation of nonresident's privilege to drive a motor vehicle in North Carolina based on a refusal to submit to a chemical analysis); *see also* State v. Streckfuss, 171 N.C. App. 81, 85–87 (2005) (implicitly recognizing that North Carolina lacks authority to prohibit a nonresident from driving in his or her home state). For this reason, the NC DMV will not accept out-of-state licenses, and the clerk must return such licenses to the license holder upon satisfaction of the civil revocation period and payment of costs. The NC DMV will, however, pursuant to the provisions of G.S. 20-16.2(f), notify both the state of the person's residence and any state in which the person is licensed of the revocation of the North Carolina driving privilege.
101. Of the total fee, 50 percent is credited to the state's general fund; 25 percent must be used for the statewide chemical alcohol testing program administered by the Forensic Tests for Alcohol Branch of the Department of Health and Human Services; and the remaining 25 percent must be remitted to the county as reimbursement for jail expenses incurred due to enforcement of the impaired driving laws. G.S. 20-16.5(j). No fee is due if a magistrate or judge orders a civil license revocation rescinded. *Id.*
102. *Id.* § 20-16.5(h).
103. *Id.*

license has expired, the clerk may return it to the person with a caution that it is no longer valid.[104] If the person has surrendered his or her copy of a limited driving privilege and is no longer eligible to use it, the clerk must make a record that the limited driving privilege was withheld.[105] The clerk must then forward that record to the clerk in the county in which the limited driving privilege was issued for inclusion in the case file.[106]

H. Nature of Revocation

When it was first enacted, G.S. 20-16.5 provided for a ten-day driver's license revocation and restoration upon payment of a $25 fee. A colleague who wrote about the revocation shortly after its enactment described the legislation as providing an immediate " 'slap in the face' to virtually all drivers charged with DWI" and as making it "more certain that a sanction will be imposed, regardless of the defendant's status or his lawyer's expertise."[107] The characterization of such revocations by the National Highway Transportation Safety Administration (NHTSA) is similar. NHTSA's 2011 Highway Safety Countermeasure Guide[108] describes such license revocations, which exist in varying forms in most states, as "provid[ing] for swift and certain penalties for DWI, rather than the lengthy and uncertain outcomes of criminal courts" and lists them as one of the most effective countermeasures to reduce alcohol-impaired driving.[109]

Given its punitive effect, it is not surprising that a constitutional challenge to North Carolina's civil revocation procedure reached the state supreme court within a few years of its enactment. The court upheld the procedure as comporting with due process and equal protection guarantees under the federal and state constitutions and, in so holding, rejected the plaintiff's claim that the revocation constituted punishment rather than a remedial highway safety measure.[110]

Ten years later, the state supreme court in *State v. Oliver*[111] rejected a defendant's challenge premised on state and federal constitutional guarantees against double jeopardy to his conviction of impaired driving after his license had been revoked pursuant to G.S. 20-16.5. The defendant argued that the ten-day civil revocation of his license was punishment for purposes of double jeopardy analysis and that his subsequent criminal conviction amounted to an impermissible second punishment for the same offense. The court concluded that the license revocation was remedial rather than punitive and described the revocation and accompanying fee as "neither excessive nor overwhelmingly disproportionate responses to the immediate dangers an impaired driver poses to the public and himself."[112] The court characterized "any deterrent effect" of the revocation as "merely incidental to the overriding purpose of protecting the public's safety" and noted that its decision accorded with the majority of states considering such challenges.[113]

---

104. *Id.*
105. *Id.*
106. *Id.*
107. James C. Drennan, *Impaired Driving: The Safe Roads Act, in* NORTH CAROLINA LEGISLATION 1983 114, 117 (Ann L. Sawyer ed., UNC Institute of Government, 1983).
108. NAT'L HIGHWAY TRANSP. SAFETY ADMIN., COUNTERMEASURES THAT WORK: A HIGHWAY SAFETY COUNTERMEASURE GUIDE FOR STATE HIGHWAY SAFETY OFFICERS (6th ed. 2011) (hereinafter *NHTSA Guide*), www.nhtsa.gov/staticfiles/nti/pdf/811444.pdf.
109. *NHTSA Guide, supra* note 108, at 1-11.
110. Henry v. Edmisten, 315 N.C. 474 (1986).
111. 343 N.C. 202 (1996).
112. *Id.* at 209.
113. *Id.* at 210.

After the legislature increased the minimum civil revocation period from ten to thirty days in 1997, the state court of appeals in *State v. Evans*[114] again considered a double jeopardy challenge to prosecution for impaired driving following a civil revocation. The *Evans* court rejected the defendant's constitutional claim, finding that the purpose of the revocation continued to be "remov[ing] from our highways drivers who either cannot or will not operate a motor vehicle safely and soberly."[115] The court noted that while it presently found "no punitive purpose on the face of" G.S. 20-16.5, "at some point, a further increase in the revocation period by the General Assembly becomes excessive . . . [and] there is a point at which the length of time can no longer serve a legitimate remedial purpose, and the revocation provision could indeed violate the Double Jeopardy Clause."[116]

The state supreme court has likewise rejected the claim that civil revocation of a defendant's commercial driver's license for impaired driving in a non-commercial vehicle amounts to punishment that bars the subsequent prosecution of the defendant for impaired driving.[117]

A civil revocation pursuant to G.S. 20-16.5 revokes a person's privilege to drive in North Carolina regardless of the source of his or her authorization to drive.[118] Revocations under G.S. 20-16.5 are independent of and run concurrently with other revocations.[119] A court that imposes a period of revocation upon conviction of an offense involving impaired driving may not give credit for any period of revocation imposed under G.S. 20-16.5.[120]

III. Impaired Driving Holds and *State v. Knoll*

The Motor Vehicle Driver Privacy Protection Act of 2006[121] created statutory provisions designed to, in the words of the task force recommending the changes, "avoid a dismissal under *Knoll*."[122] The *Knoll* reference was to the North Carolina Supreme Court's opinion in *State v. Knoll*[123] ordering that charges of impaired driving against defendants in three separate cases be dismissed. The court had found in each case that the magistrate committed substantial statutory violations related to the setting of conditions of pretrial release that prejudiced the defendant's ability to gain access to witnesses. Though *Knoll* is most widely recognized for its outcome—the dismissal of charges in three impaired driving cases—the *Knoll* court's holding at least theoretically *increased* the showing required from certain defendants to warrant dismissal of impaired driving charges. Before *Knoll*, to obtain dismissal of the charges a defendant charged with impaired driving had only to demonstrate that he or she

---

114. 145 N.C. App. 324 (2001).
115. *Id.* at 331.
116. *Id.* at 332.
117. *See* State v. Reid, 148 N.C. App. 548, 554 (2002) (determining that civil revocation of defendant's commercial license "was the exercise of reasonable regulatory authority designed for an appropriate public purpose" and that defendant's later conviction for impaired driving did not constitute double jeopardy). And the North Carolina Supreme Court held in *State v. McKenzie*, ___ N.C. ___, 750 S.E.2d 521 (2013) (per curiam) (adopting dissenting opinion below), that a one-year commercial driver's license disqualification resulting from a civil license revocation under G.S. 20-16.5 was a civil sanction rather than a criminal penalty.
118. G.S. 20-16.5(i).
119. *Id.*
120. *Id.*
121. S.L. 2006-253.
122. Governor's Task Force on Driving While Impaired, Final Report to Governor Michael F. Easley 22 (Jan. 14, 2005) (hereinafter *Task Force Report*).
123. 322 N.C. 535 (1988).

was denied access to witnesses during the time in which such witnesses might provide testimony as to his or her lack of intoxication; prejudice from such a denial was presumed. *Knoll* requires that, to establish a basis for dismissal of charges, a defendant charged with impaired driving based upon driving with an alcohol concentration that equals or exceeds the per se limit in G.S. 20-138.1(a)(2) must not only demonstrate a substantial statutory violation of the defendant's right to pretrial release, but also prove that he or she was prejudiced by the violation.

Among the implied consent offense procedures enacted in 2006 to prevent dismissals based on *Knoll* was G.S. 20-38.4, a statute governing initial appearances in implied consent cases. This statute requires, among other things, that a magistrate who finds probable cause for an offense involving impaired driving consider whether the defendant is "impaired to the extent that the provisions of G.S. 15A-534.2 should be imposed."[124] G.S. 15A-534.2, enacted by the Safe Roads Act of 1983, provides that if a magistrate "finds by clear and convincing evidence that the impairment of the defendant's physical or mental faculties presents a danger, if he is released, of physical injury to himself or others or damage to property, the judicial official must order that the defendant be held in custody and inform the defendant that he will be held in custody until" (1) the defendant is no longer impaired to the extent that the defendant poses a danger or (2) a sober, responsible adult is willing and able to assume responsibility for the defendant until the defendant is no longer impaired.[125] G.S. 20-38.4 also requires a magistrate conducting an initial appearance for an implied consent offense[126] to "[i]nform the person in writing of the established procedure to have others appear at the jail to observe his condition or to administer an additional chemical analysis if the person is unable to make bond."[127] Magistrates also must "[r]equire the person who is unable to make bond to list all persons he wishes to contact and telephone numbers on a form that sets forth the procedure for contacting the persons listed."[128]

Because of the adoption of implied consent offense procedures in 2006 and their relationship to *Knoll* motions, *Knoll* and its progeny deserve examination to determine (1) under what circumstances dismissal of impaired driving charges is warranted based upon the denial to a detained defendant of access to family and friends and (2) how the implied consent offense procedures may impact these circumstances.

A. Denial of Access to Family and Friends in Implied Consent Cases

To understand *Knoll*, one must first consider *State v. Hill*,[129] which established a defendant's right to the extraordinary remedy of dismissal based upon the denial of access to witnesses.

---

124. G.S. 20-38.4(a)(3).

125. *Id.* §§ 15A-534.2(b), (c).

126. See *supra* note 2 (listing implied consent offenses). While first-degree murder is statutorily defined as an implied consent offense, the state supreme court in *State v. Jones*, 353 N.C. 159 (2000), reversed the defendant's first-degree murder convictions, which were based upon deaths resulting from the defendant's commission of the felony offense of assault with a deadly weapon with intent to inflict serious injury. The court held that because the intent required to prove the felony assault was not actual intent but instead was intent implied from the defendant's culpable negligence in driving while impaired, the felony assault could not serve as the underlying felony for felony murder under G.S. 14-17.

127. G.S. 20-38.4(a)(4)a.

128. *Id.* § 20-38.4(a)(4)b.

129. 277 N.C. 547 (1971).

1. State v. Hill, 277 N.C. 547 (1971)

The North Carolina Supreme Court held in *Hill* that the defendant's Sixth Amendment right to obtain witnesses on his behalf was violated when his brother-in-law, who also was his attorney, was not allowed to see him after his arrest. The jailer holding Hill refused to release him after his brother-in-law posted bond and further refused to allow the brother-in-law to see Hill. From the time Hill was arrested at 11 p.m. until 7 a.m. the next morning, only law enforcement officers saw or had access to him.

The *Hill* court recognized that for offenses "of which intoxication is an essential element," the denial of immediate access to witnesses may deprive "a defendant of his only opportunity to obtain evidence which might prove his innocence."[130] Because the guilt or innocence of a defendant charged with impaired driving "depends upon whether he was intoxicated at the time of his arrest," such a defendant "must have access to his counsel, friends, relatives, or some disinterested person within a relatively short time after his arrest" in order to have "witnesses for his defense."[131] The court held that in Hill's case "the right . . . to communicate with counsel and friends implies, at the very least, the right to have them see him, observe and examine him, with reference to his alleged intoxication."[132]

The court concluded, therefore, that Hill was denied his constitutional and statutory right to communicate with counsel and friends at a time when the denial deprived him of any opportunity to confront the State's witnesses with other testimony.[133] The court held that "[u]nder these circumstances, to say that the denial was not prejudicial is to assume that which is incapable of proof."[134]

The General Assembly substantially codified the holding in *Hill* by enacting G.S. 15A-954(a)(4), which requires that a court dismiss criminal charges upon determining that "[t]he defendant's constitutional rights have been flagrantly violated and there is such irreparable prejudice to the defendant's preparation of his case that there is no remedy but to dismiss the prosecution."[135] Despite the statement in the official commentary that subdivision (a)(4) is "intended to embody the holding" in *Hill*, the provision adds the requirement that "irreparable prejudice" result from the violation. The official commentary notes the assumption "that the drastic relief called for under this motion would be granted most sparingly."[136]

2. State v. Knoll, 322 N.C. 535 (1988)

Three impaired driving cases were consolidated for hearing in *Knoll*. In each case, the defendant was charged with impaired driving in Wake County, North Carolina, and made a pretrial motion to dismiss the charge based upon a violation of statutory and constitutional rights.

a. Defendant Knoll

David Knoll was stopped at 1:15 p.m. and charged with driving while impaired. He submitted to a chemical analysis of his breath at 2:31 p.m., which revealed a breath alcohol concentration of 0.30. Knoll then appeared before a magistrate, who set bond at $300 without inquiring into any of the

130. *Id.* at 553–55.

131. *Id.* at 553.

132. *Id.*

133. Hill moved for dismissal before the superior court on the basis that he was denied counsel at a critical stage of the proceedings, but the state supreme court based its ruling on the defendant's right to communicate with counsel and friends generally, noting that these rights were "not limited to receiving professional advice from his attorney." *Id.* at 552.

134. *Id.* at 554.

135. *See* Official Commentary to G.S. 15A-954.

136. *Id.*

factors relevant to conditions of pretrial release. Between 4 p.m. and 5 p.m., Knoll made several requests to call his father. He was allowed to call him at about 5 p.m. After speaking to Knoll, Knoll's father spoke to the magistrate, telling him that he wanted to come right away to get his son. The magistrate told Knoll's father that Knoll could not be released until 11 p.m. As a result, Knoll's father waited until 11 p.m. to go to the jail to post bond. Knoll's father stated that when he talked with his son on the phone, his son was oriented and coherent and not noticeably impaired in either his manner of speech or in the substance of what he said.

b. Defendant Warren

The second defendant, Samson Warren Jr., was stopped at 10:11 p.m. and charged with driving while impaired. Warren submitted to a chemical analysis of his breath at 11:08 p.m., which revealed a breath alcohol concentration of 0.25. Warren then appeared before a magistrate, who set a $500 secured bond. The magistrate did not inform Warren of his right to communicate with counsel and friends. Two adult friends of Warren attempted to secure his release. The first, Donald Martin, arrived at the magistrate's office between 11 p.m. and 11:30 p.m., while Warren was in the breath-testing room. Martin spoke with Warren and observed his condition. Martin had $300 in cash and was willing to assume responsibility for Warren, but the magistrate told Martin that Warren would have to go to jail until 6 a.m. in order to sober up.

John Lewis went to the courthouse between 1 a.m. and 1:30 a.m. following Warren's arrest. The magistrate informed Lewis, who had $200 in cash with him, that Warren could not be released until 6 a.m. After being so advised, Lewis did not request to see Warren. Warren was released from the Wake County Jail at 8 a.m. when Martin posted bond for him.

c. Defendant Hicks

The third defendant, Bennie Hicks, was arrested for driving while impaired at 12:45 a.m. He submitted to a chemical analysis of his breath, which revealed a breath alcohol concentration of 0.18. Hicks appeared before a magistrate, who set a $200 bond without informing Hicks of his right to communicate with counsel and friends and without asking questions about matters relevant to conditions of release. Hicks had $2,200 in cash but was not allowed to post his own bond. At 1:30 a.m., Hicks called his wife at their home, which was about thirty minutes away from the Wake County courthouse. Hicks's wife did not have a vehicle at the time and could not come to the courthouse to pick him up. Hicks was released from jail at 6 a.m.

d. *Knoll* Court's Analysis

The court began its analysis in *Knoll* by reviewing "the general obligations of the magistrate" in impaired driving cases.[137] Curiously, however, this exposition failed to mention provisions of G.S. 15A-534.2 requiring in certain circumstances that a defendant charged with an offense involving impaired driving be detained. Though the court later acknowledged a magistrate's authority to "refuse to release one who is intoxicated to such a degree that he would be endangered by being released without supervision,"[138] this was a reference to G.S. 15A-534(c), which governs the setting of conditions of pretrial release generally and permits a magistrate to consider, among other factors, "whether the defendant is intoxicated to such a degree that he would be endangered by being released without supervision," rather than the more specific requirements of G.S. 15A-534.2.

---

137. 322 N.C. 535, 536.
138. *Id.* at 542 (quoting G.S. 15A-534(c)).

The court found that Knoll and Warren were unlawfully detained because they could have been released into the custody of "appropriate people who were seeking their release."[139] As for Hicks, the court concluded that though his "wife was temporarily unavailable to pick him up, he could have, by the use of a taxi, been in the presence of his wife within a short period of time."[140] The high court agreed with the superior court's determination that the magistrate failed to comply with statutory provisions governing the setting of conditions of pretrial release and that, but for these statutory deprivations, each defendant could have had access to friends and family.

The court of appeals in *State v. Knoll*[141] had distinguished *Hill*, concluding that the creation of a per se impaired driving offense meant that denial of access was "no longer inherently prejudicial to a defendant's ability to gather evidence in support of his innocence in every driving while impaired case."[142] The appellate court opined that "[p]rejudice may or may not occur since a chemical analysis result of 0.10 or more is sufficient, on its face, to convict."[143] Prejudice might result from "a denial of access or unwarranted detention," explained the court of appeals, if the "defendant was not advised of his right to have a second chemical test . . . or where his right to secure a second test was denied."[144] The court of appeals explained that "[p]rejudice might also occur . . . if pertinent evidence relating to contested elements of the offense, such as whether the defendant was in fact driving, became unavailable as a result of the denial of access."[145] The court of appeals found nothing in the record to support the trial court's finding that the statutory deprivations caused Knoll to lose significant evidence or testimony helpful to his defense, noting that the result of the chemical analysis alone was sufficient to convict Knoll.

Though the state supreme court adopted the rule articulated by the court of appeals that a defendant charged with a per se violation of the impaired driving statute must demonstrate prejudice resulting from a substantial statutory violation,[146] the supreme court, unlike the court of appeals, found that each defendant made a sufficient showing that "lost evidence or testimony would have been helpful to his defense, that the evidence would have been significant, and that the evidence or testimony was lost" because of the statutory violations.[147] The court based this determination on each defendant's confinement "during the crucial period" in which friends and family could have observed him to "form opinions as to his condition following arrest."[148] The court explained that "[t]his opportunity to gather evidence and to prepare a case in his own defense was lost to each defendant as a direct result of a lack of information during processing as to numerous important rights and because of the commitment to jail."[149] The court found that "[t]he lost opportunities, in all three cases, to secure independent proof of sobriety, and the lost chance, in one of the cases, to secure a second test for blood alcohol content" constituted prejudice to the defendants.[150]

---

139. *Id.* at 542.
140. *Id.*
141. 84 N.C. App. 228, 233 (1987), *rev'd*, 322 N.C. 535 (1988). Only Craig Raymond Knoll's case was before the court of appeals.
142. *Id.* at 233.
143. *Id.*
144. *Id.* (citations omitted).
145. *Id.* at 233–34.
146. State v. Knoll, 322 N.C. 535, 545 (1988).
147. *Id.* at 547 (internal citations, quotation marks omitted).
148. *Id.* at 547.
149. *Id.*
150. *Id.* at 547–48.

The court's reliance upon "lost opportunities" and "a lost chance" as establishing prejudice raises questions regarding whether the prejudice requirement as applied in *Knoll* requires any showing additional to that presumed prejudicial in *Hill*. Knoll, like Hill, was denied access to a witness who sought his release. One might interpret *Knoll* as adhering to the proposition that denial of sought-after access during the "crucial period" is always prejudicial. But if denial of access is presumptively prejudicial, then the rule announced in *Knoll* did not, in fact, depart from *Hill*. And while the basis for the finding of prejudice in Knoll's case is not clearly specified, it is even more difficult to ascertain in Warren's and Hicks's cases.

Shortly after he submitted to the chemical analysis, Warren spoke in person to Martin, one of the people who attempted to secure his release. Thus, Warren did not suffer a complete denial of access to witnesses. One might argue that his ability to communicate with a friend so soon after his arrest eliminated any prejudice resulting from his unlawful detention.

In Hicks's case, the finding of prejudice is difficult to reconcile with a magistrate's statutory obligation to hold certain impaired drivers. While the court held that Hicks should have been released to take a taxi home to his wife, G.S. 15A-534.2 (which the court did not discuss in its opinion) makes clear that a defendant who is detained pursuant to its provisions may only be released to the custody of a sober, responsible adult who appears before the judicial official ordering the release. And while Hicks attempted to procure his release by posting bond, there is no evidence that he requested to see anyone while confined or that anyone requested to see him.

Perhaps the court based its determination in part on the fact that neither Warren nor Hicks were informed by the magistrate that they had the right to access counsel and friends; yet, again, any determination that such a statutory violation is presumptively prejudicial does not comport with the standard articulated by the court requiring that the defendant demonstrate prejudice.

These curious aspects of the court's holding may explain why *Knoll*, which purported to increase the showing required to obtain dismissal of charges, is widely perceived as the seminal case entitling defendants charged with impaired driving to the dismissal of charges.

3. Right to Dismissal Based Upon a Constitutional, versus Statutory, Claim

Though the *Knoll* defendants argued that dismissal was warranted on the basis of a violation of constitutional as well as statutory rights, the court did not rule on the defendants' constitutional claims. In *State v. Gilbert*,[151] the court of appeals distinguished statutory violations resulting from a magistrate's failure to comply with statutory procedures governing the setting of conditions of pretrial release from constitutional violations. The *Gilbert* court found a magistrate's refusal to set conditions of release and the ensuing five-hour detention of a defendant to constitute statutory, but not constitutional, violations.[152] The court explained that Gilbert, who saw his brother shortly after he was administered a breath test, did not request and was not denied access to anyone. For this reason, the court determined that Gilbert failed to establish a constitutional violation. The court in *Gilbert* further explained that a defendant seeking dismissal of per se impaired driving charges based upon

151. 85 N.C. App. 594 (1987). *Gilbert* was decided after the decision of the court of appeals in *State v. Knoll*, 84 N.C. App. 228 (1987), but before the state supreme court's ruling reversing the court of appeals, see 322 N.C. 535 (1988). *Gilbert* is still good law, however, as it relied upon the determination of the court of appeals in *Knoll* that the presumptive prejudice rule of *Hill* did not govern in statutory per se cases—a rule adopted by the supreme court.

152. *Gilbert*, 85 N.C. App. at 596–97.

a violation of the constitutional right to access witnesses must, like a defendant seeking dismissal for a statutory violation, demonstrate irreparable prejudice resulting from the violation.[153]

4. Prejudice: Proven or Presumed?

Because the *Knoll* requirement that a defendant demonstrate prejudice resulting from a violation of statutory rights related to pretrial release or the constitutional right to have access to witnesses applies only in cases in which the defendant is charged with a per se violation of the impaired driving statute, two lines of cases exist post-*Knoll*: the *Knoll* branch, requiring proof of prejudice for dismissal of charges pursuant to G.S. 20-138.1(a)(2) (the per se prong), and the presumptive prejudice branch,[154] for cases in which a defendant prosecuted solely pursuant to G.S. 20-138.1(a)(1) (the impairment prong) is denied access to witnesses. Furthermore, post-*Knoll* jurisprudence suggests that dismissal is an appropriate remedy in an impairment-prong case only when the defendant is denied his or her constitutional right to obtain evidence in his or her defense; less serious statutory violations warrant suppression of evidence rather than dismissal of charges.

The North Carolina Court of Appeals decided *State v. Ferguson*,[155] another presumptive prejudice case, one week before the state supreme court decided *Knoll*. The court in *Knoll* made no mention of *Ferguson*. In *Ferguson*, the defendant was advised of his right to have a witness observe his breath test. Ferguson called his wife and told her to arrive at the jail in twenty minutes. When the twenty minutes expired, Ferguson refused the test because his wife was not there. Ferguson did not see his wife until he was released from jail later that evening. She had arrived at the jail within the twenty minutes and informed the desk officer that she was there to witness her husband's breath test but was told that she was too late. She waited an hour and a half before seeing her husband.

Ferguson moved to dismiss the charges because he was denied his constitutional and statutory right of access to a witness to observe the breath test. While the trial court expressed its "distress" over the "regrettable" circumstances, it denied Ferguson's motion.[156] The court of appeals remanded to the trial court noting that if, upon remand, it found "that Mrs. Ferguson's arrival to the jail was timely and she made reasonable efforts to gain access to the defendant, then defendant was denied access to a potential witness."[157] The appellate court concluded that "[t]he denial of access to a witness in this case-when the State's sole evidence of the offense is the personal observations of the authorities-would constitute a flagrant violation of the defendant's constitutional right to obtain witnesses under N.C. Const. Art. 1 Sec. 23 as a matter of law and would require that the charges be dismissed."[158] *State v. Eliason*[159] cited *Ferguson* for the proposition that "if a witness arrived timely under the breathalyzer statute and was unable to gain access to the accused despite reasonable efforts to do so, it would constitute a flagrant violation of defendant's constitutional right to gather witnesses and would require dismissal of all charges."[160] Eliason was charged with a per se violation of the impaired driving statute and alleged that the magistrate's failure to inquire into all of the statutory

153. *Id.* at 597 (citing as support State v. Curmon, 295 N.C. 453 (1978); State v. Joyner, 295 N.C. 55 (1978)); *see also* State v. Haas, 131 N.C. App. 113, 166 (1998) (citing *Gilbert* and explaining that "a motion to dismiss will only be granted when the statutory or constitutional violation caused irreparable prejudice to the development of [the defendant's] case").

154. *See* State v. Hill, 277 N.C. 547 (1971).

155. 90 N.C. App. 513 (1988).

156. *Id.* at 518, 519.

157. *Id.* at 519.

158. *Id.* (citing *Hill*, 277 N.C. 547).

159. 100 N.C. App. 313 (1990).

160. *Id.* at 317.

considerations before setting the conditions of his pretrial release violated his statutory and constitutional rights to access to counsel and friends. The court determined that Eliason failed to show that he was prejudiced by this denial, as required by *Knoll,* and was not entitled to relief on constitutional grounds as there was no showing that he was denied access to anyone. The court found that "[t]here was no violation of defendant's constitutional rights which would warrant dismissal of the charges against him."[161] In subsequent cases in which a defendant has been denied the right to have a witness observe the breath test, the court of appeals has characterized this as a denial of a statutory, rather than a constitutional, right, which requires suppression of the test results rather than dismissal of the charges. In *State v. Myers,*[162] for example, the defendant moved to suppress the results of a chemical analysis based upon an officer's statement, after Myers requested that his wife come into the breath-testing room, that "that might not be a good idea because she had been drinking also."[163] Myers's wife then left the police department. The court of appeals held that the breath test results should have been suppressed based on the refusal of Myers's request to have his wife witness the test. Myers did not argue that the case should have been dismissed because of the violation, and the court did not intimate that dismissal would have been an appropriate remedy.

In *State v. Hatley,*[164] the defendant likewise moved to suppress the results of a chemical analysis of her breath based upon the denial of her right to have a witness observe the testing procedures. The court of appeals cited *Ferguson* for the proposition that "[a] witness who has been selected to observe the testing procedures must make reasonable efforts to gain access to the defendant."[165] The court held that the denial of this right "requires suppression of the intoxilyzer results" but again did not intimate that dismissal was the appropriate remedy.[166] Thus, while the presumptive prejudice rule of *Hill* has survived, post-*Ferguson* cases suggest that while suppression of a chemical analysis is warranted when a defendant is denied the right to have a witness observe the procedures, dismissal of the case is not necessarily warranted upon such a denial. Instead, it appears that there must be outright denial of access to witnesses during the relevant time frame to warrant dismissal based upon a flagrant violation of a defendant's constitutional rights.

5. *Knoll's* Progeny

Were *Knoll* the end of the matter, one might conclude that any time a magistrate fails to comply with statutory provisions governing initial appearances and the setting of conditions of pretrial release, resulting in the detention of a defendant charged with impaired driving, a defendant suffers prejudice requiring dismissal of the charges. But cases following *Knoll* emphasize that to warrant dismissal of charges, a defendant must make more than a perfunctory showing of prejudice resulting from such a violation to be entitled to the drastic relief of dismissal.

Cases in *Knoll's* wake have identified numerous circumstances in which the complained-of violations were deemed unfounded, insubstantial, or not prejudicial to the defendant. Indeed, there are no reported appellate court opinions post-*Knoll* in which the courts have found dismissal of implied consent charges an appropriate remedy for an alleged violation of provisions governing pretrial release. Instead, the court of appeals has made the following determinations in post-*Knoll* cases:

161. *Id.* at 318.
162. 118 N.C. App. 452 (1995).
163. *Id.* at 453.
164. 190 N.C. App. 639 (2008).
165. *Id.* at 642–43 (citations omitted).
166. *Id.* at 643 (citations omitted).

- Dismissal was not warranted based upon the defendant's allegation that law enforcement officials refused to take him to the hospital for additional testing or to withdraw blood for later testing. The alleged refusal did not violate the defendant's statutory rights under G.S. 20-139.1 or his constitutional right to due process. Law enforcement officials met their statutory and constitutional obligations by providing the defendant access to a telephone and by allowing access to the defendant for purposes of conducting an additional test.[167]
- The defendant was not entitled to dismissal of charges based upon the magistrate's failure to inquire into every statutorily enumerated factor relevant to setting conditions of pretrial release where he failed to show that consideration of other factors would have required different conditions of release.[168]
- To warrant dismissal, a defendant must prove that he or she was denied access to witnesses and friends during the crucial period during which exculpatory evidence could have been gathered.[169]
- Suppression of evidence regarding field sobriety tests and dismissal of appreciable impairment theory cured any prejudice resulting from denial of the defendant's request to allow a witness to observe field sobriety tests. The defendant was not entitled to have charges under the per se prong of G.S. 20-138.1 dismissed.[170]
- Substantial violation of the defendant's right to pretrial release does not establish a basis for dismissal of charges when she was not denied access to family and friends while in jail. The defendant, who was unlawfully detained, saw her friends at the jail but did not ask to speak to them.[171]

6. State v. Labinski, 188 N.C. App. 120 (2008)

Juxtaposing *Knoll* and a more recent case in its progeny, *State v. Labinski*,[172] reveals the heightened evidentiary standard applied by the appellate courts post-*Knoll* to defendants' claims that they have suffered irreparable prejudice arising from an unlawful detention. In *Labinski*, the defendant was arrested for impaired driving and taken to the jail for a breath test. On the way to the jail, Labinski sent a text message to her friend Brian Anderson to let him know she was in trouble. The officer who administered the breath test notified Labinski of her rights, including her right to have a witness present. Labinski did not call anyone. She submitted to the chemical analysis of her breath at 3 a.m., which revealed a breath-alcohol concentration of 0.08.

Around the time Labinski was performing her breath test, four of her friends, including Anderson, arrived at the jail. Labinski saw her friends while she was walking with the officer from the breath-testing room to the magistrate's office, but she did not ask to speak with them, and they did not ask to speak to her. Labinski appeared before the magistrate at 3:25 a.m. The magistrate set a $500 secured bond and conditioned Labinski's release upon (1) release to a sober, responsible adult, (2) release when she had a breath-alcohol concentration of 0.05, or (3) release at 9 a.m.

Labinski was logged into the jail at 3:47 a.m. She was placed in an interview room with a phone and given a list of bail bondspersons. A detention officer allowed Labinski to retrieve telephone numbers

167. State v. Bumgarner, 97 N.C. App. 567 (1990).
168. State v. Haas, 131 N.C. App. 113 (1998); State v. Eliason, 100 N.C. App. 313 (1990).
169. State v. Ham, 105 N.C. App. 658 (1992).
170. State v. Rasmussen, 158 N.C. App. 544 (2003).
171. State v. Labinski, 188 N.C. App. 120 (2008).
172. *Id.*

from her mobile phone, and she called three of her friends who were already at the jail. She did not call a bail bondsperson. Ultimately, a bail bondsperson contacted by one of her friends posted bond for her release. At 5:02 a.m. she was released to the bail bondsperson and one of her friends who had been waiting at the jail.

Labinski moved to dismiss the impaired driving charges based upon violation of her right to timely pretrial release and, thus, access to family and friends. Labinski contended that the magistrate violated G.S. 15A-534.2 by ordering her detained without considering whether she was so intoxicated that she posed a danger to herself or others. She also argued that the magistrate required a secured bond without making the findings required by G.S. 15A-534(b) and considering the factors listed in G.S. 15A-534(c). Labinski alleged that the magistrate's failure to grant her timely pretrial release and access to friends and family resulted in the loss of evidence, which prejudiced her defense to the impaired driving charges. She asserted that, under *Knoll*, the appropriate remedy for the violation was dismissal of the charges.

In considering Labinski's appeal, the court noted that a noncapital defendant generally has the right to pretrial release. Citing *Knoll*, the court explained that if statutory provisions governing conditions of pretrial release in an impaired driving case are violated and the defendant can show irreparable prejudice directly resulting from a lost opportunity to gather evidence in her behalf by having family and friends observe her and form opinions about her condition after her arrest and to prepare a case in her own defense, the charges must be dismissed.

The court recognized the magistrate's authority under G.S. 15A-534.2 to hold Labinski in custody if he found clear and convincing evidence that her impairment presented a danger, were she to be released, of physical injury to herself or others or damage to property. The trial court found that "based on [the magistrate's] opinion that anyone charged with driving while impaired who blows a 0.08 or above on the Intoxilyzer 5000 would possibly hurt himself or someone else, [the magistrate] set the Defendant's bond at $500 secured."[173] The court of appeals held that this finding was not supported by the evidence. The magistrate did not testify regarding his reason for setting a $500 secured bond but said he required that Labinski be released to a sober, responsible adult " '[b]ecause that's what the statute requires me to do.' "[174] The magistrate did not testify that he had any concern about Labinski hurting herself or anyone else or to having an opinion regarding her behavior based on a particular alcohol concentration alone. Indeed, the magistrate stated that Labinski was polite and cooperative. Thus, the court concluded that the magistrate substantially violated Labinski's right to pretrial release by ordering her held without evidence that her impairment presented a danger to herself or others or of damage to property.

The court then considered whether Labinski suffered irreparable prejudice resulting from the statutory violation. Labinski alleged that her commitment to jail under improper release conditions prevented her friends from observing her physical and mental condition during the time period crucial to her defense. The court concluded, however, that even though Labinski was not timely released from detention, she was not denied access to friends and family such that she lost the opportunity to gather evidence on her behalf. The court noted that Labinski was informed of her right to have a witness present for the breath test and that she did not request a witness, even though four of her friends were at the jail and could have witnessed the test. The court further observed that these friends were at the jail by the time Labinski left the breath-testing room and remained there until she was released. The court reported that Labinski could see her friends and they could see her but that she

173. *Id.* at 124.
174. *Id.* at 126.

did not ask to speak to them or that they be permitted access to her. Finally, the court recognized that Labinski had access to a telephone and made several phone calls.

In *Knoll*, the court determined that the detention of Warren, like that of Labinski, amounted to a statutory violation. Warren's friends, like Labinski's, came to the jail notwithstanding his unlawful detention. And Warren spoke to one of his friends in person, while Labinski only observed her friends. When another of Warren's friends was informed that Warren could not be released to him, the friend did not ask to see Warren. The *Knoll* court found prejudice, but the *Labinski* court did not, reasoning in part that Labinski did not ask to speak to her friends, nor they to her. *Knoll*'s progeny, including *Labinski*, demonstrate that despite the curious circumstances in *Knoll*, prejudice will not be automatically—or even readily—inferred from a statutory violation, even one that results in the defendant's unlawful detention.

7. Reconciling Hill, Knoll, and Their Progeny

The *Hill* court held that denying an impaired driving defendant access to a witness during the crucial time period during which such a witness might form an opinion about the defendant's alleged impairment is presumptively prejudicial and amounts to a violation of the defendant's constitutional rights.

Knoll held that a defendant charged with impaired driving based on an alcohol concentration that meets or exceeds the per se threshold is entitled to dismissal of charges based on a substantial statutory violation of his or her pretrial release rights only if the defendant can establish that he or she was prejudiced by the violation. The rule *as applied* by the *Knoll* court, however, required no showing of prejudice by the defendant that was additional to the circumstances deemed prejudicial in *Hill*.

The proof required by courts in the wake of *Hill* and *Knoll* has essentially been the same for statutory and constitutional violations in both impairment prong and per se impaired driving cases. With the exception of *State v. Ferguson*,[175] the appellate courts in both contexts have, however, deemed none of the circumstances they have considered to constitute a constitutional violation or a prejudicial statutory violation that warranted dismissal of the charges.[176]

> The principles may be summarized as follows: If the State violates a defendant's statutory right to pretrial release by impermissibly holding the defendant and the defendant is, during the crucial time period following his or her arrest, denied access to all witnesses, the defendant may be entitled to dismissal of the charges.[177]
>
> Similarly, if a defendant charged with an impaired driving offense is denied access to witnesses, even though lawfully detained, the defendant may be entitled to dismissal of the charges based upon a flagrant violation of his or her constitutional rights.[178]

175. 90 N.C. App. 513 (1988).

176. See *supra* sections III.A.4–6.

177. *See* State v. Ham, 105 N.C. App. 658 (1992) (stating that to warrant dismissal, the defendant must prove that he or she was denied access to witnesses and friends during the crucial period during which exculpatory evidence could have been gathered); State v. Knoll, 322 N.C. 535 (1988) (holding that the violation of a defendant's statutory right to pretrial release in an impaired driving case that prejudices the defendant requires dismissal). *Cf. Labinski*, 188 N.C. App. 120 (concluding that substantial violation of the defendant's right to pretrial release did not establish basis for dismissal since defendant was not denied access to family and friends while in jail).

178. G.S. 15A-954(a)(4); State v. Hill, 277 N.C. 547 (1971); *see also Ferguson*, 90 N.C. App. 513 (applying *Hill* to circumstances in which defendant's wife was denied access to the breath-testing room and in which the defendant did not see his wife until he was released from jail an hour and a half later).

IV. Procedural Requirements Governing Holds and Notice in Implied Consent Cases

As previously noted, several procedural requirements enacted as part of the Motor Vehicle Driver Privacy Protection Act of 2006 and applicable in implied consent cases are designed to ensure that defendants are detained when appropriate and that detained defendants are not denied access to witnesses.

A. Impaired Driving Holds

Among these provisions is G.S. 20-38.4, which requires a magistrate, upon finding probable cause for an implied consent offense, to consider whether the defendant "is impaired to the extent that the provisions of G.S. 15A-534.2 should be imposed."[179] G.S. 15A-534.2 applies to initial appearances for *offenses involving impaired driving*. These offenses are as follows:

1. Impaired driving (G.S. 20-138.1)
2. Habitual impaired driving (G.S. 20-138.5)
3. Impaired driving in a commercial vehicle (G.S. 20-138.2)
4. Death or serious injury by vehicle based upon impaired driving (G.S. 20-141.4)
5. First- or second-degree murder under G.S. 14-17 based on impaired driving
6. Involuntary manslaughter under G.S. 14-18 based on impaired driving
7. Substantially similar offenses committed in another state or jurisdiction

If a magistrate conducting an initial appearance for an offense involving impaired driving finds clear and convincing evidence that the impairment of the defendant's physical or mental faculties presents a danger, were the defendant to be released, of physical injury to the defendant or others or damage to property, the magistrate must order that the defendant be held in custody. Such detentions commonly are referred to as "impaired driving holds." A magistrate ordering such a detention must inform the defendant that he or she will be held in custody until (a) the magistrate determines that the defendant's physical and mental faculties are no longer impaired to the extent that the defendant presents a danger of physical injury to himself, herself, or others, or of damage to property if released or (b) a sober, responsible adult is willing and able to assume responsibility for the defendant until the defendant's physical and mental faculties are no longer impaired. A magistrate who orders a defendant detained pursuant to these provisions must also determine the appropriate conditions for pretrial release in accordance with G.S. 15A-534, which governs the setting of conditions of pretrial release generally.

A defendant subject to detention under G.S. 15A-534.2 may be denied pretrial release based upon the defendant's impairment for no longer than twenty-four hours. After twenty-four hours, a defendant held pursuant to G.S. 15A-534.2 must be released upon meeting the conditions of pretrial release imposed at the initial appearance. In determining whether a defendant subject to an impaired driving hold remains impaired, a magistrate may request the defendant to submit to periodic tests to determine his or her alcohol concentration. Approved alcohol screening devices as well as other approved chemical analysis instruments may be used for this purpose. A magistrate must determine that a defendant with an alcohol concentration of 0.05 or less is no longer impaired unless there is

179. G.S. 20-38.4(a)(3).

evidence that the defendant is still impaired from a combination of alcohol and some other impairing substance or condition.

G.S. 15A-534.2 itself was unchanged by the Motor Vehicle Driver Privacy Protection Act of 2006. Its statutory provisions have authorized impaired driving holds since they were enacted in 1983. The significance of the 2006 legislation for impaired driving is its explicit requirement that magistrates consider whether such a hold be imposed. In addition, G.S. 20-38.4(b) requires that the Administrative Office of the Courts (AOC) adopt a form implementing its requirements. The implementing form is AOC-CR-270,[180] which must be completed by a magistrate who detains an impaired driver pursuant to G.S. 15A-534.2. The magistrate must set forth in writing in the "Findings" section of AOC-CR-270 the reasons for the detention. When the defendant is released, the magistrate must complete the corresponding section of the form. If release is to a sober, responsible adult, that person's name must be entered on the form. The sober, responsible adult must sign the form certifying that he or she is a sober, responsible person, at least 18 years old, and is willing and able to assume responsibility for the defendant until the defendant's physical and mental faculties are no longer impaired.

In determining whether an adult who seeks to secure a defendant's release qualifies as a "sober, responsible adult," a magistrate may rely upon his or her own observations as well as reports from others.[181] There is no statutory or case law guidance for determining whether an adult is responsible in this context. A magistrate making this determination might reasonably consider factors such as whether the person was a passenger in the car at the time the defendant was driving while impaired, whether the person has a driver's license, the person's criminal record, and the person's relationship to the defendant. The ultimate determination must be based upon the magistrate's exercise of reasonable discretion. In addition to being sober and responsible, an adult who assumes responsibility for an impaired defendant must be "willing and able" to do so. While a magistrate generally may base his or her determination that someone is willing to assume responsibility upon that person's request to assume custody, further inquiry may be necessary to determine the person's ability to secure the safety of the defendant and others. These determinations likewise are left to the magistrate's reasonable exercise of discretion.

The completion of form AOC-CR-270, which requires a magistrate ordering an impaired driving hold to provide reasons for the detention, may reduce the risk that a defendant will be unlawfully held pursuant to G.S. 15A-534.2. The "Findings" section of the form contravenes the notion that persons who commit an offense involving impaired driving are, without additional findings, subject to detention based on impairment simply based on the finding of probable cause to believe the offense occurred. The form also makes clear that it is the magistrate, rather than the jailer, who determines whether a defendant is no longer impaired such that the defendant is subject to the impaired driving hold and whether an adult meets the criteria for assuming custody of the defendant during the time the defendant is impaired.

---

180. This form, Detention of Impaired Driver, is available on the N.C. Administrative Office of the Courts' website at www.nccourts.org/Forms/Documents/842.pdf.

181. *See* State v. Haas, 131 N.C. App. 113 (1998) (finding that magistrate had no duty to release defendant to the custody of an adult who was a passenger in the car driven by the defendant when officer informed magistrate that that adult was extremely intoxicated eighty minutes earlier).

B. Procedures for Gaining Access to Witnesses

In addition to enacting procedures designed to ensure that defendants charged with implied consent offenses are detained in appropriate cases involving impaired driving, the Motor Vehicle Driver Privacy Protection Act of 2006 enacted provisions designed to ensure that defendants confined to jail are informed of the manner in which they may gain access to witnesses while detained. G.S. 20-38.4(a)(4) requires the magistrate to inform a defendant "unable to make bond" of "the established procedure to have others appear at the jail to observe his condition or to administer an additional chemical analysis."

The established procedures must be approved by the chief district court judge, the Department of Health and Human Services, the district attorney, and the sheriff.[182] County procedures vary. A magistrate who conducts an initial appearance in an implied consent case for a defendant who will be detained in jail, however briefly, must certify on form AOC-CR-271, Implied Consent Offense Notice,[183] that the magistrate has informed the defendant of the procedures to access others while in jail and that he or she has required the defendant to list all persons the defendant wishes to contact and their telephone numbers.

Some argue that the requirement that a magistrate inform a defendant charged with an implied consent offense who is "unable to make bond" of the procedures for access to witnesses while in jail does not apply to defendants subject to an impaired driving hold, but instead applies to persons detained solely because of their inability to post bond sufficient to satisfy pretrial release conditions set in G.S. 15A-534. Under this interpretation, a defendant who has posted bond but is held based upon his or her impairment is not entitled to the notice. This reading of the statute is problematic for several reasons. First, a defendant subject to an impaired driving hold could be described as "unable to make bond" given that the posting of bond will not secure the defendant's release. Moreover, interpreting G.S. 20-38.4(a)(4) as requiring notice to all defendants charged with implied consent offenses who are detained better aligns the provision with the governor's task force[184] goal of "prevent[ing] dismissals related to delays in processing and by the defendant's lack of access to witnesses."[185] Informing all defendants about how to access witnesses and health care professionals in jail serves to counter any argument that a defendant was prejudiced by his or her detention.

The magistrate must complete form AOC-CR-271 and provide the defendant, along with that form, a copy of written local procedures explaining how the defendant may contact others and how others can observe the defendant at the jail and administer an additional chemical analysis. The magistrate also must require a defendant unable to make bond to list on form AOC-CR-271 names and telephone numbers for anyone the defendant wishes to contact. If the defendant returns the AOC-CR-271, the magistrate must note the return and place a copy of the form in the case file. If the defendant does not return the form, the magistrate must note in the space provided on a separate AOC-CR-271 that the defendant failed to return the form. The magistrate must place the form on which this notation is made in the file.

---

182. G.S. 20-38.5(a)(3).

183. Available on the N.C. Administrative Office of the Courts' website at www.nccourts.org/Forms/Documents/993.pdf.

184. See the text beginning at *supra* note 121.

185. *Task Force Report*, *supra* note 122, at 21.

C. 2006 Procedures and *Knoll*

North Carolina's appellate courts have considered the application of *State v. Knoll* to cases governed by the implied consent procedures enacted in 2006 in two published opinions. In *State v. Daniel*,[186] a majority of the court of appeals determined, over a dissent, that the magistrate did not violate a defendant's statutory right to pretrial release by refusing to release her to an adult whom the magistrate did not deem sober.[187] More significantly, the court determined that even if the magistrate erred, the defendant was not prejudiced by the denial of release since she met with the person for eight minutes while she was in jail. In *State v. Kostick*,[188] the court of appeals determined that the magistrate did not violate the defendant's rights by imposing a $500 secured bond in an impaired driving case and that, even if the magistrate deviated from the statutory requirements, the defendant was not prejudiced.

1. State v. Daniel, 208 N.C. App. 364 (2010)

The defendant in *Daniel* was stopped by the Charlotte-Mecklenburg police while driving at around 8:30 p.m. on December 29, 2007. She subsequently was arrested for impaired driving. Two hours later, she submitted to a breath test, without calling an attorney or witness, which reported an alcohol concentration of 0.17. The defendant's friend, Jack Bruce, walked to the scene of her arrest to take possession of the defendant's car. A police officer gave Bruce the keys even though he smelled alcohol on Bruce.

Bruce then went to the jail to retrieve the defendant, arriving sometime between 11:00 p.m. and 12:25 a.m. He talked to an unidentified woman behind a window, presumably a magistrate, who asked him if he had anything to drink that day. Bruce said he had a beer with supper. The woman told Bruce the amount of the defendant's bond and the charges against her and "'insisted that [he] needed to get a female to get [defendant] out.'"[189] At 12:40 a.m., Bruce met for eight minutes with the defendant, who appeared upset, had been crying, and had "good" speech. The defendant was not, however, released into Bruce's custody until 6:34 p.m., nearly a full day after she initially was stopped.[190]

The defendant moved to dismiss the charges based upon prejudice resulting from her unlawful detention. The trial court denied the motion, concluding that there was some evidence to support the magistrate's determination that Bruce was not a sober, responsible adult. The jury subsequently found the defendant guilty of impaired driving. The defendant appealed from the denial of her motion to dismiss.

After noting that its review was limited to whether competent evidence supported the trial court's findings and conclusions and that dismissal of charges was a "drastic remedy," the court of appeals concluded that it was not faced with the "dilemmas" that existed in *Knoll*.[191] First, the court noted that *Knoll* differed procedurally in that the *trial court* there found substantial statutory violations and prejudice, those findings were "in no way challenged," and the evidence supported those findings.[192] In *Daniel*, in contrast, the trial court *denied* the defendant's motion to dismiss based upon its determination that the magistrate determined Bruce not to be a sober, responsible adult, a conclusion the

186. 208 N.C. App. 364 (2010).

187. The defendant in *Daniel* did not exercise his right pursuant to G.S. 7A-30(2) to appeal to the North Carolina Supreme Court from the decision of a divided panel of the court of appeals.

188. ___ N.C. App. ___, 755 S.E.2d 411 (2014).

189. 208 N.C. App. at 365.

190. *Id.* at 366.

191. *Id.* at 366, 367.

192. *Id.* at 367.

appellate court found supported by the officer's smelling of alcohol on Bruce earlier in the evening and Bruce's report that he had a beer with supper.

Next, the court of appeals noted that the trial court in *Knoll* found violations of G.S. 15A-511(b), -533(b), and -534(c), whereas the defendant in *Daniel* alleged a violation solely of G.S. 15A-534.2(c).

While the majority characterized the defendant's extensive detention in *Daniel* as "inexcusable," it did not find a statutory violation, reasoning that the magistrate wasn't required to release Daniel to Bruce's custody since she had determined that Bruce was not sober.[193] The court went on to uphold the trial court's conclusion that even if a statutory violation occurred, the defendant was not irreparably prejudiced, pointing out that Bruce met with the defendant shortly after her initial appearance. This conclusion suggests that affording a detained defendant access to witnesses in jail eliminates any prejudice that may be said to result from an unlawful detention.

The dissent found no evidence in the record to support the determination that Bruce was not deemed a sober, responsible adult. The dissent further concluded that the defendant was prejudiced by this violation, reasoning that the unlawful confinement in this case was akin to that deemed prejudicial in *Knoll*.[194]

2. State v. Kostick, ___ N.C. App. ___, 755 S.E.2d 411 (2014)

The defendant in *Kostick* was stopped at a checkpoint and subsequently arrested for impaired driving. He submitted to a breath test that resulted in an alcohol concentration of 0.15. About a half-hour later, at 1:05 a.m., the defendant appeared before a magistrate for an initial appearance. The magistrate imposed a secured bond of $500 as a condition of release. The magistrate imposed this condition because (1) he deemed the defendant "pretty drunk" based on the results of the breath test, (2) the defendant was a South Carolina resident, and (3) the defendant had a gun in his car.[195] (Charges against the defendant for carrying a concealed weapon were dismissed at trial after the defendant produced a South Carolina gun permit.) The defendant told the magistrate he did not wish to contact anyone, and he was confined in the county jail. While in jail, he was allowed to use the telephone, and he phoned a bail bondsperson. The defendant posted bond and was released at 4:50 a.m.

The defendant moved to dismiss the charges pursuant to *Knoll*. The trial court denied the motion, determining that the "'magistrate was under an obligation not to turn [the defendant] out in the public in that kind of condition,'" that the magistrate did not "'deny him any rights by setting a bond,'" and that, in any event, the defendant was not prejudiced by the nearly four-hour detention.[196] The trial court applied retrograde extrapolation,[197] a mathematical formula used to calculate a person's alcohol concentration at an earlier time, to determine whether the defendant was prejudiced. The court concluded that the defendant was not prejudiced since, had he sought an independent chemical analysis at the time he was released, he "'still would have been at or near .08, if the breathalyser [*sic*] was accurate.'"[198] Thus, the trial court concluded "that the magistrate's processing of defendant was not prejudicial because defendant was so intoxicated that his length of detention and bond amount [were] proper."[199]

---

193. *Id.* at 370–71.
194. The decision was not appealed to the North Carolina Supreme Court.
195. ___ N.C. App. ___, ___, 755 S.E.2d 411, 423–24 (2014).
196. *Id.* at ___, 755 S.E.2d at 423.
197. See chapter 2 for further discussion of retrograde extrapolation.
198. *Kostick*, ___ N.C. App. at ___, 755 S.E.2d at 423.
199. *Id.* at ___, 755 S.E.2d at 424.

The court of appeals held that the trial court's findings and conclusions were supported by competent evidence, that the magistrate followed G.S. 15A-511(b), and that any deviation from the statutory requirements was not prejudicial to the defendant. Thus, the court concluded that the trial court did not err in denying the defendant's motion to dismiss pursuant to *Knoll.*

3. Implications for Future Cases

The court's opinion in *Daniel* indicates that procedural requirements may indeed prevent dismissals pursuant to *Knoll.* This is so because a defendant seeking dismissal under *Knoll* must demonstrate a substantial statutory violation, and the requirement that a magistrate consider whether an impaired driving hold should be imposed and make written findings supporting that determination reduces the likelihood a defendant will be detained when the detainment is not statutorily authorized. In addition, to warrant dismissal of the charges, a defendant must demonstrate prejudice resulting from the violation. It will be difficult for a defendant to meet this burden if he or she is informed of the procedures for gaining access to witnesses but fails to avail himself or herself of the available access.

The take-aways from *Kostick* are less clear. While the State prevailed in *Kostick*, some aspects of the court's reasoning appear to undermine previous jurisprudence from the court of appeals. First, *Kostick* fails to distinguish between the purposes for setting bond and for imposing an impaired driving hold. Indeed, the court appeared to assume that imposing a secured bond for a defendant was an acceptable way of ensuring that he or she would not be released while impaired. That's obviously not the case, since some defendants manage to post bond fairly immediately. Moreover, when a defendant charged with an impaired driving offense is impaired to the extent that his release poses a danger, magistrates are authorized to impose an impaired driving hold.[200] To impose such a hold a magistrate must complete the detention of impaired driver form, AOC-CR-270,[201] and must make written findings about the basis for his or her conclusion that the defendant is so impaired that a hold is warranted.[202]

In addition, the *Kostick* court's analysis about the defendant's likely alcohol concentration at the time he was released seems unnecessary. While a defendant has the right to obtain an independent chemical analysis after he or she is released, he or she has no right to be released so that he or she may obtain such an analysis.[203] The prejudice with which *Knoll* primarily was concerned was a defendant's lack of access to witnesses who could form an opinion about his or her impairment rather than whether a defendant was able to obtain an independent chemical test. Thus, as the *Daniel* court intimated, informing a defendant of the procedures for gaining access to witnesses and affording that access arguably will be sufficient to extinguish any prejudice resulting from a substantial statutory violation of a defendant's right to pretrial release.[204] Future litigation will be required to provide judicial officials with a more exhaustive list of the types of errors or procedural irregularities that warrant relief under *Knoll* as well as a clearer definition of what constitutes prejudice.

---

200. G.S. 15A-534.2.

201. See *supra* note 180.

202. *See* G.S. 20-38.4(b) (requiring the Administrative Office of the Courts to adopt forms to implement statutory implied consent procedures).

203. *Cf.* State v. Bumgarner, 97 N.C. App. 567, 572–73 (1990) (holding that law enforcement officers met their statutory obligations by providing the defendant access to a telephone and by allowing access to the defendant for purposes of conducting an additional test).

204. *Cf.* State v. Daniel, 208 N.C. App. 364 (2010) (determining that even if a statutory violation occurred, the defendant was not irreparably prejudiced, since a witness met with the defendant shortly after her initial appearance).

Chapter 4

Motions and Motions Procedures in Implied Consent Cases

Chapter 4

Motions and Motions Procedures in Implied Consent Cases

I. Introduction

Special trial procedures apply to misdemeanor implied consent offenses that are litigated in district court. This chapter discusses the procedures that govern motions to suppress evidence and dismiss charges in these implied consent cases, as well as the permissible bases for such motions in implied consent cases generally.

As in other criminal cases, defendants charged with implied consent offenses frequently move to suppress evidence and dismiss charges. Procedural rules in Chapter 15A of the North Carolina General Statutes (hereinafter G.S.), the Criminal Procedure Act, generally govern the making, hearing, and consideration of such motions. In superior court, a defendant generally must move to suppress evidence prior to trial, though certain exceptions apply.[1] Motions to dismiss, in contrast, generally may be made in superior court at any time,[2] though, again, some exceptions apply.[3] In misdemeanor prosecutions in district court, motions to suppress evidence and to dismiss charges ordinarily are made upon arraignment or during the course of trial.[4] An exception to this rule applies to motions to suppress and motions to dismiss in implied consent cases.

II. Trial Procedures for Implied Consent Offenses

Article 2D of G.S. Chapter 20 sets forth procedure for the investigation, processing, and trial of implied consent offenses. The trial procedures apply to any implied consent offense[5] litigated in district court.[6] Two statutes codified in this article—G.S. 20-38.6 and 20-38.7—govern the making and consideration of motions to suppress evidence and dismiss charges in implied consent cases tried in district court, as well as the procedures for ruling upon such motions and appealing from district court determinations. In a departure from the procedures that normally apply in district court, these

1. Section 15A-975 of the North Carolina General Statutes (hereinafter G.S).
2. *Id.* § 15A-954.
3. *Id.* § 15A-952(b).
4. *Id.* § 15A-953.
5. A list of these offenses is set forth in Chapter 1, section II.
6. G.S. 20-38.1.

statutes require that motions to suppress evidence or dismiss charges in implied consent cases be raised before trial, with the exception of (1) motions based upon newly discovered facts, which may be raised during trial, and (2) motions to dismiss for insufficient evidence, which may be raised at the close of the State's evidence and at the close of all the evidence. They also afford the State an opportunity to appeal a district court's determination that a motion to suppress or dismiss should be granted.

A. Motor Vehicle Driver Privacy Protection Act of 2006

The genesis of the legislation resulting in the enactment of G.S. 20-38.6 and 20-38.7 was a 2005 report issued by the Governor's Task Force on Driving While Impaired, which made numerous recommendations for improving "North Carolina's DWI system."[7] One recommendation was that "District Court trial procedure . . . be formalized for DWI and related offenses" through the enactment of legislation requiring that motions to suppress and motions to dismiss evidence in implied consent cases litigated in district court be filed before trial.[8] The report further recommended the enactment of statutory provisions permitting the State to appeal to superior court any pretrial district court order suppressing evidence or dismissing charges. These recommendations were based upon the following observations:

- Currently in Superior Court, motions to suppress are accompanied by an affidavit and are required before the trial. There is no such law in District Court, which is where the majority of DWI cases are tried. Also, the State is not allowed to appeal orders of suppressions to the Superior Court.
- Defense attorneys are allowed to argue any motion without prior notice to the District Attorney (DA), and the DA does not have an opportunity to prepare a response to the motion as allowed in Superior Court.
- Many DWI cases are resolved when the court rules on these motions to dismiss or suppress.
    - The proceedings of District Court should be modified to require:
        a. Motions to suppress and dismiss evidence (such as Intoxilyzer results) must be made in writing and filed seven days prior to the trial.
        b. There are no statutes defining when evidence can be suppressed or dismissed as there is in Superior Court. District Court procedure should be modeled to more closely resemble Superior Court.
        c. District Court judges make written findings of fact and conclusions of law when evidence is suppressed or cases are dismissed.
        d. The State is allowed to appeal District Court orders dismissing a case or suppressing evidence to Superior Court.[9]

By requiring that motions to suppress and motions to dismiss charges generally be filed before trial begins, the implied consent offense procedures that subsequently were enacted as part of the Motor Vehicle Driver Privacy Protection Act of 2006 and codified at G.S. 20-38.6 and 20-38.7 provide for determinations of such pretrial motions before jeopardy attaches, thereby removing double jeopardy as a potential bar to the State's ability to challenge on appeal a district court order suppressing evidence or dismissing charges. Yet the enactment of these provisions did more than create

---

7. Governor's Task Force on Driving While Impaired, Final Report to Governor Michael F. Easley (Jan. 14, 2005), 24–25.
8. *Id.* at 24, 62–63.
9. *Id.* at 24–25.

a pretrial motions-and-appeals process for implied consent cases heard in district court that would mirror procedures applicable in superior court. Indeed, they created a new type of ruling for such motions—the preliminary determination.[10]

B. Summary Rulings

Not all rulings on motions to suppress and motions to dismiss entered in district court in an implied consent case must be preceded by a preliminary determination. A district court judge must summarily grant a motion to suppress evidence if the State stipulates that the evidence will not be offered in any criminal action or proceeding against the defendant.[11] A district court judge may summarily deny a motion to suppress evidence if the defendant fails to make the motion pretrial when all material facts were known to the defendant.[12]

C. Preliminary Determinations

If the motion is not determined summarily, the district court judge must conduct a hearing on the motion and make findings of fact.[13] Then, rather than entering a ruling granting or denying the motion as a court would in any other case, the judge must issue a written order, termed a *preliminary determination*, that contains findings of fact and conclusions of law and preliminarily indicates whether the motion should be granted or denied. If the preliminary ruling indicates the motion should be denied, the district court judge may enter a final judgment denying the motion.

If, on the other hand, the preliminary determination indicates the motion should be granted, the district court judge may not enter a final judgment on the motion until after the State is afforded an opportunity to appeal to superior court for review of the district court's preliminary determination.[14]

D. Appeal

A second statutory provision, G.S. 20-38.7, grants the State the right to appeal to superior court a district court's preliminary determination that a motion to suppress or dismiss should be granted. While G.S. 20-38.7 authorizes such an appeal, it does not prescribe the procedure for entering the appeal, the method for providing notice of appeal, or any time limitation for appeal. Nor does it expressly incorporate the appeal provisions of the Criminal Procedure Act. Nevertheless, a pair of

---

10. Given that pretrial rulings eviscerate any double jeopardy concerns, why would the legislature have also required district courts to rule on such motions by preliminary determination rather than in final orders? One potential explanation (which was rejected by the North Carolina Court of Appeals in *State v. Fowler*, 197 N.C. App. 1 (2009), discussed in text beginning at note 15, *infra*) is that the legislature required the entry of preliminary determinations rather than final judgments in order to preserve the State's right to file an interlocutory appeal from a district court ruling granting a motion to suppress during trial. Before the court held otherwise in *Fowler*, one might have interpreted G.S. 20-38.7(a) as allowing the State to appeal to superior court a district court's midtrial preliminary determination granting a motion to suppress, thereby allowing the superior court to review the determination before it could result in the suppression of critical evidence that might later lead to entry of a dismissal resolving factual elements of the offense. The North Carolina Court of Appeals read the provisions differently in *Fowler*, leaving unanswered, and perhaps rendering rhetorical, the query regarding the necessity of a preliminary determination of motions in implied consent cases.

11. G.S. 20-38.6(c).

12. *Id.* § 20-38.6(d).

13. *Id.* § 20-38.6(e).

14. *Id.* § 20-38.6(f).

opinions published by the court of appeals within a few years of the statute's enactment sheds light on the proper procedure for appeal.

The court of appeals' opinion in *State v. Fowler*[15] resolved several significant challenges to the then-new implied consent motions procedures, upholding G.S. 20-38.6 and 20-38.7 as constitutional and explaining the circumstances and manner in which they apply. *State v. Palmer*,[16] decided the same day, clarified the mechanism by which the State may appeal from a district court's preliminary determination.[17]

1. Time Limitation

The court of appeals in *Fowler* considered, and ultimately rejected, the defendant's contention that the implied consent procedures codified in G.S. 20-38.6 and 20-38.7 were unconstitutional. Among the arguments raised by the defendant in *Fowler* was that the absence of a time limit for appealing under G.S. 20-38.7 infringed upon the fundamental right to a speedy trial of a defendant charged with an implied consent offense in district court. The court acknowledged the absence of an express time limitation but recited one of its earlier rulings in a different context recognizing that "[i]n the absence of a statute or rule of court prescribing the time for taking and perfecting an appeal, an appeal must be taken and perfected within a reasonable time."[18] Accordingly, the court determined that the legislature's failure to establish a time by which the State must give notice of appeal requires a case-by-case examination to determine whether the State acted in violation of a defendant's right to a speedy trial by subjecting that defendant to undue delay. The court held that the mere fact of the State's appeal from a preliminary determination in an implied consent case does not infringe on a defendant's fundamental right to a speedy trial.[19]

2. No Appeal after Jeopardy Attaches

Fowler also considered whether the State may appeal under G.S. 20-38.7 from a district court's preliminary determination granting a motion to suppress or dismiss made *after jeopardy has attached.* The court first addressed rulings on motions to dismiss for insufficient evidence made at the close of evidence, holding that the State may not appeal the granting of any such motion.[20] Noting that

---

15. 197 N.C. App. 1 (2009).

16. 197 N.C. App. 201 (2009).

17. For a detailed review of both opinions, see Shea Riggsbee Denning, *Motions Procedures in Implied Consent Cases after State v. Fowler and State v. Palmer*, Admin. of Just. Bull. No. 2009/06 (Dec. 2009), http://sogpubs.unc.edu/electronicversions/pdfs/aojb0906.pdf.

18. *Fowler*, 197 N.C. App. at 23 (citations omitted).

19. *Id.* at 24.

20. *Id.* at 18; *see also* Evans v. Michigan, 133 S. Ct. 1069 (2013) (trial court's erroneous dismissal for insufficient evidence was an acquittal for double jeopardy purposes and appeal was therefore barred). *State v. Morgan*, 189 N.C. App. 716 (2008), a case involving the dismissal of implied consent charges that were not governed by the procedures enacted in 2006, demonstrates the application of the bar against double jeopardy to prevent the State from appealing the dismissal of such charges if the basis for the decision is insufficiency of the evidence, even where the lack of evidence results from erroneous findings. In *Morgan*, the district court dismissed charges of impaired driving because the notary's seal on the affidavits giving rise to probable cause seemed to be missing the date on which the notary's commission would expire. The State appealed the dismissal to superior court, which determined that although "'the State had begun to present . . . evidence on the charge in the District court when that court dismissed the case,'" the district court "'dismissed the charge on grounds unrelated to the Defendant's guilt or innocence.'" *Id.* at 718 (quoting superior court's order). The superior court held that, accordingly, the State's appeal was not barred on double jeopardy grounds. The superior court further concluded that "'the seals on the arrest affidavit and the revocation reports contain all of the necessary information, including the expiration date of the notary's commission.'"

G.S. 20-38.6(a) excepted from its pretrial requirements motions to dismiss for insufficient evidence, the court explained that a determination by the district court that the State presented insufficient evidence to establish the defendant's guilt constitutes an acquittal for purposes of the Double Jeopardy Clause. Accordingly, when a court enters such a judgment, the Double Jeopardy Clause bars an appeal by the prosecution that might result in a second trial or in further proceedings devoted to resolving the factual issues related to the elements of the offense charged.

The court then addressed the more difficult question—whether the State is statutorily and constitutionally authorized to appeal a district court's rulings on other types of motions to dismiss or suppress raised during trial. Characterizing G.S. 20-38.6(a) and (f) and 20-38.7(a) as "not expressly preclud[ing] the State from appealing motions to suppress or dismiss made by defendants *during* trial based on newly discovered facts" and noting that statutes authorizing an appeal by the State in a criminal case must be strictly construed, the court of appeals concluded that the State may appeal a district court's preliminary determination in favor of the defendant to superior court only when (1) the preliminary determination is made and decided in district court at a time before jeopardy has attached and (2) the preliminary determination is entirely unrelated to the sufficiency of the evidence as to any element of the offense or as to the defendant's guilt or innocence.[21] "In other words," the court explained, "[G.S.] 20-38.6(a), (f), and 20-38.7(a) should not be construed to grant the State a right of appeal to superior court when the district court grants a defendant's motion to suppress evidence or dismiss charges *during* trial based on 'facts not previously known' which are only discovered by defendant 'during the course of the trial.'"[22]

The test articulated by the court is stricter than that required by the Double Jeopardy Clause, which does not bar the State's appeal from an order suppressing evidence, given that such orders are founded on a legal determination that a defendant's statutory or constitutional rights have been violated

---

Id. Thus, the superior court granted the State's appeal and reinstated the impaired driving charges against the defendant, remanding the case to district court for trial.

The court of appeals reversed, determining that while the affidavits were suppressed due to perceived "technical violations . . . not substantively related to Defendant's guilt or innocence," the dismissal of the charges "arose from the lack of any evidence to support the charge of DWI once the District Court disallowed the affidavits based on what now appears to be the erroneous finding of a technical violation." *Id.* at 721. The appellate court noted that suppression of the affidavits by itself did not warrant dismissal of the charge. Instead, the dismissal resulted from the lack of any other evidence to support the charge once the affidavits were suppressed (the defendant had declined a breath test and refused to submit to any field sobriety tests). The court characterized the officer's affidavits as the "only evidence that Defendant was driving while impaired." *Id.* at 722.

The conclusion of the court of appeals that there was no evidence other than the affidavits is curious given that the arresting officer, whose affidavits were under attack, testified in district court regarding the notarization of the affidavits. The court of appeals did not explain why the officer could not have provided evidence in support of the State's case by testifying about the events he observed before arresting the defendant. It also is unclear from the court's description of the proceedings below whether the State was afforded an opportunity to present other evidence in support of its case after the district court suppressed the affidavits. Perhaps the court's conclusion may be attributed in part to the apparent agreement by the State and the defendant "that the basis [for the] decision was insufficiency of the evidence-even if for technical reasons." *Id.* Regardless of the reasons underlying the court's conclusion that the dismissal was based on sufficiency of the evidence, *Morgan* clearly stands for the proposition that dismissal of charges on sufficiency of the evidence grounds after jeopardy has attached is not reviewable on appeal.

21. *Fowler*, 197 N.C. App. at 18–19 (emphasis in original) (citation omitted).

22. *Id.* at 19 (emphasis in original) (citation omitted). Though the court relied in part upon a governor's task force report as support for its conclusion, the report made no recommendations regarding the issuance of preliminary determinations or midtrial appeals. [*Author's note*: The task force report referenced by the court is discussed in the text of this publication beginning at note 7, *supra*.]

rather than upon a defendant's factual guilt or innocence. Moreover, principles of double jeopardy do not prohibit an appeal by the State from an order dismissing charges on grounds unrelated to a defendant's factual guilt or innocence or the retrying of a defendant if such an order is reversed on appeal—even if the order dismissing the charges is entered after jeopardy has attached.[23] For example, the North Carolina Court of Appeals held in *State v. Priddy*[24] that the State's appeal from a superior court order dismissing a habitual impaired driving charge on jurisdictional grounds after trial began was not barred by double jeopardy and that the defendant could be retried on the charge. Accordingly, G.S. 15A-1432(a)(1) grants the State a right to appeal from district to superior court when there has been a decision or judgment dismissing criminal charges as to one or more counts unless the rule against double jeopardy prohibits further prosecution. Thus, the State may appeal to superior court a district court order dismissing charges on grounds unrelated to the defendant's factual guilt or innocence, even when such an order is entered after trial begins. However, as the implied consent offense procedures are interpreted in *Fowler*, the State has no such right to appeal a district court's midtrial granting of a motion to suppress.

With respect to the requirement that preliminary determinations subject to appeal by the State be entirely unrelated to the sufficiency of the evidence, the court opined that the General Assembly intended pretrial motions under G.S. 20-38.6(a) to address only procedural matters such as "delays in the processing of a defendant, limitations imposed on a defendant's access to witnesses, and challenges to the results of a [chemical analysis of the defendant's breath]."[25] Presumably the court considers a Fourth Amendment challenge such as the one raised by *Fowler* among motions addressing procedural matters rather than the sufficiency of the evidence, as the court did not indicate that the superior court lacked authority to consider the State's appeal from the preliminary determination.

Given the *Fowler* court's holding that G.S. 20-38.7 does not permit the State to appeal from motions granted midtrial, the requirement that a district court rule by "preliminary determination" affords the State no right of appeal additional to what would be constitutionally permissible were the district court to issue such pretrial rulings by final order.

3. Appeal Procedures

The court of appeals in *State v. Palmer*,[26] decided the same day as *Fowler*, considered the proper method for appealing under G.S. 20-38.7. In approving the method utilized by the State in *Fowler*, *Palmer* provides direction that is difficult to glean from the spartan appeal provisions of G.S. 20-38.7(a).

Palmer noted courts' authority, when a statute regulating appeals to the superior court fails to prescribe rules, to look to statutes regulating appeals in analogous cases and to give them such application as the particular case and statutory language warrant.[27] *Palmer* considered G.S. 15A-1432, which regulates appeals by the State to superior court from a district court's final order dismissing criminal charges, to be analogous to G.S. 20-38.7. Thus, *Palmer* looked to the procedures in G.S. 15A-1432(b) to determine whether the State properly appealed pursuant to G.S. 20-38.7(a). Following the *Fowler* court's determination that the legislature failed to establish a time by which the State must give notice

---

23. *See* United States v. Scott, 437 U.S. 82 (1978) (holding that the Double Jeopardy Clause did not bar the government's appeal of trial court's midtrial dismissal of charges upon defendant's motion that was made on grounds of preindictment delay and was unrelated to the legal sufficiency of the evidence).

24. 115 N.C. App. 547 (1994).

25. *Fowler*, 197 N.C. App. at 19.

26. 197 N.C. App. 201 (2009).

27. *Id.* at 205.

of appeal, however, *Palmer* "decline[d] to engraft upon [G.S.] 20-38.7(a) the ten-day time limit for making an appeal specified in [G.S.] 15A-1432(b)."[28]

Then, assuming without deciding that the State was required to file written notice of appeal, the *Palmer* court examined whether the State's written notice in that case sufficiently conformed to the remaining requirements of G.S. 15A-1432(b), which requires appeal by written motion specifying the basis of the appeal. Motions for appeal under this provision must be filed with the clerk and served upon the defendant.[29] The *Palmer* court found the State's appeal proper. The State filed a document captioned "State's Appeal to Superior Court," including in the caption the defendant's name and address and the case file number.[30] The document stated that the State "appeals to the superior court the district court preliminary determination granting a motion to suppress or dismiss," enumerated the issues raised in the defendant's motion, and "recited almost verbatim all of the district court's findings of fact."[31] The appellate court rejected the superior court's conclusion that the State's failure to provide the date of the preliminary determination rendered its notice of appeal insufficient. The court likewise rejected the defendant's contention that the State's failure to include the month on its certificate of service rendered the State's appeal insufficient as a matter of law, noting that the defendant was not misled or prejudiced by the error.

4. Standard of Review

If the State appeals a preliminary determination in the defendant's favor and the findings of fact are disputed, the superior court determines the matter de novo.[32] If there is no dispute, the district court's findings of fact are binding on the superior court and should be presumed to be supported by competent evidence.[33] After considering the matter according to the appropriate standard of review, the superior court does not itself enter a final ruling on the motion. Instead, the superior court must remand the matter to district court with instructions to finally grant or deny the motion.[34]

5. No Appeal from Superior Court's Remand Order

Any appeal beyond the appeal of the preliminary determination is governed by Article 90 of G.S. Chapter 15A.[35] No provision of that Article allows the State to appeal from the superior court's interlocutory order remanding an implied consent case to district court for entry of a final order on a motion to suppress or dismiss; thus, the State has no right to appeal at this juncture.[36] Nevertheless,

---

28. *Id.* at 206.

29. Service on the attorney of record of a motion specifying the basis of appeal pursuant to G.S. 15A-1432 is proper. *See* G.S. 15A-951(b) (providing for service of written motions on attorney of record or upon the defendant if he or she is not represented by counsel).

30. 197 N.C. App. at 206.

31. *Id.*

32. G.S. 20-38.7(a).

33. State v. Fowler, 197 N.C. App. 1, 11 (2009).

34. G.S. 20-38.6(f) provides that "the judge shall not enter a final judgment on the motion until after the State has appealed to superior court or has indicated it does not intend to appeal." The court of appeals in *Fowler*, 197 N.C. App. at 11–12, construed this provision to require that the superior court remand the case to district court for entry of a final judgment on the motion.

35. G.S. 20-38.7(a).

36. *Fowler*, 197 N.C. App. at 5–6 (concluding that G.S. 15A-1445(a)(1), which allows the State to appeal to the appellate division from a superior court's entry of a judgment dismissing criminal charges, did not confer upon the State the right to appeal from the superior court's interlocutory order remanding the case for entry of a dismissal by the district court; further holding that G.S. 20-38.7(a) did not confer upon the State the right to appeal the superior court's remand order to the appellate division); *Palmer*, 197 N.C. App. at 203–04

the court of appeals has, on numerous occasions, granted certiorari review of such interlocutory orders at the State's request.[37]

6. Appeal from District Court's Final Order

A defendant may not appeal a district court's denial of a pretrial motion to suppress or dismiss.[38] If the defendant is convicted, he or she may appeal to superior court for trial de novo.[39] The defendant may again move to suppress evidence or dismiss charges in that forum. As a general rule, no motion in superior court is prejudiced by any ruling upon the subject in district court.[40] It is unclear, however, how that rule comports with the special implied consent procedures that afford the superior court interlocutory review of the determinations of the district court. The appellate courts have not addressed the issue of whether a superior court has the authority, even if so inclined, to enter a subsequent ruling upon the trial of the matter that differs from the earlier interlocutory order.[41]

The State may appeal to superior court a district court's final judgment dismissing charges if the appeal does not violate the Double Jeopardy Clause.[42] If the superior court reverses a district court's dismissal of charges, it must reinstate the charges and remand the matter to district court. The defendant may appeal this order to the appellate division.[43] If the superior court affirms a district court's final judgment dismissing charges, the State may appeal to the appellate division.[44]

The State may not appeal a district court's entry of a final order suppressing evidence but, pursuant to Rule 19 of the General Rules of Practice, may file in superior court a petition for writ of certiorari.

III. Motions to Suppress

Since motions to suppress in implied consent cases must in most circumstances be raised before trial, it is important to identify what types of motions are included within this definition. Given that the term "motion to suppress" is not defined by statute, the statutory provision granting the remedy of suppression is a good point of reference for the types of motions contemplated by this term.[45] G.S. 15A-974 provides:

> . . . Upon timely motion, evidence must be suppressed if: . . . (1) Its exclusion is required by the Constitution of the United States or the Constitution of the State of North

---

(holding, pursuant to *Fowler*, that State had no statutory right of appeal from superior court's interlocutory order remanding matter to district court for entry of a final order suppressing evidence).

37. *See, e.g., Fowler*, 197 N.C. App. at 8; *Palmer*, 197 N.C. App. at 204; State v. Osterhoudt, ___ N.C. App. ___, ___, 731 S.E.2d 454, 458 (2012). *But see* State v. Rackley, 200 N.C. App. 433 (2009) (declining to issue a writ of certiorari to address merits of State's appeal from superior court order agreeing with district court's preliminary determination that defendant's motion to suppress should be granted).

38. G.S. 20-38.7(b).

39. *Id.* § 7A-290.

40. *Id.* § 15A-953.

41. For a discussion of potential arguments in favor of and opposed to additional superior court review, see Shea Denning, *State v. Osterhoudt and Motions Procedures in Implied Consent Cases*, N.C. CRIM. L., UNC SCH. OF GOV'T BLOG (Aug. 23, 2012), http://nccriminallaw.sog.unc.edu/?p=3836.

42. G.S. 15A-1432(a).

43. *Id.* § 15A-1432(d).

44. *Id.* § 15A-1432(e).

45. *See* Jeff Welty, *What's a Motion to Suppress?* N.C. CRIM. L., UNC SCH. OF GOV'T BLOG (Sept. 21, 2010), http://nccriminallaw.sog.unc.edu/?p=1612.

> Carolina; or . . . (2) It is obtained as a result of a substantial violation of the provisions of this Chapter. In determining whether a violation is substantial, the court must consider all the circumstances, including:
>
> a. The importance of the particular interest violated;
> b. The extent of the deviation from lawful conduct;
> c. The extent to which the violation was willful;
> d. The extent to which exclusion will tend to deter future violations of this Chapter.
>
> Evidence shall not be suppressed under this subdivision if the person committing the violation of the provision or provisions under this Chapter acted under the objectively reasonable, good faith belief that the actions were lawful.[46]

The statutory exposition of limited grounds for suppression distinguishes motions to suppress from more general objections to the introduction of evidence. While both motions to suppress and objections to the introduction of evidence seek the exclusion of evidence from trial, only evidence kept out under a ground for suppression is deemed "suppressed," and thus subject to the pretrial motions requirement.

G.S. 15A-974(a)(1) makes clear that motions to bar the introduction of evidence obtained in violation of a defendant's Fourth Amendment rights (and therefore subject to the Exclusionary Rule) are motions to suppress within the meaning of G.S. 20-38.6. Thus, a defendant who alleges that his or her blood was withdrawn over his or her objection and without a search warrant and that a warrant could have been obtained without significant delay must move to suppress the evidence before his or her trial on impaired driving charges begins (unless the motion is based on facts not previously known).

It likewise is clear that a defendant's request that the court exclude evidence obtained as a result of a substantial violation of his or her rights under G.S. Chapter 15A is properly deemed a motion to suppress, subject to the pretrial motions provisions of G.S. 20-38.6. So, for example, a defendant who alleges based on facts known before trial that the police officer who arrested her for impaired driving willfully acted beyond the scope of her territorial jurisdiction under G.S. 15A-402 and that all evidence resulting from the arrest should therefore be suppressed must so move before trial.

Yet, despite the broad language of G.S. 15A-974, not all attempts by defendants to bar the State from introducing evidence whose "exclusion is required by the Constitution" are properly deemed motions to suppress that must be made before trial pursuant to G.S. 20-38.6.[47] A defendant may, for example, object during trial to the introduction of a report from a chemical analyst who is not present to testify at trial on the basis that introduction of the analyst's report without testimony from the analyst violates his or her right to confront a witness under the Confrontation Clause of the Sixth Amendment.[48] Such objections generally are not considered the proper subject of a motion to suppress, even though founded on an exclusion that is required by the Constitution. Indeed, the commentary to G.S. 15A-974 indicates that the type of exclusion referred to by the rule is exclusion

46. G.S. 15A-974(a).

47. *See* Welty, *What's a Motion to Suppress? supra* note 45.

48. U.S. Const. amend. VI (providing that in all criminal prosecutions a defendant shall be afforded the right to cross examine witnesses against him (or her)). Note that a defendant may waive his or her right to object to introduction of a chemical analyst's report if the State provides notice of the report before trial pursuant to G.S. 20-139.1 and if the defendant fails to provide timely written notice of his or her objection to its introduction. The notice and demand procedures applicable to implied consent testing are discussed in chapter 1.

resulting from the *gathering* of evidence in violation of constitutional rights rather than the *introduction* of evidence in violation of constitutional rights that apply at trial.[49]

One Fourth Amendment scholar has noted that the federal courts' consideration of suppression motions as concerning "the 'application of the exclusionary rule of evidence,' or matters of 'police conduct not immediately relevant to the question of guilt' " comports with North Carolina case law,[50] lending support to the notion that " 'motion to suppress' means something like 'motion seeking to exclude evidence as a sanction for police misconduct in obtaining it . . . .' "[51]

In addition, the North Carolina courts have identified a basis for suppression of evidence in implied consent cases that is *not* expressly included in G.S. 15A-974. While G.S. 15A-974(2) requires the suppression of evidence obtained as a result of a substantial violation of G.S. Chapter 15A, no statute requires the suppression of evidence obtained in violation of G.S. Chapter 20, which contains the provisions governing implied consent. Nevertheless, in opinions spanning four decades, North Carolina's appellate courts have suppressed chemical analysis results based upon statutory violations related to their administration.[52] The line of cases providing this remedy begins with *State v. Shadding*,[53] a case decided a few years after the legislature's enactment of the statute requiring that a person be informed of certain implied consent rights before administration of a chemical analysis. In *Shadding*, the court held that upon objection by a defendant to evidence of the results of a breath test on the grounds that he or she was not notified of the right to call an attorney and select a witness, a trial court must conduct a hearing and find as a fact whether the defendant was so notified. If the trial court finds that a defendant was notified, it must also determine whether the "test was delayed (not to exceed thirty minutes from the time defendant was notified of such rights) to give defendant an opportunity to call an attorney and select a witness to view the testing procedures, or whether defendant waived such rights after being advised of them."[54] Reasoning that "[s]uch rights of notification, explicitly given by statute, would be meaningless if the breathalyzer test results could be introduced into evidence despite non-compliance with the statute," the court held that the State's failure to offer evidence regarding whether the defendant was advised of his rights under G.S. 20-16.2(a) rendered results of the breath test inadmissible.[55] Furthermore, the court explained that when a defendant is advised of such rights and does not waive them, "the results of the test are admissible in evidence only if the testing was delayed (not to exceed thirty minutes) to give defendant an opportunity to exercise such rights."[56]

In *State v. Fuller*,[57] the court relied upon *Shadding* in holding that the results of the defendant's breath test were improperly admitted into evidence. In *Fuller*, the officer who administered the test

49. *See* G.S. 15A-974, Criminal Code Commission Commentary (noting that "subdivision (1) only requires suppression of evidence if its *exclusion* is constitutionally required" and recognizing that "[i]t is possible then that evidence may be gathered in violation of constitutional rights, but suppression is not the sanction to be applied unless authoritative case law so declares"); *see also* Welty, *What's a Motion to Suppress? supra* note 45 (citing case law supporting the notion that the term " 'motion to suppress' means something like 'motion seeking to exclude evidence as a sanction for police misconduct in obtaining it' ").

50. Welty, *What's a Motion to Suppress? supra* note 45 (citation omitted).

51. *Id.*

52. The court of appeals also has concluded that a substantial violation of the checking station requirements in G.S. 20-16.3A warrants suppression. State v. White ___ N.C. App. ___, 753 S.E.2d 698 (2014).

53. 17 N.C. App. 279 (1973).

54. *Id.* at 283.

55. *Id.* at 282–83.

56. *Id.* at 283.

57. 24 N.C. App. 38 (1974).

testified that he advised the defendant of his right to refuse to take the test, his right to have witnesses and an attorney present, and that he would be afforded thirty minutes to obtain the witness. The defendant alleged, however, that he was not advised of his right to have an additional test administered by a qualified person of his own choosing. Holding that the State's failure to prove that the defendant was accorded this statutory right rendered the test results inadmissible, the court commented that if the failure to advise of the rights set forth in G.S. 20-16.2 "is not going to preclude the admission in evidence of the test results, the General Assembly must delete the requirement."[58]

Not surprisingly, the court of appeals has deemed denial of the rights promised in the notice required by G.S. 20-16.2(a), like denial of notice itself, to require suppression of test results. Thus, in *State v. Myers*,[59] the court held that breath-test results were improperly admitted, as the defendant was denied the right to have his wife witness the breath test. Myers told the officer that he wanted his wife to come into the breath-testing room and the officer said "that might not be a good idea because she had been drinking also."[60] The court found the officer's statement "tantamount to a refusal of that request," which barred admission of the results at trial.[61] Likewise, in *State v. Hatley*,[62] the court held that suppression of the defendant's breath-test results was required, as the defendant called a witness who arrived at the sheriff's office within thirty minutes and told the front desk duty officer that she was there to see the defendant and yet was not admitted to the testing room. Neither *Myers* nor *Hatley* demonstrated irregularities in the breath-testing procedures or that having a witness present would have facilitated their defense of the charges. The court of appeals required no such showing, holding that the denial of the right required suppression of the results without any corresponding demonstration of prejudice.

Yet, in a couple of limited instances, the court of appeals has required that the defendant demonstrate prejudice—or at least consequences—resulting from a statutory violation to be entitled to relief. In *State v. Buckner*,[63] the defendant argued that it was error for the court to admit the result of his breath test, which was administered after the arresting officer observed him for only twenty minutes, rather than the thirty minutes provided by statute. The defendant, who made a phone call after being advised of his implied consent rights, argued that the State was required to demonstrate that he waived the right to have an attorney or witness present to introduce the result of the test. The court rejected the defendant's argument, pointing to the defendant's failure to contend that a witness or lawyer was "on the way to the scene of the test" or "that an additional 10 minutes would have resulted in any change of status."[64] The court held that a delay of less than thirty minutes was permissible as there was no evidence "that a lawyer or witness would have arrived to witness the proceeding had the operator delayed the test an additional 10 minutes."[65] In so holding, the court effectively elevated the showing required of a defendant in such a case to include the demonstration that being afforded the right would have enabled its exercise.

The court imposed a similar requirement in *State v. Green*.[66] In that case, the officer "garbled" the notice of the defendant's right to have an independent test performed, implying that the defendant

58. *Id.* at 42.
59. 118 N.C. App. 452 (1995).
60. *Id.* at 453.
61. *Id.* at 454.
62. 190 N.C. App. 639 (2008).
63. 34 N.C. App. 447 (1977).
64. *Id.* at 450.
65. *Id.* at 451.
66. 27 N.C. App. 491 (1975).

could call a qualified person to administer the initial chemical analysis rather than informing him that he could have a subsequent independent test.[67] The court held that this irregularity did not require suppression of the breath test results, concluding that "had defendant availed himself of the right given, even as given, the officer would have gotten the person requested and would have undoubtedly known that the purpose was to have an additional test administered."[68] The court further commented: "We cannot see how the defendant could have possibly been prejudiced."[69]

What distinguishes *Buckner* from *Myers* and *Hatley*? *Green* from *Shadding* and *Fuller*? Certainly, they represent different degrees of violation. In *Myers* and *Hatley*, live witnesses were turned away or denied admittance, while in *Buckner* the defendant merely was denied the full thirty minutes afforded him by statute to procure a potential witness's appearance. And in *Shadding* and *Fuller*, notice was all together lacking, not just garbled as it was in *Green*. The court of appeals in *State v. Williams*[70] held that the trial court did not err in suppressing the result of a chemical blood test administered to a defendant who was not re-advised of his implied consent rights[71] and distinguished *Buckner* and *Green*. The *Williams* court explained that "the technical deficiencies raised by the defendants [in *Buckner* and *Green*] did not override the facts showing each defendant was advised of and given copies of his implied consent rights prior to testing."[72]

IV. Motions to Dismiss

A. Grounds

Grounds for the dismissal of charges are set forth in G.S. 15A-954. This statute requires the court on motion of the defendant to dismiss the charges in a criminal pleading if it determines that any of the following conditions are satisfied:

(1) The statute alleged to have been violated is unconstitutional on its face or as applied to the defendant.
(2) The statute of limitations has run.
(3) The defendant has been denied a speedy trial as required by the Constitution of the United States and the Constitution of North Carolina.
(4) The defendant's constitutional rights have been flagrantly violated and there is such irreparable prejudice to the defendant's preparation of his case that there is no remedy but to dismiss the prosecution.
(5) The defendant has previously been placed in jeopardy of the same offense.
(6) The defendant has previously been charged with the same offense in another North Carolina court of competent jurisdiction, and the criminal pleading charging the offense is still pending and valid.

---

67. *Id.* at 495.
68. *Id.*
69. *Id.*
70. ___ N.C. App. ___, 759 S.E.2d 350 (2014).
71. The defendant had earlier been advised of his implied consent rights and had refused to submit to a breath test.
72. *Williams*, ___ N.C. App. at ___, 759 S.E.2d at 355.

(7) An issue of fact or law essential to a successful prosecution has been previously adjudicated in favor of the defendant in a prior action between the parties.
(8) The court has no jurisdiction of the offense charged.
(9) The defendant has been granted immunity by law from prosecution.
(10) The pleading fails to charge an offense as provided in G.S. 15A-924(e).[73]

Other grounds for dismissal applicable solely to indictments are set forth in G.S. 15A-955. And, in *State v. Knoll*,[74] the North Carolina Supreme Court held that the violation of a defendant's statutory rights to pretrial release in an impaired driving case that prejudices the defendant requires dismissal of the charges. *Knoll* and its progeny are discussed in chapter 3.

Two of the grounds for relief set forth in G.S. 15A-954 frequently are alleged in implied consent cases, and their application in this context is discussed in greater detail below.

1. The Defendant Has Been Denied a Speedy Trial

a. State Crime Lab Delays

The state crime lab and other local laboratories perform nearly 10,000 blood toxicology analyses annually, the vast majority of them in impaired driving cases. Unlike breath analysis results, which the State has in hand before a person's initial appearance in an impaired driving case, several months may elapse after a person's arrest for impaired driving charges before the State receives a toxicology report analyzing the defendant's blood. The reasons for the delay are several. It takes time for the sample to reach the laboratory. The testing process itself is more time-consuming than that associated with a breath-testing instrument's analysis of a breath sample. Laboratory analysts have less time in the laboratory than they did before a defendant's constitutional right to cross examine the author of a forensic laboratory report was recognized in *Melendez-Diaz v. Massachusetts*,[75] since they often must travel to courthouses across the state to testify about their analyses. Furthermore, in recent years there has been a shortage of analysts. As the turnaround time for toxicology reports increases, many have questioned how such delays affect a defendant's right to speedy trial.

A court considering a defendant's motion to dismiss on speedy trial grounds must assess four factors: (1) length of the delay; (2) reason for the delay; (3) the defendant's assertion of his or her right to a speedy trial; and (4) prejudice to the defendant.[76] The length of the delay is a triggering mechanism. When the delay reaches a threshold that is presumptively prejudicial, the court must inquire into the other factors. Given that delays approaching one year are considered sufficient to trigger this threshold for purposes of felony charges,[77] and "the delay that can be tolerated for an ordinary street crime is considerably less than for a serious, complex conspiracy charge,"[78] the postponement of misdemeanor impaired driving trials for periods approaching a year to allow time for laboratory toxicology testing easily triggers examination of the remaining three factors.

In considering the reason-for-the-delay factor of the speedy trial motion test, the U.S. Supreme Court in *Barker v. Wingo*[79] assigned different weights to different reasons: A deliberate attempt by the State to delay trial in order to hamper the defense weighs heavily against the government. More

73. G.S. 15A-954(a).
74. 322 N.C. 535 (1988).
75. 557 U.S. 305 (2009).
76. Barker v. Wingo, 407 U.S. 514, 530 (1972).
77. *See* Doggett v. United States, 505 U.S. 647, 652 n.1 (1992).
78. *See Barker*, 407 U.S. at 531.
79. 407 U.S. 514.

neutral reasons, such as "negligence or overcrowded courts" weigh less heavily against the government but nevertheless must be considered "since the ultimate responsibility for such circumstances . . . rest[s] with the government rather than with the defendant."[80] A valid reason, such as a missing witness, justifies appropriate delay. North Carolina's appellate courts have required a defendant to offer prima facie evidence that the delay was caused by the neglect or willfulness of the prosecution.[81] Only after the defendant has met this burden must the State offer evidence explaining the reasons for the delay.[82]

Thus, a question central to determining whether a defendant's right to speedy trial has been violated by the delay of trial to obtain toxicology results is whether routine delays for purposes of forensic testing may be attributed to the neglect of the prosecution or, instead, whether such delays are neutral factors.

In a 2013 unpublished decision, the court of appeals determined that a defendant's right to a speedy trial was violated by a fourteen-month delay in her trial on impaired driving charges.[83] The trial court in *State v. Sheppard* weighed the seven months of the delay that occurred before the State received the toxicology results " 'more neutrally,' " given that the State " 'should be given a reasonable amount of time to prepare its case.' " The seven-month delay after the lab report was filed, in contrast, weighed more heavily in the balance against the State.

Several years earlier, the court of appeals in *State v. Dorton*[84] did not disturb the trial court's determination that delay caused by a backlog in testing at the State Bureau of Investigation was "not attributable to the District Attorney's office."[85] The *Dorton* court rejected the defendant's contention that the delay was attributable to the State, noting that the defendant's burden was to show prosecutorial neglect or willfulness. Similarly, the court of appeals of Maryland in *Glover v. State*[86] considered delay resulting from an eight-month wait for DNA test results "a valid justification in these circumstances," given that "DNA evidence is highly technical, often requiring courts to allow more time for completion of the tests and review, by both parties, of the results."[87] The court cautioned, however, that the State has a duty to ensure "that critical discovery materials, such as DNA evidence, are properly monitored and accounted for, and not simply collecting dust in state or federal crime labs."[88]

Courts from several other jurisdictions have weighed delays associated with laboratory testing against the State in the *Barker* balancing test, but not heavily.[89]

---

80. *Id.* at 531.

81. *See* State v. Goins, ___ N.C. App. ___, ___, 754 S.E.2d 195, 198 (2014) (stating that the defendant bears the burden of offering *prima facie* evidence that the delay was caused by the neglect or willfulness of the prosecution and that only after the defendant has carried this burden must the State offer evidence explaining the reasons for the delay that are sufficient to rebut the *prima facie* evidence); State v. Spivey, 357 N.C. 114, 119 (2003) (stating that the constitution does not outlaw good-faith delays that are reasonably necessary for the State to prepare and present its case).

82. *Id.*

83. State v. Sheppard, ___ N.C. App. ___, 738 S.E.2d 453 (2013) (unpublished).

84. 172 N.C. App. 759 (2005).

85. *Id.* at 764.

86. 792 A.2d 1160, 1169 (Md. 2002).

87. *Id.*

88. *Id. See also* State v. Goins, ___ N.C. App. ___, ___, 754 S.E.2d 195, 198 (2014) (concluding that the defendant's right to a speedy trial was not violated by twenty-seven-month delay that resulted in part from "a backlog at the . . . crime lab").

89. *See, e.g.*, Ben v. State, 95 So. 3d 1236, 1243, 1247 (Miss. 2012) (citations omitted) (noting, with respect to thirteen-month delay attributable to state crime lab, court's reluctance "to weigh heavily against the State

Thus, it seems unlikely that a defendant can establish a speedy trial violation in a misdemeanor impaired driving case based solely on a nearly year-long delay associated with the completion of a toxicology report. Yet, even if crime lab delays approaching a year weigh only slightly or not at all against the State, other factors, such as prejudice to the defendant, may tip the balance in the defendant's favor. And while delays of a year or less may be considered neutral or only slightly in the defendant's favor, at some point the delays may become so long that the factor may weigh more heavily against the State.

b. Other Speedy Trial Claims

For the court's analysis of a defendant's speedy trial claim in the context of the State's refiling of impaired driving charges following a voluntary dismissal, see *infra* section III.A.2.b.

2. The Defendant's Constitutional Rights Have Been Flagrantly Violated

G.S. 15A-954(a)(4) requires dismissal on the motion of a defendant upon the court's determination that "[t]he defendant's constitutional rights have been flagrantly violated and there is such irreparable prejudice to the defendant's preparation of his case that there is no remedy but to dismiss the prosecution." The Official Commentary to the rule notes the assumption "that the drastic relief called for under this motion would be granted most sparingly."[90]

a. Right to Communicate with Counsel and Friends

i. State v. Hill

G.S. 15A-954(a)(4) codifies the North Carolina Supreme Court's holding in *State v. Hill*[91] that the denial of a defendant's constitutional right to communicate with counsel and friends at a time when the denial deprives him of the opportunity to confront the State's witnesses with other testimony requires dismissal of the charges.[92]

The *Hill* court held that the defendant's constitutional rights[93] were violated when his brother-in-law, who also was his attorney, was not allowed to see him after his arrest for impaired driving. The jailer holding the defendant refused to release him after his brother-in-law posted bond and further refused to allow the brother-in-law to see the defendant. From the time the defendant was arrested at 11 p.m. until 7 a.m. the next morning, only law enforcement officers saw or had access to him.

---

investigative delay caused by an instrumentality of the State, such as the state crime lab," and citing relevant authority); State v. Magnusen, 646 So. 2d 1275, 1282 (Miss. 1994) (concluding, with respect to a five-month delay for serology reports from the state crime lab, that "the official neglect of an understaffed and overworked crime lab gives this portion of the delay to the defendant but barely"); State v. Tortolito, 950 P.2d 811, 815 (N.M. Ct. App. 1997) (weighing eleven-month delay attributable to the DNA testing against the State, but not heavily, where DNA and other evidence requiring scientific analysis was tested in its normal order of priority in the State's crime lab and testing was prolonged in part by the small size of the DNA samples collected from the crime scene); *see also* Vanlier v. Carroll, 535 F. Supp. 2d 467, 479–80 (D. Del. 2008) (determining that the State should not be held accountable for typical amount of time needed to conduct DNA test, which court calculated as two months, and holding that remaining ten months of DNA testing period should be weighed against the State, but not heavily, given facts of case), *aff'd*, 384 F. App'x 155 (3d Cir. 2010) (unpublished).

90. *See* Official Commentary to G.S. 15A-954.

91. 277 N.C. 547 (1971).

92. *See* Official Commentary to G.S. 15A-954. Despite the statement in the official commentary that subdivision (a)(4) is "intended to embody the holding" in *Hill*, the provision adds the requirement that "irreparable prejudice" result from the violation.

93. The *Hill* court cited the North Carolina Constitution's provision that " 'every person charged with crime has the right . . . to confront the accusers and witnesses with other testimony and to have counsel for defense.' " 277 N.C. at 552 (citing N.C. Const. art. I, § 23).

The *Hill* court recognized that for offenses "of which intoxication is an essential element," the denial of immediate access to witnesses may deprive "a defendant of his only opportunity to obtain evidence which might prove his innocence."[94] Because the guilt or innocence of a defendant charged with impaired driving "depends upon whether he was intoxicated at the time of his arrest," such a defendant "must have access to his counsel, friends, relatives, or some disinterested person within a relatively short time after his arrest" in order to have "witnesses for his defense."[95] The court held that in the *Hill* defendant's case "the right . . . to communicate with counsel and friends implies, at the very least, the right to have them see him, observe and examine him, with reference to his alleged intoxication."[96]

Under these circumstances, the court concluded that "to say that the denial was not prejudicial is to assume that which is incapable of proof."[97]

ii. State v. Ferguson

The court of appeals applied the rule from *Hill* in *State v. Ferguson*,[98] an impaired driving prosecution in which a defendant was denied the right to have a witness observe his breath test and was denied access to his wife who was waiting for him at the jail. After being advised of his right to have a witness observe his breath test, the defendant in *Ferguson* called his wife and told her to arrive at the jail in twenty minutes. When the twenty minutes expired, he refused the test because his wife was not there. He did not see his wife until he was released from jail later that evening. She had arrived at the jail within the twenty minutes and informed the desk officer that she was there to witness her husband's breath test but was told that she was too late. She waited an hour and a half before seeing her husband.

Ferguson moved to dismiss the charges because he was denied his constitutional and statutory right of access to a witness to observe the breath test. While the trial court expressed its "distress" over the "regrettable" circumstances, it denied Ferguson's motion.[99] The court of appeals remanded to the trial court noting that if, upon remand, it found "that Mrs. Ferguson's arrival to the jail was timely and she made reasonable efforts to gain access to the defendant, then defendant was denied access to a potential witness."[100] The appellate court concluded that "[t]he denial of access to a witness in this case-when the State's sole evidence of the offense is the personal observations of the authorities-would constitute a flagrant violation of the defendant's constitutional right to obtain witnesses under [Article I, Section 23 of the North Carolina Constitution] as a matter of law and would require that the charges be dismissed."[101]

The court of appeals in *State v. Eliason*[102] cited *Ferguson* for the proposition that "if a witness arrived timely under the breathalyzer statute and was unable to gain access to the accused despite reasonable efforts to do so, it would constitute a flagrant violation of defendant's constitutional right to gather witnesses and would require dismissal of all charges."[103] Eliason was charged with a per se

94. *Id.* at 553, 555.
95. *Id.* at 553.
96. *Id.*
97. *Id.* at 554.
98. 90 N.C. App. 513 (1988).
99. *Id.* at 519.
100. *Id.*
101. *Id.* (citing *Hill*, 277 N.C. 547).
102. 100 N.C. App. 313 (1990).
103. *Id.* at 317.

violation of the impaired driving statute and alleged that the magistrate's failure to inquire into all of the statutory considerations before setting the conditions of his pretrial release violated his statutory and constitutional rights to access to counsel and friends. The court determined that Eliason failed to show that he was prejudiced by this denial as required by *State v. Knoll*[104] and was not entitled to relief on constitutional grounds as there was no showing that he was denied access to anyone. The court found that "[t]here was no violation of defendant's constitutional rights which would warrant dismissal of the charges against him."[105]

In subsequent cases in which a defendant has been denied the right to have a witness observe the breath test, however, the court of appeals has characterized this as a denial of a statutory, rather than a constitutional, right. The distinction is significant, as the court has held that the denial of statutory rights of this sort requires suppression of chemical analysis results rather than dismissal of charges. In *State v. Myers*[106] the defendant moved to suppress the results of a chemical analysis based upon an officer's statement, after Myers requested that his wife come into the breath-testing room, that "that might not be a good idea because she had been drinking also."[107] Myers's wife then left the police department. The court of appeals held that the breath-test results should have been suppressed based on the refusal of Myers's request to have his wife witness the test. Myers did not argue that the case should have been dismissed because of the violation, and the court did not intimate that dismissal would have been an appropriate remedy.

In *State v. Hatley*[108] the defendant likewise moved to suppress the results of a chemical analysis of her breath based upon the denial of her right to have a witness observe the testing procedures. The court of appeals cited *Ferguson* for the proposition that "[a] witness who has been selected to observe the testing procedures must make reasonable efforts to gain access to the defendant."[109] The court held that the denial of this right "requires suppression of the intoxilyzer results" but again did not intimate that dismissal was the appropriate remedy.[110]

Thus, post-*Ferguson* cases suggest that while suppression of a chemical analysis is warranted when a defendant is denied the right to have a witness observe the procedures, dismissal of the case is not necessarily warranted upon such a denial. Instead, it appears that there must be outright denial of access to witnesses during the relevant time frame to warrant dismissal based upon a flagrant violation of a defendant's constitutional rights.

b. Dismissal and Refiling

There has long been a tension between a district attorney's authority to calendar cases and to dismiss and refile charges and a judge's control over the court's calendar. The interplay between judicial control and prosecutorial authority often are highlighted when a prosecutor moves to continue a case and the court denies the motion. One potential response by the State, assuming the statute of limitations has not expired, is to dismiss the charges and subsequently refile them. By doing so, the State effectively circumvents the court's order denying the motion to continue. Defendants have alleged

---

104. 322 N.C. 535 (1988) (holding that the violation of a defendant's statutory rights to pretrial release in an impaired driving case that prejudices the defendant requires dismissal of the charges). *Knoll* and its progeny are discussed in chapter 3.

105. *Eliason,* 100 N.C. App. at 318.

106. 118 N.C. App. 452 (1995).

107. *Id.* at 453.

108. 190 N.C. App. 639 (2008).

109. *Id.* at 642–43 (citation omitted).

110. *Id.* at 643.

that this practice violates various constitutional rights, among them the right to a speedy trial. The North Carolina Court of Appeals in *State v. Friend*,[111] however, found that this practice did not violate the defendant's constitutional rights.

The defendant in *Friend* initially was charged with impaired driving on March 7, 2006. The case was continued eleven times, several times based on the unavailability of the State's witnesses and several times upon the defendant's request. On July 18, 2007, the State again moved to continue on the basis that the arresting officer was not in court. When the district court judge denied the State's motion, the State voluntarily dismissed the charge. Nine days later, the State filed new charges based on the same March 7, 2006, incident of impaired driving. The defendant filed a motion to dismiss, which was granted by the district court on October 24, 2007. The State appealed this ruling to the superior court, which remanded the matter for entry of a written order, which the district court judge entered on April 4, 2008. The district court concluded that "a dismissal pursuant to [G.S.] 15A-931, after the prosecution, in control of the calendar, called the case at its own discretion and asked the Court for a decision [on the] Motion to Continue, involved the inherent authority of the Court, and to exercise a dismissal and reinstatement based on the facts and history of the case . . . violates the separation of powers clause and intrudes upon the authority of the Court, and violates the equal protection and due process rights of the Defendant."[112] The State again appealed to superior court. This time, the superior court reversed the district court's order dismissing the case and remanded for trial. The defendant was convicted in district court of driving while impaired on April 13, 2009. He appealed to superior court for trial de novo and moved in that forum for dismissal of the charges. On February 15, 2010, the superior court denied the defendant's motion to dismiss. The defendant was convicted in superior court on the impaired driving charges on February 17, 2010, nearly four years after the offense occurred.

The defendant argued on appeal that the State's dismissal of the original charges following the district court's denial of the State's motion for a continuance violated the separation of powers provision of the state constitution; therefore, the defendant contended, the superior court erred in not dismissing the subsequent charges. The defendant argued that the district attorney was an executive branch official who was obligated to proceed with trial when the district court denied the State's continuance motion. Allowing the State to voluntarily dismiss the charges allowed the executive branch to subvert the court's ultimate authority to manage its trial calendar, he contended. The appellate court disagreed on two alternative bases. First, the court cited *Simeon v. Hardin*[113] for the proposition that the district attorney is a judicial or quasi-judicial officer; thus, no separation of powers issue arises. Second, the court noted that the *Simeon* court deemed constitutional G.S. 15A-931's allocation to the district attorney of the power to dismiss charges and opined that, notwithstanding the dismissal, "[t]he trial court retained ultimate control over its calendar."[114] Therefore, the court reasoned, even if two branches of government are at work in the setting of the trial calendar, the defendant's separation of powers claim fails.

The *Friend* court then addressed the defendant's claims that the filing of the post-dismissal charges violated his rights to due process and a speedy trial. The time limitations imposed by the two-year statute of limitations applicable to misdemeanor criminal offenses was significant in the court's

111. 219 N.C. App. 338 (2012).

112. State v. Friend, Record on Appeal, No. COA11-572 (Apr. 4, 2008), at 22, *available at* www.ncappellatecourts.org/show-file.php?document_id=70641.

113. 339 N.C. 358 (1994).

114. 219 N.C. App. at 342.

rejection of both constitutional claims. With respect to the defendant's due process claim, the court noted that G.S. 15A-931(b) provides that dismissal of a charge does not toll the statute of limitations. Thus, while the State's dismissal in *Friend* did not preclude the filing of new charges, the statute of limitations set an outer time limit for when those charges could be filed. In the case of the *Friend* defendant, any misdemeanor charges arising from the March 7, 2006, incident had to be filed by March 7, 2008. Noting that the defendant failed to show bad faith on the part of the State or prejudice to his defense, the *Friend* court determined that the filing of a new charge within the statute of limitations did not violate due process.

The defendant further argued that the delay in his trial, which he characterized as running from the offense date until his conviction in superior court, infringed upon his constitutional right to a speedy trial. Pursuant to the four-factor analysis established in *Barker* for evaluating such a claim (see page 131, above), the court first considered the length of the delay. The court noted that the additional factors—the reason for the delay, the defendant's assertion of his or her right to a speedy trial, and prejudice to the defendant—only were considered if the delay was for a year or more. Given that the defendant in *Friend* made his sole speedy trial demand in superior court, the court computed the delay as consisting of the time that elapsed between the defendant's appeal to superior court (April 13, 2009) and his trial in superior court (February 15, 2010). Because this period was less than one year, the court stated that it was unnecessary to consider the additional factors.

Nevertheless, assuming for the sake of argument that the delay exceeded one year, the court applied the additional factors, and again concluded that the defendant's claim lacked merit. Even though the State's dismissal resulted from its failure to procure witnesses in court on the day of trial, the court noted that more than half of the earlier continuances were granted at the defendant's behest. The court considered the delays associated with the "bounc[ing] back and forth between District Court and Superior Court" based on the State's appeal of the order dismissing the case and the recusal of the original district court judge to be neutral factors.[115] The court weighed against the defendant's claim his failure to demand a speedy trial until nearly four years after the offense and a year after his conviction in district court. Finally, the court found that the defendant failed to demonstrate that he was prejudiced by the delay. While the defendant argued that he suffered " 'anxiety and concern' during the delay," the court noted that the State filed the subsequent charge nine days after dismissing the original charge and "well within the two year statute of limitations for misdemeanors."[116] The court considered the defendant's anxiety as "limited by the statute of limitations" and determined that the prejudice factor weighed against the defendant's claim.[117]

While *Friend* does not preclude or render without merit all constitutional challenges arising from the dismissal and re-filing of misdemeanor charges when the State is denied a desired continuance, it indicates that such claims are not likely to succeed absent extenuating circumstances such as bad faith or prejudice to the defendant. Thus, prosecutors may tactically use the dismissal authority conferred by G.S. 15A-931 to circumvent the denial of a motion to continue in a misdemeanor prosecution.

115. *Id.* at 344.
116. *Id.* at 345.
117. *Id.*

B. Proper Remedies

The remedies of suppression and dismissal are not interchangeable. Suppression of evidence, for example, is a proper remedy when evidence is obtained in violation of the Fourth Amendment. However, a Fourth Amendment violation, without more, does not provide a basis for dismissal of charges.[118] Likewise, though North Carolina's courts have sanctioned the suppression of chemical analysis results obtained in violation of statutory procedures, dismissal of charges for such statutory violations is not authorized. Indeed, the only context in which dismissal of DWI charges for statutory violations is authorized is when a defendant demonstrates prejudice resulting from a violation of statutory rights related to pretrial release.[119]

---

118. *See* State v. Wilson, ___ N.C. App. ___, 736 S.E.2d 614 (2013) (holding that (1) defendant had no right to dismissal of charges pursuant to G.S. 15A-954(a)(4) for alleged violation of his constitutional rights where he failed to describe the irreparable prejudice that resulted from the violation, the trial court made no finding of irreparable prejudice, and the defendant did not argue on appeal that he was irreparably prejudiced and (2) trial court erred in dismissing impaired driving charges under G.S. 15A-954(a)(1) on grounds that the implied consent testing procedures in G.S. 20-139.1 were unconstitutional as applied; for dismissal of DWI charges to be warranted under G.S. 15A-954(a)(1), a court must conclude that the impaired driving statute itself, G.S. 20-138.1, is unconstitutional).

119. See *infra* chapter 3 for a discussion of *State v. Knoll*, 322 N.C. 535 (1988).

Chapter 5

Sentencing under G.S. 20-179

Chapter 5

Sentencing under G.S. 20-179

I. Introduction

Sentencing for most misdemeanor and felony convictions in North Carolina is governed by the structured sentencing provisions set forth in Article 81B of Chapter 15A of the state's General Statutes (hereinafter G.S.).[1] The misdemeanor offense of impaired driving as defined in G.S. 20-138.1 and several related offenses, however, are excepted from structured sentencing provisions and instead are sentenced pursuant to G.S. 20-179. This chapter discusses these statutory sentencing provisions, including the determination of aggravating and mitigating factors, sentencing options for defendants sentenced at the various statutory levels, and the manner in which a sentence is served, including provisions for awarding jail credit and granting parole.

Experts writing about sentencing in impaired driving cases more than a decade ago stated that "[e]xcept for death penalty cases, no sentence requires more documentation."[2] Professors Loeb and Drennan were referring to the sentencing procedures codified in G.S. 20-179, which govern sentencing upon conviction under G.S. 20-138.1 (impaired driving) or 20-138.2 (impaired driving in a commercial vehicle) and upon a second or subsequent conviction of G.S. 20-138.2A (operating a commercial vehicle after consuming alcohol) or 20-138.2B (operating a school bus or a child care, emergency, or law enforcement vehicle after consuming). The offenses sentenced pursuant to G.S. 20-179 are referred to hereinafter as *covered offenses.*

The statutory requirements for documentation in sentencing of covered offenses—all of which are misdemeanors—have not lessened over the past decade; indeed, the entire sentencing scheme for such offenses has become more complex in recent years. Significant procedural changes to the sentencing scheme for impaired driving followed the United States Supreme Court's decision in *Blakely v. Washington*,[3] which elaborated upon its holding in *Apprendi v. New Jersey*[4] that the Sixth Amendment to the federal Constitution requires that any fact (other than a prior conviction) that increases the defendant's sentence beyond the statutory maximum must be submitted to a jury and found beyond a reasonable doubt. *Blakely* held that the statutory maximum for *Apprendi* purposes is not the maximum sentence that may be imposed for the most aggravated type of offense; instead,

---

1. *See* North Carolina General Statutes (hereinafter G.S.) 15A-1340.10.

2. Ben F. Loeb, Jr. & James C. Drennan, Motor Vehicle Law and The Law of Impaired Driving in North Carolina 81 (UNC Institute of Government, 2000) (hereinafter Motor Vehicle Law).

3. 542 U.S. 296 (2004).

4. 530 U.S. 466 (2000).

the statutory maximum is the maximum sentence a judge may impose solely on the basis of the facts reflected in the jury verdict or admitted by the defendant.

Before the statutory provisions governing sentencing in impaired driving cases were amended in 2006,[5] post-*Blakely*, aggravating factors were determined by the judge, exposing defendants to increased levels of punishment carrying increased statutory maximum sentences. The State had to prove to a jury only the elements of the covered offense and then prove to a judge, by a preponderance of the evidence, any applicable aggravating sentencing factors. The separation of offense- and offender-specific sentencing factors from the broadly defined elements of covered offenses was part of the General Assembly's effort in the Safe Roads Act of 1983[6] to curtail the charging discretion of district attorneys in prosecuting such crimes.[7] The legislature's creation of statutorily defined sentencing factors allowed judges to consider aggravating and mitigating offender and offense characteristics at sentencing and to impose a sentence tailored to the relative seriousness of the offense, while at the same time greatly limiting judges' discretion.[8] Post-*Blakely* amendments to G.S. 20-179 require that aggravating factors, other than the fact of a prior conviction, now be found by a jury (in superior court) and that all aggravating factors be proven beyond a reasonable doubt in both district and superior court.[9] The sentencing scheme was again amended in 2011 to create a new Aggravated Level One punishment for impaired driving, carrying a maximum term of three years imprisonment,

---

5. S.L. 2006-253 (H 1048).

6. 1983 N.C. Sess. Laws, ch. 435.

7. *See* James C. Drennan, *Impaired Driving: The Safe Roads Act, in* NORTH CAROLINA LEGISLATION 1983 115 (Ann L. Sawyer ed., UNC Institute of Government, 1983) (hereinafter *Safe Roads Act*) (noting that the creation of a single crime with multiple levels of narrowly prescribed punishments limits officials' discretion in charging and judges' discretion in sentencing while treating defendants in different circumstances differently).

8. *See id.*

9. Post-*Blakely* amendments render largely, but not entirely, academic the question of whether G.S. 20-138.1 and 20-179 define one offense or six offenses. While the prosecutor is required to provide notice of intent to prove aggravating factors in superior court, *see* G.S. 20-179(a1)(1) (imposing an obligation much like a pleading requirement), no such notice of the State's intent is required in district court, meaning that, for district court prosecutions, those factors are not pleaded, functionally or otherwise, as elements. Other element-like treatment does, however, apply to such factors. As has already been noted, the factors, other than those related to proof of a prior conviction, must be proved beyond a reasonable doubt. In addition, the court of appeals held in *State v. Hurt*, 208 N.C. App. 1 (2010), *rev'd on other grounds*, 367 N.C. 80 (2013) (per curiam), that the Confrontation Clause of the Sixth Amendment to the U.S. Constitution applied to the proof at sentencing of sentencing factors that "if found, increase the defendant's sentence beyond the statutory maximum." *Id.* at 6. The court of appeals' opinion in *Hurt* subsequently was reversed by the North Carolina Supreme Court on the grounds that the defendant's confrontation rights were not violated by the testifying experts' reliance on reports prepared by experts who did not testify at trial, 367 N.C. 80, 80 (2013) (per curiam). Following the reversal of the court of appeals in *Hurt*, it remains unclear whether the State may, for example, introduce at a G.S. 20-179 sentencing hearing over a defendant's objection the affidavit of a non-testifying chemical analyst to prove the aggravating factor in G.S. 20-179(d)(1) that the defendant had an alcohol concentration of 0.15. *See* Shea Denning, *What's Blakely Got to Do With It? Sentencing in Impaired Driving Cases after Melendez-Diaz*, N.C. CRIM. L., UNC SCH. OF GOV'T BLOG (July 24, 2009), http://sogweb.sog.unc.edu/blogs/ncclaw/?p=567.

and to render the presence of one specified grossly aggravating factor[10] sufficient to trigger Level One punishment.[11]

The rigors and complexities of the sentencing scheme appear at odds with the misdemeanor classification of the covered offenses, raising the question of why such exacting requirements exist for sentencing in a misdemeanor criminal case. One might question why impaired driving offenses are not punished under the structured sentencing provisions applicable to misdemeanors generally and, if further scrutiny and increased sanctions are necessary in light of the risks posed, why aggravated types of such offenses are not classified as felonies and sentenced accordingly. No official legislative commentary or historical record definitively resolves such queries, though the sentencing provisions clearly are part of a broader statutory scheme designed to deter people from driving while impaired, to prevent injury, and to punish and rehabilitate offenders.[12] Many components of that broader scheme are unrelated to sentencing; some, like provisions for immediate civil license revocations,[13] do not even require conviction. Others relate to collateral consequences imposed upon offenders, such as the seizure, impoundment, and forfeiture of vehicles,[14] the revocation of offenders' licenses upon conviction,[15] and administrative requirements that a person install an ignition interlock device in order to have his or her driver's license restored[16] or to obtain a limited driving privilege.[17] North Carolina's legislature has enacted many of the sanctions and prophylactic approaches to reduce impaired driving advocated by highway safety experts, including the National Highway Transportation Safety Administration (NHTSA). NHTSA's guide to sentencing impaired driving offenders characterizes the key to reducing incidences of impaired driving as certain, consistent, and coordinated sentencing.[18] By defining factors associated with the defendant and the offense that dictate the appropriate level of sentencing, along with a relatively limited menu of sentencing options for each level of driving while impaired (DWI), G.S. 20-179 arguably comports with NHTSA's recommendation that "[s]entencing . . . should be consistent from one court to another, . . . yet balanced with the need for matching offenders to the most appropriate sanctions and extent of treatment."[19] The sentencing scheme also integrates more traditional punitive sanctions with treatment requirements and licensure consequences. And the transmission of information between the courts and the administrative agencies responsible for treatment and licensure appears to provide some of the coordination of communication to ensure compliance with sentences that NHTSA recommends.

North Carolina's appellate courts have repeatedly held that defendants convicted of impaired driving must be sentenced in accordance with G.S. 20-179.[20] Indeed, the state supreme court has

---

10. *See* G.S. 20-179(c) (requiring a judge to impose Level One punishment if it is determined that the grossly aggravating factor in subdivision (4) applies); *id.* § 20-179(c)(4) (rendering driving by the defendant while (i) a child under the age of 18, (ii) a person with the mental development of a child under the age of 18, or (iii) a person with a physical disability preventing unaided exit from the vehicle was in the vehicle at the time of the offense a grossly aggravating factor).

11. *See* S.L. 2011-191; 2011-329.

12. *See* Drennan, *Safe Roads Act*, at 116.

13. G.S. 20-16.5.

14. *Id.* § 20-28.3.

15. *Id.* §§ 20-17(a)(2), (13), (14).

16. *Id.* § 20-17.8.

17. *Id.* § 20-179.3(c1).

18. U.S. Dep't of Transp., Nat'l Highway Traffic Safety Admin., A Guide to Sentencing DWI Offenders (2d ed. 2005), www.nhtsa.gov/people/injury/alcohol/dwioffenders/A%20Guide2.pdf.

19. *Id.* at 3 (references omitted).

20. *See In re* Tucker, 348 N.C. 677 (1998) (noting in judicial disciplinary action district court judge's mistaken belief that mandatory sentencing provisions of G.S. 20-179 did not apply if he continued prayer

interpreted G.S. 20-179 to *require* sentencing pursuant to its provisions to the exclusion of dispositions like a prayer for judgment continued,[21] despite the lack of explicit language in G.S. 20-179 barring prayers for judgment in impaired driving cases. This interpretation of G.S. 20-179 differs markedly from that applied to the misdemeanor sentencing provisions for other traffic offenses, for which a disposition of prayer for judgment is permissible except where expressly barred by statute.[22]

II. Sentencing Procedures

A. Sentencing Hearing in District Court

Because all covered impaired driving offenses are misdemeanors, the district court has exclusive, original jurisdiction over cases charging covered offenses except when (1) the charges are made in an indictment initiated by a grand jury presentment, (2) a covered offense is consolidated for trial with a felony, (3) a conviction for a covered offense results from a plea in lieu of a felony charge, or (4) a covered offense is a lesser-included offense of a felony.[23] Because there is no right to trial by jury in criminal cases in district court,[24] the district court judge makes the findings of aggravating and mitigating factors required by G.S. 20-179 in a sentencing hearing held in district court after a defendant is convicted of a covered offense.[25] A district court must likewise conduct a sentencing hearing when a covered offense is remanded to district court after an appeal to superior court.[26]

B. Sentencing Hearing in Superior Court

A sentencing hearing likewise must be held after a defendant is convicted of a covered offense in superior court, regardless of whether the covered offense was tried initially in superior court (because it was initiated by presentment or joined with a related felony charge) or was tried de novo upon an

---

for judgment to a date certain and then dismissed the case); *In re* Martin, 333 N.C. 242 (1993) (censuring district court judge for convicting defendants of reckless driving when they were charged with driving while impaired, acts that the judge knew to be improper and beyond the power of his office); *In re* Greene, 297 N.C. 305, 312 (1979) (holding that North Carolina courts do not have an "'inherent power'" to continue prayer for judgment continued on conditions or to suspend sentence when the sentence (as it is for impaired driving convictions) is mandated by the General Assembly; directing named district court judge in adjudicating convictions for offenses sentenced pursuant to G.S. 20-179 to pronounce judgment in accordance with statute); *see also* State v. Petty, 212 N.C. App. 368 (2011) (recognizing that district court judge had no authority to arrest judgment upon defendant's conviction of impaired driving—an action that amounted to the entry of an invalid judgment).

21. *Greene*, 297 N.C. at 310. The entry of a prayer for judgment continued (PJC), as its terms imply, postpones (or continues) entry of judgment following conviction. Entry of this type of order sometimes is used to postpone (that is, continue) sentencing (in other words, entry of judgment) to a date certain. That type of PJC is permissible following conviction of a covered offense. What is impermissible is entry of a PJC that postpones judgment indefinitely or with no date certain, which may result in judgment never being imposed following conviction of a covered offense, or entry of a PJC that is followed by dismissal of the charges.

22. *See, e.g.*, G.S. 20-217(e) (providing that a person who passes a stopped school bus "shall not receive a prayer for judgment continued under any circumstances").

23. *See id.* § 7A-272(a) (setting forth jurisdiction of district court); 7A-271 (prescribing jurisdiction of superior court).

24. *Id.* § 7A-196(b).

25. *See id.* § 20-179(a).

26. *Id.*

appeal from a district court conviction. In superior court, a jury must determine the existence of any aggravating factor other than the fact of a prior conviction.[27] The jury impaneled for the trial may, in the same trial, determine if one or more aggravating factors is present, unless the court determines that the interests of justice require that this determination be made in a separate sentencing proceeding.[28] If the court determines that a separate proceeding is required, the proceeding must be conducted by the trial judge before the trial jury as soon as practicable after the guilty verdict is returned.[29]

If a juror dies, becomes incapacitated or disqualified, or is discharged after the jury returns its verdict on the underlying charges but before the trial jury begins its deliberations on the issue of whether one or more aggravating factors exists, an alternate juror chosen based on the order in which alternate jurors were selected becomes a part of the jury.[30] If the trial jury is unable to reconvene for a hearing on the issue of whether one or more aggravating factors exist after having determined the guilt of the accused, the trial judge must impanel a new jury to determine the issue.[31] A jury selected to determine whether one or more aggravating factors exist must be selected in the same manner as juries are selected for the trial of criminal cases.[32]

If a defendant admits that an aggravating factor exists but pleads not guilty to the underlying charge, a jury must be impaneled to dispose of the charge only.[33] In such a case, evidence that relates solely to the establishment of an aggravating factor may not be admitted at trial.[34] If a defendant pleads guilty to the charge but contests the existence of one or more aggravating factors, a jury must be impaneled to determine if the aggravating factor or factors exist.[35]

C. Standard of Proof

In both district and superior courts, the State must prove beyond a reasonable doubt that an aggravating factor exists unless the defendant admits to the existence of the factor.[36] If the defendant does not admit to the existence of an aggravating factor (other than the fact of a prior conviction), in superior court, only the jury may determine if it is present.[37] In district court, the judge determines the existence of both aggravating and mitigating factors.[38] In both forums, the defendant bears the burden of proving by a preponderance of the evidence that a mitigating factor exists.[39]

---

27. *Id.* § 20-179(d).
28. *Id.* § 20-179(a1)(2).
29. *Id.*
30. *Id.* § 20-179(a1)(3).
31. *Id.*
32. *Id.* § 20-179(a1)(4); *see also* G.S. Chapter 15A, Article 72 (setting forth procedures for selecting and impaneling a jury).
33. G.S. 20-179(a2)(1).
34. *Id.*
35. *Id.* § 20-179(a2)(2).
36. *Id.* §§ 20-179(a)(1), (a1)(2).
37. *Id.* § 20-179(a1)(2).
38. *Id.* § 20-179(a).
39. *Id.* §§ 20-179(a)(1), (a1)(2).

D. Levels of Punishment

G.S. 20-179 sets forth six levels of punishment applicable to covered offenses committed December 1, 2011, or later: Aggravated Level One, Level One, Level Two, Level Three, Level Four, and Level Five. The discussion in this section is applicable to offenses committed on or after this date.[40] A summary of the six levels of punishment and the sanctions applicable for each, keyed to date of offense, may be found in Tables 5.1 through 5.3. For offenses committed before December 1, 2011, there are five possible levels of punishment, Levels One through Five. For those offenses, Level One applies if there are two or more grossly aggravating factors. Level Two applies if there is one grossly aggravating factor, regardless of type. A summary of the five punishment levels and their sanctions for offenses committed before December 1, 2011, may be found in Table 5.4.

Certain aggravating factors, termed "grossly aggravating factors," are deemed more serious than other factors and thus have a greater impact on the defendant's sentence. Upon sentencing pursuant to G.S. 20-179, the appropriate finder of fact must *first* determine whether any grossly aggravating factors exist.[41] If it is determined that three or more grossly aggravating factors exist, the judge must impose Aggravated Level One punishment.[42] If the grossly aggravating factor in G.S. 20-179(c)(4) exists (driving while a child, person with the mental capacity of a child, or a disabled person is in the vehicle) or if two other grossly aggravating factors exist, the judge must impose Level One punishment.[43] If only one of the other grossly aggravating factors applies, the judge must impose Level Two punishment.[44]

In imposing Aggravated Level One, Level One, or Level Two punishment, the judge may, but is not required to, consider the aggravating and mitigating factors in G.S. 20-179(d) and (e) in determining the appropriate sentence. Because a jury must determine the presence of both grossly aggravating and aggravating factors in superior court, the jury will be asked to determine whether either type of aggravating factor exists.[45] If the jury finds factors in aggravation, the court must enter those findings on the court's determination of sentencing factors form[46] or on some "comparable document."[47] In district court a judge may elect not to formally determine the presence of aggravating or mitigating factors if he or she finds that one or more grossly aggravating factors applies.[48]

If there are no grossly aggravating factors in the case, the judge in district court or the jury in superior court must determine all aggravating factors.[49] The judge must weigh the seriousness of each

---

40. Note that for offenses committed December 1, 2012, and later, recent legislative amendments have resulted in changes to certain punishments. These changes are discussed in more detail in the text at *infra* sections V.B.1. and V.C.1., and charts setting out punishments applicable after December 1, 2012, are presented as Tables 5.1 and 5.2.

41. G.S. 20-179(c).

42. *Id.*

43. *Id.*; *id.* § 20-179(c)(4) (defining, as a grossly aggravating factor, "[d]riving by the defendant while (i) a child under the age of 18 years, (ii) a person with the mental development of a child under the age of 18 years, or (iii) a person with a physical disability preventing unaided exit from the vehicle was in the vehicle at the time of the offense").

44. *Id.* § 20-179(c).

45. *See, e.g.*, N.C. Pattern Instruction—Crim. 270.15 (Aggravating Factors for Impaired Driving.—G.S. 20-179).

46. AOC-CR-311 is the "Impaired Driving Determination of Sentencing Factors Form." It is reprinted in Appendixes 5.1A and 5.1B (keyed to date of offense).

47. G.S. 20-179(c1).

48. *See id.* § 20-179(c).

49. *Id.* § 20-179(d).

aggravating factor in light of the particular circumstances of the case.[50] The judge also must determine whether any mitigating factors apply and must weigh the degree of mitigation of each factor in light of the particular circumstances of the case.[51]

All aggravating and mitigating factors must be entered in writing.[52] Aggravating factors found by a jury must be entered on the court's determination of sentencing factors form[53] or some "comparable document" used to record the findings of sentencing factors.[54]

If the judge or the jury in the sentencing hearing determines that there are no grossly aggravating factors, the judge must weigh the aggravating and mitigating factors.[55] If the judge determines that the aggravating factors "substantially outweigh" any mitigating factors, the judge must note in the judgment the factors found and his or her finding that the defendant is subject to Level Three punishment.[56] The judge must then impose a punishment within the limits defined in G.S. 20-179(i).[57]

If there are no aggravating and mitigating factors or the judge determines that the aggravating factors are "substantially counterbalanced" by mitigating factors, the judge must note in the judgment any factors found and the finding that the defendant is subject to Level Four punishment and impose a punishment within the limits defined in G.S. 20-179(j).[58]

If the judge determines that the mitigating factors substantially outweigh any aggravating factors, the judge must note in the judgment the factors found and his or her finding that the defendant is subject to Level Five punishment and impose a punishment within the limits defined in G.S. 20-179(k).[59]

E. Duties of Prosecutor in District Court

Before a sentencing hearing for a covered offense in district court, the prosecutor must make all feasible efforts to obtain the defendant's full record of traffic convictions and must present this record to the judge for consideration at the hearing.[60] Upon the defendant's request, the prosecutor must provide to the defendant or his or her attorney a copy of the defendant's record of traffic convictions at a reasonable time before introducing the record into evidence.[61] In addition, the prosecutor must present all other appropriate grossly aggravating and aggravating factors of which he or she is aware, and the defendant or his or her attorney may present all appropriate mitigating factors.[62] If a "valid

---

50. *Id.*
51. *Id.* § 20-179(e).
52. *Id.* § 20-179(c1).
53. *See* AOC-CR-311 (reprinted in Appendixes 5.1A and 5.1B (keyed to date of offense)).
54. G.S. 20-179(c1).
55. *Id.* § 20-179(f).
56. *Id.* § 20-179(f)(1).
57. *Id.*
58. *Id.* § 20-179(f)(2).
59. *Id.* § 20-179(f)(3).
60. *Id.* § 20-179(a)(2).
61. *Id.* § 20-179(a).
62. *Id.*

chemical analysis"[63] was made of the defendant, the prosecutor must present evidence of the resulting alcohol concentration.[64]

F. Duties of Prosecutor in Superior Court

Pursuant to G.S. 20-179(a1)(1), if the State intends to prove one or more aggravating factors for a covered offense that a defendant has appealed to superior court for trial de novo, the State must provide the defendant notice of its intent. The notice must be provided no later than ten days prior to trial and must contain a plain and concise factual statement indicating each factor the State plans to use. Unlike notice provisions under structured sentencing, which require the State to provide notice of aggravating factors but not prior convictions,[65] G.S. 20-179(a1)(1) requires the State to provide notice of any aggravating factor it intends to use under G.S. 20-179(c) or (d), which includes the aggravating factors premised on prior convictions.

The notice provisions of G.S. 20-179 were enacted as part of the Motor Vehicle Driver Privacy Protection Act of 2006[66] and were crafted to protect a defendant's Sixth Amendment[67] right to be informed of the charges being brought against him or her.[68] The Administrative Office of the Courts has promulgated form AOC-CR-338, Notice of Grossly Aggravating and Aggravating Factors (reprinted as Appendixes 5.2A and 5.2B (keyed to date of offense)), to facilitate compliance with the notice requirement in G.S. 20-179(a1)(1). If the State fails to provide the statutorily required notice, then neither the jury nor the judge may find the factor applicable at sentencing. The court of appeals in *State v. Mackey*[69] held that the trial court erred by sentencing a defendant in the aggravated range when the State in a structured sentencing case failed to provide proper written notice of aggravating factors pursuant to G.S. 15A-1340.16(a6). In so holding, *Mackey* noted that "[t]he State had at its disposal a form routinely used by prosecutors to comply with this minimal requirement."[70] The court of appeals in *State v. Reeves*[71] relied upon *Mackey* in vacating a defendant's Level Three DWI sentence and remanding for resentencing due to the State's failure to provide the statutorily required notice of its intent to use an aggravating factor. In *Reeves*, the defendant was convicted of reckless driving to endanger in violation of G.S. 20-140(b) in addition to impaired driving. The State relied upon the aggravating factor of "especially reckless" driving in support of an aggravated sentence. The

---

63. A chemical analysis is "[a] test or tests of the breath, blood, or other bodily fluid or substance of a person to determine the person's alcohol concentration or presence of an impairing substance, performed in accordance with G.S. 20-139.1, including duplicate or sequential analyses." G.S. 20-4.01(3a). A breath test "administered pursuant to the implied-consent law" and performed in accordance with rules of the Department of Health and Human Services (DHHS) by a person with a current DHHS permit for the type of instrument employed is an admissible chemical analysis. *Id.* § 20-139.1(b). A blood or urine test likewise is deemed an admissible chemical analysis if (1) a law enforcement officer or chemical analyst requested a blood and/or urine sample from the person charged; and (2) a chemical analysis of the person's blood was performed by a chemical analyst possessing a DHHS permit for the type of analysis performed. *See id.* § 20-139.1(c4).

64. *Id.* § 20-179(a)(2).

65. *See id.* § 15A-1340.16(a6).

66. S.L. 2006-253.

67. U.S. CONST. amend. VI.

68. For a thorough analysis of the impetus for imposing similar notice requirements upon the State in structured sentencing cases post-*Blakely*, see Jessica Smith, *North Carolina Sentencing after Blakely v. Washington and the Blakely Bill* (UNC School of Government, Sept. 2005), 10–13, www.sog.unc.edu/sites/www.sog.unc.edu/files/Blakely%20Update.pdf.

69. 209 N.C. App. 116 (2011).

70. *Id.* at 121.

71. 218 N.C. App. 570, 576 (2012).

trial judge determined that this factor substantially outweighed any mitigating factor and imposed Level Three punishment.[72]

Somewhat curiously, G.S. 20-179(a1)(1) states that it applies "If the defendant appeals to superior court, and the State intends to use one or more aggravating factors," giving rise to a question about whether it governs the trial of covered offenses within the original jurisdiction of the superior court. Though most covered offenses originate in district court, as they are all misdemeanors, a covered offense will fall within the original jurisdiction of the superior court when it (1) is consolidated for trial with a felony, (2) results from a plea in lieu of a felony charge, (3) is a lesser-included offense of a felony, or (4) results from an indictment initiated by presentment.[73] Given that there is no principled reason for requiring notice only for covered offenses appealed from district court, a court might, notwithstanding the introductory clause of G.S. 20-179(a1)(1), cited above, construe the statutory notice provision as applying to all covered offenses, regardless of where they originate. For that reason, it appears that the State is well advised to provide notice of aggravating factors for covered offenses originally tried in superior court as well as those appealed from district court. Nevertheless, in a case within the original jurisdiction of the superior court in which the State fails to provide such notice, there is a colorable argument that the State's failure to do so is not a statutory violation.

III. Aggravating Factors

A. Grossly Aggravating Factors

As previously mentioned, grossly aggravating factors are deemed more serious than mere aggravating factors and have a greater impact upon a defendant's sentence. The presence of a single grossly aggravating factor renders a defendant subject to sentencing at Level Two (or Level One, depending upon the date of the covered offense and which factor is present), which carries a maximum sentence of 12 months' imprisonment. The presence of three or more grossly aggravating factors for a covered offense committed on or after December 1, 2011, renders the offense an Aggravated Level One offense, punishable by up to 3 years' imprisonment.

There are four grossly aggravating factors: (1) a qualifying prior conviction for an offense involving impaired driving; (2) driving while license revoked for an impaired driving revocation; (3) serious injury to another person caused by the defendant's impaired driving; and (4) driving with one of the following types of individuals in the vehicle: (i) a child under the age of 18, (ii) a person with the mental development of a child under 18, or (iii) a person with a physical disability preventing unaided exit from the vehicle.[74]

72. The trial judge arrested judgment on the reckless driving conviction on the basis that it was " 'used to enhance the DWI,' " 218 N.C. App. at 571 (quoting trial court), an action that does not appear to be required as a matter of constitutional law, as discussed *infra* at section III.A.2.e.

73. *See* G.S. 7A-271(a); 7A-272(a).

74. *Id.* § 20-179(f)(1).

1. Qualifying Prior Conviction for an Offense Involving Impaired Driving

The first grossly aggravating factor is a qualifying prior conviction for an offense involving impaired driving. An *offense involving impaired driving* is defined in G.S. 20-4.01(24a) as any of the following offenses:

- Impaired driving under G.S. 20-138.1
- Habitual impaired driving under G.S. 20-138.5
- Impaired driving in commercial vehicle under G.S. 20-138.2
- Any offense under G.S. 20-141.4 (felony and misdemeanor death by vehicle and serious injury by vehicle) based on impaired driving
- First- or second-degree murder under G.S. 14-17 based on impaired driving
- Involuntary manslaughter under G.S. 14-18 based on impaired driving
- Substantially similar offenses committed in another state or jurisdiction

A prior conviction for an offense involving impaired driving qualifies as a grossly aggravating factor if

a. The conviction occurred within seven years before the date of the offense for which the defendant is being sentenced; or
b. The conviction occurs after the date of the offense for which the defendant is presently being sentenced, but prior to or contemporaneously with the present sentencing; or
c. The conviction occurred in district court; the case was appealed to superior court; the appeal has been withdrawn or the case has been remanded back to district court; and a new sentencing hearing has not been held pursuant to G.S. 20-38.7.[75]

Each prior conviction is a separate grossly aggravating factor.[76]

a. What Counts as a Conviction?

The term "conviction" is defined in G.S. 20-4.01(4a) to include, among other adjudications, a "final conviction of a criminal offense, including a no contest plea."[77] Typically, for sentencing purposes, a defendant is said to have been convicted when he or she has been adjudged guilty or has entered a plea of guilty,[78] though sentencing may not occur and the conviction may not become final until some later date. The term "final conviction," as used in G.S. Chapter 20, has been construed to mean

---

75. *Id.* § 20-179(c)(1).

76. *Id.*.

77. *Id.* § 20-4.01(4a)a.1. "Conviction," when referring to an offense committed in North Carolina, also means any of the following: (1) "[a]n unvacated forfeiture of cash in the full amount of a bond required by Article 26 of Chapter 15A of the General Statutes," *id.* § 20-4.01(4a)a.3.; (2) "[a] third or subsequent prayer for judgment continued within any five-year period," *id.* § 20-4.01(4a)a.4.; or (3) "[a]ny prayer for judgment continued if the offender holds a commercial drivers license or if the offense occurs in a commercial motor vehicle." *Id.* § 20-4.01(4a)a.5. When referring to an offense committed outside North Carolina, the term "conviction" means (1) "[a]n unvacated adjudication of guilt;" (2) "[a] determination that a person has violated or failed to comply with the law in a court of original jurisdiction or an authorized administrative tribunal;" (3) "[a]n unvacated forfeiture of bail or collateral deposited to secure the person's appearance in court;" (4) "[a] violation of a condition of release without bail, regardless of whether or not the penalty is rebated, suspended, or probated;" (5) "[a] final conviction of a criminal offense, including a no contest plea;" or (6) "[a]ny prayer for judgment continued, including any payment of a fine or court costs, if the offender holds a commercial drivers license or if the offense occurs in a commercial motor vehicle." *Id.* §§ 20-4.01(4a)b.1.–6.

78. *Id.* § 15A-1331(b) (providing that "a person has been convicted when he has been adjudged guilty or has entered a plea of guilty or no contest").

an adjudication of guilt plus the entry of a judgment from which a defendant can exercise his or her right to appeal.[79]

Under structured sentencing, a district court conviction that occurs before the date a criminal judgment is entered for the current offense is deemed a "prior conviction" if the defendant has not given notice of appeal and the time for appeal has expired.[80] Superior court convictions that occur before the date of judgment for the current structured sentencing offense, in contrast, are deemed prior convictions regardless of whether they are appealed to the appellate division.[81] The additional requirements necessary for a district court conviction to qualify as a prior conviction stem from a defendant's right to appeal a misdemeanor district court conviction to superior court for trial de novo by jury—a statutory right afforded by G.S. 15A-1431(b) to effectuate the constitutional right to trial by jury.[82] Arguably, the term "final conviction" in G.S. 20-4.01(4a) likewise protects a defendant's constitutional right to trial by jury by permitting a defendant's sentence to be enhanced by, and collateral consequences to ensue from, only those district court convictions that are not subject to a pending appeal to superior court. It appears, however, that in some circumstances, district court convictions that would not qualify as "prior convictions" under structured sentencing may be final convictions for purposes of G.S. 20-179.

G.S. 20-179(c)(1) defines qualifying prior convictions to include convictions that occur "prior to or contemporaneously with" the current offense. If those convictions could not be considered as qualifying prior convictions until the time for appeal expired, this would, in effect, prevent convictions entered within ten days before sentencing for the current offense from being considered at all in the event those prior convictions were not appealed.

Consider this example. Defendant Dane is charged with impaired driving on November 3, 2012, and again on December 8, 2012. On February 20, 2013, Dane pleads guilty to and is sentenced at Level Five for the November 3, 2012, DWI. He doesn't orally provide notice of appeal. Later that day, Dane pleads guilty to and is sentenced for the December 8, 2012, DWI. Is the conviction for the November 3 offense a grossly aggravating factor? It appears to be a qualifying prior conviction entered either "prior to or contemporaneously with" the current sentencing. But if it cannot be considered a "final conviction" until after the time for appealing has expired, it cannot be counted. The outcome is that, by not appealing the conviction for the November 3 offense, Dane would be sentenced for two Level 5 DWIs. The General Assembly's inclusion of "contemporaneous" convictions as grossly aggravating factors strongly indicates that the legislature did not intend this result.

The apparent legislative intent and the protection of a defendant's right to a jury trial both are effectuated if one interprets the term "conviction," as used in G.S. 20-179(c)(1), to include district court convictions from which no notice of appeal has been filed—regardless of whether the time for filing

---

79. *See* Barbour v. Scheidt, 246 N.C. 169, 173 (1957) (holding that the North Carolina Division of Motor Vehicles lacked authority to revoke the petitioner's driver's license upon adjudication of guilt for speeding offense followed by entry of a prayer for judgment continued as "the conviction alone, without the imposition of a judgment from which an appeal might be taken, is not a final conviction" for purposes of license revocation statutes). The matter at issue in *Barbour* could now be resolved by statute, which defines a conviction as "[a] third or subsequent prayer for judgment continued within any five-year period" or "[a]ny prayer for judgment continued if the offender holds a commercial drivers license or if the offense occurs in a commercial motor vehicle." G.S. 20-4.01(4a)a.4. As noted earlier, a judge may not lawfully dispose of a covered offense by granting a prayer for judgment continued. *See In re* Greene, 297 N.C. 305 (1979).

80. G.S. 15A-1340.11(7)a.

81. *Id.* § 15A-1340.11(7)b.

82. U.S. Const. amend. VI ("In all criminal prosecutions, the accused shall enjoy the right to a speedy and public trial, by an impartial jury . . . ."); G.S. 7A-196(b) ("In criminal cases there shall be no jury trials in the district court. Upon appeal to superior court trial shall be de novo, with jury trial as provided by law.")

a notice of appeal has yet expired. If a defendant's sentence is elevated based upon a prior conviction that subsequently is appealed and the defendant is acquitted upon trial de novo in superior court, the defendant presumably would be entitled to resentencing for the conviction that it enhanced, though, in many cases, the sentence may already have been served and collateral consequences suffered by the defendant as a result of the enhanced conviction.[83]

A prior conviction for an offense involving impaired driving may have been entered in superior court. This could occur, for example, upon a defendant's conviction for a misdemeanor impaired driving conviction appealed from district court; upon conviction of a felony offense involving impaired driving; or upon a defendant's conviction for a misdemeanor impaired driving offense initiated by presentment, tried in superior court as a lesser-included offense of a felony or consolidated for trial with a felony.[84] Whether a conviction in superior court from which an appeal has been entered to the court of appeals may be considered a final conviction is not entirely free from doubt, though the most plausible legislative interpretation is that entry of judgment in superior court renders a conviction in that tribunal final regardless of whether the matter has been appealed to the court of appeals. This interpretation accords with the structured sentencing rule defining a "prior conviction" in part as a previous conviction in superior court "regardless of whether the conviction is on appeal to the appellate division."[85] If the rule were otherwise, a defendant with a qualifying prior conviction appealed from superior court could be sentenced for a later conviction as though he or she had no prior conviction. The matter could not be redressed if the prior conviction was affirmed on appeal as the affirmance would, at most, trigger execution of the judgment (if it was stayed while the matter was pending before the appellate courts) and would not require resentencing. In contrast, if a prior conviction used to enhance a subsequent sentence is reversed on appeal, the defendant arguably has the right to a new sentencing hearing for the subsequent conviction.[86]

b. What Is the Date of a Prior Conviction?

A "prior conviction for an offense involving impaired driving" is a grossly aggravating factor if "[t]he conviction occurred within seven years before the date of the offense for which the defendant is being sentenced."[87] Determining the date a "conviction occurred" when a conviction and judgment are entered in district court and not appealed or when a conviction and judgment are entered in superior court is straightforward. Identifying the date of conviction in the case of a district court conviction for a covered offense that is appealed to superior court and subsequently remanded to district court for resentencing (for offenses committed on or after December 1, 2006) or for execution of the sentence (for earlier convictions) is more complicated. For covered offenses committed on or after December 1, 2006, giving notice of appeal from a conviction in district court vacates the sentence imposed.[88] In contrast, giving notice of appeal from a conviction for a structured sentencing misdemeanor merely stays the execution of all portions of the judgment; if the appeal subsequently is withdrawn, the case is remanded to district court for execution of the judgment.[89] When an appeal from a conviction

---

83. *See* State v. Bidgood, 144 N.C. App. 267, 276 (2001) (finding that "it would be unjust to permit an enhanced sentence to stand where it is made to appear that the Prior Record Level has been erroneously calculated due to a subsequent reversal of a conviction on appeal" and remanding to the trial court "for entry of judgment which accurately reflects defendant's Prior Record Level").
84. G.S. 7A-271(a)(1), (2), (3).
85. *Id.* § 15A-1340.11(7)b.
86. *See Bidgood*, 144 N.C. App. at 276.
87. G.S. 20-179(c)(1)a.
88. *Id.* § 20-38.7(c).
89. *Id.* §§ 15A-1431(f1), (g), (h).

for a covered offense committed December 1, 2006, or later is withdrawn, the district court must hold a new sentencing hearing and must consider any new convictions.[90] This divergent procedure was enacted to prevent a defendant with two pending covered offenses from avoiding application of a grossly aggravating factor for either conviction by appealing the conviction for the first covered offense and, while the case was on appeal, pleading guilty to and being sentenced for the second covered offense. The first conviction is not considered a prior conviction at the time of sentencing for the second covered offense because it is not a "final conviction" so long as the case is the subject of a pending appeal to superior court.[91] Before the 2006 statutory changes, a defendant could, after the second conviction was entered, withdraw the appeal of the first conviction, triggering execution of a sentence that did not take into account the second conviction.

When a defendant initially is convicted of and sentenced for an impaired driving offense on one date but the judgment becomes final on a later date and, in the case of post–December 1, 2006, offenses, judgment and sentence actually are entered at a later date, a question arises regarding the date on which the prior conviction "occurred" for purposes of considering the seven-year look-back period under G.S. 20-179(c)(1). Given that the term "conviction," when used in connection with sentencing, generally means the determination of a defendant's guilt,[92] it seems likely that the date on which the defendant was adjudicated guilty is the date of conviction.[93] Moreover, if the term "final conviction" primarily is a mechanism to protect a defendant's right to trial de novo by jury in superior court, then the counting of a final conviction as having occurred on the date of the initial conviction and sentencing in district court, even if it *became final* at some later date, does not compromise that right.

c. Proof of Prior Convictions

While a judge may accept any evidence as to the presence or absence of prior convictions that he or she finds reliable, a judge must give prima facie effect to convictions recorded by the North Carolina Division of Motor Vehicles (NC DMV) or any other state agency.[94] A copy of such conviction records transmitted by the police information network is admissible in evidence without further authentication.[95] If a judge decides to impose an active sentence of imprisonment that would not have been imposed but for a prior conviction of an offense, the judge must afford the defendant an opportunity to introduce evidence and satisfy the defendant's burden of proving that the prior conviction was obtained when the defendant was indigent, had no counsel, and had not waived his or her right to counsel.[96]

---

90. *Id.* § 20-179(c).

91. *See id.* § 20-4.01(4a) (defining conviction as a "final conviction of a criminal offense," *id.* § 20-4.01(4a)a.1.).

92. *See id.* § 15A-1331(b) ("a person has been convicted when he has been adjudged guilty or has entered a plea of guilty or no contest"); State v. Canellas, 164 N.C. App. 775, 778 (2004); State v. Wilkins, 128 N.C. App. 315 (1998).

93. *See, as to multiple convictions, Wilkins,* 128 N.C. App. 315 (determining, for purposes of G.S. 15A-1340.14(d), which provides that for purposes of determining a defendant's prior record level for felony sentencing purposes, if an offender is convicted of more than one offense in a single session of district court, only one of the convictions is used, that when a defendant is convicted in district court, appeals the conviction to superior court, and subsequently withdraws the appeal causing the case to be remanded to district court for execution of the judgment, the conviction occurs on the date when the offender was originally convicted in district court).

94. G.S. 20-179(o).

95. *Id.*

96. *Id.*; *see also id.* § 15A-980(a) (affording a defendant the right to suppress a prior conviction obtained in violation of his or her right to counsel).

2. Driving While License Revoked for an Impaired Driving Revocation under G.S. 20-28.2(a)

The second grossly aggravating factor is "[d]riving by the defendant at the time of the offense while his driver's license was revoked under G.S. 20-28, and the revocation was an impaired driving revocation under G.S. 20-28.2(a)."[97] For this factor to apply, each of the elements of driving while revoked as that offense is defined in G.S. 20-28 must be satisfied, though there is no requirement that the defendant be charged with or convicted of the offense of driving while license revoked.[98]

To commit the offense of driving while license revoked under G.S. 20-28(a), a person must drive a motor vehicle on a highway while his or her license is revoked. Because a bicycle is a *vehicle*[99] but is not a *motor vehicle*,[100] a defendant who commits the offense of impaired driving on a bicycle does not also commit the offense of driving while license revoked in violation of G.S. 20-28(a). Thus, the grossly aggravating factor set forth in G.S. 20-179(c)(2) does not apply to a person who commits a covered offense on a bicycle or some other vehicle, such as a moped,[101] that is not also a motor vehicle. Likewise, the aggravating factor does not apply to a defendant who, while his or her license was revoked for an impaired driving license revocation, commits a covered offense in a public vehicular area, such as a parking lot. Because the offense of driving while license revoked under G.S. 20-28(a) must be committed on a street or highway, commission of a covered offense in a public vehicular area does not render the grossly aggravating factor in G.S. 20-179(c)(2) applicable.

In addition to satisfying the elements of G.S. 20-28(a), for the grossly aggravating factor in G.S. 20-179(c)(2) to apply, the defendant's license must be revoked for "an impaired driving revocation under G.S. 20-28.2(a)."

G.S. 20-28.2(a) defines an *"impaired driving license revocation"* as a revocation made under any of the following statutes:

- G.S. 20-13.2: consuming alcohol/drugs or willful refusal by driver under 21
- G.S. 20-16(a)(8b): military driving while impaired
- G.S. 20-16.2: refused chemical test
- G.S. 20-16.5: pretrial civil license revocation
- G.S. 20-17(a)(2): impaired driving or impaired driving in a commercial motor vehicle
- G.S. 20-138.5: habitual impaired driving
- G.S. 20-17(a)(12): transporting open container
- G.S. 20-17.2: court order not to operate (repealed effective December 1, 2006)
- G.S. 20-16(a)(7): impaired driving out of state resulting in N.C. revocation
- G.S. 20-17(a)(1): manslaughter or second-degree murder involving impaired driving
- G.S. 20-17(a)(3): felony involving use of motor vehicle, involving impaired driving
- G.S. 20-17(a)(9): felony or misdemeanor death or serious injury by vehicle involving impaired driving

---

97. *Id.* § 20-179(c)(2).

98. *Cf.* State v. Dewalt, 209 N.C. App. 187 (2011) (interpreting the aggravating factor of "[d]riving when the person's drivers license is revoked" set forth in G.S. 20-141.5(b)(5) for purposes of elevating the misdemeanor offense of speeding to elude arrest to a felony offense pursuant to G.S. 20-141.5 not to require proof of driving on a street or highway, as required by G.S. 20-28(a), because driving while license revoked, unlike several other aggravating factors listed in G.S. 20-141.5(b), did not incorporate a reference to the statute defining it as a crime).

99. G.S. 20-4.01(49).

100. *Id.* § 20-4.01(23).

101. *Id.* (providing that the term "motor vehicle" "shall not include mopeds as defined in G.S. 20-4.01(27)d1").

- G.S. 20-17(a)(11): assault with motor vehicle involving impaired driving
- G.S. 20-28.2(a)(3): cases where the laws of another state and the offense for which the person's license is revoked prohibit substantially similar conduct which, if committed in this State, would result in a revocation listed under any of the above statutes

The last category of revocations warrants some discussion. G.S. 20-179(c)(2) borrows its definition of an impaired driving revocation from the statutory provisions providing for seizure, impoundment, and forfeiture of motor vehicles driven in the commission of an impaired driving offense by a person with an impaired driving license revocation.[102] Thus, revocation of a person's driver's license by another state for an impaired driving event may render the motor vehicle driven by the person in the commission of an impaired driving offense in North Carolina subject to seizure, impoundment, and forfeiture.[103] Revocation by another state with no corresponding action by the North Carolina Division of Motor Vehicles (NC DMV) likely does not, however, constitute a revocation for purposes of driving while license revoked pursuant to G.S. 20-28(a), which arguably requires a North Carolina order of revocation and notification by NC DMV. The terms "revocation" and "suspension" are defined in G.S. 20-4.01(36) and 20-4.01(47) to mean "[t]ermination of a licensee's or permittee's privilege to drive . . . for a period of time stated in an order of revocation or suspension." The requirement that the termination be stated in an order of revocation or suspension corresponds to the requirement that the State prove that a defendant had actual or constructive knowledge of the revocation to obtain a conviction under G.S. 20-28(a).[104] While not free from ambiguity, both *revocation* and *suspension* have been interpreted in practice to require an order issued by a North Carolina court or by NC DMV.[105] In light of separate statutory provisions (1) authorizing NC DMV to suspend or revoke the driving privileges of nonresidents in the same manner as it may for residents[106] and (2) prohibiting a person from operating under a foreign license while subject to such a revocation order,[107] interpreting G.S. 20-28(a) as applicable only when a North Carolina revocation is in effect best accords with the whole of G.S. Chapter 20.

Finally, a person who violates the restrictions of a limited driving privilege issued under G.S. 20-179.3 commits "the offense of driving while . . . license . . . revoked under G.S. 20-28(a)." G.S. 20-179.3(j). Thus, the grossly aggravating factor in G.S. 20-179(c)(2) applies to a person who commits a covered offense while driving in violation of the restrictions of a G.S. 20-179.3 limited driving privilege if the person's driver's license is revoked for an impaired driving revocation.

a. Conviction-Based Revocations

Questions also arise regarding whether a defendant's license is revoked for an impaired driving revocation when the time period set forth for the original revocation pursuant to G.S. 20-19(c1) (one year) or 20-19(d) (four years) had expired at the time of the current offense but the defendant's driver's license has not been restored. Whether the grossly aggravating factor in G.S. 20-179(c)(2) applies depends on whether the revocation remains in effect or, instead, whether the defendant simply is

---

102. *Id.* § 20-28.2(a).

103. *Id.* § 20-28.2(a)(3).

104. *See* State v. Atwood, 290 N.C. 266, 271 (1976).

105. *See* Loeb & Drennan, Motor Vehicle Law, *supra* note 2, at 84; *see also* N.C. Pattern Jury Instruction—Crim. 271.10 (stating that for jury to find that notice of revocation was given, the State must prove beyond a reasonable doubt that (1) notice was personally delivered, (2) the defendant surrendered license to an official of the court (pursuant to G.S. 20-24(a)), or (3) NC DMV provided notice by mail in accordance with G.S. 20-48).

106. *See* G.S. 20-22(a).

107. *See id.* § 20-21.

deemed unlicensed. If the defendant failed to obtain a certificate of completion for receiving a substance abuse assessment and completing the recommended training or treatment, the revocation period is extended until NC DMV receives the certificate of completion.[108] If the revocation period was extended for this reason at the time the person committed the instant offense, then his or her license was revoked for an impaired driving revocation. The grossly aggravating factor thus applies if the defendant met the other requirements for the offense of driving while license revoked under G.S. 20-28(a) by having driven a motor vehicle on a street or highway knowing that his or her license was revoked.[109] If, however, the defendant had obtained a certificate of completion but simply failed to seek restoration of his or her license, which requires proof of insurance[110] and payment of a $100 restoration fee,[111] then the defendant's license was not revoked at the time of the driving. In such a circumstance, the grossly aggravating factor does not apply. An "indefinite" end date for a driver's license suspension for a conviction of impaired driving under G.S. 20-138.1 noted on a defendant's driving record, accompanied by an asterisk beside the suspension, reflects that the term of revocation applicable under G.S. 20-19 has expired but NC DMV has not received a certificate of completion; thus the revocation continues to be in effect.

b. Civil License Revocations

Similar questions arise when, at the time of the covered offense, the defendant's license was civilly revoked pursuant to G.S. 20-16.5. In most circumstances, it is readily apparent that the grossly aggravating factor applies, since impaired driving license revocations are defined by G.S. 20-28.2(a) to include G.S. 20-16.5 revocations. The analysis is rendered slightly more complicated when the minimum revocation period has expired pursuant to G.S. 20-16.5 but the defendant's license still is revoked because he or she has not paid the fee necessary to end the civil revocation. G.S. 20-28(a1) provides that a person convicted of driving while license revoked for driving while subject to revocation under G.S. 20-16.5 after the minimum revocation period has expired but before reclaiming his or her license is *punished* as if the person has been convicted of the less serious offense of driving without a license. Regardless of the defendant's eligibility for reduced punishment for the offense of driving while license revoked on these facts, however, the underlying offense remains driving while license revoked. Accordingly, the nature of the underlying revocation—a civil license revocation pursuant to G.S. 20-16.5—remains unchanged. Thus, the grossly aggravating factor in G.S. 20-179(c)(2) applies if the defendant commits the current offense and simultaneously satisfies the elements of driving while license revoked while subject to a G.S. 20-16.5 revocation, regardless of the reason the G.S. 20-16.5 revocation remains in place.

c. Previous Impaired Driving Revocations

Questions also arise regarding whether G.S. 20-179(c)(2) applies when a defendant's license is revoked for driving while license revoked while subject to an earlier impaired driving revocation. If the revocation in effect at the time of the instant impaired driving offense was for driving while license revoked (as contrasted with the earlier-entered revocation for an impaired driving offense), the grossly aggravating factor in G.S. 20-179(c)(2) does not apply. This is so because regardless of the reason for which the defendant was revoked at the time he or she committed the earlier offense of driving while license revoked, the revocation in effect at the time of the instant impaired driving offense was

---

108. *See id.* § 20-17.6(b).

109. *See* Shea Denning, *Proving Knowledge of a License Revocation*, N.C. Crim. L., UNC Sch. of Gov't Blog (Apr. 12, 2010), http://sogweb.sog.unc.edu/blogs/ncclaw/?p=1195.

110. G.S. 20-19(k).

111. *Id.* § 20-7(i1).

pursuant to G.S. 20-28(a), which is not among the "impaired driving license revocations" set forth in G.S. 20-28.2(a). Note, however, that the aggravating factor of driving by the defendant while his or her driver's license was revoked as set forth in G.S. 20-179(d)(4) *does* apply on these facts.

d. NC DMV Records

The status of a person's driver's license may be proved by the driving records maintained by NC DMV.[112] A certified copy of such records is prima facie evidence of a revoked license, and certified copies may be transmitted over the Police Information Network.[113]

e. Double Punishment, but No Double Jeopardy

A defendant whose punishment for a covered offense is enhanced based upon a finding of the grossly aggravating factor of driving at the time of the offense while his or her license was revoked and the revocation was an impaired driving revocation,[114] also may be convicted of driving while revoked in violation of G.S. 20-28(a).[115] In similar fashion, a defendant's punishment for a covered offense may be aggravated by (1) his or her conviction under G.S. 20-141.5 of speeding to elude;[116] (2) his or her conviction under G.S. 20-141 of speeding by at least 30 miles per hour over the legal limit;[117] or (3) his or her conviction for passing a stopped school bus in violation of G.S. 20-217,[118] an offense for which he or she also may be convicted, when the conduct occurs during the same transaction as the covered offense.[119]

In such circumstances, a question arises as to whether the Double Jeopardy Clause of the Fifth Amendment,[120] which secures a person's right to be free from multiple punishments for the same offense,[121] permits the person to be punished additionally for the conduct constituting the aggravating factor while at the same time being punished for the covered offense at an aggravated level. A defendant may argue that when a covered offense is aggravated by conduct that is itself a separate crime or by conviction of a separate crime, that conduct or conviction is an element, and thus a lesser-included offense, of the aggravated covered offense. Because, under the test derived from *Blockburger v. United States*,[122] offenses are the same for double jeopardy purposes if all of the elements of one offense are subsumed in the other,[123] the argument continues that a defendant punished for the covered offense and the aggravating conduct or conviction is receiving multiple punishments for the same offense. The contrary argument is that while aggravating factors may be treated as the functional equivalent of elements for Sixth Amendment purposes, they are not elements for purposes of determining whether

---

112. *Id.* § 20-26(b).
113. *Id.*
114. *Id.* § 20-179(c)(2).
115. If the defendant committed the covered offense while driving with a revoked license but the revocation was not an impaired driving revocation, the aggravating factor in G.S. 20-179(d)(4) applies. A defendant subject to this aggravating factor also may be convicted of driving while license revoked in violation of G.S. 20-28(a) for the same conduct.
116. G.S. 20-179(d)(6).
117. *Id.* § 20-179(d)(7).
118. *Id.* § 20-179(d)(8).
119. *Id.* § 20-179(d).
120. U.S. Const. amend. V.
121. For further discussion of the double jeopardy bar to prosecution and punishment, see Jessica Smith, North Carolina Crimes: A Guidebook on the Elements of Crime 13 (UNC School of Government, 7th ed. 2012).
122. 284 U.S. 299 (1932).
123. Offenses are not the same for double jeopardy purposes if each contains an element that is not in the other. *See* United States v. Dixon, 509 U.S. 688 (1993).

the Double Jeopardy Clause bars punishment for both offenses.[124] The United States Supreme Court has not determined whether sentencing factors that must be determined by the jury beyond a reasonable doubt are elements of an offense for purposes of double jeopardy analysis,[125] and no North Carolina court has weighed in on the question.

Even if aggravating factors are elements of an aggravated covered offense for purpose of the Fifth Amendment double jeopardy analysis as well as the Sixth Amendment jury trial analysis, there still are circumstances in which a defendant may be punished in a single prosecution for an aggravated covered offense and lesser-included offenses. The Double Jeopardy Clause does not prohibit multiple punishments for offenses when one is included within the other under the *Blockburger* test if both are tried at the same time and if the legislature specifically authorizes cumulative punishment for both offenses.[126] Thus, even if the elements of two crimes are the same, a defendant may in a single trial be convicted of and punished for both crimes if it is found that the legislature intended for multiple punishments to apply.[127] And, while *Missouri v. Hunter* (see note 126) referred to specific authorization for cumulative punishment, the North Carolina Supreme Court has found such authorization in the absence of an explicit statutory rule by examining legislative and judicial history and by inferring that inaction from the legislature constitutes "acquiesce[nce]" as to the conviction and punishment of both crimes in a single trial.[128]

Prior to *Blakely v. Washington*,[129] sentencing factors in G.S. 20-179 were not considered elements of the substantive covered offense. Thus, for example, driving while license revoked was not considered a lesser-included offense of impaired driving aggravated by driving while license revoked, and cumulative punishment frequently was imposed for both offenses. When the General Assembly amended G.S. 20-179 in 2006 to require that aggravating factors be submitted to the fact-finder and proved beyond a reasonable doubt, it did recast the sentencing factors under G.S. 20-179 as elements of a covered offense. The legislature's continued treatment of these aggravators as sentencing factors, the requirement of a separate conviction for certain of the factors without mention of a bar against multiple punishment, and the legislature's inaction in the face of the long-standing view that cumulative punishment under G.S 20-179 is permissible evince the General Assembly's intent to allow for

---

124. *See* United States v. O'Brien, 560 U.S. 218, 224–25 (2010) (explaining that while judge-found sentencing factors cannot increase the maximum sentence a defendant might otherwise receive based purely on the facts found by the jury, subject to this constitutional constraint, whether a given fact is an element of the crime itself or a sentencing factor is a question for the legislature).

125. *See* Sattazahn v. Pennsylvania, 537 U.S. 101, 111 (2003) (plurality op.) (finding, in the context of determining whether the Double Jeopardy Clause applied to capital sentencing proceedings so as to preclude imposition of the death penalty in a subsequent trial if a jury in an earlier proceeding concludes that the State has failed to prove an aggravating circumstance, "no principled reason to distinguish . . . between what constitutes an offense for purposes of the Sixth Amendment's jury-trial guarantee and what constitutes an 'offense' for purposes of the Fifth Amendment's Double Jeopardy Clause"); *compare* People v. Hogan, 114 P.3d 42 (2004), *cert. denied* (Colo. App. 2005) (holding that second-degree kidnapping, when enhanced by a factor of aggravated robbery, does not require that separate conviction for the aggravated robbery be merged into the kidnapping conviction and declining to construe plurality opinion in *Sattazahn* as a constitutional mandate that any fact increasing the maximum penalty becomes an essential element of the offense for both double jeopardy and merger purposes), *and* State v. Stephenson, 195 S.W.3d 574 (Tenn. 2006) (holding that the plurality opinion in *Sattazahn* cannot be read to hold that aggravating circumstances must be included as elements of the offense of capital murder for purposes of *Blockburger*), *with* Thomas v. Commonwealth, No. 2003-CA-000166-MR, 2004 WL 405951 (Ky. Ct. App. Mar. 5, 2004) (unpublished) (concluding that DUI was a lesser-included offense of driving while license suspended for DUI and that offenses were the same under *Blockburger*).

126. *See* Missouri v. Hunter, 459 U.S. 359 (1983).

127. State v. Gardner, 315 N.C. 444 (1986).

128. *Gardner*, 315 N.C. at 462.

129. 542 U.S. 296 (2004).

cumulative punishment to be imposed for conviction of an aggravated covered offense and for the aggravating conduct itself.

3. Serious Injury to Another Person Caused by the Defendant's Impaired Driving at the Time of the Offense

The third grossly aggravating factor is serious injury to another person caused by the defendant's impaired driving at the time of the offense.[130] The plain language of the statute makes clear that a person other than the defendant must suffer serious injury for this factor to apply. In the assault context, the state supreme court has stated that serious injury is injury that is serious but falls short of causing death and has characterized "[f]urther definition" as "neither wise nor desirable."[131] And while the courts similarly have declined to define "serious injury" in the context of G.S. 20-179,[132] they have, contrary to the assault-based definition stated above, concluded that it may be based upon injuries so serious as to result in death.[133]

The courts have identified several relevant factors for purposes of assault prosecutions that may guide the determination of whether serious injury has been inflicted.[134] Those factors, which likewise appear applicable to determining whether a covered offense has caused serious injury, include, but are not limited to, pain and suffering, loss of blood, hospitalization, and time lost from work.[135] Any one of the factors is sufficient by itself to constitute substantial evidence of serious injury.[136] Thus, whether a serious injury has been inflicted depends upon the facts of each case[137] and is generally for the jury to decide under appropriate instructions.[138]

---

130. G.S. 20-179(c)(3). A person who unintentionally causes serious injury to another person while engaged in the offense of impaired driving under G.S. 20-138.1 or impaired driving in a commercial vehicle under G.S. 20-138.2 where the impaired driving offense is the proximate cause of the other's serious injury commits the offense of felony serious injury by vehicle, a Class F felony. *See id.* § 20-141.4(a3).

131. State v. Jones, 258 N.C. 89, 91 (1962).

132. *See* State v. Barber, 93 N.C. App. 42, 49 (1989) (finding serious injury based upon the victim's (1) treatment for a cut on the heel and for a broken right leg, (2) hospitalization for blood clots in his lungs and for a compressed vertebra, (3) more than $8,000 in medical expenses, and (4) absence from work due to his injuries).

133. State v. Speight, 186 N.C. App. 93, 100 (2007) (finding "overwhelming and uncontroverted" evidence supporting the aggravating factor of serious injury under G.S. 20-179(c)(3) where the defendant, who was driving while impaired, crossed the median and crashed head-on into a vehicle heading in the opposite direction, killing both of its occupants).

134. State v. McLean, 211 N.C. App. 321, 325 (2011).

135. *Id.*

136. *Id.* (citing State v. Bagley, 183 N.C. App. 514, 526 (2007) ("Substantial evidence of a serious injury that is sufficient to survive a motion to dismiss includes, but is not limited to, evidence of 'hospitalization, pain, blood loss, and time lost at work.' "); State v. Joyner, 295 N.C. 55, 65 (1978) (citing State v. Ferguson, *infra* note 137) ("Evidence that the victim was hospitalized is not necessary for the proof of serious injury.")).

137. *See* State v. Ferguson, 261 N.C. 558, 559 (1964) (finding sufficient evidence to submit element of serious injury to the jury based upon evidence that the defendant, in a pickup truck, rammed the back of an automobile driven by the victim, causing him to suffer a whiplash injury that prevented the victim from turning his head without pain and "caused pains to run down his back into the back of his legs," injuries for which the victim was not hospitalized); State v. Field, 75 N.C. App. 647 (1985) (court ruled on constitutionality of judge determining grossly aggravating factor, finding it constitutional, a holding since overruled by *Blakely v. Washington*, 542 U.S. 296 (2004); judge found serious injury based on (1) injury to one person consisting of a severe cut to the head requiring twenty-nine stitches and fractures of the knee that required surgery and (2) injury to another person consisting of a blow to the head and a broken nose, requiring surgery and a skin graft to cover a hole in the membrane).

138. *See* State v. James, 321 N.C. 676 (1988) (stating general standard and finding evidence that defendant shot victim with a rifle and that victim was hospitalized as a result of injuries received during the assault sufficient to go to the jury on the element of "serious injury"); *see also McLean*, 211 N.C. App. at 326, (holding that trial judge's failure to give North Carolina Pattern Jury Instruction—Crim. 120.12, defining

G.S. 20-179 does not address whether more than one grossly aggravating factor exists if more than one person other than the defendant is seriously injured as a result of the defendant's impaired driving. The specification in G.S. 20-179(c)(1) that each qualifying prior conviction counts as a separate grossly aggravating factor and the lack of any similar statement with respect to this factor, along with the other grossly aggravating factors, may indicate that only one grossly aggravating factor of a given type applies for a single covered offense regardless of how many separate occurrences might constitute that type of grossly aggravating factor. On the other hand, one might argue that the legislature's reference to a serious injury to "another person" rather than serious injury to *another person or other persons* evinces its intent for application of a separate grossly aggravating factor for each person seriously injured.

4. Driving by the Defendant While a Child, Person with the Mental Capacity of a Child, or a Disabled Person Was in the Vehicle

The fourth and final grossly aggravating factor for offenses committed after December 1, 2011, is commission of a covered offense with any of the following persons in the vehicle: (1) a child under the age of 18; (2) a person with the mental development of a child under 18; or (3) a person with a physical disability that prevents the person from getting out of the vehicle without assistance.[139] For covered offenses committed December 1, 2011, or later, Level One punishment is required if this factor is found.

It is unclear whether more than one grossly aggravating factor exists if more than one qualifying child, person with the mental capacity of a child, or disabled person is in the vehicle at the time of the offense. G.S. 20-179(c)(4), like subdivision (c)(3), discussed above, is silent on the matter. Before this factor was amended and broadened, effective for offenses committed on or after December 1, 2011, it applied if the defendant drove with a child under the age of 16 in the vehicle.[140] Then, as now, the statute did not specify whether the presence of more than one child supported the finding of more than one aggravating factor. Some experts interpreted the former version of the factor to have singular application regardless of the number of children in the vehicle[141] since this subdivision, unlike G.S. 20-179(c)(1), was silent on the matter.[142] As with the grossly aggravating factor for serious injury to another, discussed above, a contrary argument may be made based on the subdivision's reference to "a child" or "a person." One might contend that had the legislature intended one factor to apply regardless of the number of children or disabled persons present in the vehicle, the subdivision would contain the plural form of those nouns.

The amendment of the grossly aggravating factor to render it applicable, for offenses committed on or after December 1, 2011, when a person from one of three distinct categories is present in the vehicle at the time of the offense further complicates matters. The court of appeals has construed "especially reckless or dangerous driving"—an aggravating factor in G.S. 20-179(d)(2), which is similarly worded in the disjunctive—to permit a finding of two separate aggravating factors, one based on

---

"serious injury" as an injury that "causes great pain and suffering," was not error, as the appellate courts have chosen not to narrowly define "serious injury" in the context of assaults).

139. G.S. 20-179(c)(4).

140. *Id.* § 20-179(c)(4) (2009).

141. Loeb & Drennan, Motor Vehicle Law, *supra* note 2, at 85; *see also* Jeff Welty, *DWI for the Whole Family,* N.C. Crim. L., UNC Sch. of Gov't Blog (June 15, 2009), http://sogweb.sog.unc.edu/blogs/ncclaw/?p=428.

142. See *supra* section III.A.3 (discussing this argument in the context of the serious injury to another factor codified in G.S. 20-179(c)(3)).

especially reckless driving, the other based on especially dangerous driving.[143] The court of appeals in *State v. Mack*[144] explained that "there would need to be at least one item of evidence not used to prove either an element of the offense or any other factor in aggravation to support each additional aggravating factor."[145] If *Mack*'s reasoning were applied to G.S. 20-179(c)(4), as amended, it would allow for the determination of more than one grossly aggravating factor based on the presence of more than one person in the car, each of whom satisfied a separate category. So, for example, a finding of one grossly aggravating factor under G.S. 20-179(c)(4) would be appropriate for a defendant who committed a covered offense with more than one child under the age of 18 in the vehicle. And if a person with a qualifying disability or a person with the mental development of a child under the age of 18 also was present in the vehicle, a separate grossly aggravating factor would apply. As discussed above, whether more than one grossly aggravating factor under G.S. 20-179(c)(4) may apply based on the presence of individuals within the same category remains unsettled.

B. Aggravating Factors

There are nine aggravating factors, eight of them defined and a ninth "catch-all" aggravating factor. Except for the fifth factor (which involves prior convictions), the conduct constituting the aggravating factor must occur during the same transaction or occurrence as the impaired driving offense.

In district court, the judge determines whether an aggravating factor exists. With the exception of the fifth aggravating factor set forth below, in superior court the jury determines whether any factor exists. The judge in superior court determines whether the fifth aggravating factor applies, as this involves the determination of a prior conviction.[146] Any aggravating factor, whether found by the judge in district court or the jury or judge in superior court, must be entered in writing on the court's determination of sentencing factors form or some comparable document.[147] As previously mentioned, the State bears the burden of proving beyond a reasonable doubt that any aggravating factor exists.[148]

The aggravating factors are set forth below as subsections (1)–(9).

1. Gross Impairment of the Defendant's Faculties While Driving or an Alcohol Concentration of 0.15 or More within a Relevant Time after the Driving

"Gross impairment" is a high level of impairment, higher than that impairment which must be shown to prove the offense of DWI.[149] No minimum alcohol concentration is required to prove gross impairment. Given that there is no bright line marking "where 'impairment' ends and 'gross impairment' begins," the determination of whether a defendant is grossly impaired depends on the facts of each individual case.[150] The court of appeals in *State v. Harrington*[151] found sufficient evidence of gross impairment where the defendant had an alcohol concentration of 0.14, drove erratically, was unsteady on his feet, had slurred speech, had difficulty answering routine questions, and could not satisfactorily

143. *See* State v. Mack, 81 N.C. App. 578 (1986).
144. *Id.*
145. *Id.* at 585.
146. G.S. 20-179(c).
147. *Id.* § 20-179(c1). AOC-CR-311, the "Impaired Driving Determination of Sentencing Factors" form, is reprinted in Appendixes 5.1A and 5.1B (the first applies to offenses committed before December 1, 2011, the second to offenses committed on or after December 1, 2011).
148. G.S. 20-179(a)(1).
149. State v. Harrington, 78 N.C. App. 39, 46 (1985).
150. *Id.* at 46–47.
151. 78 N.C. App. 39.

perform any field sobriety tests. The court in *State v. Gunter*[152] found sufficient evidence of gross impairment based on an alcohol concentration of 0.27, the defendant's slurred speech and difficulty standing, and the defendant's asking for the whereabouts of a woman who was not present.

For purposes of determining whether a defendant has an alcohol concentration of 0.15 or more within a relevant time after the driving, the results of a chemical analysis[153] "presented at trial or sentencing" are sufficient proof.[154] Moreover, such results are deemed "conclusive" and are not subject to modification, even by order of the court.[155] The term "presented" is not defined by statute, though one might reasonably construe the provision to deem conclusive only those results that are admitted into evidence at trial or sentencing. Under this view, chemical analysis results that are suppressed pursuant to a trial judge's conclusion that the State violated the defendant's statutory or constitutional rights[156] in obtaining the evidence do not conclusively establish a defendant's alcohol concentration for purposes of this aggravating factor. Likewise, under this view, chemical analysis results that are excluded from trial or sentencing on evidentiary or Confrontation Clause grounds do not conclusively establish this factor.[157]

2. Especially Reckless or Dangerous Driving

The State may prove both especially reckless and especially dangerous driving in connection with a single covered offense.[158] If it does so, two aggravating factors are present.[159] To prove two factors in connection with a single offense, at least one item of evidence not used to support an element of the offense or any other aggravating factor must be present. Moreover, because impaired driving itself is a reckless and dangerous act, to establish this factor the State must prove excessive aspects of recklessness or of dangerousness not normally present in the offense of impaired driving.[160] Falling asleep at the wheel while driving, as the result of an impairing substance, has been found to be especially dangerous.[161] Driving into a telephone pole without braking while speeding has been found to be especially reckless.[162]

---

152. 111 N.C. App. 621, 628 (1993).

153. A chemical analysis is defined as "[a] test or tests of the breath, blood, or other bodily fluid or substance of a person to determine the person's alcohol concentration or presence of an impairing substance, performed in accordance with G.S. 20-139.1, including duplicate or sequential analyses." G.S. 20-4.01(3a).

154. *Id.* § 20-179(d)(1).

155. *Id.*

156. *See* State v. Shadding, 17 N.C. App. 279 (1973) (holding that the State's failure to offer evidence regarding whether the defendant was advised of his implied consent rights rendered results of breath test inadmissible); *see also* G.S. 15A-974(a)(1) (providing for the suppression of evidence if its exclusion is required by the federal or state constitution).

157. *See* State v. Hurt, 208 N.C. App. 1 (2010) (holding that the Confrontation Clause applies to sentencing proceedings where a jury determines facts that, if found, increase the defendant's sentence beyond the statutory maximum), *rev'd on other grounds*, ___ N.C. ___, 743 S.E.2d 173 (2013) (per curiam); *see also* Jamie Markham, *Confrontation Rights Apply at Sentencing in Noncapital Cases*, N.C. Crim. L., UNC Sch. of Gov't Blog (Nov. 23, 2010), http://nccriminallaw.sog.unc.edu/?p=1771; Shea Denning, *What's Blakely Got to Do with It? Sentencing in Impaired Driving Cases after Melendez-Diaz*, N.C. Crim. L., UNC Sch. of Gov't Blog (July 24, 2009), http://sogweb.sog.unc.edu/blogs/ncclaw/?p=567.

158. State v. Mack, 81 N.C. App. 578, 584–85 (1986).

159. *Id.*

160. *Id.*

161. *Id.* at 585.

162. State v. Gunter, 111 N.C. App. 621, 628 (1993).

3. Negligent Driving that Led to a Reportable Accident

A "reportable crash" is one that results in (1) a person's injury or death, (2) property damage of at least $1,000, or (3) property damage to a vehicle seized pursuant to G.S. 20-28.3 for forfeiture in an impaired driving case.[163] A crash is any event that results in injury or property damage attributable directly to the motion of a motor vehicle or its load.[164] For this factor to be present, the accident must have occurred during the same act of driving as the impaired driving offense for which the defendant is being sentenced.

4. Driving by the Defendant While His or Her Driver's License Was Revoked

Unlike the related grossly aggravating factor in G.S. 20-179(c)(2), this factor apparently does not require proof of each element of driving while license revoked under G.S. 20-28, though it is not clear precisely what the State may prove short of a violation of G.S. 20-28(a) to establish this factor.[165] In addition, this factor applies when the defendant commits a covered offense while driving while his or her license is revoked for something other than an impaired driving revocation.

5. A Specified Conviction Record

For the aggravating factor in G.S. 20-179(d)(5) to apply, the defendant must have a driving record consisting of:

(a) two or more prior convictions of a motor vehicle offense not involving impaired driving that require the assessment of at least three driver's license points;[166]
(b) two or more prior convictions of a motor vehicle offense not involving impaired driving that, standing alone, would require or authorize NC DMV to revoke the person's license;
(c) one conviction described in (a) and one conviction described in (b); or
(d) one or more prior convictions of an offense involving impaired driving that occurred more than seven years before the date of the offense for which the defendant is being sentenced, thus making the conviction(s) too remote to qualify as grossly aggravating factors.

---

163. G.S. 20-4.01(33b).

164. *Id.* § 20-4.01(4b). "The terms collision, accident, and crash and their cognates are synonymous." *Id.*

165. *Cf.* State v. Dewalt, 209 N.C. App. 187, 190–92 (2011) (interpreting the aggravating factor of "[d]riving when the person's drivers license is revoked" set forth in G.S. 20-141.5(b)(5) for purposes of elevating the misdemeanor offense of speeding to elude arrest to a felony offense pursuant to G.S. 20-141.5 not to require proof of driving on a street or highway, as required by G.S. 20-28(a), because driving while license revoked, unlike several other aggravating factors listed in G.S. 20-141.5(b), did not incorporate a reference to the statute defining it as a crime); *see also* Shea Denning, *State v. Dewalt and Speeding to Elude*, N.C. Crim. L., UNC Sch. of Gov't Blog (Jan. 12, 2011), http://sogweb.sog.unc.edu/blogs/ncclaw/?p=1872.

166. Three driver's license points are assigned for conviction of any of the following offenses:

a. Running through a stop sign
b. Speeding in excess of 55 miles per hour
c. Failing to yield right of way
d. Running through red light
e. No driver's license or license expired more than one year
f. Failure to stop for siren
g. Driving through safety zone
h. No liability insurance
i. Failure to report accident where such report is required
j. Speeding in a school zone in excess of the posted school zone speed limit
k. Any moving violation committed while driving a commercial motor vehicle

G.S. 20-16(c).

For purposes of (a), (b), or (c) above, the final conviction date of the qualifying conviction must have been within five years of the date of the covered offense. The statute does not specify whether those convictions must occur within the five years immediately *preceding* the commission of the covered offense or whether they may occur after commission of the covered offense. The former interpretation appears to have been the shared view historically and arguably is the most straightforward reading of the statute.[167]

6. Conviction under G.S. 20-141.5 of Speeding by the Defendant While Fleeing or Attempting to Elude Apprehension

Pursuant to G.S. 20-141.5, it is a Class 1 misdemeanor to operate a motor vehicle on a street, highway, or public vehicular area while fleeing or attempting to elude a law enforcement officer who is in the lawful performance of his or her public duties. If two or more specified aggravating factors are present at the time of the offense, or if the violation causes the death of another person, the offense is elevated to a Class H felony.[168] If there are two qualifying aggravating factors and a death, the offense is a Class E felony.[169] Speeding more than 15 miles per hour over the speed limit and speeding in a school or work zone are among the aggravating factors that may lead to an offense elevation,[170] though speeding is not an element of the misdemeanor offense. The reference to "speeding" in G.S. 20-179(d)(7) likely is a reference to the caption of G.S. 20-141.5, "Speeding to elude arrest; seizure and sale of vehicles," and not a requirement that speeding be proved for the factor to apply.

For this aggravating factor to apply, the defendant must have been convicted of a violation of G.S. 20-141.5 based upon conduct that occurred during the commission of the covered offense.

7. Conviction under G.S. 20-141 of Speeding by the Defendant by at Least 30 Miles per Hour Over the Legal Limit

This aggravating factor applies when the defendant has been convicted of speeding at least 30 miles over the speed limit and the speeding occurred in the commission of the covered offense.

A person can violate the speed restrictions that apply on North Carolina roads in one of three ways: (1) by driving at a speed greater than is reasonable and prudent under existing conditions; (2) by exceeding maximum speed limits; or (3) by operating a vehicle at less than a minimum posted speed.[171] Generally speaking, speeding is an infraction—a noncriminal violation of the law—punishable by a penalty of not more than $100. Driving on a highway at a speed of more than 15 miles per hour over the speed limit or over 80 miles per hour, however, is a Class 2 misdemeanor, punishable by up to 60 days imprisonment, depending upon the person's prior record level.

Charges involving the second variety of speeding (which is commonly referred to as exceeding the posted speed) require only a determination of whether the person drove a vehicle on a highway in excess of the maximum speed limit by driving more than 15 miles per hour or by driving more than 80 miles per hour, in which case the person committed a misdemeanor criminal offense. Otherwise, the offense is an infraction.

In practice, however, in many speeding cases involving charges of exceeding the maximum speed, the process of stating the charges and determining the person's responsibility (in the case

167. Loeb & Drennan, Motor Vehicle Law, *supra* note 2, at 87.
168. G.S. 20-141.5(b), (b1).
169. *Id.* § 20-141.5(b1).
170. *Id.* §§ 20-141.5(b)(1), (6).
171. *Id.* § 20-141.

of an infraction) or guilt (in the case of a misdemeanor) is far more precise. The citation issued to a defendant often specifies the rate of speed. When a defendant pleads guilty to a speeding charge in which the specific speed is alleged, the defendant pleads not just to speeding but to driving a specific speed in a specific speed zone. If a defendant is found guilty or responsible in district court for a violation of G.S. 20-141, the judge may find the defendant guilty or responsible not only for speeding but also for driving a particular speed, which, again, is a determination that may have collateral licensure and insurance consequences. The same holds true for the jury in superior court.

8. Passing a Stopped School Bus in Violation of G.S. 20-217

The driver of any vehicle who approaches a school bus that is displaying its mechanical stop signal or flashing red light and is stopped to receive or discharge passengers must stop and remain stopped until after the mechanical stop signal has been withdrawn, the flashing red stoplights have been turned off, and the bus has started to move.[172] An exception applies for the driver of a vehicle traveling in the opposite direction from a school bus on a divided roadway.[173] This aggravating factor applies to a defendant who passes a stopped school bus in the commission of a covered offense; there is no requirement that the defendant be charged with or convicted of violating G.S. 20-217.

9. Any Other Factor that Aggravates the Seriousness of the Offense

The final aggravating factor, the so-called "catch-all," must involve conduct that occurred during the same transaction or occurrence as the covered offense.[174] It may apply, for example, when the driver behaves uncooperatively or is belligerent upon being stopped.

IV. Mitigating Factors

Mitigating factors are set forth in subsections (e)(1)–(7) of G.S. 20-179. There are eight mitigating factors (one is set forth in G.S. 20-179(e)(6a)), including a catch-all factor. The judge in both district and superior courts determines the existence of any mitigating factor. The defendant bears the burden of proving by a preponderance of the evidence that a mitigating factor exists. Except for the factors in subdivisions (4), (6), (6a), and (7), the conduct constituting the mitigating factor must occur during the same transaction or occurrence as the covered offense.

A. List of Mitigating Factors by Reference to G.S. 20-179(e) Subdivisions

1. Slight Impairment of the Defendant's Faculties, Resulting Solely from Alcohol, and an Alcohol Concentration that Did Not Exceed 0.09 at any Relevant Time after the Driving

In some ways this factor is analogous to the first aggravating factor, but it varies in one significant way. Unlike the aggravating factor, which is present if a judge determines a person to be grossly impaired even if his or her alcohol concentration is under 0.15, this factor may not be found if the person's alcohol concentration is more than 0.09. Put another way, the 0.15 alcohol concentration is not a minimum level for aggravation, but the 0.09 alcohol concentration is a maximum level for

172. *Id.* § 20-217(a).
173. *Id.* § 20-217(c).
174. *Id.* § 20-179(d)(9).

mitigation. No one with an alcohol concentration above 0.09 can be deemed slightly impaired as a matter of law. In addition, the impairment must be solely from alcohol for this factor to be present.

2. Slight Impairment of the Defendant's Faculties, Resulting Solely from Alcohol, with No Chemical Analysis Having Been Available to the Defendant

This factor and mitigating factor (1), above, are mutually exclusive. If one is present, the other is not. For this factor to be present, no chemical analysis must have been available to the defendant. A defendant who willfully refuses a chemical analysis may not claim the benefit of this factor. If drug impairment is present, this factor may not be found.

3. Driving at the Time of the Offense that Was Safe and Lawful Except for the Impairment of the Defendant's Faculties

Though there are no appellate court cases considering this factor, apparently it would apply if the defendant was stopped at a checkpoint or, perhaps, was pulled over for a registration violation, and no faulty driving was observed. It is less certain whether the factor would apply if, for instance, the defendant was stopped for an equipment violation such as the failure to have an operational brake light, a violation that creates a safety hazard unrelated to the driver's impairment. Because *lawful* driving is required, this factor apparently may not be found when a violation of the rules of the road[175] other than impaired driving has been proved.

4. A Safe Driving Record

For purposes of this mitigating factor, a safe driving record is defined as having (a) no conviction for any offense requiring the assessment of four or more driver's license points or (b) no conviction that would require or authorize the North Carolina Division of Motor Vehicles (NC DMV) to revoke the person's license.[176]

As set out in G.S. 20-16(c), convictions for the following offenses carry four or more driver's license points:

- Passing a stopped school bus
- Aggressive driving
- Reckless driving
- Hit and run, property damage only
- Following too close
- Driving on the wrong side of the road
- Illegal passing
- Failure to yield the right of way to a pedestrian pursuant to G.S. 20-158(b)(2)b.
- Failure to yield the right of way to a bicycle, motor scooter, or motorcycle

In addition, also per G.S. 20-16(c), convictions for the following offenses for violations that occur while operating a commercial motor vehicle carry four or more driver's license points:

- Rail-highway crossing violation
- Careless and reckless driving in violation of G.S. 20-140(f)
- Speeding in violation of G.S. 20-141(j3)
- Running through a stop sign

---

175. Part 10 of G.S. Chapter 20 governs the "Operation of Vehicles and Rules of the Road."
176. G.S. 20-179(e)(4).

- Speeding in excess of 55 miles per hour
- Failing to yield the right of way
- Running through a red light
- No driver's license or license expired more than one year
- Failure to stop for a siren
- Driving through a safety zone
- No liability insurance
- Failure to report an accident where such report is required
- Speeding in a school zone in excess of the posted school zone speed limit
- Possessing alcoholic beverages in the passenger area of a commercial motor vehicle

Only offenses that have a final conviction date occurring within five years of the date of the current covered offense may be considered in determining whether this factor is present. As with G.S. 20-179(d)(5), the statute fails to specify whether it encompasses only those convictions occurring in the five years immediately *preceding* the commission of the covered offense or whether convictions that occur *subsequent to* the commission of the covered offense also qualify. The former interpretation appears to have been the shared view historically and arguably is the most straightforward reading of the statute.[177]

There are some circumstances in which both the "safe driving" mitigating factor and the aggravating factor in G.S. 20-179(d)(5) based upon a defendant's record of traffic convictions will apply. For example, the mitigating factor would apply in the case of a defendant with ten prior convictions for speeding 65 miles per hour in a 55 mile per hour zone—convictions that result in the assessment of three driver's license points each but which, standing alone, cannot result in license revocation. Because each conviction requires the assessment of three driver's license points, the aggravating factor in G.S. 20-179(d)(5) also would apply.

The safe driving mitigating factor and the aggravating factor in G.S. 20-179(d)(5) are mutually exclusive in their application to convictions for which a defendant's driver's license is subject to revocation. No such conviction satisfies that prong of the mitigating factor. One such conviction precludes application of the mitigating factor. Two or more such convictions render the aggravating factor present.

On occasion, a defendant who has never been licensed and for whom NC DMV has no record of convictions will claim that this mitigating factor applies. No appellate court has considered this issue. Nevertheless, construing the "safe driving record" mitigator as applicable to a person who has no official driving record arguably contradicts the legislature's apparent desire to mitigate punishment for drivers with demonstrably safe driving histories.

---

177. Loeb & Drennan, Motor Vehicle Law, *supra* note 2, at 87.

5. Impairment of the Defendant's Faculties, Caused Primarily by a Lawfully Prescribed Drug for an Existing Medical Condition, and the Amount of Drug Taken Was within the Prescribed Dosage

While the fact that a person committed the offense of impaired driving while impaired by alcohol or a drug that he or she was legally entitled to use is not a defense to a charge of impaired driving,[178] a defendant's impairment from a prescribed dose of a drug lawfully prescribed for a medical condition is a mitigating factor at sentencing.[179]

6. Voluntary Submission to a Substance Abuse Assessment and to Treatment

This factor applies if a defendant, after being charged with the covered offense, voluntarily submits to a mental health facility for treatment and, if recommended by the facility, voluntarily participates in the recommended treatment. There is no requirement that the defendant have completed treatment by the date of sentencing for the mitigating factor to apply, though the defendant must have participated in any treatment or education required up to the time of sentencing. The court of appeals in *State v. Gunter*[180] determined that the mitigating factor was not satisfied by the defendant's obtaining of a substance abuse assessment the day before sentencing, under which he had not yet participated in treatment.[181]

The mitigating factor does not require that the assessment be performed by an individual authorized to conduct a substance abuse assessment under G.S. 20-17.6.[182] If, however, a defendant desires the voluntary assessment to double as the mandatory assessment required after conviction, as a condition of both probation and restoration of a driver's license, the assessment must be performed by a qualified individual.[183]

6a. Completion of a Substance Abuse Assessment, Compliance with Its Recommendations, and 60 Days of Continuous Abstinence from Alcohol Consumption, as Proven by a Continuous Alcohol Monitoring (CAM) System

This factor requires completion of a substance abuse assessment and compliance with its recommendations, as is required for mitigating factor (6), above, and contains the additional requirement that the defendant simultaneously maintain sixty days of continuous abstinence from alcohol consumption, as proven by a continuous alcohol monitoring (CAM) system. A CAM system is "a device that is worn by a person that can detect, monitor, record, and report the amount of alcohol within

---

178. G.S. 20-138.1(b).

179. *Id.* § 20-179(e)(5).

180. 111 N.C. App. 621 (1993).

181. *Id.* at 627.

182. G.S. 20-17.6 requires that the substance abuse assessment be conducted by one of the entities authorized by the Department of Health and Human Services to conduct assessments. The following individuals are authorized to conduct such assessments: (1) a certified substance abuse counselor; (2) a licensed clinical addiction specialist; (3) a person licensed by the North Carolina Medical Board or the North Carolina Psychology Board; (4) a physician certified by the American Society of Addiction Medicine. *See id.* § 122C-142.1(b1).

183. *Id.* § 20-17.6(c). G.S. 20-17.6 does not specifically authorize pretrial assessments to satisfy the requirement for a post-conviction assessment. Nevertheless, many courts, as well as the Department of Health and Human Services, consider qualified pretrial assessments as satisfying this requirement.

the wearer's system over a continuous 24-hour daily basis."[184] For its use to establish this mitigating factor, the system must be of a type approved by the Division of Adult Correction.[185]

7. Any Other Factor that Mitigates the Seriousness of the Offense

This factor is similar to the catch-all aggravating factor, with one notable exception: It is not limited to conduct that occurred during the commission of the covered offense.[186] The universe of qualifying conduct is, however, limited to conduct that in some way mitigates the seriousness of the offense.

It is not a mitigating factor that the driver of the vehicle was suffering from alcoholism, drug addiction, diminished capacity, or mental disease or defect.[187] Evidence of these matters may be received at the sentencing hearing, however, and used by the judge to formulate the terms and conditions of a sentence under the applicable punishment level.

V. Levels of Punishment

As noted earlier, G.S. 20-179 sets forth six levels of punishment applicable to covered offenses committed December 1, 2011, or later: Aggravated Level One, Level One, Level Two, Level Three, Level Four, and Level Five. As with earlier sections, the discussion that follows is applicable to offenses committed on or after this date unless otherwise specified. A summary of the six levels of punishment and the sanctions applicable for each, keyed to date of offense, may be found in Tables 5.1 through 5.3. A summary of the five punishment levels and their accompanying sanctions for offenses committed before December 1, 2011, is set forth in Table 5.4.

A. Aggravated Level One

Aggravated Level One punishment is the most severe of the punishments applicable to a covered offense. If three or more grossly aggravating factors apply for a covered offense committed December 1, 2011, or later, the judge must impose punishment at the Aggravated Level One level (hereinafter Level A1).[188] A defendant sentenced at Level A1 may be fined up to $10,000 and must be sentenced to a term of imprisonment that includes a minimum term of not less than 12 months and a maximum term of not more than 36 months. The term of imprisonment may be suspended only if a condition of special probation is imposed to require the defendant to serve a term of imprisonment of at least 120 days. If the defendant is placed on probation, the judge must require as a condition of probation that the defendant (1) abstain from alcohol consumption for a minimum of 120 days to a maximum of the term of probation, as verified by a continuous alcohol monitoring (CAM) system and (2) obtain a substance abuse assessment and the education or treatment required by G.S. 20-17.6.

---

184. *Id.* § 15A-1343.3(a); *see also* Ames Alexander, *DWI Tool Is Curbed in NC*, News & Observer, Aug. 13, 2010, www.newsobserver.com/2010/08/13/626823/dwi-tool-is-curbed-in-nc.html (describing technology and chronicling past controversy regarding use of CAM).

185. G.S. 20-179(e)(6a).

186. *See id.* § 20-179(e)(7).

187. *Id.* § 20-179(f).

188. For covered offenses committed before December 1, 2011, Level One is the most severe level of punishment and must be imposed when at least two grossly aggravating factors are present.

A defendant sentenced at Level A1 is not eligible for parole.[189] However, the defendant must be released to post-release supervision four months before the expiration of his or her maximum term.[190] During this four-month period of post-release supervision, the defendant must abstain from alcohol consumption, as verified by a CAM system.[191] As noted in the earlier discussion of the mitigating factor for abstinence from alcohol, a CAM system is "a device that is worn by a person that can detect, monitor, record, and report the amount of alcohol within the wearer's system over a continuous 24-hour daily basis."[192] The system used must be of a type approved by the Division of Adult Correction.[193]

As explained later in this chapter,[194] a defendant sentenced to a term of imprisonment for a covered offense is eligible to have his or her sentences reduced by good time credit. State corrections regulations award credit to persons "convicted of Driving While Impaired" at the rate of one day of credit for each day spent in custody without a violation, and Level A1 sentences are not explicitly excepted from these provisions.[195]

Nevertheless, the North Carolina Attorney General's Office has opined in an advisory letter to the general counsel for the Department of Public Safety that "no sentence credits are available" to a defendant sentenced at Aggravated Level One.[196] The attorney general reasons that "[t]he exclusion of Aggravated Level One impaired driving offenses from parole indicates the legislature's intent that no sentence credits apply" and that an "offender is simply released on post-release supervision four months before completion of the maximum term."[197]

The Division of Adult Correction has accordingly determined that good time credit does not apply to Level A1 sentences. This means that a defendant sentenced at Level A1 serves the maximum term of imprisonment imposed, less four months. As a result, regardless of how he or she behaves, a defendant sentenced to 36 months imprisonment for Level A1 DWI will be released to post-release supervision after serving 32 months. A defendant sentenced to 12 months imprisonment for Level A1 DWI will be released to post-release supervision after serving 8 months' imprisonment.

B. Level One

For covered offenses committed before December 1, 2011, Level One was the most severe level of punishment, and it applied whenever there were at least two grossly aggravating factors. For covered offenses committed on or after December 1, 2011, Level One punishment applies if the grossly aggravating factor under G.S. 20-179(c)(4) (child, person with the mental capacity of a child, or disabled

---

189. G.S. 20-179(f3).

190. *Id.* (providing that a Level A1 defendant, upon release, must be supervised by the Section of Community Supervision of the Division of Adult Correction under and subject to the post-release supervision provisions of G.S. Chapter 15A, Article 84A). For Level A1 sentences imposed before January 1, 2015, defendants must be supervised by the Section of Prisons of the Division of Adult Correction. *See* G.S. 20-179(f3) (2013).

191. G.S. 20-179(f3).

192. See *supra* note 184.

193. G.S. 20-179(f3), (h1).

194. *See infra* section VIII.B.2.

195. *See* State of North Carolina, Dep't of Pub. Safety, Div. of Prisons, Policy & Procedure Manual (issue date 9/5/13), Ch. B. (Inmate Conduct Rules, Discipline), Sec. .0100 (Sentence Credits), p. 2, www.doc.state.nc.us/dop/policy_procedure_manual/b0100.pdf.

196. Advisory Letter from Assistant Attorney General Elizabeth Parsons and Special Deputy Attorney General Joseph Finarelli to Casandra White, General Counsel, North Carolina Department of Public Safety 2 (June 27, 2012) (on file with author).

197. *Id.* at 3.

person in vehicle) is found[198] or if two other grossly aggravating factors apply.[199] A defendant sentenced to Level One punishment may be fined up to $4,000 and must be sentenced to a term of imprisonment that includes a minimum term of at least 30 days and a maximum term of not more than 24 months. The term of imprisonment may be suspended only if a condition of special probation is imposed to require the defendant to serve a term of imprisonment of at least 30 days. If a defendant is placed on probation, the judge must require as a condition of probation that the defendant obtain a substance abuse assessment and the education or treatment required by G.S. 20-17.6.[200] For offenses committed before December 1, 2011, the judge also may impose a condition of probation requiring that the defendant abstain from alcohol consumption for a minimum of 30 days to a maximum of the term of probation as verified by a CAM system.[201]

1. Amendments Effective December 1, 2012

For covered offenses committed on or after December 1, 2012, and sentenced at Level One, a judge may "reduce the minimum term of imprisonment required to a term of not less than 10 days if a condition of special probation is imposed to require that a defendant abstain from alcohol consumption and be monitored by a continuous alcohol monitoring system, of a type approved by the Division of Adult Correction of the Department of Public Safety, for a period of not less than 120 days."[202] If a defendant is monitored on an approved CAM system during the pretrial period, up to 60 days of pretrial monitoring may be credited against the 120-day monitoring requirement for probation.[203] The reference to 10 days as the minimum term of imprisonment, rather than the *minimum term of imprisonment that must be imposed as a condition of special probation*, gives rise to a question about whether a judge may satisfy the mandatory statutory sentencing provisions in G.S. 20-179(g) by imposing a 10-day sentence that is suspended on the condition that the defendant abstain from alcohol consumption and submit to CAM for 120 days. This seems unlikely to have been the legislature's intent. First, the authorization for a sentence suspended on these conditions appears directly after the authorization for suspension of a sentence on condition that a term of imprisonment of at least 30 days be imposed as a condition of special probation. Second, if the 10 days refers to the underlying minimum term of imprisonment rather than a minimum period of imprisonment as a condition of special probation, Level One punishment can be satisfied by a defendant's service of 10 days of imprisonment upon his or her refusal to abstain from alcohol, be monitored by CAM, or comply with any other condition of probation. Finally, such a construction would fail to account for the General Assembly's use of the term "special probation," a term defined by G.S. 15A-1351 as a type of probationary sentence in which the court requires, among other conditions, that the defendant

---

198. If, for an offense committed December 1, 2011, or later, the grossly aggravating factor in G.S. 20-179(c)(4) is found along with two or more additional grossly aggravating factors, Level A1 punishment is required.

199. G.S. 20-179(g).

200. *Id.*

201. *Id.* § 20-179(h1). The defendant's abstinence from alcohol must be verified by a CAM system of a type approved by the Division of Adult Correction. *Id.* For offenses committed on or after December 1, 2007, but before December 1, 2011, the maximum period for which CAM could be imposed was 60 days. *See* G.S. 20-179(h1) (2009); S.L. 2007-165. Other provisions, repealed for offenses committed on or after December 1, 2011, limited the total cost of CAM to the defendant to $1,000 and prohibited CAM if the court found that the defendant should not be required to pay for it unless the costs were paid by the local government entity responsible for the defendant's incarceration. *See* G.S. 20-179(h1), (h2) (2009); S.L. 2011-191.

202. S.L. 2012-146 (H 494), *as amended by* S.L. 2012-194 (S 847) (amending G.S. 20-179(g)) (July 12, 2012); *see also* Shea Denning, *Authorization for Continuous Alcohol Monitoring Expanded by S.L. 2012-146*, N.C. Crim. L., UNC Sch. of Gov't Blog (July 17, 2012), http://nccriminallaw.sog.unc.edu/?p=3726.

203. S.L. 2012-146, cited in full immediately above.

submit to a period or periods of imprisonment at times and intervals within the period of probation.[204] Because it seems nearly certain that the legislature intended for the alcohol-abstinence and CAM condition to be coupled with a requirement that the defendant serve 10 days of imprisonment as a condition of special probation, Table 5.2 reflects this interpretation.

A court may not impose CAM pursuant to G.S. 20-179(g) if it finds good cause that the defendant should not be required to pay the costs of CAM "unless the local governmental entity responsible for the incarceration of the defendant in the local confinement facility agrees to pay the costs of the system."[205]

C. Level Two

For offenses committed on or after December 1, 2011, the judge must impose Level Two punishment if only one grossly aggravating factor applies and it is not the factor set forth in G.S. 20-179(c)(4).[206] For offenses committed before December 1, 2011, Level Two punishment is required whenever only one grossly aggravating factor is present.[207] A defendant subject to Level Two punishment may be fined up to $2,000 and must be sentenced to a term of imprisonment that includes a minimum term of not less than 7 days and a maximum term of not more than 12 months. The term of imprisonment may be suspended only if a condition of special probation is imposed to require the defendant to serve a term of imprisonment of at least 7 days.[208] If a defendant is placed on probation, the judge must require as a condition of probation that the defendant obtain a substance abuse assessment and the education or treatment required by G.S. 20-17.6.[209] For offenses committed on or after December 1, 2011, the judge also may impose a condition of probation requiring that the defendant abstain from alcohol consumption for a minimum of 30 days to a maximum of the term of probation, as verified by a CAM system.[210]

1. Amendments Effective October 1, 2013

Federal law requires that a portion of federal highway funds that would otherwise be apportioned to a state be reserved from any state that has not enacted a repeat intoxicated driver law.[211] These state laws must require that a person convicted of a second impaired driving offense be required to perform at least 30 days of community service or be imprisoned for at least five days. A person convicted of a third or subsequent impaired driving offense must be required to perform at least 60 days of com-

---

204. *See* G.S. 15A-1351(a). It bears noting, however, that the General Assembly used the term "special probation" elsewhere in S.L. 2012-146 to refer to a probationary sentence for a Level Two offender that did not require periods of imprisonment. *See infra* section V.C.1.

205. G.S. 20-179(k4); *see* S.L. 2012-146 (H 494), *as amended by* S.L. 2012-194 (S 847) (enacting new G.S. 20-179(k4), effective for offenses committed on or after December 1, 2012) (July 12, 2012).

206. G.S. 20-179(c).

207. *Id.*

208. *Id.* § 20-179(h).

209. *Id.*

210. *Id.* § 20-179(h1). The defendant's abstinence from alcohol must be verified by a CAM system of a type approved by the Division of Adult Correction. *Id.* For offenses committed on or after December 1, 2007, but before December 1, 2011, the maximum period for which CAM could be imposed was 60 days. *See* G.S. 20-179(h1) (2009); S.L. 2007-165. Other provisions, repealed for offenses committed on or after December 1, 2011, limited the total cost of CAM to the defendant to $1,000 and prohibited CAM if the court found that the defendant should not be required to pay for it unless the costs were paid by the local government entity responsible for the defendant's incarceration. *See* G.S. 20-179(h1), (h2) (2009); S.L. 2011-191.

211. 23 U.S.C. §§ 164(a)(4), (b)(2).

munity service or serve at least 10 days of imprisonment. The North Carolina legislature amended G.S. 20-179(h) in 2013 to satisfy these minimum requirements.

For covered offenses committed on or after October 1, 2013, G.S. 20-179(h) (Level Two punishment for various DWI convictions) provides that if the defendant is subject to Level Two punishment based on grossly aggravating factors in G.S. 20-179(c)(1) (prior conviction) or -179(c)(2) (driving while license revoked for an impaired driving revocation), the prior DWI conviction occurred within five years before the date of the offense for which the defendant is being sentenced, and the judge suspends all active terms of imprisonment and imposes abstention from alcohol as verified by a continuous alcohol monitoring system, then the judge must also impose as a special probation condition that the defendant must complete 240 hours of community service.[212]

2. Amendments Effective December 1, 2012

For covered offenses committed on or after December 1, 2012, and sentenced at Level Two, a judge may suspend the sentence if he or she imposes a condition of special probation requiring that the defendant serve a term of imprisonment of at least 7 days or that the defendant "abstain from consuming alcohol for at least 90 consecutive days, as verified by a continuous alcohol monitoring system, of a type approved by the Division of Adult Correction of the Department of Public Safety."[213] If the defendant is monitored on an approved CAM system during the pretrial period, up to 60 days of pretrial monitoring may be credited against the 90-day monitoring requirement for probation.[214]

A court may not impose CAM pursuant to G.S. 20-179(h) if it finds good cause that the defendant should not be required to pay the costs of CAM "unless the local governmental entity responsible for the incarceration of the defendant in the local confinement facility agrees to pay the costs of the system."[215]

D. Level Three

Level Three punishment is required if the judge determines that the aggravating factors "substantially outweigh" the mitigating factors.[216] A defendant subject to Level Three punishment may be fined up to $1,000 and must be sentenced to a term of imprisonment that includes a minimum term of not less than 72 hours and a maximum term of not more than 6 months.[217] The term of imprisonment may be suspended but must include the condition that the defendant (1) be imprisoned for a term of at least 72 hours as a condition of special probation; (2) perform community service for a term of at least 72 hours; or (3) any combination of these conditions.[218]

The Division of Adult Correction of the Department of Public Safety is authorized by G.S. 143B-708 to "conduct a community service program" to provide oversight of offenders ordered to perform

---

212. S.L. 2013-348 (S 659).

213. S.L. 2012-146 (H 494), *as amended by* S.L. 2012-194 (S 847) (amending G.S. 20-179(h)) (July 12, 2012). As noted earlier, see *supra* section V.B.1, a probationary sentence that does not require service of a term of imprisonment is not "special probation" as that term is defined in G.S. 15A-1351. Thus, a condition requiring that a defendant abstain from alcohol consumption for 90 days, as verified by CAM, that is not coupled with a requirement that the defendant serve intervals of imprisonment is more appropriately characterized as a *special condition of probation* rather than as "special probation."

214. S.L. 2012-146 (H 494), *as amended by* S.L. 2012-194 (S 847) (amending G.S. 20-179(h)) (July 12, 2012).

215. G.S. 20-179(k4); *see* S.L. 2012-146 (H 494), *as amended by* S.L. 2012-194 (S 847) (enacting new G.S. 20-179(k4), effective for offenses committed on or after December 1, 2012).

216. G.S. 20-179(f)(1).

217. *Id.*

218. *Id.*

community service as a condition of probation for criminal violations, "including driving while impaired violations under G.S. 20-138.1."[219] The program assigns offenders to perform service in the local community. Each defendant who participates in the program must pay a $250 fee.[220]

The community service program for persons sentenced under G.S. 20-179(i), (j), or (k) formerly was codified in G.S. 20-179.4, which made clear that the community service requirements for covered offenses had to be served under the supervision of community service coordinators as part of the statutorily prescribed program. G.S. 20-179.4 was repealed in 2009,[221] and references to the community service program for impaired driving offenders were combined with provisions governing the Department of Correction's community service program for all offenders.[222] The provisions were again recodified in 2011[223] in G.S. 143B-708, which provides:

> The Division of Adult Correction of the Department of Public Safety may conduct a community service program. The program shall provide oversight of offenders placed under the supervision of the Section of Community Corrections of the Division of Adult Correction and ordered to perform community service hours for criminal violations, including driving while impaired violations under G.S. 20-138.1. This program shall assign offenders, either on supervised or on unsupervised probation, to perform service to the local community in an effort to promote the offender's rehabilitation and to provide services that help restore or improve the community. The program shall provide appropriate work site placement for offenders ordered to perform community service hours. The Division may adopt rules to conduct the program. Each offender shall be required to comply with the rules adopted for the program.[224]

The repeal of G.S. 20-179.4 has given rise to an argument that while "community service" under G.S. 20-179 may be satisfied by service performed pursuant to the statewide community service program, qualifying community service also may be performed outside of the program. This issue arises most often in the case of defendants who reside outside of North Carolina and who are sentenced to probation at Levels Three, Four, or Five. For obvious practical reasons, many such defendants would prefer to avoid returning to North Carolina to satisfy community service requirements.[225] It seems unlikely that the recodification of the community service references in 2009 and 2011 reflects the legislature's intent to eliminate the long-standing requirement that community service be performed through the community service program. Moreover, covered offenses are subject to the probation provisions of Article 82 of G.S. Chapter 15A, which include, as a special condition of probation, "community or reparation service under the supervision of the Section of Community Corrections of the Division of Adult Correction,"[226] further indicating that community service as a condition of probation means community service under the program established pursuant to G.S. 143B-708.

---

219. *Id.* § 143B-708(a).

220. *Id.* § 143B-708(c).

221. S.L. 2009-372.

222. *See* G.S. 143B-262.4 (2009) (providing that the Department of Correction may conduct a community service program that "shall provide oversight of offenders placed under the supervision of the Division of Community Corrections and ordered to perform community service hours for criminal violations, including driving while impaired violations under G.S. 20-138.1").

223. *See* S.L. 2011-145.

224. *See* G.S. 143B-708(a).

225. And for equally obvious reasons, such defendants frequently prefer community service to jail—the other condition that can satisfy the requirements for a suspended sentence.

226. G.S. 15A-1343(b1)(6).

If a defendant sentenced at Level Three is placed on probation, the judge must require as a condition of probation that the defendant obtain a substance abuse assessment and the education or treatment required by G.S. 20-17.6.[227]

E. Level Four

Level Four punishment is required if the judge determines that there are no aggravating and mitigating factors or that aggravating factors are "substantially counterbalanced by mitigating factors."[228] A defendant subject to Level Four punishment may be fined up to $500 and must be sentenced to a term of imprisonment that includes a minimum term of not less than 48 hours and a maximum term of not more than 120 days.[229] The term of imprisonment may be suspended but must include the condition that the defendant (1) be imprisoned for a term of 48 hours as a condition of special probation; (2) perform community service for a term of 48 hours; or (3) any combination of these conditions.[230] Note that the conditions of probation for a Level Four sentence, unlike Levels A1 through Three, specify the precise number of hours that must be served as a condition of special probation or for which community service must be performed. Those hours may not be raised or lowered by the judge.[231]

If a defendant sentenced at Level Four is placed on probation, the judge must require as a condition of probation that the defendant obtain a substance abuse assessment and the education or treatment required by G.S. 20-17.6.[232]

---

227. *Id.* § 20-179(i).

228. *Id.* § 20-179(f)(2). The court of appeals in *State v. Green,* 209 N.C. App. 669, 681 (2011), characterized Level Four punishment as "tantamount to a sentence within the presumptive range;" thus, the *Green* court determined that no *Blakely* error (see the section entitled "Introduction," *supra,* for further context) occurred when the defendant was punished at Level Four based on the trial court's finding of an aggravating factor not found by the jury. *Green* cited as support structured sentencing cases noting that a trial court may sentence anywhere within the presumptive range without findings other than those in the jury verdict. *Id.* at 681 (citing State v. Norris, 360 N.C. 507, 513 (2006)). *See also* State v. Hagans, 177 N.C. App. 17, 31–32 (2006). Nevertheless, the treatment of mitigating factors under G.S. 20-179 differs in an important respect from their treatment under structured sentencing. In a structured sentencing case, a judge may, but is not required to, impose a sentence within the mitigated range upon finding that mitigating factors are present and are sufficient to outweigh any aggravating factors. In contrast, under G.S. 20-179(f)(3), a judge must impose a Level Five sentence if he or she determines that the mitigating factors substantially outweigh any aggravating factors. As noted above, Level Four punishment is prescribed only if there are no aggravating or mitigating factors or if aggravating factors are substantially counterbalanced by mitigating factors. Thus, at a sentencing hearing for a covered offense involving one or more mitigating factors, a judge's consideration of an aggravating factor not found by the jury does, in fact, expose a defendant to enhanced punishment under G.S. 20-179.

The court of appeals recognized this distinction in State v. Geisslercrain, ___ N.C. App. ___, 756 S.E.2d 92 (2014). The *Geisslercrain* court explained that when only aggravating factors are present, the trial court must impose a Level Three punishment; when only mitigating factors are present, the trial court must impose a Level Five punishment; and when no aggravating or mitigating factors are present or when such factors substantially counterbalance one another, the trial court must impose a Level Four punishment. *Geisslercrain* held that the trial court erred in sentencing the defendant to Level Four punishment based on a single aggravating factor that was found by the judge and not the jury as required by *Blakely v. Washington,* 542 U.S. 296 (2004), and by G.S. 20-179 itself. The appellate court explained that given the absence of any properly found aggravating factors, the trial court "had no discretion but to sentence Defendant to a Level Five punishment." *Geisslercrain,* ___ N.C. App. at ___, 756 S.E.2d at 97.

229. G.S. 20-179(j).

230. *Id.*

231. *See* State v. Magee, 75 N.C. App. 357 (1985).

232. G.S. 20-179(j).

F. Level Five

Level Five punishment is required when the mitigating factors substantially outweigh any aggravating factors.[233] A defendant subject to Level Five punishment may be fined up to $200 and must be sentenced to a term of imprisonment that includes a minimum term of not less than 24 hours and a maximum term of not more than 60 days.[234] The term of imprisonment may be suspended on condition that the defendant (1) be imprisoned for a term of 24 hours as a condition of special probation; (2) perform community service for a term of 24 hours; or (3) any combination of those conditions.[235]

If a defendant sentenced at Level Five is placed on probation, the judge must require as a condition of probation that the defendant obtain a substance abuse assessment and the education or treatment required by G.S. 20-17.6.[236]

G. Aider and Abettor Punishment

As a rule, a person who aids and abets another to commit a covered offense is him or herself guilty of the principal offense.[237] However, because the sentencing factors are focused on the conduct of the driver, they are difficult to apply to a person convicted of a covered offense as an aider and abettor. Accordingly, G.S. 20-179 provides that a person convicted of impaired driving under G.S. 20-138.1 under the common law concept of aiding and abetting is subject to Level Five punishment.[238] In such a case, the judge need not make any findings of grossly aggravating, aggravating, or mitigating factors.[239]

VI. Probationary Sentences

A. Incidents of Probation

Any lawful condition of probation may be imposed under any level of punishment for a covered offense.[240] Among the permissible conditions of probation is that the defendant "[s]atisfy any other conditions determined by the court to be reasonably related to his rehabilitation."[241] Courts have substantial discretion in devising conditions under this section.[242] The appellate courts have upheld conditions of probation in impaired driving cases preventing the defendant from driving,[243] preventing the defendant from being present during certain hours at an establishment licensed to sell

---

233. *Id.* § 20-179(f)(3).
234. *Id.* § 20-179(k).
235. *Id.* §§ 20-179(k)(1)–(4).
236. *Id.* § 20-179(k).
237. For a general discussion of the common law concept of aiding and abetting, see SMITH, NORTH CAROLINA CRIMES, *supra* note 121, at 31–34.
238. G.S. 20-179(f1). Note that Section 20-179(f1) applies only to the covered offense of impaired driving under G.S. 20-138.1.
239. *Id.*
240. *Id.* §§ 20-179(f3), (g), (h), (i), (j), (k); *see id.* § 15A-1343 (setting out permissible conditions of probation).
241. *Id.* § 15A-1343(b1)(10).
242. State v. Harrington, 78 N.C. App. 39, 48 (1985).
243. State v. Smith, 233 N.C. 68 (1950) (upholding condition preventing a person from driving on the highways for 12 months); State v. Cooper, 304 N.C. 180 (1981) (upholding condition preventing a probationer from operating a motor vehicle during certain hours).

alcoholic beverages,[244] and preventing the defendant from using, possessing, or consuming alcohol.[245] One condition traditionally imposed and previously sanctioned by the court of appeals—mandatory participation in a Twelve-Step program such as Alcoholics Anonymous or Narcotics Anonymous[246]—has been held unconstitutional by several federal courts of appeals on the basis that it violates the First Amendment's clause prohibiting the establishment of religion.[247]

B. Continuous Alcohol Monitoring

For covered offenses committed on or after December 1, 2011, continuous alcohol monitoring (CAM) is required as a condition of probation under Aggravated Level One[248] and is authorized as a condition of probation for Level One and Level Two punishment.[249] For covered impaired driving offenses committed on or after December 1, 2012, new G.S. 20-179(k2) permits a judge to order "as a condition of special probation" for any level of punishment under G.S. 20-179 that "the defendant abstain from alcohol consumption, as verified by a continuous alcohol monitoring system, of a type approved by the Division of Adult Correction of the Department of Public Safety."[250] As noted earlier, the reference to alcohol abstinence and CAM as a "condition of special probation" does not square with the meaning ascribed to the term "special probation" in G.S. 15A-1351.[251]

In addition, for covered offenses committed on or after December 1, 2012, G.S. 20-179(k3) permits a court in its sentencing order to authorize a probation officer to require a defendant to submit to CAM for assessment purposes if the defendant is required, as a condition of probation, not to consume alcohol and the probation officer believes the defendant is consuming alcohol.[252] If the probation officer orders the defendant to submit to CAM pursuant to this provision, the defendant must bear the costs of CAM.[253]

A court may not impose CAM pursuant to G.S. 20-179(k2) or (k3) if it finds good cause that the defendant should not be required to pay the costs of CAM "unless the local governmental entity responsible for the incarceration of the defendant in the local confinement facility agrees to pay the costs of the system."[254]

C. Limits on Special Probation

While each level of punishment under G.S. 20-179 requires that probationary sentences contain specified conditions—including, in the case of Levels A1, One, and Two, a mandatory term of imprisonment as a condition of special probation—G.S. 20-179 does not specify the maximum term of imprisonment that may be imposed as a condition of special probation. That limitation is established

244. *Harrington*, 78 N.C. App. at 48.

245. State v. James, 166 N.C. App. 761 (2004).

246. State v. McGill, 114 N.C. App. 479, 483–84 (1994).

247. *See* Jamie Markham, *Does Mandatory AA/NA Violate the First Amendment?*, N.C. Crim. L., UNC Sch. of Gov't Blog (Oct. 16, 2009), http://sogweb.sog.unc.edu/blogs/ncclaw/?p=784&print=1.

248. G.S. 20-179(f3).

249. *Id.* § 20-179(h1).

250. *Id.* § 20-179(k2); *see also* S.L. 2012-146 (H 494), *as amended by* S.L. 2012-194 (S 847) (enacting new G.S. 20-179(k2), effective for offenses committed on or after December 1, 2012) (July 12, 2012).

251. See *supra* section V.B.1.

252. G.S. 20-179(k3); *see* S.L. 2012-146 (H 494), *as amended by* S.L. 2012-194 (S 847) (enacting new G.S. 20-179(k3), effective for offenses committed on or after December 1, 2012).

253. *Id.*

254. *Id.* § 20-179(k4); *see* S.L. 2012-146 (H 494), *as amended by* S.L. 2012-194 (S 847) (enacting new G.S. 20-179(k4), effective for offenses committed on or after December 1, 2012).

by G.S. 15A-1351(a), which requires that "[f]or probationary sentences for impaired driving under G.S. 20-138.1, the total of all periods of confinement imposed as an incident of special probation, but not including an activated suspended sentence, shall not exceed one-fourth the maximum penalty allowed by law."[255] This rule differs from that applicable in structured sentencing, which limits a period of special probation to no more than one-fourth of the sentence imposed.[256] It is not entirely clear whether the maximum penalty allowed by law under G.S. 15A-1351(a) is the maximum for any level of impaired driving (3 years, which would result in a 9-month maximum period of special probation) or the maximum penalty for the level at which the defendant was convicted. The latter interpretation seems the one most likely intended by the legislature as, under the former interpretation, the limitation imposed by G.S. 15A-1351(a) would exceed the statutory maximum for covered offenses sentenced at Levels Three, Four, or Five.[257]

D. Length of Probation

The period of probation initially imposed for a covered offense may not exceed five years.[258] The period may be extended with the consent of the defendant beyond the original period (1) for the purpose of allowing the defendant to complete restitution or (2) to allow the defendant to continue medical or psychiatric treatment ordered as a condition of probation.[259] The period of the extension shall not exceed three years beyond the original period of probation and may be ordered only in the last six months of the original period of probation.[260]

E. Substance Abuse Assessment

When a defendant is sentenced to probation for a covered offense, a substance abuse assessment and completion of recommended education or treatment must be required as a condition of probation.[261] The required assessment and education or treatment for these sentences is the same as that required for a defendant whose license is revoked upon conviction of certain alcohol-related offenses to have his or her driver's license restored after a period of revocation.

---

255. The Criminal Procedure Act is peppered with exceptions for "impaired driving under G.S. 20-138.1," like this one, which generally are interpreted to apply to all covered offenses. *See* G.S. 15A-1351(a) (setting forth permissible periods of confinement for special probation "[f]or probationary sentences for impaired driving under G.S. 20-138.1" that differ from those for other criminal offenses); *id.* § 15A-1351(b) (providing that sentencing for a felony or misdemeanor "other than impaired driving under G.S. 20-138.1" that occurred on or after the effective date of G.S. Chapter 15A, Article 81B is subject thereto); *id.* § 15A-1340.10 (providing that structured sentencing under Article 81B "applies to criminal offenses . . . other than impaired driving under G.S. 20-138.1"). Absent that interpretation, offenses other than impaired driving under G.S. 20-138.1 sentenced under G.S. 20-179 would be subject to provisions of the Structured Sentencing Act that conflict with G.S. 20-179.

256. *Id.* § 15A-1351(a). In addition, confinement as a condition of special probation ordered for criminal offenses other than "impaired driving under G.S. 20-138.1" may not be required beyond two years of conviction. *Id.* There is no such time limitation on special probation confinement pursuant to a probationary sentence for "impaired driving under G.S. 20-138.1," a reference that, as discussed *supra* note 259, likely includes all covered offenses sentenced under G.S. 20-179.

257. *See* Jamie Markham, *Sentence Reduction Credits and Parole for DWI Inmates*, N.C. Crim. L., UNC Sch. of Gov't Blog (Jan. 13, 2010), http://sogweb.sog.unc.edu/blogs/ncclaw/?p=988 (stating that construing the "maximum penalty allowed by law for the offense" under G.S. 15A-1371 to mean the maximum punishment for the applicable level of punishment under G.S. 20-179 makes sense in the context of calculating parole eligibility).

258. G.S. 15A-1342(a).

259. *Id.*

260. *Id.*

261. *Id.* §§ 20-179(g), (h), (i), (j), (k).

These assessments must be completed by facilities authorized by the state Department of Health and Human Services.[262] An assessment consists of a face-to-face clinical interview, administration of an approved standardized test to determine chemical dependency, review of the person's driving record, and verification of the person's alcohol concentration at the time of the offense.[263] After the assessment is completed, the facility recommends the level of service to be completed, which can range in intensity from completion of a sixteen-hour alcohol and drug education traffic school (ADETS)—the least intensive requirement—to inpatient treatment.[264]

ADETS—the resulting recommendation in 20 percent of the assessments performed in the 2012–13 fiscal year—is recommended if all of the following apply:[265]

- the assessment does not identify a "substance abuse handicap,"
- the person has no previous convictions for impaired driving or driving after consuming while under 21,
- the person's alcohol concentration at the time of the offense is .14 or less,
- the person did not refuse a chemical analysis, and
- the person meets certain placement criteria established by the American Society of Addiction Medicine (ASAM).

If the above criteria are not met, one of the following four levels of treatment will be recommended (from least to most intensive): short-term outpatient treatment, longer-term outpatient treatment, day treatment/intensive outpatient treatment, or inpatient and residential treatment. The largest percentage of assessments in 2012–13 (48 percent) recommended short-term outpatient treatment.[266]

A person who obtains a substance abuse assessment for purposes of obtaining a certificate of completion for license restoration reasons (see *supra* section III.A.2.a) must pay to the assessing agency a fee of $100.[267] If the person needs more than one certificate of completion, which would be the case if his or her license was revoked for more than one conviction covered by G.S. 20-17.6, the person must pay a $100 fee for each certificate sought, though only one assessment will be performed and a single course of treatment required.[268]

The fee for ADETS is statutorily prescribed at $160.[269] Fees for treatment vary, depending upon the provider and level of treatment. In 2012–13, fees for short-term treatment averaged $360 and fees for longer-term treatment averaged $630.[270]

---

262. *Id.* § 20-17.6(c); 122C-142.1(a).

263. Title 10A of the North Carolina Administrative Code (hereinafter N.C.A.C.), Subchapter 27G, Section .3807, Subsections (b), (c).

264. *See* North Carolina Department of Health & Human Services, Division of Mental Health, Developmental Disabilities and Substance Abuse Services, Driving While Impaired (DWI) Substance Abuse Services Report: G.S. 122C-142.1 6 (Feb. 2012) (hereinafter Substance Abuse Services Report), www.ncdhhs.gov/mhddsas/statspublications/Reports/reports-generalassembly/generalreports/dwireport2-2012.pdf.

265. G.S. 122C-142.1(c); 10A N.C.A.C., ch. 27G, sec. .3813(c)(1). *See also* North Carolina Department of Health & Human Services, Division of Mental Health, Developmental Disabilities and Substance Abuse Services, Driving While Impaired (DWI) Substance Abuse Services Report: G.S. 122C-142.1 3 (Feb. 1, 2014) (hereinafter Substance Abuse Services Report 2014), http://www.ncleg.net/documentsites/committees/JLOCHHS/Handouts%20and%20Minutes%20by%20Interim/2013-14%20Interim%20HHS%20Handouts/February%2011,%202014/Reports/Substance%20Abuse%20Services%20Report.pdf.

266. *See* Substance Abuse Services Report 2014, at 3.

267. G.S. 122C-142.1(f1).

268. *Id.*

269. *Id.*

270. Substance Abuse Services Report 2014, at 4.

F. Limits on Use of Supervised Probation

G.S. 20-179(r) provides that any person convicted of impaired driving and placed on probation must be placed on unsupervised probation if he or she is sentenced at Levels Three through Five, has no impaired driving convictions in the seven years preceding the current offense date, and has been assessed and completed any recommended treatment, unless the judge makes specific findings in the record about the need for probation supervision. If a judge places a convicted impaired driver on supervised probation under this subsection based on a finding that supervised probation is necessary, the judge must authorize the probation officer to transfer the defendant to unsupervised probation after he or she completes any ordered community service and pays any fines.

VII. Appeal

A. Vacating of Sentence

As noted in the discussion about what constitutes a prior conviction, above, the General Assembly in 2006 enacted provisions designed to prevent defendants from manipulating the procedure for appealing district court convictions to superior court in order to escape enhanced punishment based upon prior convictions. G.S. 20-38.7(c), applicable for offenses committed December 1, 2006, or later, provides:

> Notwithstanding the provisions of G.S. 15A-1431, for any implied-consent offense that is first tried in district court and that is appealed to superior court by the defendant for a trial de novo as a result of a conviction, the sentence imposed by the district court is vacated upon giving notice of appeal. The case shall only be remanded back to district court with the consent of the prosecutor and the superior court. When an appeal is withdrawn or a case is remanded back to district court, the district court shall hold a new sentencing hearing and shall consider any new convictions.

The first item of note related to this provision is that it purports to apply to all implied consent offenses, not just to offenses sentenced under G.S. 20-179. This broad application is surprising given that the appeal/sentencing manipulation to which it was addressed occurred in connection with sentencing under G.S. 20-179, which sets forth a graduated punishment scheme that significantly increases a defendant's punishment if the defendant has a qualifying prior conviction. A qualifying prior conviction renders a defendant subject to punishment at Level Two, which requires a minimum term of imprisonment of not less than 7 days and a maximum term of not more than 12 months. Because each qualifying prior conviction counts as a grossly aggravating factor, a defendant with two qualifying prior convictions is subject to punishment at Level One. A defendant with three prior convictions is subject to punishment at Level A1, which requires that the defendant be sentenced to a term of imprisonment that includes a minimum term of not less than 12 months and a maximum term of not more than 36 months. For misdemeanor implied consent offenses sentenced under structured sentencing, the impact of a single prior conviction is far less.[271] Given the impetus for the provision and the reference in G.S. 20-38.7(d) to facts determined by a jury under G.S. 20-179, it is unclear whether the legislature intended for the statute to apply to implied consent offenses other than

---

271. *See* G.S. 15A-1340.21(b) (providing that a defendant who has at least one but not more than four prior convictions is at prior conviction level II).

those sentenced under G.S. 20-179. Furthermore, it is unclear whether the provision ever is applied in practice to implied consent offenses other than covered offenses.

B. Remand for Resentencing

In addition to providing that convictions for implied consent offenses are vacated upon giving notice of appeal, G.S. 20-38.7(c) provides that cases "shall only be remanded back to district court with the consent of the prosecutor and the superior court." This language calls into question whether a defendant who appeals from a district court conviction for an implied consent offense may withdraw the appeal before the case is transferred to superior court without the consent of the prosecutor or the court as a defendant may for other types of district court convictions.[272] The next sentence of G.S. 20-38.7(c) implies that consent may not be necessary in this circumstance, as it requires that a new sentencing hearing be held "[w]hen an appeal is withdrawn *or* a case is remanded back to district court."[273] Once an implied consent case appealed to superior court is transferred to that court, it is clear that the prosecutor and the superior court must consent to the remand.[274] At a new sentencing hearing held after an appeal is withdrawn or a case is remanded, the district court must consider any new convictions.[275]

C. Appeal from Resentencing

G.S. 20-38.7(d) provides for a limited right to appeal following a new sentencing hearing. It is unclear whether the General Assembly's intent was to allow a defendant to appeal for trial de novo or instead to appeal only the sentence imposed. The statute permits a defendant to appeal to superior court only if (1) the new sentence is based upon additional facts considered by the district court that were not considered in the previously vacated sentence and (2) the defendant would be entitled to a jury determination of those facts "pursuant to G.S. 20-179."[276] Because the fact of a prior conviction is determined by a judge, not a jury,[277] the finding of a new conviction (that is, a conviction that became final after the date of the earlier sentencing) at the new sentencing hearing does not trigger a statutory right to appeal. In contrast, the finding of another type of fact, such as the presence of a child under the age of 18 in the vehicle at the time of the offense, is a fact for which the defendant has a right to a jury determination. A defendant would, therefore, be statutorily entitled to appeal from a new sentence imposed after remand for a covered offense based upon the court's consideration of such a fact.

Thus, G.S. 20-38.7(d) clearly contemplates that a judge permissibly may impose judgment at a new sentencing hearing based upon factors other than new convictions, regardless of whether those factors were considered in the previously vacated sentence. Notwithstanding the broad language of the statute, a defendant's right to due process may constrain a judge's ability at a new sentencing hearing to find additional sentencing factors that result in a more severe sentence.

---

272. *See id.* § 15A-1431(c).

273. *Id.* § 20-38.7(c) (emphasis added). If a defendant is permitted to withdraw an appeal from a conviction of a covered offense without consent pursuant to G.S. 15A-1431, remand is automatic, though the remand is for resentencing, whereas in structured sentencing cases remand is for execution of the judgment. *See id.* § 15A-1431(g).

274. *See id.* § 15A-1431(h) (permitting a defendant to withdraw an appeal after the calendaring of the case for trial de novo in superior court only by consent of the court).

275. *Id.* § 20-38.7(c).

276. *Id.* § 20-38.7(d).

277. *See id.* § 20-179(c).

D. Due Process Considerations

The United States Supreme Court held in *North Carolina v. Pearce*[278] that the Due Process Clause of the Fourteenth Amendment to the U.S. Constitution requires that vindictiveness against a defendant for having successfully attacked his or her first conviction "must play no part in the sentence he receives after a new trial."[279] Noting that a defendant's exercise of a right to appeal must be "free and unfettered,"[280] *Pearce* reasoned that imposing a heavier sentence upon a defendant for the explicit purpose of punishing the defendant for having succeeded in getting his or her conviction set aside "would be a flagrant violation of the Fourteenth Amendment."[281] And, since fear of such vindictiveness can unconstitutionally deter a defendant's exercise of his or her right to appeal from or to collaterally attack a conviction, "due process also requires that a defendant be freed of apprehension of such a retaliatory motivation on the part of the sentencing judge."[282] To assure the absence of such motivation, the *Pearce* court adopted a prophylactic rule requiring that "whenever a judge imposes a more severe sentence upon a defendant after a new trial, the reasons for his doing so must affirmatively appear [and] [t]hose reasons must be based upon objective information concerning identifiable conduct on the part of the defendant occurring after the time of the original sentencing proceeding."[283] The high Court subsequently has limited the applicability of *Pearce*'s prophylactic rule, holding that it does not apply to the imposition of an increased sentence in a trial de novo system,[284] to an increased sentence by a jury upon reconviction after a new trial,[285] or to imposition of a harsher sentence following trial than was imposed pursuant to a guilty plea.[286]

In 1977 the North Carolina General Assembly enacted a statute governing resentencing in superior court after appellate review, G.S. 15A-1335, which embodies generally the rule of *Pearce* but is more restrictive in that it does not allow imposition of a more severe sentence at resentencing based upon aggravating factors that occurred after the date of the original sentence.[287] New sentencing hearings conducted pursuant to G.S. 20-38.7 are not controlled by G.S. 15A-1335 and occur in a procedurally different context from the sentencing at issue in *Pearce* in that resentencing under G.S. 20-38.7 does not follow a new trial or a reversal of the judge's earlier determinations. Instead, a new sentencing hearing follows a defendant's withdrawal of his or her appeal to superior court. Thus, it is not clear that the *Pearce* rule applies in this context.

Nevertheless, the concerns about penalizing a defendant for exercising the right to appeal and about placing the defendant in apprehension of such a retaliatory motivation that underlay the holding in *Pearce* do appear relevant to resentencing under G.S. 20-38.7. Arguably, the possibility of an increased sentence imposed by a district court upon withdrawal of an appeal to superior court could

278. 395 U.S. 711 (1969), *overruled on other grounds by* Alabama v. Smith, 490 U.S. 794 (1989) (holding that no presumption of vindictiveness arises when the first sentence was based upon a guilty plea and the second sentence follows a trial).

279. *Id.* at 725.

280. *Id.* at 724 (internal quotation marks, citations omitted).

281. *Id.* at 723–24.

282. *Id.* at 725 (footnote omitted).

283. *Id.* at 726.

284. Colten v. Kentucky, 407 U.S. 104 (1972).

285. Chaffin v. Stynchcombe, 412 U.S. 17 (1973).

286. Alabama v. Smith, 490 U.S. 794 (1989).

287. *See* State v. Mitchell, 67 N.C. App. 549, 551 (1984). S.L. 2013-385, sec. 3.1 amended G.S. 15A-1335 to limit its application to cases in which the original conviction resulted from a guilty verdict rendered by a jury. For analysis of this change, see Jessica Smith, *A 2013 Rollback of State Procedural Protections for Defendants*, N.C. CRIM. L., UNC SCH. OF GOV'T BLOG (Apr. 7, 2014), http://nccriminallaw.sog.unc.edu/?p=4706.

chill the defendant's exercise of that statutory right. And the rationale for the U.S. Supreme Court's determination in *Colten v. Kentucky*[288] that the superior court in a two-tier system may impose a harsher sentence, free of the *Pearce* rule, is that the superior court conducts a trial de novo representing a "fresh determination of guilt or innocence," not an appeal on the record. This distinction does not support a *Pearce* exception for resentencing by the district court.

If *Pearce* is applicable to resentencing under G.S. 20-38.7, and if aggravating factors in impaired driving cases are indeed sentencing factors and not elements of the offense,[289] the district court upon resentencing under G.S. 20-38.7 may make a "fresh determination of the presence in the evidence of aggravating and mitigating factors,"[290] but "in the process of weighing and balancing the factors found"[291] may not impose a sentence greater than the original sentence unless the increase results from a finding of convictions that became final after the date of the initial sentencing.[292] If *Pearce* does not apply, the defendant may receive a harsher sentence upon resentencing, and the defendant's right to appeal is limited by G.S. 20-38.7(d).

Regardless of *Pearce*'s applicability, the district court upon resentencing under G.S. 20-38.7 may impose a harsher sentence without running afoul of due process if that sentence is statutorily mandated.[293] So, for instance, if a defendant sentenced for a Level One DWI initially was sentenced to a term of imprisonment of 15 days, the judge upon resentencing could impose a Level One sentence that required a term of imprisonment of 30 days, the minimum term required by G.S. 20-179(g).

E. Withdrawal of an Appeal Following Resentencing

G.S. 20-38.7(d) provides that if a defendant who has the right to appeal from a new sentence imposed in district court upon remand from superior court gives notice of appeal and subsequently withdraws the appeal, the district court must reinstate the sentence as a final judgment that is not subject to further appeal. This provision implies that giving notice of appeal from resentencing in district court vacates the sentence, though this matter is not all together clear since the rule vacating sentences imposed in district court applies to cases appealed to the superior court for trial de novo.[294]

---

288. 407 U.S. 104.

289. *Cf.* United States v. O'Brien, 560 U.S. 218, 225 (2010) (citations omitted) (noting in context of federal statute that "whether a given fact is an element of the crime itself or a sentencing factor is a question for Congress. When Congress is not explicit, as is often the case because it seldom directly addresses the distinction between sentencing factors and elements, courts look to the provisions and the framework of the statute to determine whether a fact is an element or a sentencing factor.").

290. *See Mitchell*, 67 N.C. App. at 551 (1984).

291. *Id.*

292. *See* Wasman v. United States, 468 U.S. 559, 569–70 (1984) ("Consideration of a criminal conviction obtained in the interim between an original sentencing and a sentencing after retrial is manifestly legitimate").

293. *See* State v. Branch, 134 N.C. App. 637, 641 (1999) (holding that trial courts have the authority to vacate an invalid sentence and resentence a defendant even if the term of court has ended); *see also* Jessica Smith, *Trial Judge's Authority to Sua Sponte Correct Errors After Entry of Judgment in a Criminal Case*, Admin. of Just. Bull. No. 2003/02 (UNC Institute of Government, May 2003), www.sog.unc.edu/sites/www.sog.unc.edu/files/aoj200302.pdf.; *cf.* State v. Williams, 74 N.C. App. 728 (1985) (holding that G.S. 15A-1335 did not apply to a situation in which the judge imposed the minimum and presumptive sentence of 14 years at resentencing when the initial sentence was 12 years).

294. *See* G.S. 20-38.7(c) (providing that "for any implied-consent offense that is first tried in district court and that is appealed to superior court . . . for a trial de novo . . ., the sentence imposed by the district court is vacated upon giving notice of appeal").

VIII. Service of a Sentence: Jail or Prison, Jail Credit and Parole

A. Jail or Prison

1. Sentences Imposed on or after January 1, 2015

Defendants sentenced to imprisonment for misdemeanor impaired driving (and, presumably, other covered offenses)[295] on or after January 1, 2015, must serve that time in a local confinement facility—a jail—rather than in prison, regardless of the length of the sentence.[296]

The General Assembly in 2014 repealed G.S. 20-176(c1), the statutory provision that formerly governed the place of confinement for imprisonment under such sentences.[297] The former rule is discussed in the next section.

A person sentenced January 1, 2015, or later to imprisonment of any duration for impaired driving under G.S. 20-138.1, other than imprisonment required as a condition of special probation, must be committed to the Statewide Misdemeanant Confinement Program (SMCP).[298] Under this program, the North Carolina Sheriffs' Association identifies space in local confinement facilities that is available for housing misdemeanants.[299] While a defendant serving a term of imprisonment for a covered offense will serve that time in a local confinement facility rather than in a Division of Adult Correction (DAC) facility,[300] the local facility will not necessarily be located in the same county in which the defendant was convicted.[301]

For misdemeanor impaired driving sentences imposed on or after January 1, 2015, all imprisonment imposed as a condition of special probation must be served in a designated local confinement or treatment facility—regardless of whether the imprisonment is for continuous or noncontinuous periods.[302]

2. Sentences Imposed before January 1, 2015

The starting point for determining where sentences for impaired driving and other covered offenses sentenced before January 1, 2015, were served was G.S. 20-176(c1) (repealed by S.L. 2014-100), which provided:

> Notwithstanding any other provision of law, no person convicted of a misdemeanor for the violation of any provision of this Chapter except G.S. 20-28(a) and (b), G.S. 20-141(j), G.S. 20-141.3(b) and (c), G.S. 20-141.4, or a second or subsequent conviction of G.S. 20-138.1 shall be imprisoned in the State prison system unless the person previously has been imprisoned in a local confinement facility, as defined by G.S. 153A-217(5), for a violation of this Chapter.

Thus, the rule formerly applicable to sentences for all G.S. Chapter 20 offenses (including misdemeanor impaired driving under G.S. 20-138.1) was that terms of imprisonment for active sentences,

---

295. *See* supra note 255.
296. *See* S.L. 2014-100, sec. 16C.1 (amending G.S. 15A-1351(a) and -1352(f) to so provide).
297. S.L. 2014-100.
298. G.S. 15A-1352(f).
299. *Id.* § 148-32.1.
300. The SMCP allows a misdemeanant to be transferred to a DAC facility upon court order in certain limited circumstances. G.S. 148-32.1(b3), (b4).
301. *See Id.* § 148-32.1(b2) (providing that any county that voluntarily agrees to house misdemeanants from that county or from other counties pursuant to the SMCP may enter into a written agreement with the DAC to do so).
302. *Id.* § 15A-1351(a).

regardless of length, were served in local confinement facilities rather than in the custody of the DAC. That rule did not apply to a defendant who previously had been imprisoned in a local confinement facility for a Chapter 20 offense. The general rule also did not apply to convictions for certain offenses, among them a second or subsequent conviction of driving while impaired in violation of G.S. 20-138.1.

When an exception to the general rule of local confinement in G.S. 20-176(c1) applied, G.S. 15A-1352, which governs the appropriate place of confinement for criminal offenses generally, established the framework for where a term of imprisonment was served. Applying that framework to impaired driving sentences became less straightforward after the legislature in 2011 created a Statewide Misdemeanant Confinement Program but excluded impaired driving sentences from its purview.[303] The rule for defendants sentenced on or after January 1, 2012, appeared to be that a person sentenced to imprisonment for a second or subsequent conviction of misdemeanor impaired driving had to serve that time in a local jail if the sentence was 90 days or less.[304] Judges had discretion regarding the place of confinement for such sentences of more than 90 and up to 180 days.[305] Sentences of this type ordering imprisonment for 181 days or more required imprisonment in a DAC facility.[306]

Yet another set of rules formerly applied to imprisonment served as a condition of special probation. Pursuant to former G.S. 15A-1351(a), noncontinuous periods of special probation for any criminal offense could be served only in a designated local confinement or treatment facility.[307] If imprisonment as a condition of special probation was instead ordered for a continuous period, the judge had discretion over whether to order the defendant confined to a local or to a DAC facility.[308]

B. Jail Credit

1. Time Served

Generally, the minimum and maximum term of a criminal sentence must be credited with and diminished by the total amount of time a defendant has spent committed to or in confinement in any State or local correctional, mental, or other institution as a result of the charge that culminated in the sentence.[309] An exception applies for covered offenses, barring a defendant from receiving credit for the first 24 hours spent in jail pending trial.[310] This rule precludes the application of credit for such time against either an active term of imprisonment or a term of imprisonment imposed as a condition of special probation.[311] So, for example, a defendant who served 24 hours in jail upon being arrested for a covered offense may not be awarded credit for that time against the minimum period of imprisonment required as a condition of special probation.[312]

Credit for time spent committed or confined as a result of the charge (other than the first 24 hours of incarceration pending trial) may be credited to either the suspended sentence or to the imprisonment required for special probation.[313]

---

303. *See generally* JAMES M. MARKHAM, THE NORTH CAROLINA JUSTICE REINVESTMENT ACT 93–103 (2012).
304. G.S. 15A-1352(a) (2013).
305. *Id.* §§ 15A-1352(a), (e).
306. *Id.* § 15A-1351(a).
307. *Id.*
308. *Id.*
309. *Id.* § 15-196.1.
310. *Id.* § 20-179(p)(1).
311. *Id.* § 20-179(p).
312. *Id.* § 20-179(p)(1).
313. *Id.* § 15A-1351(a).

2. Good Time Credit

G.S. 15A-1355(c) provides that "[f]or sentences of imprisonment imposed for convictions of impaired driving under G.S. 20-138.1," a defendant may receive credit toward service of the maximum term and any minimum term of imprisonment and toward eligibility for parole as provided in rules and regulations made under G.S. 148-13.

G.S. 148-13(b) permits the Secretary of Public Safety to issue regulations "[w]ith respect to prisoners who are serving sentences for impaired driving offenses under G.S. 20-138.1" providing for "deductions of time from the terms of such prisoners for good behavior, meritorious conduct, work or study, participation in rehabilitation programs, and the like." It appears that this reference is intended to refer to all covered offenses sentenced under G.S. 20-179, not simply to the offense of impaired driving under G.S. 20-138.1.[314]

Regulations issued by the Secretary of Public Safety provide that inmates "convicted of Driving While Impaired" are awarded "Good Time at the rate of one day deducted from their prison or jail term for each day they spend in custody without a conviction through the Disciplinary Process of a violation of inmate conduct rules."[315] These credits also are awarded to inmates sentenced as felons for crimes they committed prior to October 1, 1994. A defendant convicted of a covered offense is eligible for good time credit regardless of the place of confinement.[316] No portion of a term of special probation for a covered offense may be reduced by Good Time credit.[317]

C. Credit for Inpatient Treatment

One of the purposes for sentencing for impaired driving, like sentencing generally, is to rehabilitate offenders so that they may be restored to the community as lawful citizens.[318] The rehabilitative aims of the sentencing scheme for impaired driving are evident in the requirement that offenders obtain substance abuse assessments and treatment or education as conditions of probation. They likewise are evident in the provisions of G.S. 20-179(k1) that allow a court to order that a defendant serve a term of special probation as an inpatient at a state-operated or -licensed facility for the treatment of alcoholism or substance abuse. The latter provision accords with structured sentencing provisions that allow a judge to order that a defendant serve a period of special probation at a designated treatment facility.[319] Unlike its structured sentencing counterpart, however, G.S. 20-179(k1) explicitly requires the defendant to bear the expense of any treatment unless the trial judge orders that the

---

314. This interpretation accords with construing G.S. Chapter 15A provisions applicable to sentences for impaired driving under G.S. 20-138.1 as controlling all sentences under G.S. 20-179. See *supra* note 255. It also explains the use of the plural "impaired driving offenses" rather than a reference to the singular offense of impaired driving under G.S. 20-138.1.

315. *See* State of North Carolina, Dep't of Pub. Safety, Div. of Prisons, Policy & Procedure Manual (issue date 9/5/13), Ch. B. (Inmate Conduct Rules, Discipline), Secs. .0100, .0111(a) (Sentence Credits), p. 2 (hereinafter Policy & Procedure Manual 2013), www.doc.state.nc.us/dop/policy_procedure_manual/b0100.pdf.

316. *See* G.S. 148-13(e) (effective for sentences for impaired driving under G.S. 20-138.1 imposed January 1, 2015, or later and providing that the Secretary's regulations concerning good time credit be distributed to and followed by local jail administrators with regard to sentenced jail prisoners); *see also id.* § 148-13(b) (2013) (authorizing Secretary of Public Safety to issue regulations applicable to "prisoners who are serving prison or jail terms for impaired driving offenses"); Policy & Procedure Manual 2013, Ch. B., Sec. .0111(a), at 2 (providing for "Good Time at the rate of one day deducted from . . . prison or jail term").

317. G.S. 148-13(f).

318. *See id.* § 15A-1340.12.

319. *See id.* § 15A-1351(a).

costs be absorbed by the State. In ordering a defendant convicted of a covered offense to serve time at a treatment facility, the judge may impose restrictions on the defendant's ability to leave the premises of the treatment facility and may require that the defendant follow the facility's rules.[320]

G.S. 20-179(k1) also permits a judge to "credit against the active sentence imposed on a defendant the time the defendant was an inpatient at the treatment facility, provided such treatment occurred after the commission of the offense for which the defendant is being sentenced." This provision is subject to a few interpretations. One narrow interpretation is that the clause means simply that when a judge orders that a period of imprisonment imposed as a condition of special probation be served at a treatment facility, the judge may credit this time against any suspended sentence that later is activated. Given that the general rules for crediting time served in a treatment facility only award credit for time spent in a state or local institution,[321] such a provision is necessary to allow for credit when the inpatient time is served in a private facility. Thus, even under this narrow view, G.S. 20-179(k1)'s rules about awarding sentencing credit for inpatient treatment are significantly broader than the rules for awarding such credit to sentences generally, including sentences for offenses involving impaired driving that are not sentenced under G.S. 20-179, such as habitual impaired driving. Yet this relatively restrictive interpretation of subsection (k1) has two flaws. First, it renders surplusage language requiring that the credited treatment occur "after the commission of the offense for which the defendant is being sentenced," since treatment ordered at sentencing always will be completed after the offense. Second, subsection (k1) makes no reference to sentences subsequently activated upon violation of probation, which would be the logical time at which post-sentencing treatment credit would be ordered.

Alternatively, G.S. 20-179(k1) might be interpreted as permitting a judge to award credit for qualifying inpatient treatment at a licensed facility only against a sentence that imposes "active punishment" as that term is defined by G.S. 15A-1340.11—that is, a sentence that requires a term of imprisonment and is not suspended. Another still-yet broader reading, and the view held by the author, is that a defendant may receive credit for qualifying inpatient treatment against periods of imprisonment imposed as a condition of special probation as well as against an active sentence. Under this interpretation, the term "active" in the context of G.S. 20-179(k1) refers to a period of imprisonment rather than "active punishment" pursuant to G.S. 15A-1340.11. The pairing of the credit provision in subsection (k1) with authorization for service of a term of imprisonment imposed as a condition of special probation at such a treatment facility provides support for the view that the legislature intended to allow for credit against periods of imprisonment served pursuant to active or probationary sentences. If this interpretation is correct, then credit awarded for qualifying inpatient treatment may satisfy the minimum terms of imprisonment required for active sentences or as a condition of special probation for each level of impaired driving. Thus, a defendant who serves 30 days as an inpatient at a licensed treatment facility after committing an impaired driving offense sentenced at Level One may, in the judge's discretion, be awarded credit for this time against a term of special probation requiring a term of imprisonment of 30 days. In this circumstance, the defendant will not be required to serve any

---

320. *See id.* § 20-179(k1).

321. *See id.* § 15-196.1 (requiring credit against the minimum and maximum term of a sentence for "the total amount of time a defendant has spent, committed to or in confinement in any State or local correctional, mental or other institution as a result of the charge that culminated in the sentence"); State v. Stephenson, 213 N.C. App. 621, 623–24 (2011) (holding that the defendant was not entitled to credit in structured sentencing case for time spent at Potter's House, an "independent Christian faith-based rehabilitation program . . . not affiliated with or operated by either a State or local government agency").

time in jail unless he or she violates conditions of probation and imprisonment is ordered in response to such a violation.

D. Service on Weekends

The judge in his or her discretion may order a term of imprisonment imposed pursuant to G.S. 20-179 to be served on "weekends," even if the sentence cannot be served in consecutive sequence.[322] Active terms of imprisonment for covered offenses as well as special probation may be served in this manner.[323] The statutory reference to "weekends" rather than to "noncontinuous periods" gives rise to a question regarding whether a judge may order that imprisonment be served for noncontinuous periods on days other than Friday through Sunday. Given that weekend service of jail time presumably is permitted to mitigate the disruption of a defendant's work and school schedule, there appears to be no principled reason for adopting a literal construction that would disallow service of noncontinuous periods of imprisonment on weekdays, particularly when such an arrangement is necessary to permit a defendant to complete work and school obligations that occur on weekend days.

If a defendant is ordered to serve 48 hours or more or has 48 hours or more remaining on a term of imprisonment, he or she must be required to serve 48 continuous hours of imprisonment to be given credit.[324] Credit for jail time may only be awarded hour for hour for time actually served.[325] The jail must maintain a log showing the number of hours served. A defendant who reports to the jail for service of a term of imprisonment with alcohol remaining in his or her body (as shown by an alcohol screening device) or a controlled substance previously consumed (unless lawfully obtained and taken in therapeutically appropriate amounts) must not be allowed to enter the jail and must be reported to the court.[326] If the defendant is reported back to the court for this reason, the court must hold a hearing.[327] If the court determines that at the time of the defendant's entrance to the jail he or she had alcohol remaining in his or her body or had a previously consumed controlled substance in his or her body, the defendant must be ordered to serve jail time immediately and is ineligible to serve jail time on weekends.[328] It is a defense to immediate service of jail time and ineligibility for weekend service if the alcohol or controlled substance was lawfully obtained and taken in therapeutically appropriate amounts.[329]

E. Concurrent, Consolidated, and Consecutive Sentences

Under structured sentencing, a judge may consolidate convictions for multiple felony offenses entered at the same time or multiple misdemeanor offenses entered in the same session of court and impose a single judgment that is consistent with the punishment required for the most serious of the consoli-

---

322. G.S. 20-179(s).

323. While G.S. 15A-1351(a) authorizes a sentence of special probation for any criminal offense to be served "at whatever time or intervals within the period of probation, consecutive or nonconsecutive, the court determines," a court may not order that an active sentence for a structured sentencing offense be served in noncontinuous periods. *See* State v. Miller, 205 N.C. App. 291 (2010). *See also* Jamie Markham, *Noncontinuous Active Sentences*, N.C. Crim. L., UNC Sch. of Gov't Blog (July 7, 2010), http://nccriminallaw.sog.unc.edu/?p=1398.

324. G.S. 20-179(s).

325. *Id.* § 20-179(s)(1).

326. *Id.* § 20-179(s)(2).

327. *Id.* § 20-179(s)(3).

328. *Id.*

329. *Id.*

dated offenses based on the defendant's prior record level.[330] A different rule governs the consolidation of impaired driving offenses sentenced pursuant to G.S. 20-179.

Two or more impaired driving charges may not be consolidated for judgment.[331] So, for example, a defendant convicted of impaired driving in a commercial vehicle in violation of G.S. 20-138.2 and impaired driving in violation of 20-138.1 must be sentenced for both offenses, even if the convictions arose from a single incident of driving or were entered on the same day. Such sentences may, however, run concurrently. A separate statutory sentencing rule provides that if the conviction for G.S. 20-138.2 and 20-138.1 arose from the same incident, the aggregate punishment may not exceed the maximum punishment applicable to the offense of impaired driving under G.S. 20-138.1.[332]

Furthermore, for each conviction of impaired driving, save for two exceptions, a judge must determine whether any of the statutory aggravating or mitigating factors that dictate the applicable level of punishment exist. No such finding of factors is required if the defendant's conviction of impaired driving is premised upon the common law concept of aiding and abetting or if the impaired driving charge is consolidated with a charge carrying a greater punishment.[333]

Thus, G.S. 20-179(f2) expressly acknowledges the propriety of consolidating an impaired driving conviction with a charge carrying greater punishment, implicitly authorizing the consolidation of impaired driving convictions subject to sentencing under G.S. 20-179 with convictions subject to greater punishment under the Structured Sentencing Act.[334] Determining whether another conviction carries a greater punishment is complicated by the multiple levels of punishment applicable to impaired driving sentences under G.S. 20-179, each of which carries its own maximum punishment. Perhaps the maximum punishment under G.S. 20-179 is the statutory maximum for the most serious level of DWI (which, for offenses committed on or after December 1, 2011, is 3 years). On the other hand, the maximum may be that applicable to the level at which the defendant is subject to being sentenced, something the court may be unable to determine without finding aggravating and mitigating factors. While jurisprudence prior to *Blakely v. Washington*[335] suggests that the statutory maximum for the most aggravated level of impaired driving establishes the relevant statutory maximum,[336] it is doubtful that the court would reach the same conclusion if the issue were considered today, given the changed constitutional landscape.

Some experts have suggested that notwithstanding the authorization to do so, impaired driving convictions subject to sentencing under G.S. 20-179 should not be consolidated with structured sentencing convictions because different rules govern the calculation of the defendant's release date under the two schemes. Such consolidation across sentencing schemes may not, however, prove

---

330. *See id.* § 15A-1340.15(b) (applicable to sentences for felonies); 15A-1340.22(b) (applicable to sentences for misdemeanors).

331. *See id.* § 20-179(f2).

332. *Id.* § 20-138.2(e) (so limiting aggregate punishment); *see also id.* § 20-138.3(c) (setting forth a similar limitation for aggregated punishment imposed for a single incident of impaired driving and driving by a person less than 21 after consuming alcohol or drugs, though the latter offense, unlike impaired driving, is subject to structured sentencing).

333. *Id.* § 20-179(f2).

334. *Cf.* State v. Branch, 134 N.C. App. 637, 641 (1999) (holding that offenses governed by the Fair Sentencing Act could not be consolidated with offenses punished under the Structured Sentencing Act).

335. 542 U.S. 296 (2004).

336. *See* State v. Santon, 101 N.C. App. 710, 712 (1991) (holding that a conviction of driving while impaired under G.S. 20-138.1, regardless of the level of punishment imposed, constitutes a prior conviction of an offense punishable by more than 60 days' imprisonment for purposes of sentencing under the Fair Sentencing Act).

problematic so long as the "lead" offense—the greater offense with which the impaired driving conviction is consolidated—is clearly indicated on the judgment. Since the sentencing scheme for the lead offense controls the defendant's service of the sentence, the jail or Division of Adult Correction need only concern itself with the sentencing, credit, and release rules applicable to the lead offense.

A related question is whether a lesser misdemeanor that is not subject to sentencing under G.S. 20-179 may be consolidated with an impaired driving offense sentenced under G.S. 20-179. This practice appears to be permissible, as the judge still would be required to determine whether aggravating and mitigating factors apply and to sentence in accordance with the provisions of G.S. 20-179.

There is no requirement that the sentence for impaired driving run consecutively to a felony sentence being served at the time of the DWI sentencing. G.S. 15A-1354(a), which applies to sentences imposed pursuant to G.S. 20-179 as well as to Structured Sentencing Act sentences, provides that in the absence of a statutory provision requiring a consecutive sentence or specification in the judgment that the sentences are to run consecutively, sentences imposed at the same time or upon a person already subject to an undischarged term of imprisonment run concurrently.

F. Parole

Defendants sentenced to "a term of imprisonment for a conviction of impaired driving under G.S. 20-138.1"[337] are eligible for parole under Article 85 of G.S. Chapter 15A. As noted earlier, the most reasonable and consistent construction of the sentencing provisions of Chapter 15A that refer to convictions of impaired driving under G.S. 20-138.1 is that they apply broadly to all convictions sentenced under G.S. 20-179.[338] This section, like the preceding ones, is written based on the assumption that these provisions apply to sentencing for all covered offenses.

As previously mentioned, G.S. 20-179 sets forth minimum and maximum terms of imprisonment applicable to each level of punishment. A corresponding provision, G.S. 15A-1351(b), states that a sentence to imprisonment "[f]or persons convicted of impaired driving under G.S. 20-138.1 . . . must impose a maximum term and may impose a minimum term." G.S. 15A-1351(b) further provides that "[t]he impaired driving judgment may state the minimum term or may state that a term constitutes both the minimum and maximum terms." If a judgment imposed pursuant to G.S. 20-179 for a covered offense states no minimum term, a defendant becomes eligible for parole in accordance with G.S. 15A-1371(a).

G.S. 15A-1371(a) provides that if no minimum sentence is imposed for a prisoner serving an active term of imprisonment for a conviction of impaired driving, the person is eligible for release on parole at any time, subject to the limitations below. If the sentence includes a minimum term of imprisonment, the person is eligible for release on parole upon completion of the minimum term or one-fifth the maximum penalty allowed by law for the offense for which the prisoner is sentenced, whichever is less.[339] Good time credit allowed under G.S. 15A-1355 reduces the term that must expire before a defendant becomes eligible for release on parole.[340] Because good time credit is awarded day for day,[341] the time that must expire before a defendant is parole-eligible effectively is halved.

The release of an otherwise parole-eligible defendant is limited by G.S. 20-179(p)(3), which prevents a defendant from being released on parole until he or she has served the mandatory minimum term

337. G.S. 15A-1371(a).
338. See *supra* note 255.
339. G.S. 15A-1371(a).
340. *Id.* § 15A-1355(c).
341. See *supra* note 315.

of imprisonment. In addition, to be released on parole, the defendant must have obtained a substance abuse assessment and have completed any recommended treatment or training program or must be paroled into a residential treatment program.[342] A defendant paroled from a sentence of imprisonment imposed pursuant to G.S. 20-179 who has completed substance abuse treatment or training and who is not being paroled to a residential treatment program must, as a condition of parole, receive community service parole pursuant to G.S. 15A-1371(h)[343] or be required to "[r]emain in one or more specified places for a specified period or periods each day and wear a device that permits the defendant's compliance with the condition to be monitored electronically."[344]

An example may help illustrate when a defendant sentenced under G.S. 20-179 is eligible for parole. Defendant Daniels is sentenced under G.S. 20-179 to a minimum term of 12 months and a maximum term of 24 months for a Level One DWI. Assuming a full award of good time credit, Daniels is eligible for release on parole after serving 2.4 months imprisonment, a term constituting one-fifth of 12 months (the maximum sentence reduced by good time credit, which is less than the minimum term reduced by good time credit, or 6 months), if she has obtained a substance abuse assessment and has completed any recommended treatment or training program or if she is paroled into a residential treatment program.

Suppose instead that Defendant Daniels' sentence was for a minimum term of 30 days and a maximum term of 24 months. Again assuming a full award of good time credit, G.S. 15A-1371 renders Daniels parole-eligible after serving 15 days imprisonment (the minimum term reduced by good time credit, which is less than one-fifth of the statutory maximum reduced by good time credit). G.S. 20-179(p)(3) requires, however, that Daniels serve the mandatory minimum term of imprisonment for a Level One DWI—30 days—before being released on parole. In addition and as noted in the previous example, Daniels must obtain a substance abuse assessment and complete any recommended treatment or training program before being released or Daniels must be paroled into a residential treatment program.

Notwithstanding the parole-eligibility rules of G.S. 15A-1371(a), a defendant serving a sentence of imprisonment of not less than 30 days nor as great as 18 months for impaired driving[345] may be released on parole after serving one-third of the maximum sentence unless the Post-Release Supervision and Parole Commission finds in writing that:

(1) There is a substantial risk that he [or she] will not conform to reasonable conditions of parole; or
(2) His [or her] release at that time would unduly depreciate the seriousness of his [or her] crime or promote disrespect for law; or
(3) His [or her] continued correctional treatment, medical care, or vocational or other training in the institution will substantially enhance his [or her] capacity to lead a law-abiding life if he [or she] is released at a later date; or
(4) There is a substantial risk that he [or she] would engage in further criminal conduct.[346]

342. G.S. 20-179(p)(3).

343. Community service parole pursuant to G.S. 15A-1371(h) is "early parole for the purpose of participation in community service under the supervision of the Section of Community Corrections of the Division of Adult Correction."

344. *Id.* §§ 15A-1374(a1), (b)(8a).

345. For the same reasons that the provisions of G.S. Chapter 15A that refer to sentences for impaired driving under G.S. 20-138.1 encompass all offenses sentenced under G.S. 20-179, see *supra* note 255, this provision presumably applies to all covered offenses sentenced pursuant to G.S. 20-179.

346. G.S. 15A-1371(g).

The term of parole under G.S. 15A-1371(g) is the unserved portion of the sentence of imprisonment. To provide the Post-Release Supervision and Parole Commission an adequate opportunity to determine whether parole under G.S. 15A-1371(g) should be denied, a defendant eligible for parole under subsection (g) may not be released from confinement before the fifth full working day after he or she is placed in the custody of the Secretary of Public Safety or the custodian of a local confinement facility.

Again, an example may help illustrate the application of the parole provisions under G.S. 15A-1371(g) and their interplay with the parole eligibility rules in subsection (a) of this same statute, discussed earlier. Suppose Defendant Diamond is sentenced to a minimum term of 30 days imprisonment and a maximum term of 12 months for a Level One DWI. Assuming a full award of good time credit and completion of a substance abuse assessment and any recommended treatment or training, Diamond is eligible for parole under G.S. 15A-1371(a) and 20-179(p) after serving 30 days imprisonment—the statutory mandatory minimum.[347] Had Diamond received this sentence for a Level Two DWI, he would have been parole-eligible after serving only 15 days of imprisonment, the minimum sentence reduced by good time credit, as that term exceeds the statutory mandatory minimum sentence of 7 days for a defendant sentenced for a Level Two DWI.[348]

Furthermore, Diamond may be paroled after completing one-third of his maximum sentence (which, in his case, is 4 months), absent a written determination from the Post-Release Supervision and Parole Commission that one of the four statutorily enumerated reasons for denying parole is present. The periods of imprisonment for purposes of determining parole eligibility under G.S. 15A-1371(g) are not reduced by the application of good time credit.

Statistics from the Department of Correction for the 2009–2010 fiscal year reflect that the 3,188 non–Structured Sentencing misdemeanants released from prison during that period, most of whom were convicted of impaired driving,[349] served an average of 6.5 months and 48 percent of the sentence imposed "due to good time, gain time and parole eligibility rules."[350] Given that good time alone would reduce a sentence of imprisonment for a covered offense by 50 percent, these statistics indicate that defendants infrequently are released on the earliest date at which they are parole-eligible. Moreover, because defendants sentenced for covered offenses must have either completed substance abuse treatment or training or been paroled into a residential treatment program, defendants who are paroled before their outright release date typically are paroled into DART Cherry's 90-day treatment program (for men)[351] or the Black Mountain Substance Abuse Treatment Center for Women.

---

347. *See id.* § 20-179(p)(3).

348. *Id.* § 15A-1371(a); 20-179(h).

349. Other than covered offenses, the only misdemeanor offense that is excluded from Structured Sentencing Act provisions is the failure to comply with public health control measures under G.S. 130A-25. Far more defendants are convicted of covered offenses than public health control violations each year. In 2010–2011, for example, more than 40,000 defendants were convicted of covered offenses and fewer than 50 of violations of G.S. Chapter 130A.

350. North Carolina Department of Correction, 2009–10 Statistical Report 26 (hereinafter DOC 2009–10 Statistical Report), http://randp.doc.state.nc.us/pubdocs/0007066.PDF.

351. "DART Cherry is a 300-bed residential treatment facility responsible for the delivery of chemical dependency treatment services to probationers sent by the courts, and to parolees released from the state prison system and transitioning back to the community." N.C. Dep't of Pub. Safety, "Dart Cherry," https://www.ncdps.gov/index2.cfm?a=000003,002372,002379.

Table 5.1. Punishment for Covered Offenses Committed on or after October 1, 2013

Punishment Level/ Controlling Statute	Factors	Imprisonment and Mandatory Probation Conditions	Fine
Aggravated Level One/ G.S. 20-179(f3)	Three or more grossly aggravating factors	• 12 months minimum to 36 months maximum • If suspended ◦ Imprisonment of at least 120 days as a condition of special probation ◦ Requirement that defendant abstain from alcohol consumption for a minimum of 120 days to a maximum of the term of probation, as verified by continuous alcohol monitoring (CAM) system ◦ Requirement that defendant obtain a substance abuse assessment and education or treatment required by G.S. 20-17.6	Up to $10,000
Level One/ G.S. 20-179(g)	Grossly aggravating factor in G.S. 20-179(c)(4) or two other grossly aggravating factors	• 30 days minimum to 24 months maximum • If suspended ◦ Special probation requiring (1) imprisonment of at least 30 days or (2) imprisonment of at least 10 days and alcohol abstinence and CAM for at least 120 days ◦ Requirement that defendant obtain a substance abuse assessment and education or treatment required by G.S. 20-17.6	Up to $4,000
Level Two/ G.S. 20-179(h)	One grossly aggravating factor, other than the grossly aggravating factor in G.S. 20-179(c)(4)	• 7 days minimum to 12 months maximum • If suspended ◦ Special probation requiring (1) imprisonment of at least 7 days or (2) alcohol abstinence and CAM for at least 90 days - If Level Two based on prior conviction or driving while license revoked (DWLR) for an impaired driving revocation and prior conviction occurred within five years, sentence must require 240 hours of community service if no imprisonment imposed ◦ Requirement that defendant obtain a substance abuse assessment and education or treatment required by G.S. 20-17.6	Up to $2,000
Level Three/ G.S. 20-179(i)	Aggravating factors substantially outweigh any mitigating factors	• 72 hours minimum to 6 months maximum • If suspended ◦ Must require one or both of the following - Imprisonment for at least 72 hours as a condition of special probation - Community service for a term of at least 72 hours ◦ Requirement that defendant obtain a substance abuse assessment and education or treatment required by G.S. 20-17.6	Up to $1,000
Level Four/ G.S. 20-179(j)	No aggravating and mitigating factors or aggravating factors are substantially counterbalanced by mitigating factors	• 48 hours minimum to 120 days maximum • If suspended ◦ Must require one or both of the following - Imprisonment for 48 hours as a condition of special probation - Community service for a term of 48 hours ◦ Requirement that defendant obtain a substance abuse assessment and education or treatment required by G.S. 20-17.6	Up to $500
Level Five/ G.S. 20-179(k)	Mitigating factors substantially outweigh aggravating factors	• 24 hours minimum to 60 days maximum • If suspended ◦ Must require one or both of the following - Imprisonment for 24 hours as a condition of special probation - Community service for a term of 24 hours ◦ Requirement that defendant obtain a substance abuse assessment and education or treatment required by G.S. 20-17.6	Up to $200

Table 5.2. Punishment for Covered Offenses Committed on or after December 1, 2012, and before October 1, 2013

Punishment Level/ Controlling Statute	Factors	Imprisonment and Mandatory Probation Conditions	Fine
Aggravated Level One/ G.S. 20-179(f3)	Three or more grossly aggravating factors	• 12 months minimum to 36 months maximum • If suspended ◦ Imprisonment of at least 120 days as a condition of special probation ◦ Requirement that defendant abstain from alcohol consumption for a minimum of 120 days to a maximum of the term of probation, as verified by continuous alcohol monitoring (CAM) system ◦ Requirement that defendant obtain a substance abuse assessment and education or treatment required by G.S. 20-17.6	Up to $10,000
Level One/ G.S. 20-179(g)	Grossly aggravating factor in G.S. 20-179(c)(4) or two other grossly aggravating factors	• 30 days minimum to 24 months maximum • If suspended ◦ Special probation requiring (1) imprisonment of at least 30 days or (2) imprisonment of at least 10 days and alcohol abstinence and CAM for at least 120 days ◦ Requirement that defendant obtain a substance abuse assessment and education or treatment required by G.S. 20-17.6	Up to $4,000
Level Two/ G.S. 20-179(h)	One grossly aggravating factor, other than the grossly aggravating factor in G.S. 20-179(c)(4)	• 7 days minimum to 12 months maximum • If suspended ◦ Special probation requiring (1) imprisonment of at least 7 days or (2) alcohol abstinence and CAM for at least 90 days ◦ Requirement that defendant obtain a substance abuse assessment and education or treatment required by G.S. 20-17.6	Up to $2,000
Level Three/ G.S. 20-179(i)	Aggravating factors substantially outweigh any mitigating factors	• 72 hours minimum to 6 months maximum • If suspended ◦ Must require one or both of the following - Imprisonment for at least 72 hours as a condition of special probation - Community service for a term of at least 72 hours ◦ Requirement that defendant obtain a substance abuse assessment and education or treatment required by G.S. 20-17.6	Up to $1,000
Level Four/ G.S. 20-179(j)	No aggravating and mitigating factors or aggravating factors are substantially counterbalanced by mitigating factors	• 48 hours minimum to 120 days maximum • If suspended ◦ Must require one or both of the following - Imprisonment for 48 hours as a condition of special probation - Community service for a term of 48 hours ◦ Requirement that defendant obtain a substance abuse assessment and education or treatment required by G.S. 20-17.6	Up to $500
Level Five/ G.S. 20-179(k)	Mitigating factors substantially outweigh aggravating factors	• 24 hours minimum to 60 days maximum • If suspended ◦ Must require one or both of the following - Imprisonment for 24 hours as a condition of special probation - Community service for a term of 24 hours ◦ Requirement that defendant obtain a substance abuse assessment and education or treatment required by G.S. 20-17.6	Up to $200

Table 5.3. Punishment for Covered Offenses Committed on or after December 1, 2011, and before December 1, 2012

Punishment Level/ Controlling Statute	Factors	Imprisonment and Mandatory Probation Conditions	Fine
Aggravated Level One/ G.S. 20-179(f3)	Three or more grossly aggravating factors	• 12 months minimum to 36 months maximum • If suspended ◦ Imprisonment of at least 120 days as a condition of special probation ◦ Requirement that defendant abstain from alcohol consumption for a minimum of 120 days to a maximum of the term of probation as verified by continuous alcohol monitoring (CAM) system ◦ Requirement that defendant obtain a substance abuse assessment and education or treatment required by G.S. 20-17.6	Up to $10,000
Level One/ G.S. 20-179(g)	Grossly aggravating factor in G.S. 20-179(c)(4) or two other grossly aggravating factors	• 30 days minimum to 24 months maximum • If suspended ◦ Imprisonment of at least 30 days as a condition of special probation ◦ Requirement that defendant obtain a substance abuse assessment and education or treatment required by G.S. 20-17.6	Up to $4,000
Level Two/ G.S. 20-179(h)	One grossly aggravating factor, other than the grossly aggravating factor in G.S. 20-179(c)(4)	• 7 days minimum to 12 months maximum • If suspended ◦ Imprisonment of at least 7 days as a condition of special probation ◦ Requirement that defendant obtain a substance abuse assessment and education or treatment required by G.S. 20-17.6	Up to $2,000
Level Three/ G.S. 20-179(i)	Aggravating factors substantially outweigh any mitigating factors	• 72 hours minimum to 6 months maximum • If suspended ◦ Must require one or both of the following - Imprisonment for at least 72 hours as a condition of special probation - Community service for a term of at least 72 hours ◦ Requirement that defendant obtain a substance abuse assessment and education or treatment required by G.S. 20-17.6	Up to $1,000
Level Four/ G.S. 20-179(j)	No aggravating and mitigating factors or aggravating factors are substantially counterbalanced by mitigating factors	• 48 hours minimum to 120 days maximum • If suspended ◦ Must require one or both of the following - Imprisonment for 48 hours as a condition of special probation - Community service for a term of 48 hours ◦ Requirement that defendant obtain a substance abuse assessment and education or treatment required by G.S. 20-17.6	Up to $500
Level Five/ G.S. 20-179(k)	Mitigating factors substantially outweigh aggravating factors	• 24 hours minimum to 60 days maximum • If suspended ◦ Must require one or both of the following - Imprisonment for 24 hours as a condition of special probation - Community service for a term of 24 hours ◦ Requirement that defendant obtain a substance abuse assessment and education or treatment required by G.S. 20-17.6	Up to $200

Table 5.4. Punishment for Covered Offenses Committed on or after December 1, 2007, and before December 1, 2011

Punishment Level/ Controlling Statute	Factors	Imprisonment and Mandatory Probation Conditions	Fine
Level One/ G.S. 20-179(g)	Two or more grossly aggravating factors	• 30 days minimum to 24 months maximum • If suspended ◦ Imprisonment of at least 30 days as a condition of special probation ◦ Requirement that defendant obtain a substance abuse assessment and education or treatment required by G.S. 20-17.6 ◦ Defendant may be required to abstain from alcohol for a minimum of 30 days up to a maximum of 60 days, as verified by a continuous alcohol monitoring (CAM) system - Total cost of CAM may not exceed $1,000	Up to $4,000
Level Two/ G.S. 20-179(h)	One grossly aggravating factor	• 7 days minimum to 12 months maximum • If suspended ◦ Imprisonment of at least 7 days as a condition of special probation ◦ Requirement that defendant obtain a substance abuse assessment and education or treatment required by G.S. 20-17.6 ◦ Defendant may be required to abstain from alcohol for a minimum of 30 days up to a maximum of 60 days, as verified by a CAM system - Total cost of CAM may not exceed $1,000	Up to $2,000
Level Three/ G.S. 20-179(i)	Aggravating factors substantially outweigh any mitigating factors	• 72 hours minimum to 6 months maximum • If suspended ◦ Must require one or both of the following - Imprisonment for at least 72 hours as a condition of special probation - Community service for a term of at least 72 hours ◦ Requirement that defendant obtain a substance abuse assessment and education or treatment required by G.S. 20-17.6	Up to $1,000
Level Four/ G.S. 20-179(j)	No aggravating and mitigating factors or aggravating factors are substantially counterbalanced by mitigating factors	• 48 hours minimum to 120 days maximum • If suspended ◦ Must require one or both of the following - Imprisonment for 48 hours as a condition of special probation - Community service for a term of 48 hours ◦ Requirement that defendant obtain a substance abuse assessment and education or treatment required by G.S. 20-17.6	Up to $500
Level Five/ G.S. 20-179(k)	Mitigating factors substantially outweigh aggravating factors	• 24 hours minimum to 60 days maximum • If suspended ◦ Must require one or both of the following - Imprisonment for 24 hours as a condition of special probation - Community service for a term of 24 hours ◦ Requirement that defendant obtain a substance abuse assessment and education or treatment required by G.S. 20-17.6	Up to $200

Appendix 5.1A. Impaired Driving Determination of Sentencing Factors (for Offenses Committed before December 1, 2011)

STATE OF NORTH CAROLINA

File No.

_______________________ County

In The General Court Of Justice
☐ District ☐ Superior Court Division

STATE VERSUS

Name Of Defendant

IMPAIRED DRIVING
DETERMINATION OF SENTENCING FACTORS
(For Offenses Committed Before Dec. 1, 2011)

G.S. 20-179

☐ **District Court:** The defendant has been convicted of impaired driving (G.S. 20-138.1). Based upon the evidence presented at the trial and sentencing hearing in District Court, the Court determines that (1) the State has proved the grossly aggravating factors and aggravating factors marked below beyond a reasonable doubt and (2) the defendant has proved the mitigating factors marked below by a preponderance of the evidence.

☐ **Superior Court:** The defendant has been convicted of impaired driving (G.S. 20-138.1). Based upon the evidence presented at the trial and sentencing hearing in Superior Court, (1) the jury has determined that the State has proved the grossly aggravating factors and aggravating factors marked below beyond a reasonable doubt, or the defendant has admitted to these grossly aggravating factors and aggravating factors, and (2) the Court determines that the defendant has proved the mitigating factors marked below by a preponderance of the evidence. If grossly aggravating factor No. 1.a., 1.b., 1.c., 1.d., 1.e., or 1.f. is marked below, the Court determines that the State has proved that grossly aggravating factor beyond a reasonable doubt. If aggravating factor No. 8 or 9 is marked below, the Court determines that the State has proved that aggravating factor beyond a reasonable doubt *(applies to offenses committed on or after August 30, 2007)*.

I. GROSSLY AGGRAVATING FACTORS - G.S. 20-179(c)

(**NOTE:** *Either Nos. 1 and 2 or No. 3 apply in each case except aiders and abettors. If No. 1 is checked, No. 2.a. or No. 2.b. must also be checked.*)

☐ 1. The defendant
- ☐ a. has been convicted of a prior offense involving impaired driving which conviction occurred within seven (7) years before the date of this offense.
- ☐ b. has two or more convictions as described in No. 1.a. (Level One punishment is required.)
- ☐ c. has been convicted of an offense involving impaired driving which conviction occurred after the date of the offense for which the defendant is being sentenced but before or contemporaneously with the sentencing in this case.
- ☐ d. has two or more convictions as described in No. 1.c. (Level One punishment is required.)
- ☐ e. has a prior conviction in District Court for an offense involving impaired driving, the conviction was appealed to Superior Court, the appeal has been withdrawn or the case has been remanded back to District Court, and a new sentencing hearing for the case has not been held pursuant to G.S. 20-38.7. *(Applies to offenses committed on or after August 30, 2007.)*
- ☐ f. has two or more convictions as described in No.1.e. (Level One punishment is required.) *(Applies to offenses committed on or after August 30, 2007.)*
- ☐ g. drove, at the time of the current offense, while the defendant's drivers license was revoked under G.S. 20-28 and the revocation was an impaired driving revocation under G.S. 20-28.2(a).
- ☐ h. caused, by the defendant's impaired driving at the time of the current offense, serious injury to another person.
- ☐ i. drove, at the time of the current offense, while a child under the age of 16 years was in the vehicle.

☐ 2. Therefore, the following level of punishment shall be imposed:
- ☐ a. **Level One** punishment, because at least two grossly aggravating factors in No. 1 apply to this defendant. (**NOTE:** *Each prior conviction is a separate grossly aggravating factor.*)
- ☐ b. **Level Two** punishment, because only one grossly aggravating factor in No. 1 applies to this defendant.

☐ 3. There are no grossly aggravating factors.

II. AGGRAVATING AND MITIGATING FACTORS - G.S. 20-179(d) AND (e)

AGGRAVATING FACTORS - G.S. 20-179(d):
(**NOTE:** *Except for the factors in subdivisions 8 and 9 below, the conduct constituting the aggravating factor must occur during the same transaction or occurrence as this impaired driving offense.*)

☐ 1. The defendant's faculties were grossly impaired at the time the defendant was driving.

☐ 2. The defendant had an alcohol concentration of at least ☐ 0.16 ☐ 0.15 *(use for offenses committed on or after December 1, 2007)* within a relevant time after the driving.

☐ 3. The driving of the defendant was especially reckless.

☐ 4. The driving of the defendant was especially dangerous.

☐ 5. The negligent driving of the defendant led to an accident causing property damage of $1,000.00 or more, or property damage of any amount to a vehicle seized pursuant to G.S. 20-28.3.

☐ 6. The negligent driving of the defendant led to an accident causing personal injury.

☐ 7. The defendant was driving while the defendant's drivers license was revoked.

☐ 8. The defendant had at least two prior convictions of a motor vehicle offense not involving impaired driving, which occurred within five (5) years of this offense, and
- ☐ a. all were offenses for which at least three (3) points were assigned under G.S. 20-16.
- ☐ b. all were offenses for which the defendant's drivers license was subject to revocation.
- ☐ c. at least one was an offense for which at least three (3) points were assigned under G.S. 20-16 and at least one was an offense for which the defendant's drivers license was subject to revocation.

☐ 9. The defendant had at least one prior conviction of an offense involving impaired driving that occurred more than seven (7) years before the date of this offense.

☐ 10. The defendant has been convicted under G.S. 20-141.5 of speeding while fleeing or attempting to elude apprehension.

☐ 11. The defendant has been convicted under G.S. 20-141 of speeding by at least 30 m.p.h. over the legal limit.

Original - File
Material opposite unmarked squares is to be disregarded as surplusage.
(Over)

AOC-CR-311, Rev. 12/07

☐ 12. The defendant passed a stopped school bus in violation of G.S. 20-217.

☐ 13. Additional factors that aggravate the seriousness of this offense:

☐ 14. There are no aggravating factors.

MITIGATING FACTORS - G.S. 20-179(e):

NOTE: *Except for the factors in subdivisions 4, 6, and 7 below, the conduct constituting the mitigating factor must occur during the same transaction or occurrence as this impaired driving offense.*

☐ 1. There was a slight impairment of the defendant's faculties resulting solely from alcohol; and, the defendant's alcohol concentration did not exceed 0.09 at any relevant time after the driving.

☐ 2. There was a slight impairment of the defendant's faculties resulting solely from alcohol; and, no chemical test was made available to the defendant.

☐ 3. The driving of the defendant was safe and lawful except for the impairment of the defendant's faculties.

☐ 4. The defendant has a safe driving record, having no convictions of any motor vehicle offense for which at least four points are assigned under G.S. 20-16 or for which the defendant's license is subject to revocation within five (5) years of the date of this offense.

☐ 5. The impairment of the defendant's faculties was caused primarily by a lawfully prescribed drug for an existing medical condition, and the amount of the medical drug taken was within the prescribed dosage.

☐ 6. After being charged in this case with impaired driving, the defendant voluntarily submitted himself/herself to a mental health facility for assessment and has voluntarily participated in any treatment recommended by such facility, if such treatment was recommended.

☐ 6a. The defendant completed a substance abuse assessment, complied with its recommendations, and simultaneously maintained 60 days of continuous abstinence from alcohol consumption, as proven by a continuous alcohol monitoring system of a type approved by the Division of Adult Correction. *(Applies to offenses committed on or after December 1, 2007.)*

☐ 7. Additional factors that mitigate the seriousness of this offense:

☐ 8. There are no mitigating factors.

DETERMINATION - G.S. 20-179(f):

(**NOTE:** *Check only one.*)

☐ 1. The aggravating factors marked above substantially outweigh any mitigating factors marked above. Therefore, Level Three punishment shall be imposed.

☐ 2. There are no aggravating or mitigating factors. Therefore, Level Four punishment shall be imposed.

☐ 3. The aggravating factors marked above are substantially counterbalanced by the mitigating factors marked above. Therefore, Level Four punishment shall be imposed.

☐ 4. The mitigating factors marked above substantially outweigh any aggravating factors marked above. Therefore, Level Five punishment shall be imposed.

☐ 5. No findings of mitigating or aggravating factors were made because the defendant is an aider and abetter. Therefore, Level Five punishment shall be imposed.

Date	Name Of Presiding Judge (Type Or Print)	Signature Of Presiding Judge

AOC-CR-311, Side Two, Rev. 12/07

Material opposite unmarked squares is to be disregarded as surplusage.

Appendix 5.1B. Impaired Driving Determination of Sentencing Factors (for Offenses Committed on or after December 1, 2011)

STATE OF NORTH CAROLINA

File No.

______________________ County

In The General Court Of Justice
☐ District ☐ Superior Court Division

STATE VERSUS

Name Of Defendant

IMPAIRED DRIVING DETERMINATION OF SENTENCING FACTORS
(For Offenses Committed On Or After Dec. 1, 2011)

G.S. 20-179

☐ **District Court:** Based upon the evidence presented at the trial and sentencing hearing in District Court, the Court determines that (1) the State has proved the grossly aggravating factors and aggravating factors marked below beyond a reasonable doubt and (2) the defendant has proved the mitigating factors marked below by a preponderance of the evidence.

☐ **Superior Court:** Based upon the evidence presented at the trial and sentencing hearing in Superior Court, (1) the jury has determined that the State has proved the grossly aggravating factors and aggravating factors marked below beyond a reasonable doubt, or the defendant has admitted to these grossly aggravating factors and aggravating factors, and (2) the Court determines that the defendant has proved the mitigating factors marked below by a preponderance of the evidence. If grossly aggravating factor No. 1.a., 1.b., 1.c., 1.d., 1.e., or 1.f. is marked below, the Court determines that the State has proved that grossly aggravating factor beyond a reasonable doubt. If aggravating factor No. 8 or 9 is marked below, the Court determines that the State has proved that aggravating factor beyond a reasonable doubt.

I. GROSSLY AGGRAVATING FACTORS - G.S. 20-179(c)

(**NOTE:** *Either Nos. 1 and 2 or No. 3 apply in each case except aiders and abettors. If No. 1 is checked, No. 2.a., 2.b., or 2.c. must also be checked.)*

☐ 1. The defendant

- ☐ a. has been convicted of a prior offense involving impaired driving which conviction occurred within seven (7) years before the date of this offense.
- ☐ b. has ☐ two ☐ three or more convictions as described in No. 1.a.
- ☐ c. has been convicted of an offense involving impaired driving which conviction occurred after the date of the offense for which the defendant is being sentenced but before or contemporaneously with the sentencing in this case.
- ☐ d. has ☐ two ☐ three or more convictions as described in No. 1.c.
- ☐ e. has a prior conviction in District Court for an offense involving impaired driving, the conviction was appealed to Superior Court, the appeal has been withdrawn or the case has been remanded back to District Court, and a new sentencing hearing for the case has not been held pursuant to G.S. 20-38.7.
- ☐ f. has ☐ two ☐ three or more convictions as described in No.1.e.
- ☐ g. drove, at the time of the current offense, while the defendant's drivers license was revoked under G.S. 20-28 and the revocation was an impaired driving revocation under G.S. 20-28.2(a).
- ☐ h. caused, by the defendant's impaired driving at the time of the current offense, serious injury to another person.
- ☐ i. drove, at the time of the current offense, while a child under the age of 18 years was in the vehicle.
- ☐ j. drove, at the time of the current offense, while a person with the mental development of a child under the age of 18 years was in the vehicle.
- ☐ k. drove, at the time of the current offense, while a person with a physical disability preventing unaided exit from the vehicle was in the vehicle.

☐ 2. Therefore, the following level of punishment shall be imposed:

- ☐ a. **Aggravated Level One** punishment, because three or more grossly aggravating factors in No. 1 apply to this defendant. (**NOTE:** *Each prior conviction is a separate grossly aggravating factor.*)
- ☐ b. **Level One** punishment, because
  - ☐ grossly aggravating factor No. 1.i., 1.j., or 1.k. applies to this defendant.
  - ☐ two and only two grossly aggravating factors in No. 1 (other than grossly aggravating factor No. 1.i., 1.j., or 1.k.) apply to this defendant.

  (**NOTE:** *Each prior conviction is a separate grossly aggravating factor.*)
- ☐ c. **Level Two** punishment, because only one grossly aggravating factor in No. 1 (other than grossly aggravating factor No. 1.i., 1.j., or 1.k.) applies to this defendant.

☐ 3. There are no grossly aggravating factors.

II. AGGRAVATING AND MITIGATING FACTORS - G.S. 20-179(d) AND (e)

AGGRAVATING FACTORS - G.S. 20-179(d):
(**NOTE:** *Except for the factors in subdivisions 8 and 9 below, the conduct constituting the aggravating factor must occur during the same transaction or occurrence as this impaired driving offense.*)

☐ 1. The defendant's faculties were grossly impaired at the time the defendant was driving.
☐ 2. The defendant had an alcohol concentration of at least 0.15 within a relevant time after the driving.
☐ 3. The driving of the defendant was especially reckless.
☐ 4. The driving of the defendant was especially dangerous.
☐ 5. The negligent driving of the defendant led to an accident causing property damage of $1,000.00 or more, or property damage of any amount to a vehicle seized pursuant to G.S. 20-28.3.
☐ 6. The negligent driving of the defendant led to an accident causing personal injury.
☐ 7. The defendant was driving while the defendant's drivers license was revoked.

Original - File
Material opposite unmarked squares is to be disregarded as surplusage.
(Over)

AOC-CR-311, Rev. 12/11

☐ 8. The defendant had at least two prior convictions of a motor vehicle offense not involving impaired driving, which occurred within five (5) years of this offense, and
  ☐ a. all were offenses for which at least three (3) points were assigned under G.S. 20-16.
  ☐ b. all were offenses for which the defendant's drivers license was subject to revocation.
  ☐ c. at least one was an offense for which at least three (3) points were assigned under G.S. 20-16 and at least one was an offense for which the defendant's drivers license was subject to revocation.

☐ 9. The defendant had at least one prior conviction of an offense involving impaired driving that occurred more than seven (7) years before the date of this offense.

☐ 10. The defendant has been convicted under G.S. 20-141.5 of speeding while fleeing or attempting to elude apprehension.

☐ 11. The defendant has been convicted under G.S. 20-141 of speeding by at least 30 m.p.h. over the legal limit.

☐ 12. The defendant passed a stopped school bus in violation of G.S. 20-217.

☐ 13. Additional factors that aggravate the seriousness of this offense:

☐ 14. There are no aggravating factors.

MITIGATING FACTORS - G.S. 20-179(e):

NOTE: *Except for the factors in subdivisions 4, 6, and 7 below, the conduct constituting the mitigating factor must occur during the same transaction or occurrence as this impaired driving offense.*

☐ 1. There was a slight impairment of the defendant's faculties resulting solely from alcohol; and, the defendant's alcohol concentration did not exceed 0.09 at any relevant time after the driving.

☐ 2. There was a slight impairment of the defendant's faculties resulting solely from alcohol; and, no chemical test was made available to the defendant.

☐ 3. The driving of the defendant was safe and lawful except for the impairment of the defendant's faculties.

☐ 4. The defendant has a safe driving record, having no convictions of any motor vehicle offense for which at least four points are assigned under G.S. 20-16 or for which the defendant's license is subject to revocation within five (5) years of the date of this offense.

☐ 5. The impairment of the defendant's faculties was caused primarily by a lawfully prescribed drug for an existing medical condition, and the amount of the medical drug taken was within the prescribed dosage.

☐ 6. After being charged in this case with impaired driving, the defendant voluntarily submitted himself/herself to a mental health facility for assessment and has voluntarily participated in any treatment recommended by such facility, if such treatment was recommended.

☐ 6a. The defendant completed a substance abuse assessment, complied with its recommendations, and simultaneously maintained 60 days of continuous abstinence from alcohol consumption, as proven by a continuous alcohol monitoring system of a type approved by the Division of Adult Correction.

☐ 7. Additional factors that mitigate the seriousness of this offense:

☐ 8. There are no mitigating factors.

DETERMINATION - G.S. 20-179(f):

(**NOTE:** *Check only one.*)

☐ 1. The aggravating factors marked above substantially outweigh any mitigating factors marked above. Therefore, Level Three punishment shall be imposed.

☐ 2. There are no aggravating or mitigating factors. Therefore, Level Four punishment shall be imposed.

☐ 3. The aggravating factors marked above are substantially counterbalanced by the mitigating factors marked above. Therefore, Level Four punishment shall be imposed.

☐ 4. The mitigating factors marked above substantially outweigh any aggravating factors marked above. Therefore, Level Five punishment shall be imposed.

☐ 5. No findings of mitigating or aggravating factors were made because the defendant is an aider and abetter. Therefore, Level Five punishment shall be imposed.

Date	*Name Of Presiding Judge (Type Or Print)*	*Signature Of Presiding Judge*

AOC-CR-311, Side Two, Rev. 12/11

Material opposite unmarked squares is to be disregarded as surplusage.

Appendix 5.2A. Notice of Grossly Aggravating and Aggravating Factors (DWI) (for Offenses Committed before December 1, 2011)

STATE OF NORTH CAROLINA

File No.

_______________ County

In The General Court Of Justice
Superior Court Division

STATE VERSUS

Name Of Defendant

NOTICE OF GROSSLY AGGRAVATING AND AGGRAVATING FACTORS (DWI)
(For Offenses Committed Before Dec. 1, 2011)
G.S. 20-179

Pursuant to G.S. 20-179(a1), the defendant is hereby notified that the State of North Carolina intends to prove the existence of grossly aggravating and aggravating factors under G.S. 20-179(c) and (d), as indicated below.

GROSSLY AGGRAVATING FACTORS - G.S. 20-179(c)

☐ 1. The State intends to prove that the defendant
- ☐ a. has been convicted of a prior offense involving impaired driving which conviction occurred within seven (7) years before the date of this offense.
- ☐ b. has two or more convictions as described in No. 1.a.
- ☐ c. has been convicted of an offense involving impaired driving which conviction occurred after the date of the offense for which the defendant is being sentenced but before or contemporaneously with the sentencing in this case.
- ☐ d. has two or more convictions as described in No. 1.c.
- ☐ e. has a prior conviction in District Court for an offense involving impaired driving, the conviction was appealed to Superior Court, the appeal has been withdrawn or the case has been remanded back to District Court, and a new sentencing hearing for the case has not been held pursuant to G.S. 20-38.7. *(Applies to offenses committed on or after August 30, 2007.)*
- ☐ f. has two or more convictions as described in No. 1.e. *(Applies to offenses committed on or after August 30, 2007.)*
- ☐ g. drove, at the time of the current offense, while the defendant's drivers license was revoked under G.S. 20-28 and the revocation was an impaired driving revocation under G.S. 20-28.2(a).
- ☐ h. caused, by the defendant's impaired driving at the time of the current offense, serious injury to another person.
- ☐ i. drove, at the time of the current offense, while a child under the age of 16 years was in the vehicle.

☐ 2. The State does not intend to prove any grossly aggravating factors.

AGGRAVATING FACTORS - G.S. 20-179(d)

☐ 1. The State intends to prove the following:
- ☐ a. The defendant's faculties were grossly impaired at the time the defendant was driving.
- ☐ b. The defendant had an alcohol concentration of at least ☐ 0.16 ☐ 0.15 *(use for offenses committed on or after December 1, 2007)* within a relevant time after the driving.
- ☐ c. The driving of the defendant was especially reckless.
- ☐ d. The driving of the defendant was especially dangerous.
- ☐ e. The negligent driving of the defendant led to an accident causing property damage of $1,000.00 or more, or property damage of any amount to a vehicle seized pursuant to G.S. 20-28.3.
- ☐ f. The negligent driving of the defendant led to an accident causing personal injury.
- ☐ g. The defendant was driving while the defendant's drivers license was revoked.
- ☐ h. The defendant had at least two prior convictions of a motor vehicle offense not involving impaired driving, which occurred within five (5) years of this offense, and
  - ☐ 1. all were offenses for which at least three (3) points were assigned under G.S. 20-16.
  - ☐ 2. all were offenses for which the defendant's drivers license was subject to revocation.
  - ☐ 3. at least one was an offense for which at least three (3) points were assigned under G.S. 20-16 and at least one was an offense for which the defendant's drivers license was subject to revocation.
- ☐ i. The defendant had at least one prior conviction of an offense involving impaired driving that occurred more than seven (7) years before the date of this offense.
- ☐ j. The defendant has been convicted under G.S. 20-141.5 of speeding while fleeing or attempting to elude apprehension.
- ☐ k. The defendant has been convicted under G.S. 20-141 of speeding by at least 30 m.p.h. over the legal limit.
- ☐ l. The defendant passed a stopped school bus in violation of G.S. 20-217.
- ☐ m. Additional factors that aggravate the seriousness of this offense:

☐ 2. The State does not intend to prove any aggravating factors.

SIGNATURE OF PROSECUTOR

Date	*Name Of Prosecutor (Type Or Print)*	*Signature Of Prosecutor*

(See REVERSE for Certificate Of Service)

AOC-CR-338, Rev. 8/07

CERTIFICATE OF SERVICE

I certify that a copy of this notice was served by:

☐ delivering a copy personally to the ☐ defendant's attorney. ☐ defendant.

☐ depositing a copy, enclosed in a postpaid properly addressed envelope, in a post office or official depository under the exclusive care and custody of the U. S. Postal Service directed to the ☐ defendant's attorney ☐ defendant at the address shown below.

Address

☐ leaving a copy at the office of the defendant's attorney with a partner or employee.

Name And Title Of Person With Whom Copy Left

☐ Other: ______________________

Date Served	*Signature Of Person Serving*	*Title*

ACCEPTANCE OF SERVICE

☐ Service accepted by: ☐ defendant's attorney. ☐ defendant.

Date Service Accepted	*Signature Of Person Accepting Service*

AOC-CR-338, Side Two, Rev. 8/07

Appendix 5.2B. Notice of Grossly Aggravating and Aggravating Factors (DWI) (for Offenses Committed on or after December 1, 2011)

STATE OF NORTH CAROLINA

File No.

____________________ County

In The General Court Of Justice
Superior Court Division

STATE VERSUS

Name Of Defendant

NOTICE OF GROSSLY AGGRAVATING AND AGGRAVATING FACTORS (DWI)
(For Offenses Committed On Or After DEC. 1, 2011)
G.S. 20-179

Pursuant to G.S. 20-179(a1), the defendant is hereby notified that the State of North Carolina intends to prove the existence of grossly aggravating and aggravating factors under G.S. 20-179(c) and (d), as indicated below.

GROSSLY AGGRAVATING FACTORS - G.S. 20-179(c)

☐ 1. The State intends to prove that the defendant
- ☐ a. has been convicted of a prior offense involving impaired driving which conviction occurred within seven (7) years before the date of this offense.
- ☐ b. has ☐ two ☐ three or more convictions as described in No. 1.a.
- ☐ c. has been convicted of an offense involving impaired driving which conviction occurred after the date of the offense for which the defendant is being sentenced but before or contemporaneously with the sentencing in this case.
- ☐ d. has ☐ two ☐ three or more convictions as described in No. 1.c.
- ☐ e. has a prior conviction in District Court for an offense involving impaired driving, the conviction was appealed to Superior Court, the appeal has been withdrawn or the case has been remanded back to District Court, and a new sentencing hearing for the case has not been held pursuant to G.S. 20-38.7.
- ☐ f. has ☐ two ☐ three or more convictions as described in No. 1.e.
- ☐ g. drove, at the time of the current offense, while the defendant's drivers license was revoked under G.S. 20-28 and the revocation was an impaired driving revocation under G.S. 20-28.2(a).
- ☐ h. caused, by the defendant's impaired driving at the time of the current offense, serious injury to another person.
- ☐ i. drove, at the time of the current offense, while a child under the age of 18 years was in the vehicle.
- ☐ j. drove, at the time of the current offense, while a person with the mental development of a child under the age of 18 years was in the vehicle.
- ☐ k. drove, at the time of the current offense, while a person with a physical disability preventing unaided exit from the vehicle was in the vehicle.

☐ 2. The State does not intend to prove any grossly aggravating factors.

AGGRAVATING FACTORS - G.S. 20-179(d)

☐ 1. The State intends to prove the following:
- ☐ a. The defendant's faculties were grossly impaired at the time the defendant was driving.
- ☐ b. The defendant had an alcohol concentration of at least 0.15 within a relevant time after the driving.
- ☐ c. The driving of the defendant was especially reckless.
- ☐ d. The driving of the defendant was especially dangerous.
- ☐ e. The negligent driving of the defendant led to an accident causing property damage of $1,000.00 or more, or property damage of any amount to a vehicle seized pursuant to G.S. 20-28.3.
- ☐ f. The negligent driving of the defendant led to an accident causing personal injury.
- ☐ g. The defendant was driving while the defendant's drivers license was revoked.
- ☐ h. The defendant had at least two prior convictions of a motor vehicle offense not involving impaired driving, which occurred within five (5) years of this offense, and
  - ☐ 1. all were offenses for which at least three (3) points were assigned under G.S. 20-16.
  - ☐ 2. all were offenses for which the defendant's drivers license was subject to revocation.
  - ☐ 3. at least one was an offense for which at least three (3) points were assigned under G.S. 20-16 and at least one was an offense for which the defendant's drivers license was subject to revocation.
- ☐ i. The defendant had at least one prior conviction of an offense involving impaired driving that occurred more than seven (7) years before the date of this offense.
- ☐ j. The defendant has been convicted under G.S. 20-141.5 of speeding while fleeing or attempting to elude apprehension.
- ☐ k. The defendant has been convicted under G.S. 20-141 of speeding by at least 30 m.p.h. over the legal limit.
- ☐ l. The defendant passed a stopped school bus in violation of G.S. 20-217.
- ☐ m. Additional factors that aggravate the seriousness of this offense:

☐ 2. The State does not intend to prove any aggravating factors.

(See REVERSE for Signature Of Prosecutor and Certificate Of Service)

AOC-CR-338, Rev. 12/11

Appendix 5.2B. Notice of Grossly Aggravating and Aggravating Factors (DWI) (for Offenses Committed on or after December 1, 2011) (*continued*)

SIGNATURE OF PROSECUTOR

Date	Name Of Prosecutor (Type Or Print)	Signature Of Prosecutor

CERTIFICATE OF SERVICE

I certify that a copy of this notice was served by:

☐ delivering a copy personally to the ☐ defendant's attorney. ☐ defendant.

☐ depositing a copy, enclosed in a postpaid properly addressed envelope, in a post office or official depository under the exclusive care and custody of the U. S. Postal Service directed to the ☐ defendant's attorney ☐ defendant at the address shown below.

Address

☐ leaving a copy at the office of the defendant's attorney with a partner or employee.

Name And Title Of Person With Whom Copy Left

☐ Other: ______

Date Served	Signature Of Person Serving	Title

ACCEPTANCE OF SERVICE

☐ Service accepted by: ☐ defendant's attorney. ☐ defendant.

Date Service Accepted	Signature Of Person Accepting Service

AOC-CR-338,Side Two, Rev. 12/11

Chapter 6

Refusal Revocations, Limited Driving Privileges, and License Restoration

Chapter 6

Refusal Revocations, Limited Driving Privileges, and License Restoration

I. Introduction

The license consequences that result from conviction of an implied consent offense are set forth in chapter 2 in the "License Revocation" section for each offense. The revocation that may be imposed by a magistrate or clerk before trial based upon a defendant's willful refusal to submit to testing or a specified alcohol concentration is discussed in chapter 3.

This chapter discusses the license revocation that results from a person's willful refusal to submit to a chemical analysis in an implied consent case, commercial driver's license disqualifications, the eligibility requirements for a limited driving privilege that permits driving of a non-commercial motor vehicle during periods of revocation resulting from charges or conviction of an implied consent offense, and the requirements for having one's license restored following a conviction for impaired driving.

II. Revocation for Willfully Refusing a Chemical Test

North Carolina's implied consent laws, like their sister provisions in other states, are designed to encourage persons suspected of driving while impaired and other alcohol-related offenses to participate in chemical testing without being physically forced to do so by law enforcement officers. The incentive for suspects to "voluntarily" submit to compulsory testing is provided by their desire to remain licensed; suspects are informed that if they refuse testing, their driver's licenses will be revoked for a period of one year.[1]

When a suspect nevertheless refuses to submit to implied consent testing, the law enforcement officer and chemical analyst complete affidavits[2] averring that the implied consent testing procedures

1. *See* Section 20-16.2(a)(1) of the North Carolina Statutes (hereinafter G.S.) (requiring that before a chemical analysis is administered a defendant be advised: "Under the implied-consent law, you can refuse any test, but your drivers license will be revoked for one year and could be revoked for a longer period of time under certain circumstances . . . .").

2. When the law enforcement officer also is the chemical analyst, only one affidavit is completed.

have been followed and stating that the person willfully refused[3] to submit to a chemical analysis. This affidavit, which also serves as a revocation report used in determining whether the defendant's license will be civilly revoked pursuant to Section 20-16.5 of the North Carolina General Statutes (hereinafter G.S.),[4] typically is sworn and subscribed before the magistrate at the initial appearance. The current form affidavit and revocation report is denominated as AOC-CVR-1A. The form is designed to allow the chemical analyst to incorporate by reference the test record ticket from the breath-testing instrument. If the chemical analyst recorded the refusal by entering it into the instrument, the test record ticket will state "TEST REFUSED."

When a person refuses to submit to a chemical analysis, the law enforcement officer must immediately mail the affidavit to the North Carolina Division of Motor Vehicles (NC DMV). Upon receiving a "properly executed affidavit" pursuant to G.S. 20-16.2(c1), NC DMV must "expeditiously notify the person charged that [his or her] license to drive is revoked for 12 months, effective on the tenth calendar day after the mailing of the revocation order unless, before the effective date of the order, the person requests in writing a hearing before [NC DMV]."[5]

A. NC DMV Hearing

If the person properly requests a hearing as described immediately above, the person retains his or her license unless it is revoked for some other reason until (1) the hearing is held, (2) the person withdraws the request, or (3) the person fails to appear at the scheduled hearing.[6] An NC DMV hearing officer conducts the hearing in the county where the charge was issued. The hearing officer may subpoena any witnesses or documents that the hearing officer deems necessary. The driver whose license is subject to revocation "may request the hearing officer to subpoena the charging officer, the chemical analyst, or both to appear at the hearing."[7]

The hearing is limited to consideration of whether:

(1) The person was charged with an implied consent offense or the driver had an alcohol concentration restriction on his or her driver's license pursuant to G.S. 20-19;[8]

---

3. For a discussion of the distinction between a willful refusal and a refusal, *see* Shea Denning, *Lee v. Gore: Round Two*, N.C. Crim. L., UNC Sch. of Gov't Blog (Aug. 19, 2010), http://nccriminallaw.sog.unc.edu/?p=1516.

4. *See* chapter 3.

5. G.S. 20-16.2(d). *See* Lee v. Gore, 365 N.C. 227 (2011) (concluding that a "willful refusal" must specifically be averred in the affidavit for NC DMV to have the authority to revoke the person's license pursuant to G.S. 20-16.2). Other sorts of deficiencies in an affidavit do not deprive NC DMV of authority. *See, e.g.*, Hoots v. Robertson, 214 N.C. App. 181 (2011) (holding that an affidavit that erroneously stated that the petitioner refused testing two minutes before the time listed for the refusal on the test record ticket was properly executed, as there is no requirement that an affidavit state when the refusal occurred). If NC DMV receives a facially deficient affidavit, its practice is to return the affidavit to the law enforcement officer along with a form DL-168 on which an NC DMV employee identifies the items that need to be corrected or completed. The state supreme court in *Lee* implicitly endorsed this practice, noting that NC DMV could have asked the officer in that case whether the affidavit omitted information. *Lee*, 365 N.C. at 234. If the officer responded affirmatively, NC DMV then could have requested that the officer swear out a new, properly executed affidavit. *Id.*

6. G.S. 20-16.2(d).

7. *Id.* The person must request that the hearing officer issue any such subpoena in writing at least three days before the hearing. In addition, the person "may subpoena any other witness whom the person deems necessary, and the provisions of G.S. 1A-1, Rule 45, apply to the issuance and service of all subpoenas issued under [G.S. 20-16.2(d)]." *Id.*

8. As discussed in section V.B.3, *infra*, a person whose license has been restored following a revocation for impaired driving and certain other alcohol-related offenses must agree to submit to a chemical analysis

(2) A law enforcement officer had reasonable grounds to believe that the person had committed an implied consent offense or violated the alcohol concentration restriction on his or her driver's license;
(3) The implied consent offense charged involved death or critical injury to another person (if this allegation is contained in the affidavit);
(4) The person was notified of his or her rights as required by G.S. 20-16.2(a); and
(5) The person willfully refused to submit to a chemical analysis.[9]

The hearing officer must enter written findings of fact and conclusions of law. If the hearing officer finds that the five aforementioned conditions are met, he or she must order that the revocation be sustained.[10] If the hearing officer finds that any of conditions 1, 2, 4, or 5 is not met, he or she must rescind the revocation.[11] If the hearing officer finds that condition 3 is alleged in the affidavit but is not met, he or she must order that the revocation be sustained, but the additional consequences for refusal of a chemical analysis in a case involving death or critical injury do not apply.[12] If the revocation is sustained, the person charged must surrender his or her license immediately upon being notified by NC DMV.[13]

B. Right to Hearing in Superior Court

If the revocation for a willful refusal is sustained after an NC DMV hearing, the person whose license has been revoked may file a petition in superior court within 30 days thereafter for a hearing on the record.[14] The superior court's review is limited to whether there is sufficient evidence in the record to support the hearing officer's findings of fact and whether the hearing officer committed an error of law in revoking the license.[15]

C. Revocation for Willful Refusal by Person under 21

If a person willfully refuses to submit to a chemical analysis pursuant to G.S. 20-16.2 while he or she is less than 21 years old, his or her license must be revoked under G.S. 20-13.2 in addition to any other applicable revocation provision. A revocation order entered under G.S. 20-13.2 becomes effective at the same time as a revocation order issued under G.S. 20-16.2. The chief effect of the dual revocation is to render the person ineligible for a limited driving privilege during the period of the willful refusal revocation.

---

in accordance with G.S. 20-16.2 at the request of a law enforcement officer who has reasonable grounds to believe that the person is driving in violation of the restriction.

9. G.S. 20-16.2(d).
10. *Id.*
11. *Id.*
12. *Id.*
13. *Id.*
14. *Id.* § 20-16.2(e).
15. *Id.*

III. Commercial Driver's License Disqualifications

The driving of commercial motor vehicles is regulated by both state and federal law.[16] The regulatory scheme for commercial license holders is more restrictive than that governing the driving of non-commercial vehicles, which is not surprising given the increased public safety risks associated with commercial vehicles, which often are larger than regular passenger vehicles[17] and which sometimes carry hazardous freight.[18] Commercial drivers who commit certain traffic violations or other specified offenses are disqualified from driving a commercial motor vehicle for the period of time specified by statute. Disqualification differs from revocation in that it applies only to the operation of a commercial motor vehicle. When a disqualification is in place, the person may, if properly licensed, continue to drive a regular, non-commercial motor vehicle. In contrast, the revocation of a person's regular or commercial driver's license, for any reason, disqualifies the person from driving a commercial motor vehicle for the period during which the person's regular or commercial driver's license is revoked.[19]

The following implied consent offenses and related acts disqualify a person from driving a commercial motor vehicle for one year if committed by a person holding a commercial driver's license or committed while operating a commercial motor vehicle by a person who does not hold a commercial driver's license:

- A first conviction under G.S. 20-138.1, driving while impaired, for any person who holds a commercial driver's license where the conviction occurred while the person was driving a motor vehicle that was not a commercial motor vehicle
- A first conviction under G.S. 20-138.2, driving a commercial motor vehicle while impaired
- Refusal to submit to a chemical test when charged with an implied consent offense
- A second or subsequent conviction, as those terms are defined in G.S. 20-138.2A(d), of driving a commercial motor vehicle after consuming alcohol under G.S. 20-138.2A
- Either (1) a civil license revocation under G.S. 20-16.5 or (2) a substantially similar revocation ordered in another jurisdiction, arising out of a charge that occurred while the person facing revocation was either (a) operating a commercial motor vehicle or (b) while the person was holding a commercial driver's license[20]
- A first conviction of vehicular homicide under G.S. 20-141.4 or vehicular manslaughter under G.S. 14-18 occurring while the person facing revocation was operating a commercial motor vehicle.[21]

---

16. *See* G.S. Chapter 20, Article 2C; 49 U.S.C. Subtitle VI, Part B, Chapter 313.
17. G.S. 20-4.01(3d).
18. *Id.* § 20-4.01(3d)c.2.
19. *Id.* § 20-17.4(f). When a person is disqualified as the result of a conviction that requires both disqualification and revocation, the following rules apply: (1) the person must surrender his or her driver's license to the court or to the North Carolina Division of Motor Vehicles (NC DMV); (2) the person may obtain a limited driving privilege to drive a non-commercial motor vehicle during the revocation period to the extent that the law would allow a limited driving privilege if the person had been driving a non-commercial motor vehicle when the offense occurred; and (3) if the disqualification lasts longer than the revocation, the person may apply for a regular Class C driver's license at the end of the revocation period. *Id.* § 20-17.5(b).
20. The state supreme court in *State v. McKenzie*, 367 N.C. 112 (2013), rejected the defendant's double jeopardy argument that the disqualification of his commercial driver's license for one year based upon charges that he drove while impaired in a passenger vehicle barred his subsequent prosecution on the impaired driving charges.
21. G.S. 20-17.4(a). *See also id.* § 20-17.4(e): "A person is disqualified from driving a commercial motor vehicle for three years if that person is convicted of an offense or commits an act requiring disqualification under

In addition, a person who is convicted for a first offense of driving a commercial motor vehicle after consuming alcohol under G.S. 20-138.2A is disqualified from driving a commercial motor vehicle for ten days.[22] A person who has been disqualified from driving a commercial motor vehicle for a conviction or refusal set forth in G.S. 20-17.4(a) who, as the result of a separate incident, is subsequently convicted of an offense or commits an act, such as refusal, requiring disqualification under G.S. 20-17.4(a) is disqualified from driving a commercial motor vehicle for life, though the North Carolina Division of Motor Vehicles (NC DMV) may adopt guidelines under which the disqualification can be reduced to ten years.[23]

IV. Limited Driving Privileges

A. Generally

The North Carolina Division of Motor Vehicles (NC DMV) has the exclusive power to issue, suspend, or revoke a person's North Carolina driver's license.[24] The General Statutes confer upon the courts, however, the authority to issue limited driving privileges—judgments that authorize a person with a revoked driver's license to drive for certain essential purposes. To be eligible for a limited driving privilege, a person must satisfy eligibility requirements defined by statute and demonstrate good cause for the issuance of the privilege. Thus, a limited driving privilege is a judgment issued in the discretion of the court authorizing a person with a revoked driver's license to drive, for limited purposes and at limited times, during the period of the revocation. The limited driving privileges available to counteract implied consent revocations are summarized in Table 6.1 at the end of this chapter.

Copies of all limited driving privileges that are issued must be sent to NC DMV.[25] Upon receiving a privilege that is invalid on its face, NC DMV must immediately notify the court and the holder of the privilege that it considers the privilege void and that NC DMV records will not indicate that the holder has a limited driving privilege.[26]

B. Willful Refusal Privilege

As noted earlier, the penalty of having one's license revoked for failure to submit to chemical testing in an implied consent case is intended to encourage suspects to participate in testing. Obviously, the incentive to submit to testing would be greatly reduced if the ensuing refusal-based revocation had

---

[G.S. 20-17.4(a)] and the offense or act occurred while the person was transporting a hazardous material that required the motor vehicle driven to be placarded."

22. *Id.* § 20-17.4(a1).

23. *Id.* § 20-17.4(b).

24. *See* Joyner v. Garrett, 279 N.C. 226 (1971); Smith v. Walsh, 34 N.C. App. 287 (1977).

25. G.S. 20-179.3(k).

26. *Id.* The North Carolina Court of Appeals held in *State v. Bowes*, 159 N.C. App. 18 (2003), that the provision in G.S. 20-179.3(k) allowing NC DMV to declare void a limited privilege—a judgment of the court—gave NC DMV the power to reverse the district court. The court of appeals concluded that this grant of authority violated the separation of powers clause in the state constitution, though it agreed with NC DMV's determination that Bowes, who was under 21 at the time of the impaired driving offense, was ineligible for a limited driving privilege. However, the state supreme court vacated the court of appeals' decision and dismissed the appeal as moot. *See* 360 N.C. 55 (2005). Thus, NC DMV continues to abide by the provisions of G.S. 20-179.3(k).

little impact on a person's ability to drive. For that reason, it is not surprising that while G.S. 20-16.2(e1) authorizes judges to issue limited driving privileges to authorize driving for certain essential purposes during a refusal-based revocation period, that authority is closely circumscribed.

1. Eligibility Requirements

A person whose license is revoked for willfully refusing chemical testing becomes eligible for a limited driving privilege only after his or her license has been revoked for at least six months for the refusal and the underlying charge has been resolved.[27] To satisfy the latter requirement, the underlying charge must have been disposed of other than by a conviction or the person must have been convicted of impaired driving under G.S. 20-138.1 and punished at Level Three, Four, or Five.[28] Moreover, if the person was convicted, he or she must have complied with at least one of the mandatory conditions of probation for the level of punishment imposed.

To be eligible for a limited driving privilege, the person also must satisfy the following requirements:

1. At the time of the refusal, he or she must have held a valid driver's license or a license that had been expired for less than a year;
2. At the time of the refusal, he or she must not have been convicted within the preceding seven years of an offense involving impaired driving;
3. At the time of the instant refusal, he or she must not have willfully refused to submit to a chemical analysis under G.S. 20-16.2 in the preceding seven years;
4. Subsequent to the refusal, he or she must not have any unresolved pending charges for or additional convictions of an offense involving impaired driving;
5. He or she must have obtained a substance abuse assessment from a mental health facility and have successfully completed any recommended training or treatment program; and
6. He or she must furnish proof of financial responsibility or establish that he or she is exempt from this requirement. A person who does not own a currently registered motor vehicle and who does not operate uninsured non-fleet private passenger vehicles owned by others—and who signs a certificate to this effect—is not required to furnish proof of financial responsibility.[29]

If the refusal occurred in a case involving death or criminal injury to another person, no limited driving privilege may be issued.[30]

A limited driving privilege issued pursuant to G.S. 20-16.2(e1) authorizes a person to drive if the person's license is revoked solely under G.S. 20-16.2 and 20-17(a)(2) (requiring revocation upon conviction of impaired driving in violation of G.S. 20-138.1 or impaired driving in a commercial vehicle in violation of G.S. 20-138.2).[31] If the person's license is revoked under any other provision, such as G.S. 20-13.2(b) or (c), which impose separate license revocations for persons under 21 who are convicted of impaired driving or who willfully refuse a chemical analysis, no limited driving privilege may be issued under G.S. 20-16.2(e1).

---

27. G.S. 20-16.2(e1).
28. See chapter 5 for discussion of the levels of punishment applicable to impaired driving in violation of G.S. 20-138.1.
29. *See* G.S. 20-16.2(e1) (also incorporating restrictions in G.S. 20-179.3).
30. *Id.*
31. *Id.*

2. Application and Hearing

The provisions of G.S. 20-179.3 relating to the procedure for application for and conduct of the hearing and to the restrictions required or authorized to be included in the limited driving privilege apply to applications for a limited privilege under G.S. 20-16.2(e1). Thus, an application for a limited driving privilege under G.S. 20-16.2 must be filed with the clerk in duplicate, and a hearing on the petition may not be scheduled until "a reasonable time after the clerk files a copy of the application with the district attorney's office."[32] If the criminal charge giving rise to the refusal was finally disposed of in district court, any district court judge in the district in which the refusal occurred may hold the hearing. If the criminal charge was finally disposed of in superior court, the limited driving privilege hearing may be held by any superior court judge in the district or set of districts in which the refusal occurred.[33]

3. Permissible Driving

A limited driving privilege issued pursuant to G.S. 20-16.2(e1) following a willful refusal may permit a person to drive solely for essential purposes related to

- his or her employment,
- maintenance of his or her household,
- his or her education,
- his or her court-ordered treatment or assessment,
- community service ordered as a condition of probation, and
- emergency medical care.[34]

Driving that is not related to these purposes is unlawful even if done at times and upon routes authorized by the privilege.[35]

a. Driving for Work-Related Purposes in Willful Refusal Cases

A limited driving privilege may authorize driving for work-related purposes during standard working hours—6:00 a.m. to 8:00 p.m. on Monday through Friday—without specifying the times and routes in which the driving must occur.[36] If the applicant is not required to drive for essential work-related purposes except during standard working hours, the limited driving privilege must prohibit driving during nonstandard working hours unless the driving (1) is for emergency medical care or (2) is authorized as essential to the completion of any community work assignments, course of instruction at an Alcohol and Drug Education Traffic School, or substance abuse assessment or treatment that is ordered by the court as a condition of probation for the impaired driving conviction.[37]

Thus, a person may not drive for any of the other permissible essential purposes, such as for maintenance of his or her household, outside of standard working hours.[38] The limited driving privilege

---

32. *Id.* § 20-179.3(d).
33. *See id.* § 20-16.2(e1).
34. *Id.* § 20-179.3(a).
35. *Id.* § 20-179.3(f).
36. *Id.* § 20-179.3(g).
37. *Id.*
38. *Id.*; *id.* § 20-179.3(g2) (stating that a limited driving privilege may not allow driving for maintenance of the household except during standard working hours). The judge may exercise his or her discretion to further restrict driving for maintenance of household.

must state the name and address of the applicant's place of work or employer, and it may include other information and restrictions applicable to work-related driving in the discretion of the court.

i. Driving for Work during Nonstandard Hours

If the person is required to drive for an essential work-related purpose outside of standard working hours, he or she must present documentation of that fact before the judge may authorize driving for this purpose during those hours.[39] If the person is self-employed, "the documentation must be attached to or made a part of the limited driving privilege."[40] If the judge determines that it is necessary for the applicant to drive during nonstandard hours for a work-related purpose, he or she may authorize such driving subject to the following limitations:

- If the person is required to drive to and from a specific place of work at regular times, the limited driving privilege must specify the general times and routes during/on which the person will be driving to and from work and restrict driving to those times and routes.
- If the person is required to drive to and from work at a specific place but is unable to specify the times at which that driving will occur, the limited driving privilege must specify the general routes on which the person will be driving to and from work and restrict the driving to those general routes.
- If the person is required to drive to and from work at regular times but is unable to specify the places at which work is to be performed, the limited driving privilege must specify the general times and geographic boundaries during/in which the applicant will be driving and restrict driving to those times and within those boundaries.
- If the person can specify neither the times nor places in which he or she will be driving to and from work, or if the person is required to drive during nonstandard working hours as a condition of employment, the limited driving privilege must specify the geographic boundaries in which the person will be driving and restrict driving to within those boundaries.[41]

b. Maintenance of Household Driving in Willful Refusal Cases

The term "maintenance of household" is not defined by statute. Presumably it includes driving for purposes of (1) household errands such as grocery shopping, (2) non-emergency medical care for the driver and other family members, (3) transporting dependents to school and other activities, (4) transporting dependents pursuant to child custody agreements, as well as driving for other purposes related to household maintenance. As previously noted, driving for maintenance of household is permitted only during standard working hours.

c. Alcohol Restriction in Willful Refusal Cases

The limited driving privilege also must prohibit the driver from consuming alcohol while driving and from driving at any time while he or she has remaining in his or her body any alcohol or controlled substance previously consumed, unless the controlled substance was lawfully obtained and taken in therapeutically appropriate amounts.[42]

---

39. *Id.* § 20-179.3(g1).
40. *Id.*
41. *Id.* §§ 20-179.3(g1)(1)–(4).
42. *Id.* § 20-179.3(h).

d. Ignition Interlock

If, notwithstanding the person's willful refusal to submit to testing, a chemical analysis was obtained reflecting an alcohol concentration of 0.15 or more,[43] the limited privilege must restrict the person to operating only a designated motor vehicle, require that the designated motor vehicle be equipped with an approved ignition interlock system set to prohibit driving with an alcohol concentration of greater than 0.00, and require that the person personally activate the ignition interlock system before driving the motor vehicle.[44]

e. Form Order

The Administrative Office of the Courts has promulgated a form order, AOC-CR-313, for use by judges in granting limited driving privileges under G.S. 20-16.2(e1).

C. Civil License Revocation Privilege

As discussed in chapter 3, G.S. 20-16.5 provides for the immediate revocation of the driver's license of a person charged with an implied consent offense who willfully refuses to submit to a chemical analysis (discussed in detail in the sections immediately above) or who has an alcohol concentration of 0.08 or more within any relevant time after driving.[45] Civil license revocations begin when ordered and continue until the person's license has been revoked for the minimum period of time specified by statute (30 or 45 days, depending upon the circumstances[46]) and the person has paid the applicable costs.[47] If, at the time of the current offense, the person has one or more pending offenses for which his or her license had been or is revoked under G.S. 20-16.5, the revocation remains in effect until final judgment, including all appeals, is entered for the current offense and all pending offenses.[48] In no event may the revocation be shorter than the otherwise applicable minimum period.

1. Revocations for Minimum Periods of 30 or 45 Days

A person whose license has been revoked under G.S. 20-16.5 for a specified period of 30 or 45 days may apply for a limited driving privilege if he or she satisfies the following requirements:

- At the time of the alleged offense the person held a valid driver's license or a license that had been expired for less than a year;
- The person does not have a pending charge involving impaired driving other than the charge for which his or her license currently is revoked, nor does he or she have additional convictions of an offense involving impaired driving since being charged for the instant offense;

---

43. *See id.* § 20-16.2(c) (providing that a "refusal does not preclude testing under other applicable procedures of law"); 20-139.1(b3) (providing that "[a] person's refusal to give the sequential breath samples necessary to constitute a valid chemical analysis is a refusal under G.S. 20-16.2(c)" and that "[a] person's refusal to give the second or subsequent breath sample shall make the result of the first breath sample, or the result of the sample providing the lowest alcohol concentration if more than one breath sample is provided, admissible in any judicial or administrative hearing").

44. *Id.* § 20-179.3(g5).

45. Lower alcohol concentration thresholds result in immediate license revocations for persons who are driving commercial motor vehicles or who are under 21 years of age. *Id.* § 20-16.5(b)(4).

46. See *supra* chapter 3.

47. G.S. 20-16.5(f).

48. *Id.*

- The person's license has been revoked for at least 10 days if the revocation is for 30 days or for at least 30 days if the revocation is for 45 days; and
- The person has obtained a substance abuse assessment from a mental health facility and registers for and agrees to participate in any recommended training or treatment program.[49]

2. Indefinite Civil License Revocation

A person whose license has been indefinitely revoked under G.S. 20-16.5 may, after passage of the minimum period for the revocation, apply for a limited driving privilege. A judge of the trial division in which the current offense is pending may issue the limited driving privilege only if it is necessary to overcome undue hardship and the person meets the following eligibility requirements:

- At the time of the offense he or she held either a valid driver's license or a license that had been expired for less than one year;
- At the time of the offense he or she had not within the preceding seven years been convicted of an offense involving impaired driving;
- Subsequent to the offense he or she has not been convicted of, or had an unresolved charge lodged against him or her for, an offense involving impaired driving; and
- The person's driver's license is revoked solely under G.S. 20-16.5.[50]

3. Application for Privilege

An application for a limited driving privilege to permit driving during the period of a civil license revocation must be filed with the clerk in duplicate, and a hearing on the matter may not be held until a reasonable time after the clerk files a copy of the application with the district attorney's office.[51] Any district court judge authorized to hold court in the judicial district is authorized to issue a limited driving privilege under G.S. 20-16.5(p) to allow driving during a 30- or 45-day civil license revocation.[52] As previously noted, in the case of an indefinite revocation, the limited driving privilege may be issued by a judge of the division in which the current offense is pending.[53]

4. Authorized Driving

Just as in willful refusal cases, a limited driving privilege issued pursuant to G.S. 20-16.5 may permit a person to drive solely for essential purposes related to

- his or her employment,
- maintenance of his or her household,
- his or her education,
- his or her court-ordered treatment or assessment,
- community service ordered as a condition of probation, and
- emergency medical care.[54]

Driving that is not related to these purposes is unlawful even if done at times and upon routes authorized by the privilege.[55]

---

49. *Id.* §§ 20-16.5(p)(1)–(4).
50. *Id.* § 20-16.5(p).
51. *Id.* (incorporating by reference application and hearing procedures from G.S. 20-179.3).
52. *Id.*
53. *Id.*
54. *Id.* § 20-179.3(a).
55. *Id.* § 20-179.3(f).

a. Driving for Work-Related Purposes

A limited driving privilege may authorize driving for work-related purposes during standard working hours—6:00 a.m. to 8:00 p.m. on Monday through Friday—without specifying the times and routes in which the driving must occur.[56] If the applicant is not required to drive for essential work-related purposes except during standard working hours, the limited driving privilege must prohibit driving during nonstandard working hours unless the driving (1) is for emergency medical care or (2) is authorized as essential to the completion of any community work assignments, course of instruction at an Alcohol and Drug Education Traffic School, or substance abuse assessment or treatment that is ordered by the court as a condition of probation for the impaired driving conviction.[57]

Thus, a person may not drive for any of the other permissible essential purposes, such as for maintenance of his or her household, outside of standard working hours.[58] The limited driving privilege must state the name and address of the applicant's place of work or employer, and it may include other information and restrictions applicable to work-related driving in the discretion of the court.

i. Driving for Work during Nonstandard Hours

If the person is required to drive for an essential work-related purpose outside of standard working hours, he or she must present documentation of that fact before the judge may authorize driving for this purpose during those hours. If the person is self-employed, the documentation must be attached to or made a part of the limited driving privilege. If the judge determines that it is necessary for the applicant to drive during nonstandard hours for a work-related purpose, he or she may authorize such driving subject to the following limitations:

- If the person is required to drive to and from a specific place of work at regular times, the limited driving privilege must specify the general times and routes during/on which the person will be driving to and from work and restrict driving to those times and routes.
- If the person is required to drive to and from work at a specific place but is unable to specify the times at which that driving will occur, the limited driving privilege must specify the general routes on which the person will be driving to and from work and restrict the driving to those general routes.
- If the person is required to drive to and from work at regular times but is unable to specify the places at which work is to be performed, the limited driving privilege must specify the general times and geographic boundaries during/in which the applicant will be driving and restrict driving to those times and within those boundaries.
- If the person can specify neither the times nor places during/to which he or she will be driving for work, or if the person is required to drive during nonstandard working hours as a condition of employment, the limited driving privilege must specify the geographic boundaries in which the person will drive and restrict driving to within those boundaries.[59]

---

56. *Id.* § 20-179.3(g).

57. *Id.*

58. *Id.*; *id.* § 20-179.3(g2) (stating that a limited driving privilege may not allow driving for maintenance of the household except during standard working hours). The judge may exercise his or her discretion to further restrict driving for maintenance of household.

59. *Id.* §§ 20-179.3(g1)(1)–(4).

b. Alcohol Restriction

The limited driving privilege also must prohibit the driver from consuming alcohol while driving and from driving at any time while he or she has remaining in his or her body any alcohol or controlled substance previously consumed, unless the controlled substance was lawfully obtained and taken in therapeutically appropriate amounts.[60]

c. Form Petition and Order

The form petition for a limited driving privilege to allow driving during a civil license revocation is AOC-CVR-09. The form for a limited driving privilege to allow driving during the period of a 30- or 45-day civil license revocation is AOC-CVR-10, and the form for a privilege to allow driving during an indefinite civil license revocation is AOC-CVR-11.

D. Privilege Following DWI Conviction

1. Generally

As discussed in chapter 2, G.S. 20-17(a)(2) requires NC DMV to revoke the license of any driver convicted for impaired driving under G.S. 20-138.1. The revocation may be for one or four years or may be permanent, depending upon whether the person previously has been convicted of an offense involving impaired driving, when that offense occurred, and the level at which a person is sentenced.

2. Application for Privilege

A person convicted of impaired driving may apply for a limited driving privilege at the time judgment is entered or at a later time during the revocation period.[61] If the person applies after sentencing, he or she must file the application with the clerk in duplicate.[62] The clerk may not schedule a hearing on the matter until a reasonable time after the clerk files a copy of the application with the district attorney's office.[63]

The hearing must be scheduled before the presiding judge at the applicant's trial if that judge is assigned to a court in the district court district or superior court district in which the conviction for impaired driving was imposed.[64] If the presiding judge is not available within the district and the conviction was imposed in superior court, the hearing must be scheduled before the senior regular resident superior court judge of the superior court district.[65] If the presiding judge is not available within the district and the conviction was imposed in district court, the hearing must be scheduled before the chief district court judge.[66] The hearing may be scheduled in any county within the district.[67]

---

60. *Id.* § 20-179.3(h).
61. *Id.* § 20-179.3(c).
62. *Id.* § 20-179.3(d).
63. *Id.*
64. *Id.* § 20-179.3(d)(1).
65. *Id.* § 20-179.3(d)(2).
66. *Id.* § 20-179.3(d)(3).
67. *Id.* § 20-179.3(d).

3. Eligibility

a. Person Convicted of DWI in North Carolina

A person whose license is revoked for impaired driving under G.S. 20-138.1 is eligible for a limited driving privilege only if he or she is sentenced at Level Three, Four, or Five under G.S. 20-179.[68] The person also must satisfy each of the following additional conditions:

- The person must be revoked solely under G.S. 20-17(a)(2).
- At the time of the offense, the person must have been validly licensed or have had a license that had been expired for less than a year.
- The person must not have been convicted of an offense involving impaired driving within the seven years preceding the offense.
- Subsequent to the offense, the person must not have been convicted of or have an unresolved charge of an offense involving impaired driving.
- The person must have obtained and filed with the court a substance abuse assessment of the type required by G.S. 20-17.6.[69]
- Finally, the person must furnish proof of financial responsibility, or establish that he or she is exempt from this requirement,[70] and must, upon issuance of the privilege, pay a processing fee of $100.[71]

b. Drivers under 21 Not Eligible

A person who is under the age of 21 at the time he or she committed the offense of impaired driving that resulted in the revocation of his or her license under G.S. 20-17(a)(2) is not eligible for a limited driving privilege. This is because such persons also are revoked under G.S. 20-13.2(b),[72] and G.S. 20-179.3 authorizes a limited driving privilege for a person whose license is revoked "solely under G.S. 20-17(a)(2)."[73] Thus, limited driving privileges may not be issued under G.S. 20-179.3 for drivers whose licenses are revoked upon conviction of impaired driving for an offense committed when the person had not yet attained 21 years of age.[74]

c. DWI Convictions in Another State or in Federal Court

A person whose North Carolina driver's license is revoked because of a conviction in another jurisdiction that is substantially similar to impaired driving under G.S. 20-138.1 is eligible for a limited driving privilege if he or she would have been eligible for it had the conviction occurred in North Carolina.[75] The eligibility requirements for such a privilege are set forth above in section IV.D.3.a.

---

68. *Id.*
69. *Id.* § 20-179.3(b)(1).
70. *See id.* § 20-179.3(l).
71. *See id.* § 20-20.2.
72. This revocation applies regardless of whether the driver is charged with or convicted of the separate offense of driving after consuming by a person under 21. A separate provision, G.S. 20-13.2(a), requires NC DMV to revoke the license of a person convicted of violating G.S. 20-138.3(a).
73. G.S. 20-179.3(e).
74. The North Carolina Court of Appeals held in *State v. Bowes*, 159 N.C. App. 18 (2003), that NC DMV could not declare void a limited driving privilege granted by the court, though it agreed with NC DMV's determination that Bowes, who was under 21 at the time of the impaired driving offense, was ineligible for a limited driving privilege. However, the state supreme court vacated the court of appeals' decision and dismissed the appeal as moot. *See* 360 N.C. 55 (2005). Thus, NC DMV continues to abide by the provisions of G.S. 20-179.3(k), which permit it to void a limited driving privilege that is invalid on its face.
75. G.S. 20-179.3(b).

In general, they require that the person (1) have been punished at Level Three, Four, or Five, (2) have been validly licensed at the time of the offense, (3) not have a qualifying prior impaired driving conviction, (4) not have a subsequent conviction or unresolved charge for impaired driving, (5) have a substance abuse assessment, and (6) furnish proof of financial responsibility. Even if a person's out-of-state conviction satisfies the "substantially similar" criteria and the person meets the enumerated eligibility requirements, the person still must demonstrate that his or her North Carolina driving privileges were revoked, a requirement that significantly reduces the universe of eligible persons.

A few examples may help demonstrate the impact of this limitation.

Howard Henderson: An N.C. Resident with an Out-of-State DWI Conviction. Suppose that Howard Henderson, a North Carolina resident with a North Carolina driver's license, drives while impaired while vacationing in Pennsylvania. Henderson subsequently is convicted in Pennsylvania of driving while impaired. Pennsylvania, one of the 46 states[76] that is a member of the Drivers License Compact,[77] reports[78] the conviction to NC DMV.[79]

After receiving the report, NC DMV revokes Henderson's driver's license pursuant to G.S. 20-4.24(b), which requires that North Carolina give the same effect to a report of a conviction in a member state of driving a motor vehicle while impaired that it would give to a North Carolina conviction of impaired driving, and G.S. 20-17(a)(2), which requires NC DMV to revoke the license of any driver upon receiving a record for his or her conviction of impaired driving under G.S. 20-138.1.[80]

Given that Henderson's North Carolina driver's license was revoked, he is eligible for a limited driving privilege under G.S. 20-179.3 if he meets the other eligibility requirements noted above. Henderson must file his application for a privilege with the clerk in duplicate, and a hearing on his application may be held a reasonable time after the clerk files a copy of the application with the district attorney's office.[81]

Since Henderson was convicted of impaired driving in a jurisdiction other than North Carolina, the hearing must be scheduled before the chief district court judge of the district court district in which Henderson resides.[82] If the Pennsylvania court imposed a term of nonoperation of a motor vehicle, then Henderson may apply for the limited driving privilege only after having completed at least 60 days of that term.[83]

---

76. Pa. Dep't of Transp., Driver License Compact Fact Sheet (July 2011), www.dmv.state.pa.us/pdotforms/fact_sheets/fs-dlc.pdf.

77. G.S. Chapter 20, Article 1C.

78. *See* Driver License Compact Fact Sheet, *supra* note 76.

79. *See* 75 Pa. Cons. Stat. § 1581, Art. III (requiring the "licensing authority of a party state [to] report each conviction of a person from another party state occurring within its jurisdiction to the licensing authority of the home state of the licensee"); *cf.* G.S. 20-4.24(a) (requiring that member states report a conviction for "[d]riving a motor vehicle while impaired").

80. *Cf.* Hoenisch v. Pa. Dep't of Transp., Bureau of Driver Licensing, 785 A.2d 969, 973 (Pa. 2001) (concluding that a conviction under G.S. 20-138.1 provides a sufficient basis for a reciprocal driver's license suspension in Pennsylvania).

81. G.S. 20-179.3(d).

82. *Id.*

83. *Id.* § 20-179.3(c).

Howard Henderson: An N.C. Resident with an Out-of-State DWI Conviction in His Former Home State. Suppose instead that Henderson was a Pennsylvania resident licensed in Pennsylvania at the time he drove while impaired in Pennsylvania. Assume further that Henderson's alcohol concentration at the time he drove while impaired was 0.10, which resulted in a one-year revocation of his Pennsylvania driver's license.[84] Pennsylvania will not report Henderson's conviction to any other state, since Henderson is a Pennsylvania resident with a Pennsylvania driver's license. Suppose Henderson moves to North Carolina two months after his Pennsylvania conviction for impaired driving. Henderson is ineligible to obtain a North Carolina driver's license because of the Pennsylvania revocation.[85] And Henderson will not be eligible for a limited driving privilege under G.S. 20-179.3 because, even though he has no North Carolina driver's license and no reciprocal privilege to drive in North Carolina, his North Carolina driving privileges have not been revoked.[86]

Charlene Connor: An N.C. Resident with a DWI Conviction in Federal Court. Consider next the circumstances of Charlene Connor, a North Carolina resident with a North Carolina driver's license who is convicted in federal court of driving while impaired on the U.S. Army base at Fort Bragg in Fayetteville, North Carolina.[87] Upon receiving notice of Connor's conviction, NC DMV is authorized to revoke Connor's license.[88] As a person whose North Carolina driver's license is revoked because of a conviction in another jurisdiction, Connor is eligible, upon satisfying other requirements, to obtain a limited driving privilege under G.S. 20-179.3. Her application, like Henderson's in the first example above, must be filed with the chief district court judge in the district in which she resides.

Charlene Connor: An Out-of-State Resident with a DWI Conviction in Federal Court. Next, suppose that Connor is an active-duty soldier stationed at the Army base at Fort Bragg in Fayetteville, North Carolina. Connor is licensed to drive by her home state of Texas. In this example, Connor is ineligible to obtain a limited driving privilege under G.S. 20-179.3 following her conviction of impaired driving in federal court because her North Carolina driving privileges have not been revoked.[89]

84. *See* 75 Pa. Cons. Stat. § 3804(e).

85. *See* G.S. 20-4.25 (prohibiting member state from issuing a license if the applicant has held a license in another member state that has been revoked and the revocation period has not ended).

86. *Cf. id.* § 20-22(a) (permitting NC DMV to revoke the driving privileges of nonresidents "in like manner and for like cause as a driver's license" issued by NC DMV); 20-23.1 (permitting NC DMV to revoke the operating privileges of a person who does not have a driver's license "in like manner as it could suspend or revoke his license if such person held a driver's license"). Perhaps Henderson could spur NC DMV to act to revoke his driving privileges under G.S. 20-23.1 and thereby render himself eligible for a privilege under G.S. 20-179.3, but this seems an impractical solution.

87. *See* 18 U.S.C. § 13 (assimilating state law crimes for areas within federal jurisdiction).

88. *See* G.S. 20-23.2.

89. Perhaps Connor could spur NC DMV to act to revoke her driving privileges as a nonresident under G.S. 20-22 and thereby render herself eligible for a privilege under G.S. 20-179.3, but this seems an impractical solution.

4. Revocations Extended Pursuant to G.S. 20-17.6

Even if the requisite revocation period passes, the license revocation for a person convicted of impaired driving in violation of G.S. 20-138.1 may not end until NC DMV receives a certificate of completion reflecting that the person obtained a substance abuse assessment and completed the recommended education or treatment.[90] A person whose license remains revoked pursuant to the provisions of G.S. 20-17.6 solely because NC DMV has not obtained a certificate of completion is not eligible for a limited driving privilege.[91]

5. Authorized Driving

A limited driving privilege issued to a person pursuant to G.S. 20-179.3 may authorize driving of a non-commercial motor vehicle within the State of North Carolina for

- essential purposes related to the person's employment,
- maintenance of the person's household,
- the person's education,
- the person's court-ordered treatment or assessment.
- community service ordered as a condition of the person's probation, and
- emergency medical care.[92]

Driving that is not related to these purposes is unlawful even if done at times and on routes authorized by the privilege.[93]

a. Driving for Work-Related Purposes

A limited driving privilege may authorize driving for work-related purposes during standard working hours—6:00 a.m. to 8:00 p.m. on Monday through Friday—without specifying the times and routes during/on which the driving must occur.[94] If the applicant is not required to drive for essential work-related purposes except during standard working hours, the limited driving privilege must prohibit driving during nonstandard working hours unless the driving (1) is for emergency medical care or (2) is authorized as essential to the completion of any community work assignments, course of instruction at an Alcohol and Drug Education Traffic School, or substance abuse assessment or treatment that is ordered by the court as a condition of probation for the impaired driving conviction.[95]

Thus, a person may not drive for any of the other permissible essential purposes, such as for maintenance of his or her household, outside of standard working hours.[96] The limited driving privilege must state the name and address of the applicant's place of work or employer, and it may include other information and restrictions applicable to work-related driving in the discretion of the court.

---

90. *See* G.S. 20-17.6(b), (c). This statute also applies to any person whose license was revoked as a result of a conviction of G.S. 20-138.2; 20-138.3; 20-138.2A (if the person's driver's license was revoked under G.S. 20-17(a)(13)); and 20-138.2B (if the person's driver's license was revoked under G.S. 20-17(a)(14)).

91. G.S. 20-17.6(e).

92. *Id.* § 20-179.3(a).

93. *Id.* § 20-179.3(f).

94. *Id.* § 20-179.3(g).

95. *Id.*

96. *Id.*; *id.* § 20-179.3(g2) (stating that a limited driving privilege may not allow driving for maintenance of the household except during standard working hours). The judge may exercise his or her discretion to further restrict driving for maintenance of the household.

i. Driving for Work during Nonstandard Hours

If the person is required to drive for an essential work-related purpose outside of standard working hours, he or she must present documentation of that fact before the judge may authorize driving for this purpose during those hours. If the person is self-employed, the documentation must be attached to or made a part of the limited driving privilege. If the judge determines that it is necessary for the applicant to drive during nonstandard hours for a work-related purpose, he or she may authorize such driving subject to the following limitations:

- If the person is required to drive to and from a specific place of work at regular times, the limited driving privilege must specify the general times and routes during/on which the person will be driving to and from work and restrict driving to those times and routes.
- If the person is required to drive to and from work at a specific place but is unable to specify the times at which that driving will occur, the limited driving privilege must specify the general routes on which the person will be driving to and from work and restrict the driving to those general routes.
- If the person is required to drive to and from work at regular times but is unable to specify the places at which work is to be performed, the limited driving privilege must specify the general times and geographic boundaries during/in which the applicant will be driving and restrict driving to those times and within those boundaries.
- If the person can specify neither the times nor places during/to which he or she will be driving for work, or if the person is required to drive during nonstandard working hours as a condition of employment, the limited driving privilege must specify the geographic boundaries in which the person will drive and restrict driving to within those boundaries.[97]

b. Alcohol Restriction

The limited driving privilege also must prohibit the driver from consuming alcohol while driving and from driving at any time while he or she has remaining in his or her body any alcohol or controlled substance previously consumed, unless the controlled substance was lawfully obtained and taken in therapeutically appropriate amounts.[98]

c. Form Petition and Order

The form order for a limited driving privilege for a person convicted of impaired driving under G.S. 20-138.1 is AOC-CR-312. The form petition for seeking a limited privilege for a person revoked for an out-of-state or federal conviction of impaired driving is AOC-CV-350. The form privilege for such out-of-state convictions is AOC-CV-352.

6. High-Risk Drivers

As is the case for any person convicted of impaired driving in violation of G.S. 20-138.1, a person so convicted based on an alcohol concentration of 0.15 is subject to a license revocation of at least one year.[99] And if evidence that the person had an alcohol concentration of 0.15 or more was presented at trial or sentencing, the limited privilege must contain additional restrictions that reflect the person's status as a "high-risk driver."[100]

---

97. *Id.* §§ 20-179.3(g1)(1)–(4).
98. *Id.* § 20-179.3(h).
99. *Id.* § 20-17(a)(2); 20-19(c1).
100. *Id.* § 20-179.3(c1).

For purposes of determining whether the person qualifies as a high-risk driver, G.S. 20-179.3(c1) provides that the results of a chemical analysis presented at trial or sentencing are sufficient to prove a person's alcohol concentration, are conclusive, and are not subject to modification by any party, with or without approval of the court.

a. Limited Driving Privilege Requirements for High-Risk Drivers

A limited privilege issued to a person whose license is revoked upon conviction of impaired driving in violation of G.S. 20-138.1 and who had an alcohol concentration of 0.15 is subject to the following restrictions:

1. The limited driving privilege may not become effective until at least 45 days after the final conviction under G.S. 20-138.1.
2. The limited driving privilege must restrict the driver to operating only a designated motor vehicle.
3. The limited driving privilege must require that the designated motor vehicle be equipped with a functioning ignition interlock system of a type approved by NC DMV, which is set to prohibit driving with an alcohol concentration greater than 0.00.
4. The limited driving privilege must require that the driver personally activate the ignition interlock system before driving the motor vehicle.
5. Finally, the limited driving privilege must restrict the applicant to driving only to and from the applicant's place of employment, the place the applicant is enrolled in school, any court-ordered treatment or substance abuse education, and any ignition interlock service facility.[101]

b. Form Order

AOC-CR-340 is the form for such privileges.

c. Exception for Employer-Owned Motor Vehicles

The ignition interlock restrictions for a limited driving privilege that are set forth as requirements (2), (3), and (4) above do not apply to a motor vehicle that is owned by the driver's employer and that the driver operates solely for work-related purposes.[102] For this exception to apply, the owner of the vehicle must file with the court a written document authorizing the driver to drive the motor vehicle for work-related purposes under the authority of the limited driving privilege.[103] This exception to ignition interlock requirements is unique to the limited privilege; there is no such exception to ignition interlock requirements that apply after the period of revocation ends and a person's license is restored.[104]

E. Privilege Following Driving after Consuming Conviction

When a person is convicted of driving after consuming while under age 21 in violation of G.S. 20-138.3, the person's license is revoked pursuant to G.S. 20-13.2(a). Revocations under G.S. 20-13.2 endure for one year and run concurrently with any other revocations. The statute is somewhat misleadingly captioned "Grounds for revoking provisional license," though its license revocation provisions apply to persons under 21, rather than exclusively to provisional license-holders, all of whom are

---

101. *Id.* § 20-179.3(c1); 20-179.3(g5).
102. *Id.* § 20-179.3(g4).
103. *Id.*
104. *See id.* § 20-17.8.

under 18.[105] The incongruous reference resulted from the General Assembly's failure to amend the title of G.S. 20-13.2, which formerly applied only to provisional licensees, when it raised from 18 to 21 the age below which a person is prohibited from driving after consuming.[106]

1. Eligibility Requirements

A person whose driver's license is revoked solely for conviction of driving by a person under 21 after consuming alcohol or drugs in violation of G.S. 20-138.3 is eligible for a limited driving privilege if he or she meets all of the following eligibility requirements:

- The person must have been 18, 19, or 20 years old on the date of the offense.
- The person must not previously have been convicted of a violation of G.S. 20-138.3.
- At the time of the offense, the person must have held a valid driver's license or a license that had been expired for less than a year.
- At the time of the offense, the person must not have been convicted within the preceding seven years of an offense involving impaired driving.
- Subsequent to the offense, the person must not have any unresolved pending charges for or convictions for an offense involving impaired driving.
- The person must have obtained and filed with the court a substance abuse assessment of the type required by G.S. 20-17.6.
- The person must furnish proof of financial responsibility or establish that he or she is exempt from this requirement.[107]

A person convicted of impaired driving based upon the same incident of driving that led to the driving after consuming conviction is ineligible for a limited driving privilege because his or her license also will be revoked pursuant to G.S. 20-17(a)(2). Other than G.S. 20-138.3(d), there is no limited privilege that authorizes driving during a period of revocation imposed pursuant to G.S. 20-13.2. Indeed, G.S. 20-138.3(d) provides that "G.S. 20-179.3, rather than this subsection, governs the issuance of a limited driving privilege to a person who is convicted of [driving by a person under 21 after consuming] and of driving while impaired as a result of the same transaction." As previously noted, G.S. 20-179.3, in turn, authorizes a privilege only when a person is revoked solely under G.S. 20-17(a)(2).

F. Privilege Following Second or Subsequent Open Container Conviction

NC DMV must revoke a person's license upon receiving notice of a second or subsequent conviction of transporting an open container of alcoholic beverage under G.S. 20-138.7.[108] The term "s

econd or subsequent" is not defined for purposes of this revocation or for the underlying offense. It is, however, defined in G.S. 20-138.2A (prohibiting driving a commercial motor vehicle after consuming alcohol) and 20-138.2B (prohibiting driving a school bus, school activity bus, or child care vehicle after consuming alcohol) as a previous conviction that occurred in the seven years immediately preceding the date of the current offense.[109] Perhaps this definition from similar statutes likewise applies here.

---

105. *See id.* § 20-4.01(31a).
106. *See* S.L. 1995-506.
107. G.S. 20-138.3(d) (incorporating eligibility requirements of G.S. 20-179.3).
108. *Id.* § 20-17(a)(12).
109. *Id.* § 20-138.2A(d); 20-138.2B(d). *See also id.* § 20-17(a)(16) (defining second or subsequent conviction of larceny of motor fuel under G.S. 14-72.5 as a prior conviction in the seven years immediately preceding the

In any event, it is clear that NC DMV may not consider for purposes of this revocation any conviction more than ten years old.[110]

A person whose driver's license is revoked solely for conviction of transporting an open container of alcohol in violation of G.S. 20-138.7 is eligible for a limited driving privilege if he or she meets each of the following eligibility requirements:

1. At the time of the offense, the person must have held a valid driver's license or a license that had been expired for less than a year.
2. At the time of the offense, the person must not have been convicted within the preceding seven years of an offense involving impaired driving.
3. Subsequent to the offense, the person must not have any unresolved charges lodged against him or her for, or additional convictions of, an offense involving impaired driving.
4. The person must furnish proof of financial responsibility or establish that he or he is exempt from this requirement.[111]

The terms, conditions, and restrictions provided for in G.S. 20-179.3 and discussed above in connection with limited driving privileges issued to negate revocations for conviction of impaired driving apply to limited driving privileges issued pursuant to G.S. 20-138.7(h).

V. License Restoration

A. Generally

Limited driving privileges issued by a court pursuant to the provisions of G.S. Chapter 20 authorize driving only during a period of revocation imposed by the North Carolina Division of Motor Vehicles (NC DMV). Once the period of revocation ends, the person may apply to NC DMV to have his or her license restored.[112] The license restoration fee generally is $50.[113] However, if the person's driver's license was revoked pursuant to G.S. 20-17(a)(2) for conviction of impaired driving under G.S. 20-138.1 or impaired driving under G.S. 20-138.2, the restoration fee is $100.[114] Twenty-five dollars of this enhanced fee is used to fund the statewide chemical alcohol testing program administered by the Forensic Tests for Alcohol Branch of the Chronic Disease and Injury Section of the Department of Health and Human Services.[115]

B. Alcohol Concentration Restrictions

When NC DMV restores a person's license that was revoked for (1) conviction of driving after consuming by a person under 21 years of age in violation of G.S. 20-138.3, (2) conviction in federal court or in another state of an offense involving impaired driving, (3) conviction of impaired driving in violation of G.S. 20-138.1 or impaired driving in a commercial motor vehicle in violation of

date of the current offense).

110. *Id.* § 20-36.

111. *Id.* § 20-138.7(h) (incorporating eligibility requirements of G.S. 20-179.3).

112. *Id.* § 20-7(i1).

113. *Id.*

114. *Id.*

115. *Id.*

G.S. 20-138.2,[116] (4) conviction of manslaughter or negligent homicide based on impaired driving, or (5) conviction of felony death or serious injury by vehicle in violation of G.S. 20-141.4, NC DMV must prohibit the person from operating a vehicle with an alcohol concentration of 0.04 or more or more than 0.00, depending on the circumstances, at any relevant time after the driving. The license restoration provisions and restrictions discussed below are summarized in Table 6.2 at the end of this chapter.

1. 0.04 Restriction

For the following types of license restorations, the applicable alcohol concentration restriction is one that prohibits the person from driving with an alcohol concentration of 0.04 or more at any relevant time after the driving:

- The first restoration of a driver's license for a person convicted of driving while impaired in violation of G.S. 20-138.1 or
- The first restoration of a driver's license revoked pursuant to G.S. 20-23 (revoking resident's license upon conviction in another state) or 20-23.2 (revoking driver's license upon conviction of impaired driving in federal court) when the offense for which the person's license was revoked prohibits substantially similar conduct which if committed in this State would result in conviction of driving while impaired under G.S. 20-138.1.

2. 0.00 Restriction

For the restorations listed below, the applicable alcohol concentration restriction must prohibit the person from driving with an alcohol concentration of greater than 0.00 at any relevant time after the driving:

- The second or subsequent restoration of a driver's license for a person convicted of driving while impaired;
- The second or subsequent restoration of a driver's license revoked pursuant to G.S. 20-23 (revoking resident's license upon conviction in another state) or 20-23.2 (revoking driver's license upon conviction of impaired driving in federal court) when the offense for which the person's license was revoked prohibits substantially similar conduct which if committed in this State would result in conviction of driving while impaired under G.S. 20-138.1;
- Any restoration of a driver's license for a person convicted of
  - driving while impaired in a commercial motor vehicle (G.S. 20-138.2),
  - habitual impaired driving (G.S. 20-138.5),
  - driving while less than 21 years old after consuming alcohol or drugs (G.S. 20-138.3),
  - felony death by vehicle (G.S. 20-141.4(a1)), or
  - manslaughter or negligent homicide based on impaired driving;[117]
- Any restoration for a person whose license was revoked under G.S. 20-19(c3) for violation of an alcohol concentration restriction;[118]
- Any restoration of a driver's license revoked pursuant to G.S. 20-23 or 20-23.2 when the offense for which the person's license was revoked prohibits substantially similar conduct which if committed in this State would result in a conviction of

---

116. Note that the person must have an alcohol concentration of 0.06 to trigger this revocation.
117. G.S. 20-19(c3)(2).
118. *Id.*

- driving while impaired in a commercial motor vehicle (G.S. 20-138.2),
- driving while less than 21 years old after consuming alcohol or drugs (G.S. 20-138.3)
- death or serious injury by vehicle (G.S. 20-141.4), or
- manslaughter or negligent homicide based on impaired driving.[119]

3. Chemical Testing and Duration of Restriction

The person seeking restoration of his or her license must agree to submit to a chemical analysis in accordance with G.S. 20-16.2 at the request of a law enforcement officer who has reasonable grounds to believe that the person is operating a motor vehicle on a highway or public vehicular area in violation of the alcohol restriction.[120] The restriction remains in effect for seven years from the date of restoration if the person's license was permanently revoked, until the person's twenty-first birthday if the revocation was for a conviction under G.S. 20-138.3, and three years in all other cases.[121]

4. Reports of Violation

A law enforcement officer who has reasonable grounds to believe that a person violated an alcohol concentration restriction placed on his or her driver's license or willfully refused to submit to a chemical analysis must complete an affidavit pursuant to G.S. 20-16.2(c1).[122] On the basis of information reported pursuant to G.S. 20-16.2, NC DMV must revoke the driver's license of any person who violates a condition of restoration imposed pursuant to G.S. 20-19(c3).[123] An alcohol concentration report from an ignition interlock system may not be used as the basis for revocation.[124] A violation of an alcohol concentration restriction or the willful refusal to submit to a chemical analysis results in a one-year revocation.[125] If the period of revocation was imposed pursuant to G.S. 20-19(d) (four-year revocation) or 20-19(e) (permanent revocation), any remaining period of the original revocation, prior to its reduction, must be reinstated and the one-year revocation begins after all other periods of revocation have terminated.[126]

When a person has violated a condition of restoration by refusing a chemical analysis, the notice and hearing procedures of G.S. 20-16.2 apply.[127] When a person has submitted to a chemical analysis and the results show a violation of the alcohol concentration restriction, the notification and hearing procedures of G.S. 20-19(c3) apply.

5. NC DMV Action and Hearing on Reported Alcohol Concentration Violation

When it receives a properly executed affidavit required by G.S. 20-16.2(c1), NC DMV must expeditiously notify the person charged that his or her license to drive is revoked for the period of time specified in G.S. 20-19(c3), effective on the tenth calendar day after mailing the revocation order unless, before the effective date of the order, the person requests a hearing in writing.[128] If the person properly requests a hearing, the person retains his or her license, unless it is revoked under some other provision of law, until the hearing is held, the person withdraws the request for the hearing, or

---

119. *Id.* § 20-19(c3)(4).
120. *Id.* § 20-19(c3).
121. *Id.*
122. *Id.*; *id.* § 20-16.2(c1).
123. *Id.* § 20-19(c3).
124. *Id.*
125. *Id.*
126. *Id.*
127. See *supra* section II.B (section on notice and hearing related to willful refusal revocations).
128. G.S. 20-19(c5).

the person fails to appear at a scheduled hearing. The hearing must be held in the county where the violation occurred.[129] The hearing officer may subpoena any witnesses or documents that he or she deems necessary. The person charged may request that the hearing officer subpoena the charging officer, the chemical analyst, or both to appear at the hearing. The person must make such a request in writing at least three days before the hearing. The person may subpoena any other witness he or she deems necessary pursuant to the provisions of G.S. 1A-1, Rule 45.

The hearing is limited to consideration of the following four issues:

1. Did the charging officer have reasonable grounds to believe that the person violated the alcohol concentration restriction?
2. Was the person notified of his or her implied consent rights as required by G.S. 20-16.2(a)?
3. Did the person's driver's license in fact have an alcohol concentration restriction?
4. Did the person submit to a chemical analysis upon the request of the charging officer? If so, did the analysis reveal an alcohol concentration in excess of the restriction on the person's driver's license?[130]

If the NC DMV hearing officer finds that these conditions are satisfied, he or she must order that the revocation be sustained. If NC DMV finds that any of the conditions is not met, it must rescind the revocation. If the revocation is sustained, the person must surrender his or her driver's license immediately upon notification by NC DMV.[131]

A person has no right to appeal NC DMV's decision.[132] However, the person may, within 30 days of the date on which NC DMV's decision is mailed, petition the superior court of the county in which the hearing took place for discretionary review on the record of the revocation.[133] The superior court may stay the imposition of the revocation only if the court finds that the person is likely to succeed on the merits of the case and will suffer irreparable harm if such a stay is not granted. The stay may not exceed 30 days. The reviewing court may review only the record and is limited to determining if the NC DMV hearing officer followed proper procedures and if the hearing officer made sufficient findings of fact to support the revocation.[134]

C. Ignition Interlock Restriction

When NC DMV restores the license of a person whose license was revoked based upon a conviction of impaired driving in violation of G.S. 20-138.1, it must impose an ignition interlock restriction if any of the following conditions exist:

1. The person had an alcohol concentration of 0.15 or more;
2. The person was convicted of another offense involving impaired driving, and that other offense occurred within seven years immediately preceding the date of the offense for which the person's license has been revoked; or

---

129. G.S. 20-19(c5) requires that the hearing be held in the county where the charge was brought. In this context, "the charge" appears to refer to the allegation that the person violated an alcohol concentration restriction. In many circumstances, no criminal charge will accompany the alleged violation of the alcohol restriction.

130. G.S. 20-19(c5).

131. *Id.*

132. *Id.* § 20-19(c6).

133. *Id.*

134. *Id.*

3. The person was sentenced at Aggravated Level One pursuant to G.S. 20-179(f3).[135]

An ignition interlock restriction also is required as a condition of restoration for any driver's license revoked as a result of a conviction of habitual impaired driving in violation of G.S. 20-138.5.[136]

An ignition interlock restriction imposes the following limitations:

- The driver may operate only a vehicle that is equipped with a functioning ignition interlock system of a type approved by NC DMV;
- The driver must personally activate the ignition interlock system before driving the vehicle; and
- The driver may not drive with an alcohol concentration that meets or exceeds a specified level.[137]

If ignition interlock is required solely because the person had an alcohol concentration of 0.15 or more, the person is prohibited from driving with an alcohol concentration of 0.04 or greater. If, however, ignition interlock is required because the person had a prior offense within seven years or was sentenced at Aggravated Level One, the person is prohibited from driving with an alcohol concentration of greater than 0.00. Moreover, if the driver also was convicted, based on the same circumstances, of (1) driving while impaired in a commercial vehicle; (2) driving while less than 21 years old after consuming alcohol or drugs; (3) death by vehicle or serious injury by vehicle; or (4) manslaughter or negligent homicide resulting from the operation of a vehicle when the offense involved impaired driving, the person is prohibited from driving with an alcohol concentration of more than 0.00.

An alcohol concentration restriction of 0.04 combined with an ignition interlock restriction is noted on a person's license as restriction 20. An alcohol concentration restriction of 0.00 combined with an ignition interlock restriction is noted on a person's license as restriction 22.

The ignition interlock and alcohol concentration restrictions remain in effect for (1) one year from the date of restoration if the original revocation period was one year; (2) three years from the date of restoration if the original revocation period was four years; or (3) seven years from the date of restoration if the original revocation was a permanent revocation.[138] If the person was eligible for and received a limited driving privilege under G.S. 20-179.3, with the ignition interlock requirement contained in G.S. 20-179.3(g5), the period of time for which the limited driving privilege was held must be applied toward the requirements of G.S. 20-179.3(c). Thus, a high-risk driver subject to a one-year revocation who was issued a limited driving privilege on the forty-sixth day after the revocation is required to maintain ignition interlock for only forty-five additional days post-restoration.

A person subject to the ignition interlock requirement as a condition of license restoration must equip all the vehicles he or she owns with ignition interlock.[139] NC DMV may grant an exception to the requirement that all vehicles be so equipped for vehicles that are relied upon by another member of the person's family for transportation and are not in the possession of the affected driver.[140]

---

135. *Id.* § 20-17.8(a).
136. *Id.* § 20-17.8(a1). This provision, like the restoration provisions for habitual impaired driving generally, expires December 1, 2014. S.L. 2009-369.
137. G.S. 20-17.8(b).
138. *Id.* § 20-17.8(c).
139. *Id.* § 20-17.8(c1).
140. *Id.* See chapter 2 for further discussion of the offense of driving in violation of an ignition interlock restriction.

D. Conditional Restoration after Specified Number of Years

1. Four-Year Revocations

When a person's license is revoked under G.S. 20-17(a)(2) (requiring revocation upon conviction of impaired driving under G.S. 20-138.1 or impaired driving in a commercial vehicle under G.S. 20-138.2 based on an alcohol concentration of 0.06 or more) and the person has been convicted of another offense involving impaired driving within three years of the date of the offense for which his or her license is being revoked, the revocation period is four years.[141] The period of revocation likewise is four years if the person's license is revoked for conviction of felony serious injury by vehicle in violation of G.S. 20-141.4(a3). Notwithstanding the four-year revocation period, NC DMV may conditionally restore the person's license after it has been revoked for two years if the person provides NC DMV with satisfactory proof that

- he or she has not in the period of revocation been convicted in North Carolina or any other state or federal jurisdiction of
  - a motor vehicle offense,
  - an alcoholic beverage control law offense,
  - a drug law offense, or
  - any other criminal law offense involving the possession or consumption of alcohol or drugs and
- he or she is not currently an excessive user of alcohol, drugs, or prescription drugs and is not unlawfully using any controlled substance.[142]

If NC DMV restores the person's license, it may place reasonable conditions or restrictions on the person for the duration of the original revocation period.[143]

NC DMV must, in addition to any other applicable restriction or condition, place the applicable alcohol concentration restriction discussed above as well as any applicable ignition interlock restriction on the person's driver's license.

E. Permanent Revocation

When a person's license is revoked under G.S. 20-17(a)(2) (requiring revocation upon conviction of impaired driving under G.S. 20-138.1 or impaired driving in a commercial vehicle under G.S. 20-138.2 based on an alcohol concentration of 0.06 or more) and the person has been convicted of two or more previous offenses involving impaired driving with the most recent offense occurring within five years of the date of the offense for which his or her license is being revoked, the revocation period is permanent.[144] The revocation period likewise is permanent if the person was revoked pursuant to G.S. 20-17(a)(2) and was sentenced at Aggravated Level One under G.S. 20-179(f3).[145] Conviction

141. G.S. 20-19(d).

142. *Id.* The person may voluntarily submit to continuous alcohol monitoring by an approved system in order to prove that he or she has abstained from alcohol during the period of revocation immediately prior to the restoration consideration. G.S. 20-19(d)(2). NC DMV must accept monitoring periods of 120 days or longer as evidence of abstinence if it receives sufficient documentation that the person abstained from alcohol use during the monitoring period. *Id.*

143. *Id.* § 20-19(d).

144. *Id.* § 20-19(e).

145. *Id.*

of aggravated felony serious injury by vehicle under G.S. 20-141.4(a4) also requires permanent revocation.[146]

1. Restoration after Three Years

Notwithstanding the permanent revocation, NC DMV may conditionally restore the license of a person permanently revoked pursuant to G.S. 20-19(e) after the license has been revoked for at least three years if the person provides NC DMV with satisfactory proof of the following:

- In the three years immediately preceding the person's application for a restored license, the person has not been convicted in North Carolina or in any other state or federal court of
  - a motor vehicle offense,
  - an alcohol beverage control law offense,
  - a drug law offense, or
  - any criminal offense involving the consumption of alcohol or drugs and
- The person is not currently an excessive user of alcohol, drugs, or prescription drugs and is not unlawfully using any controlled substance.[147]

The person may voluntarily submit to continuous alcohol monitoring for the purpose of proving abstinence from alcohol consumption during a period of revocation immediately prior to the restoration consideration.[148]

2. Restoration after Twenty-Four Months

NC DMV may conditionally restore a driver's license that is permanently revoked pursuant to G.S. 20-19(e) after it has been revoked for at least twenty-four months if the person provides NC DMV with satisfactory proof of all of the following:

- The person has not consumed any alcohol for the twelve months preceding the restoration while being monitored by a continuous alcohol monitoring device of a type approved by the Division of Adult Correction of the Department of Public Safety.
- The person has not in the period of revocation been convicted in North Carolina or any other state or federal jurisdiction of
  - a motor vehicle offense,
  - an alcoholic beverage control law offense,
  - a drug law offense, or
  - any other criminal offense involving the possession or consumption of alcohol or drugs.
- The person is not currently an excessive user of drugs or prescription drugs.
- The person is not unlawfully using any controlled substance.[149]

---

146. *Id.*
147. *Id.* § 20-19(e1).
148. *Id.* The person may voluntarily submit to continuous alcohol monitoring by an approved system in order to prove that he or she has abstained from alcohol during the period of revocation immediately prior to the restoration consideration. *Id.* § 20-19(e1)(2). NC DMV must accept monitoring periods of 120 days or longer as evidence of abstinence if it receives sufficient documentation that the person abstained from alcohol use during the monitoring period. *Id.* § 20-19(e1)(2)(a).
149. *Id.* § 20-19(e2).

If NC DMV restores a person's license pursuant to G.S. 20-19(e1), (e2), or (e4), it may place reasonable conditions or restrictions on the person for any period up to five years from the date of restoration.[150]

F. Conditional Restoration Following Conviction of Habitual Impaired Driving

Conviction of habitual impaired driving under G.S. 20-138.5 results in the permanent revocation of the defendant's driver's license.[151] Notwithstanding the "permanent" revocation, legislation enacted in 2009 permits NC DMV to conditionally restore the license of a person that is revoked for habitual impaired driving.[152] NC DMV may restore the person's license after it has been revoked for at least ten years after the completion of any sentence imposed by the court if the person provides NC DMV with proof that

- in the ten years immediately preceding the person's application for a restored license, he or she has not been convicted in North Carolina or in any other state or federal court of
  - a motor vehicle offense,
  - an alcohol beverage control law offense,
  - a drug law offense, or
  - any other criminal offense; and
- he or she is not currently a user of alcohol, is not unlawfully using any controlled substance, and is not an excessive user of prescription drugs.[153]

Upon restoration, NC DMV must restrict the person from operating a vehicle with an alcohol concentration of greater than 0.00 at any time after the driving.[154] The person also must agree to submit to a chemical analysis in accordance with G.S. 20-16.2 at the request of a law enforcement officer who has reasonable grounds to believe that the person is operating a motor vehicle on a highway or public vehicular area in violation of the alcohol concentration restriction.[155]

NC DMV must restrict the person to driving only vehicles equipped with a functioning ignition interlock system and must require the person to personally activate the ignition interlock system before driving the vehicle.[156] These restrictions remain in effect for seven years from the date of restoration.[157]

G. Conditional Restoration Following Impaired Driving and a Fatality

When a person's license is revoked under G.S. 20-17(a)(1) (requiring revocation upon conviction for manslaughter or negligent homicide resulting from the operation of a motor vehicle) or 20-17(a)(9) (requiring revocation for conviction under G.S. 20-141.4) and the offense is one involving impaired driving and a fatality, G.S. 20-19(i) provides that the revocation is permanent. NC DMV may, however,

---

150. *Id.* § 20-19(e3).
151. *Id.* § 20-138.5(d).
152. This legislation is set to expire December 1, 2014. S.L. 2009-369.
153. G.S. 20-19(e4).
154. *Id.* § 20-19(c3)(3).
155. *Id.* § 20-19(c3).
156. *Id.* § 20-17.8(a1).
157. *Id.* § 20-17.8(c); 20-19(c3).

conditionally restore the person's license after it has been revoked for at least five years under G.S. 20-19(i) if the person provides NC DMV with satisfactory proof that

- in the five years immediately preceding the person's application for a restored license, he or she has not been convicted in North Carolina or in any other state or federal court of
  - a motor vehicle offense,
  - an alcohol beverage control law offense,
  - a drug law offense, or
  - any criminal offense involving the consumption of alcohol or drugs and
- he or she is not currently an excessive user of alcohol or drugs.

If NC DMV restores the person's license, it may place reasonable conditions or restrictions on the person for any period up to seven years from the date of restoration.[158]

158. *Id.* § 20-19(i).

Table 6.1. Limited Driving Privileges for Implied Consent Offense Revocations

Type of Revocation	Revocation Statute	Limited Privilege Statute	Eligibility Requirements for Limited Driving Privilege	Authorized Driving	Judge Who May Issue	AOC Form Privilege
Willful Refusal	G.S. 20-16.2(d)	G.S. 20-16.2(e1); 20-179.3	• Revocation in place for at least six months • Underlying charge is resolved ◦ If convicted of DWI, person was sentenced at Level Three, Four, or Five ◦ If convicted, person has complied with at least one mandatory condition of probation • At the time of the refusal, the person held a valid driver's license or a license that had been expired for less than a year • At the time of the refusal, the person had not been convicted within the preceding seven years of an offense involving impaired driving • At the time of the refusal, the person had not willfully refused to submit to a chemical analysis in the preceding seven years • Subsequent to the refusal, person has no unresolved pending charges for or additional convictions of an offense involving impaired driving • The person has obtained a substance abuse assessment from a mental health facility and has successfully completed any recommended training or treatment program • The person furnishes proof of financial responsibility or establishes exemption from this requirement	• Driving for essential purposes related to: ◦ employment ◦ maintenance of household ◦ education ◦ court-ordered treatment or assessment ◦ community service ordered as a condition of probation ◦ emergency medical care • Generally, privilege may permit driving only during standard working hours; exceptions apply to driving for emergencies and other specifically authorized purposes. • Must restrict the person from driving while consuming alcohol or driving at any time while the person has remaining in his or her body any alcohol or controlled substance previously consumed, unless the controlled substance was lawfully obtained and taken in therapeutically appropriate amounts	• If underlying criminal charge was finally disposed of in district court, any district court judge in district where refusal occurred • If underlying criminal charge was finally disposed of in superior court, any superior court judge in district where refusal occurred	AOC-CR-313

Table 6.1. Limited Driving Privileges for Implied Consent Offense Revocations (*continued*)

Type of Revocation	Revocation Statute	Limited Privilege Statute	Eligibility Requirements for Limited Driving Privilege	Authorized Driving	Judge Who May Issue	AOC Form Privilege
Willful Refusal and Alcohol Concentration of 0.15	G.S. 20-16.2(d)	G.S. 20-16.2(e1); 20-179.3	• Revocation has been in place for at least six months • Underlying charge is resolved ◦ If convicted of DWI, the person was sentenced at Level Three, Four, or Five ◦ If convicted, the person must have complied with at least one mandatory condition of probation • At the time of the refusal, the person held a valid driver's license or a license that had been expired for less than a year • At the time of the refusal, the person had not been convicted within the preceding seven years of an offense involving impaired driving • At the time of the instant refusal, person had not willfully refused to submit to a chemical analysis in the preceding seven years • Subsequent to the refusal, the person has no unresolved pending charges for or additional convictions of an offense involving impaired driving • The person has obtained a substance abuse assessment from a mental health facility and has successfully completed any recommended training or treatment program • The person furnishes proof of financial responsibility or establishes exemption from this requirement	• Driving for essential purposes related to ◦ employment ◦ maintenance of household ◦ education ◦ court-ordered treatment or assessment ◦ community service ordered as a condition of probation ◦ emergency medical care • Generally, privilege may permit driving only during standard working hours; exceptions apply to driving for emergencies and other specifically authorized purposes • Must restrict the person from driving while consuming alcohol or driving at any time while the person has remaining in his or her body any alcohol or controlled substance previously consumed, unless the controlled substance was lawfully obtained and taken in therapeutically appropriate amounts • Must include ignition interlock restrictions in G.S. 20-179.3(g5)	• If underlying criminal charge was finally disposed of in district court, any district court judge in district where refusal occurred • If underlying criminal charge was finally disposed of in superior court, any superior court judge in district where refusal occurred	AOC-CR-313

Table 6.1. Limited Driving Privileges for Implied Consent Offense Revocations (*continued*)

Type of Revocation	Revocation Statute	Limited Privilege Statute	Eligibility Requirements for Limited Driving Privilege	Authorized Driving	Judge Who May Issue	AOC Form Privilege
Willful Refusal by Person under 21	G.S. 20-16.2(d); 20-13.2(b)	No Limited Privilege	N/A	N/A	N/A	N/A
Civil License Revocation for Mandatory Minimum of 30 or 45 days	G.S. 20-16.5	G.S. 20-16.5(p)	• At the time of the alleged offense, the person held a valid driver's license or a license that had been expired for less than a year • The person does not have a pending charge involving impaired driving other than the charge for which his or her license currently is revoked or additional convictions of an offense involving impaired driving since being charged with the instant offense • The person's license has been revoked for at least 10 days if the revocation is for 30 days or at least 30 days if the revocation is for 45 days • The person has obtained a substance abuse assessment from a mental health facility and registers for and agrees to participate in any recommended training or treatment program	• Driving for essential purposes related to ◦ employment ◦ maintenance of household ◦ education ◦ court-ordered treatment or assessment ◦ community service ordered as a condition of probation ◦ emergency medical care • Generally, privilege may permit driving only during standard working hours; exceptions apply to driving for emergencies and other specifically authorized purposes • Must restrict the person from driving while consuming alcohol or driving at any time while the person has remaining in his or her body any alcohol or controlled substance previously consumed, unless the controlled substance was lawfully obtained and taken in therapeutically appropriate amounts	• Any district court judge in district where underlying case is pending	AOC-CVR-10; AOC-CVR-09 (petition)

Table 6.1. Limited Driving Privileges for Implied Consent Offense Revocations (*continued*)

Type of Revocation	Revocation Statute	Limited Privilege Statute	Eligibility Requirements for Limited Driving Privilege	Authorized Driving	Judge Who May Issue	AOC Form Privilege
Indefinite Civil License Revocation	G.S. 20-16.5	G.S. 20-16.5(p)	• At the time of the offense the person held either a valid driver's license or a license that had been expired for less than one year • At the time of the offense the person had not within the preceding seven years been convicted of an offense involving impaired driving • Subsequent to the offense the person has not been convicted of, or had an unresolved charge lodged against him or her for an offense involving, impaired driving • The person's driver's license is revoked solely under G.S. 20-16.5 • Privilege is necessary to overcome undue hardship	• Driving for essential purposes related to ◦ employment ◦ maintenance of household ◦ education ◦ court-ordered treatment or assessment ◦ community service ordered as a condition of probation ◦ emergency medical care • Generally, privilege may permit driving only during standard working hours; exceptions apply to driving for emergencies and other specifically authorized purposes • Must restrict the person from driving while consuming alcohol or driving at any time while the person has remaining in his or her body any alcohol or controlled substance previously consumed, unless the controlled substance was lawfully obtained and taken in therapeutically appropriate amounts	• A judge of the division in which the current offense is pending	AOC-CVR-11; AOC-CVR-09 (petition)

Table 6.1. Limited Driving Privileges for Implied Consent Offense Revocations (*continued*)

Type of Revocation	Revocation Statute	Limited Privilege Statute	Eligibility Requirements for Limited Driving Privilege	Authorized Driving	Judge Who May Issue	AOC Form Privilege
Conviction of Impaired Driving under G.S. 20-138.1	G.S. 20-17(a)(2)	G.S. 20-179.3	• The person was sentenced at Level Three, Four, or Five • The person is revoked solely under G.S. 20-17(a)(2) • At the time of the offense, the person was validly licensed or had a license that had been expired for less than a year • The person has not been convicted of an offense involving impaired driving within the seven years preceding the instant offense • Subsequent to the offense, the person has not been convicted of, or had an unresolved charge of an offense involving, impaired driving • The person has obtained and filed with the court a substance abuse assessment • The person furnishes proof of financial responsibility or establishes exemption from that requirement	• Driving for essential purposes related to ◦ employment ◦ maintenance of household ◦ education ◦ court-ordered treatment or assessment ◦ community service ordered as a condition of probation ◦ emergency medical care • Generally, privilege may permit driving only during standard working hours; exceptions apply to driving for emergencies and other specifically authorized purposes • Must restrict the person from driving while consuming alcohol or driving at any time while the person has remaining in his or her body any alcohol or controlled substance previously consumed, unless the controlled substance was lawfully obtained and taken in therapeutically appropriate amounts	• Trial judge if judge is assigned to a court in the district in which conviction was imposed • If trial judge is not available and conviction was imposed in superior court, senior regular resident superior court judge • If trial judge is not available and conviction was imposed in district court, chief district court judge	AOC-CR-312

Table 6.1. Limited Driving Privileges for Implied Consent Offense Revocations *(continued)*

Type of Revocation	Revocation Statute	Limited Privilege Statute	Eligibility Requirements for Limited Driving Privilege	Authorized Driving	Judge Who May Issue	AOC Form Privilege
Conviction of Impaired Driving under G.S. 20-138.1 and Alcohol Concentration of 0.15 or More	G.S. 20-17(a)(2)	G.S. 20-179.3	• The person was sentenced at Level Three, Four, or Five • The person is revoked solely under G.S. 20-17(a)(2) • At the time of the offense, the person was validly licensed or had a license that had been expired for less than a year • The person has not been convicted of an offense involving impaired driving within the seven years preceding the instant offense • Subsequent to the offense, the person has not been convicted of, or had an unresolved charge of an offense involving, impaired driving • The person has obtained and filed with the court a substance abuse assessment • The person furnishes proof of financial responsibility or establishes exemption from that requirement	• Privilege may authorize driving to and from ◦ the person's place of employment ◦ place the person is enrolled in school ◦ any court-ordered treatment or substance abuse education ◦ any ignition interlock service facility • Generally, privilege may permit driving only during standard working hours; exceptions apply for specifically authorized purposes. • Privilege must restrict the person from driving while consuming alcohol or driving at any time while the person has remaining in his or her body any alcohol or controlled substance previously consumed, unless the controlled substance was lawfully obtained and taken in therapeutically appropriate amounts • Privilege not effective until 45 days after final conviction • The person must comply with ignition interlock requirements in G.S. 20-179.3(g5)	• Trial judge if judge is assigned to a court in the district in which conviction was imposed • If trial judge is not available and conviction was imposed in superior court, senior regular resident superior court judge • If trial judge is not available and conviction was imposed in district court, chief district court judge	AOC-CR-340
Conviction of Impaired Driving under G.S. 20-138.1 for Offense Committed by Person under 21	G.S. 20-17(a)(2); 20-13.2(b)	No Limited Privilege	N/A	N/A	N/A	N/A

Table 6.1. Limited Driving Privileges for Implied Consent Offense Revocations (*continued*)

Type of Revocation	Revocation Statute	Limited Privilege Statute	Eligibility Requirements for Limited Driving Privilege	Authorized Driving	Judge Who May Issue	AOC Form Privilege
Conviction of Impaired Driving in Another State	G.S. 20-23	G.S. 20-179.3	• The person was sentenced at Level Three, Four, or Five • The person is revoked solely under G.S. 20-17(a)(2) • At the time of the offense, the person was validly licensed or had a license that had been expired for less than a year • The person has not been convicted of an offense involving impaired driving within the seven years preceding the instant offense • Subsequent to the offense, the person has not been convicted of, or had an unresolved charge of an offense involving, impaired driving • The person has obtained and filed with the court a substance abuse assessment • The person furnishes proof of financial responsibility or establishes exemption from that requirement	• Driving for essential purposes related to ◦ employment ◦ maintenance of household ◦ education ◦ court-ordered treatment or assessment ◦ community service ordered as a condition of probation ◦ emergency medical care • Generally, privilege may permit driving only during standard working hours; exceptions apply to driving for emergencies and other specifically authorized purposes • Must restrict the person from driving while consuming alcohol or driving at any time while the person has remaining in his or her body any alcohol or controlled substance previously consumed, unless the controlled substance was lawfully obtained and taken in therapeutically appropriate amounts	• Chief district court judge of the district in which the person resides	AOC-CV-352 Form petition: AOC-CV-350

Table 6.1. Limited Driving Privileges for Implied Consent Offense Revocations (*continued*)

Type of Revocation	Revocation Statute	Limited Privilege Statute	Eligibility Requirements for Limited Driving Privilege	Authorized Driving	Judge Who May Issue	AOC Form Privilege
Conviction of Impaired Driving in Federal Court	G.S. 20-23.2	G.S. 20-179.3	• The person was sentenced at Level Three, Four, or Five • The person is revoked solely under G.S. 20-17(a)(2) • At the time of the offense, the person was validly licensed or had a license that had been expired for less than a year • The person has not been convicted of an offense involving impaired driving within the seven years preceding the instant offense • Subsequent to the offense, the person has not been convicted of, or had an unresolved charge of an offense involving, impaired driving • The person has obtained and filed with the court a substance abuse assessment • The person furnishes proof of financial responsibility or establishes exemption from that requirement	• Driving for essential purposes related to ◦ employment ◦ maintenance of household ◦ education ◦ court-ordered treatment or assessment ◦ community service ordered as a condition of probation ◦ emergency medical care • Generally, privilege may permit driving only during standard working hours; exceptions apply to driving for emergencies and other specifically authorized purposes • Must restrict the person from driving while consuming alcohol or driving at any time while the person has remaining in his or her body any alcohol or controlled substance previously consumed, unless the controlled substance was lawfully obtained and taken in therapeutically appropriate amounts	• Chief district court judge	AOC-CV-352 Form petition: AOC-CV-350

Table 6.1. Limited Driving Privileges for Implied Consent Offense Revocations (*continued*)

Type of Revocation	Revocation Statute	Limited Privilege Statute	Eligibility Requirements for Limited Driving Privilege	Authorized Driving	Judge Who May Issue	AOC Form Privilege
Conviction of Driving after Consuming Alcohol or Drugs by Person under 21 in violation of G.S. 20-138.3	G.S. 20-13.2(a)	G.S. 20-138.3(d); 20-179.3	• The person was 18, 19, or 20 years old on the date of the offense • The person has not previously been convicted of a violation of G.S. 20-138.3 • At the time of the offense, the person held a valid driver's license or a license that had been expired for less than a year • At the time of the offense, the person had not been convicted within the preceding seven years of an offense involving impaired driving • At the time of the offense, the person had not willfully refused to submit to a chemical analysis under G.S. 20-16.2 in the preceding seven years • Subsequent to the refusal, the person has no unresolved pending charges for, or additional convictions of an offense involving, impaired driving • The person has obtained a substance abuse assessment from a mental health facility and has successfully completed any recommended training or treatment program • The person furnishes proof of financial responsibility or establishes exemption from this requirement	• Driving for essential purposes related to ◦ employment ◦ maintenance of household ◦ education ◦ court-ordered treatment or assessment ◦ community service ordered as a condition of probation ◦ emergency medical care • Generally, privilege may permit driving only during standard working hours; exceptions apply to driving for emergencies and other specifically authorized purposes • Must restrict the person from driving while consuming alcohol or driving at any time while the person has remaining in his or her body any alcohol or controlled substance previously consumed, unless the controlled substance was lawfully obtained and taken in therapeutically appropriate amounts	• Trial judge if judge is assigned to a court in the district in which conviction was imposed • If trial judge is not available and conviction was imposed in superior court, senior regular resident superior court judge • If trial judge is not available and conviction was imposed in district court, chief district court judge	AOC-CR-312

Table 6.1. Limited Driving Privileges for Implied Consent Offense Revocations (*continued*)

Type of Revocation	Revocation Statute	Limited Privilege Statute	Eligibility Requirements for Limited Driving Privilege	Authorized Driving	Judge Who May Issue	AOC Form Privilege
Second or Subsequent Conviction for Transporting Open Container under G.S. 20-138.7	G.S. 20-17(12)	G.S. 20-138.7(h); 20-179.3	• At the time of the offense, the person was validly licensed or had a license that had been expired for less than a year • The person has not been convicted of an offense involving impaired driving within the seven years preceding the instant offense • Subsequent to the offense, the person has not been convicted of, or had an unresolved charge of an offense involving, impaired driving • The person has obtained and filed with the court a substance abuse assessment • The person furnishes proof of financial responsibility or establishes exemption from that requirement	• Driving for essential purposes related to ◦ employment ◦ maintenance of household ◦ education ◦ court-ordered treatment or assessment ◦ community service ordered as a condition of probation ◦ emergency medical care • Generally, privilege may permit driving only during standard working hours; exceptions apply to driving for emergencies and other specifically authorized purposes • Must restrict the person from driving while consuming alcohol or driving at any time while the person has remaining in his or her body any alcohol or controlled substance previously consumed, unless the controlled substance was lawfully obtained and taken in therapeutically appropriate amounts	• Trial judge if judge is assigned to a court in the district in which conviction was imposed • If trial judge is not available and conviction was imposed in superior court, senior regular resident superior court judge • If trial judge is not available and conviction was imposed in district court, chief district court judge	AOC-CR-312

If the applicant is not required to drive for essential work-related purposes except during standard working hours, the limited driving privilege must prohibit driving during nonstandard working hours unless the driving is (1) for emergency medical care or (2) authorized as essential to the completion of any community work assignments, course of instruction at an Alcohol and Drug Education Traffic School, or substance abuse assessment or treatment that is ordered by the court as a condition of probation for the impaired driving conviction.

Table 6.2. License Revocations for Convictions of Implied Consent Offenses and Restoration Conditions

Conviction Statute	Offense Description	Revocation Statute	Length of Revocation	Number of Restorations	Alcohol Concentration Restriction under G.S. 20-19(c3)	Duration of G.S. 20-19(c3) Alcohol Concentration Restriction	Ignition Interlock (II) and Alcohol Concentration (AC) Restriction under G.S. 20-17.8	Length of Ignition Interlock Restriction
G.S. 20-138.1	Impaired driving	G.S. 20-17(a)(2)	One year	First restoration	0.04	Three years	If alcohol concentration of 0.15 or more, II required with 0.04 AC restriction[a] If convicted of another impaired driving offense that occurred within seven years of current offense, II required with 0.00 AC restriction	One year
G.S. 20-138.1	Impaired driving and person has been convicted of another offense involving impaired driving that occurred within three years preceding date of current offense	G.S. 20-17(a)(2)	Four years	Second or subsequent restoration	0.00	Three years	II required, 0.00 AC	Three years
G.S. 20-138.1	Impaired driving and person has two or more previous offenses for which person has been convicted, one of which occurred within five years immediately preceding date of current offense	G.S. 20-17(a)(2)	Permanent	Second or subsequent restoration	0.00	Seven years	II required, 0.00 AC	Seven years
G.S. 20-138.1	Impaired driving sentenced at Aggravated Level One pursuant to G.S. 20-179(f3)	G.S. 20-17(a)(2)	Permanent	First restoration	0.04	Seven years	II required, 0.00 AC	One year
G.S. 20-138.1	Impaired driving sentenced at Aggravated Level One pursuant to G.S. 20-179(f3)	G.S. 20-17(a)(2)	Permanent	Second or subsequent restoration	0.00	Seven years	II required, 0.00 AC	Seven years

Table 6.2. License Revocations for Convictions of Implied Consent Offenses and Restoration Conditions (*continued*)

Conviction Statute	Offense Description	Revocation Statute	Length of Revocation	Number of Restorations	Alcohol Concentration Restriction under G.S. 20-19(c3)	Duration of G.S. 20-19(c3) Alcohol Concentration Restriction	Ignition Interlock (II) and Alcohol Concentration (AC) Restriction under G.S. 20-17.8	Length of Ignition Interlock Restriction
	Out-of-state or federal DWI	G.S. 20-23; 20-23.2	One year	First restoration	0.04	Three years	No II requirement	N/A
	Out-of-state or federal DWI and person has been convicted of another offense involving impaired driving that occurred within three years preceding date of current offense	G.S. 20-23; 20-23.2	Four years	Second or subsequent restoration	0.00	Three years	No II requirement	N/A
	Out-of-state or federal DWI and person has two or more previous offenses for which person has been convicted, one of which occurred within five years immediately preceding date of current offense	G.S. 20-23; 20-23.2	Permanent	Second or subsequent restoration	0.00	Seven years	No II requirement	N/A
G.S. 20-138.2	Driving a commercial motor vehicle while impaired with alcohol concentration of 0.06 or higher	G.S. 20-17(a)(2)	One year	Any restoration	0.00	Three years	No II requirement	N/A

Table 6.2. License Revocations for Convictions of Implied Consent Offenses and Restoration Conditions (*continued*)

Conviction Statute	Offense Description	Revocation Statute	Length of Revocation	Number of Restorations	Alcohol Concentration Restriction under G.S. 20-19(c3)	Duration of G.S. 20-19(c3) Alcohol Concentration Restriction	Ignition Interlock (II) and Alcohol Concentration (AC) Restriction under G.S. 20-17.8	Length of Ignition Interlock Restriction
G.S. 20-138.2	Driving a commercial motor vehicle while impaired with alcohol concentration of 0.06 or higher and person has been convicted of another offense involving impaired driving that occurred within three years preceding date of current offense	G.S. 20-17(a)(2)	Four years	Any restoration	0.00	Three years	No II requirement	N/A
G.S. 20-138.2	Driving a commercial motor vehicle while impaired with alcohol concentration of 0.06 or higher and person has two or more previous offenses for which person has been convicted, one of which occurred within five years immediately preceding date of current offense	G.S. 20-17(a)(2)	Permanent	Any restoration	0.00	Seven years	No II requirement	N/A

Table 6.2. License Revocations for Convictions of Implied Consent Offenses and Restoration Conditions (*continued*)

Conviction Statute	Offense Description	Revocation Statute	Length of Revocation	Number of Restorations	Alcohol Concentration Restriction under G.S. 20-19(c3)	Duration of G.S. 20-19(c3) Alcohol Concentration Restriction	Ignition Interlock (II) and Alcohol Concentration (AC) Restriction under G.S. 20-17.8	Length of Ignition Interlock Restriction
G.S. 20-138.2	Driving a commercial motor vehicle while impaired sentenced at Aggravated Level One pursuant to G.S. 20-179(f3)	G.S. 20-17(a)(2)	Permanent	Any restoration	0.00	Seven years	No II requirement	N/A
	Out-of-state or federal DWI in a commercial motor vehicle with alcohol concentration of 0.06 or higher	G.S. 20-23; 20-23.2	One year	Any restoration	0.00	Three years	No II requirement	N/A
	Out-of-state or federal DWI in a commercial motor vehicle with alcohol concentration of 0.06 or higher and person has been convicted of another offense involving impaired driving that occurred within three years preceding date of current offense	G.S. 20-23; 20-23.2	Four years	Any restoration	0.00	Three years	No II requirement	N/A

Table 6.2. License Revocations for Convictions of Implied Consent Offenses and Restoration Conditions (*continued*)

Conviction Statute	Offense Description	Revocation Statute	Length of Revocation	Number of Restorations	Alcohol Concentration Restriction under G.S. 20-19(c3)	Duration of G.S. 20-19(c3) Alcohol Concentration Restriction	Ignition Interlock (II) and Alcohol Concentration (AC) Restriction under G.S. 20-17.8	Length of Ignition Interlock Restriction
	Out-of-state or federal DWI in a commercial motor vehicle with alcohol concentration of 0.06 or higher and person has two or more previous offenses for which person has been convicted, one of which occurred within five years immediately preceding date of current offense	G.S. 20-23; 20-23.2	Permanent	Any restoration	0.00	Seven years	No II requirement	N/A
G.S. 20-138.2A	Second or subsequent conviction (within seven years) of driving a commercial motor vehicle after consuming alcohol	G.S. 20-17(a)(13)	One year	Any restoration	N/A	N/A	No II requirement	N/A
G.S. 20-138.23B	Driving a school bus, school activity bus, child care vehicle, ambulance or other EMS vehicle, firefighting vehicle, or law enforcement vehicle after consuming alcohol	G.S. 20-17(a)(14)	First conviction: 10 days; second or subsequent conviction: One year	Any restoration	N/A	N/A	No II requirement	N/A

Table 6.2. License Revocations for Convictions of Implied Consent Offenses and Restoration Conditions (*continued*)

Conviction Statute	Offense Description	Revocation Statute	Length of Revocation	Number of Restorations	Alcohol Concentration Restriction under G.S. 20-19(c3)	Duration of G.S. 20-19(c3) Alcohol Concentration Restriction	Ignition Interlock (II) and Alcohol Concentration (AC) Restriction under G.S. 20-17.8	Length of Ignition Interlock Restriction
G.S. 20-138.3	Driving after consuming alcohol or drugs by person under 21	G.S. 20-13.2	One year	Any restoration	0.00	Until the person is 21	No II requirement	N/A
[redacted]								
G.S. 20-138.5	Habitual impaired driving	G.S. 20-138.5(d)	Permanent	Any restoration[b]	0.00	Seven years	No II requirement	N/A
G.S. 20-138.7	Second or subsequent conviction of transporting an open container of alcoholic beverage under G.S. 20-138.7	G.S. 20-17(a)(12)	One year	Any restoration	N/A	N/A	No II requirement	N/A
[redacted]								
G.S. 20-141.4(a1)	Felony death by vehicle	G.S. 20-17(a)(9)	Permanent	Any restoration	0.00	Seven years	No II requirement	N/A
	Out-of-state felony death by vehicle	G.S. 20-23; G.S. 20-23.2	Permanent	Any restoration	0.00	Seven years	No II requirement	N/A
[redacted]								
G.S. 20-141.4(a3)	Felony serious injury by vehicle	G.S. 20-17(a)(9)	Four years	Unclear[c]	Unclear[d]	Three years	No II requirement	N/A
	Out-of-state felony serious injury by vehicle	G.S. 20-23; 20-23.2	Four years	Any restoration	0.00	Three years	No II requirement	N/A
[redacted]								
G.S. 20-141.4(a4)	Aggravated felony serious injury by vehicle	G.S. 20-17(a)(9)	Permanent	Unclear[e]	Unclear[f]	Seven years	No II requirement	N/A

Table 6.2. License Revocations for Convictions of Implied Consent Offenses and Restoration Conditions (*continued*)

Conviction Statute	Offense Description	Revocation Statute	Length of Revocation	Number of Restorations	Alcohol Concentration Restriction under G.S. 20-19(c3)	Duration of G.S. 20-19(c3) Alcohol Concentration Restriction	Ignition Interlock (II) and Alcohol Concentration (AC) Restriction under G.S. 20-17.8	Length of Ignition Interlock Restriction
	Out-of-state or federal felony serious injury by vehicle	G.S. 20-23; 20-23.2	Permanent	Any restoration	0.00	Seven years	No II requirement	N/A
G.S. 20141.4(a5)	Aggravated felony death by vehicle	G.S. 20-17(a)(9)	Permanent; G.S. 20-19(i)	Any restoration[g]	0.00	Seven years	No II requirement	N/A
	Out-of-state or federal felony death by vehicle	G.S. 20-17(a)(9)	Permanent	Any restoration	0.00	Seven years	No II requirement	N/A
G.S. 20-141.4(a6)	Repeat felony death by vehicle	G.S. 20-17(a)(9)	Permanent; G.S. 20-19(i)	Any restoration[h]	0.00	Seven years	No II requirement	N/A
	Out-of-state or federal repeat or felony death by vehicle	G.S. 20-23; G.S. 20-23.2	Permanent	Any restoration	0.00	Seven years	No II requirement	N/A
[redacted]								
Common law offense	Involuntary manslaughter based on impaired driving	G.S. 20-17(a)(1)	Permanent	Any restoration	0.00	Seven years	No II requirement	N/A
	Out-of-state or federal involuntary manslaughter based on impaired driving	G.S. 20-23; 20-23.2	Permanent	Any restoration	0.00	Seven years	No II requirement	N/A

a. If ignition interlock is required because the person had an alcohol concentration of 0.15 or more and the person also is convicted, based on the same set of circumstances, of (1) driving while impaired in a commercial vehicle in violation of G.S. 20-138.2, (2) driving while less than 21 years old after consuming alcohol or drugs in violation of G.S. 20-138.3, (3) death or serious injury by vehicle in violation of G.S. 20-141.4, or (4) manslaughter or negligent homicide based on impaired driving, the restriction must prohibit driving with an alcohol concentration of greater than 0.00. G.S. 20-17.8(b)(3)c.

b. The provision allowing conditional restoration of a driver's license revoked under G.S. 20-138.5(d) expires December 1, 2014. *See* S.L.2009-369.

c. No alcohol concentration restriction is specified by statute for license restorations following convictions of felony serious injury by vehicle under G.S. 20-141.4(a3). In contrast, G.S. 20-19(c3)(4) imposes an alcohol concentration restriction of 0.00 for any license restoration following a revocation for an out-of-state or federal conviction of an offense that is substantially similar to a violation of G.S. 20-141.4—the statute that defines both death by vehicle and serious injury by vehicle offenses.

d. No alcohol concentration restriction is specified by statute for license restorations following convictions of felony serious injury by vehicle under G.S. 20-141.4(a3). In contrast, G.S. 20-19(c3)(4) imposes an alcohol concentration restriction of 0.00 for any license restoration following a revocation for an out-of-state or federal conviction of an offense that is substantially similar to a violation of G.S. 20-141.4—the statute that defines both death by vehicle and serious injury by vehicle offenses.

e. No alcohol concentration restriction is specified by statute for license restorations following convictions of felony serious injury by vehicle under G.S. 20-141.4(a3). In contrast, G.S. 20-19(c3)(4) imposes an alcohol concentration restriction of 0.00 for any license restoration following a revocation for an out-of-state or federal conviction of an offense that is substantially similar to a violation of G.S. 20-141.4—the statute that defines both death by vehicle and serious injury by vehicle offenses.

f. No alcohol concentration restriction is specified by statute for license restorations following convictions of felony serious injury by vehicle under G.S. 20-141.4(a3). In contrast, G.S. 20-19(c3)(4) imposes an alcohol concentration restriction of 0.00 for any license restoration following a revocation for an out-of-state or federal conviction of an offense that is substantially similar to a violation of G.S. 20-141.4—the statute that defines both death by vehicle and serious injury by vehicle offenses.

g. G.S. 20-19(c3)(3) requires an alcohol concentration restriction of 0.00 for any restoration for a person convicted of "felony death by vehicle, G.S. 20-141.4(a1), [or] manslaughter or negligent homicide resulting from the operation of a motor vehicle when the offense involved impaired driving." Given that felony death by vehicle is a lesser-included offense of aggravated felony death by vehicle, it seems beyond dispute that these restrictions apply to persons convicted of the greater offense.

h. G.S. 20-19(c)(3)(3) requires an alcohol concentration restriction of 0.00 for any restoration for a person convicted of "felony death by vehicle, G.S. 20-141.4(a1), [or] manslaugher or negligent homicide resulting from the operation of a motor vehicle when the offense involved impaired driving." Given that felony death by vehicle is a lesser-included offense of repeat felony death by vehicle, it seems beyond dispute that these restrictions apply to persons convicted of the greater offense.

Chapter 7

Vehicle Seizure and Forfeiture

Chapter 7

Vehicle Seizure and Forfeiture

I. Introduction

This chapter reviews the laws requiring the seizure, impoundment, and forfeiture of motor vehicles driven by drivers in certain impaired driving cases.[1] Generally, these laws require law enforcement officers to seize a motor vehicle driven in the commission of an impaired driving offense if the driver committed the offense while his or her license already was revoked for impaired driving or if the driver drove the motor vehicle without a valid driver's license and without being covered by an automobile liability policy. Lienholders and certain types of owners may subsequently secure the release of a seized motor vehicle and, in some circumstances, may prevent it from being forfeited and sold. When motor vehicles are ordered forfeited and sold, the county schools are the beneficiaries of any net proceeds.[2]

The preceding descriptions provide only an overview of the general law. The sections that follow discuss in detail the laws and procedures applicable at each stage of the seizure, impoundment, and forfeiture process.

Like the pretrial driver's license revocation law,[3] vehicle seizure is a measure separate from the criminal prosecution of impaired drivers that is designed to "keep[] impaired drivers and their cars off

---

1. This chapter does not cover other laws authorizing the seizure and forfeiture of motor vehicles, such as Section 90-112 of the North Carolina General Statutes (hereinafter G.S.) (authorizing the seizure and forfeiture of vehicles used to conceal, convey, or transport controlled substances), G.S. 20-141.3 (authorizing the seizure of a motor vehicle operated willfully in a prearranged speed competition), and G.S. 20-141.5 (authorizing the seizure and forfeiture of a motor vehicle driven in the commission of felony speeding to elude). In some cases, a motor vehicle will be subject to seizure under more than one provision. Since none of the seizure statutes address this circumstance, it appears that all of the applicable seizure statutes apply when a motor vehicle subject to seizure under more than one statute is seized.

2. Accordingly, G.S. 20-28.3(k) mandates that the attorney for the county board of education be given notice of all proceedings regarding offenses related to a motor vehicle subject to forfeiture under G.S. 20-28.3. G.S. 20-28.3(k) (excepting from this blanket notice requirement proceedings for release of a motor vehicle to an innocent owner pursuant to G.S. 20-28.3(e1)). The attorney for the county board of education also has the right to appear and be heard on all issues related to the seizure, possession, release, forfeiture, sale, and other matters regarding the seized motor vehicle. *Id.* With the prior consent of the county board of education, the district attorney may delegate to the attorney for the county board of education any or all of the duties of the district attorney under G.S. 20-28.3. *Id.* Clerks of superior court, law enforcement agencies, and all other agencies with information relevant to the seizure, impoundment, release, or forfeiture of motor vehicles are authorized and directed to provide county boards of education with access to that information and to do so by electronic means when possible. *Id.*

3. *See id.* § 20-16.5.

of the roads."[4] Indeed, the National Highway Traffic Safety Administration (NHTSA) has concluded that vehicle impoundment for DWI offenders "reduces recidivism while the vehicle is in custody and to a lesser extent after the vehicle has been released."[5] NHTSA reported that "[a]n evaluation of California's impoundment law found both first-time and repeat offenders whose vehicles were impounded had fewer subsequent arrests for driving with a suspended license and fewer crashes."[6] The North Carolina Court of Appeals in *State v. Chisholm* upheld the forfeiture provisions as constitutional, determining that the statutes had a legitimate objective, keeping impaired drivers and their cars off the roads, and that "seizing the cars to remove them from the roads" was directly related to that goal.[7]

II. Key Terms

As noted in the introduction, a motor vehicle driven by a person charged with an offense involving impaired driving is subject to seizure if at the time of the violation (1) the driver's license of the person driving the motor vehicle was revoked as a result of a prior impaired driving license revocation or (2) the person was not validly licensed and was not covered by an automobile liability policy.[8] A judge later determines at a defendant's sentencing or other hearing whether a motor vehicle driven by an impaired driver and seized and impounded is subject to an order of forfeiture.[9] The proceeds of any forfeiture sale are disbursed to the county board of education.[10]

An understanding of several terms is required to determine whether a motor vehicle driven in an impaired driving offense is subject to seizure and possibly a subsequent forfeiture. The terms "motor vehicle," "offenses involving impaired driving," "prior impaired driving license revocations," "driving without a valid drivers license," and driving while "not covered by an automobile liability policy" are defined and discussed in this section.

A. Motor Vehicle

The term "motor vehicle" is defined as "[e]very vehicle which is self-propelled and every vehicle designed to run upon the highways which is pulled by a self-propelled vehicle."[11] The term does not include mopeds,[12] which are vehicles with "two or three wheels, no external shifting device, and a motor that does not exceed 50 cubic centimeters piston displacement and cannot propel the vehicle at a speed greater than 30 miles per hour on a level surface."[13] Only *motor vehicles* are subject to seizure pursuant to G.S. 20-28.3. Therefore, mopeds are not subject to seizure under G.S. 20-28.3.

4. State v. Chisholm, 135 N.C. App. 578, 584 (1999).
5. NHTSA, Countermeasures That Work: A Highway Safety Countermeasure Guide for State Highway Safety Officers 1-34 6th ed. (2011), www.nhtsa.gov/staticfiles/nti/pdf/811444.pdf.
6. *Id.* at 1-35 (reference omitted).
7. 135 N.C. App. at 584.
8. G.S. 20-28.3.
9. *Id.* § 20-28.2.
10. *Id.* § 20-28.2(d).
11. *Id.* § 20-4.01(23).
12. *Id.*
13. *See id.* § 105-164.3(22); *see also id.* § 20-4.01(21a).

B. Offenses Involving Impaired Driving

Vehicles may be seized pursuant to G.S. 20-28.3 only when driven in the commission of an offense involving impaired driving. These offenses are a subset of the broader category of implied consent offenses and consist of the following offenses:

- impaired driving under G.S. 20-138.1;
- habitual impaired driving under G.S. 20-138.5;
- impaired driving in commercial vehicle under G.S. 20-138.2;
- any offense under G.S. 20-141.4 based on impaired driving (felony death by vehicle and felony serious injury by vehicle);
- first- or second-degree murder under G.S. 14-17 based on impaired driving;
- involuntary manslaughter under G.S. 14-18 based on impaired driving; and
- substantially similar offenses committed in another state or jurisdiction.[14]

Thus, a motor vehicle driven by a person in the commission of one of these offenses is subject to seizure if, at the time of the offense, (1) the person's driver's license was revoked as a result of a prior impaired driving license revocation or (2) the person was not validly licensed and was not covered by an automobile liability policy.

1. Impaired Driving License Revocations

The term "impaired driving license revocation" is defined by G.S. 20-28.2(a) as a revocation made pursuant to any of the following provisions:

- G.S. 20-13.2: consuming alcohol or drugs by driver less than 21 years old or willful refusal by driver under age 21 to submit to chemical analysis;
- G.S. 20-16(a)(8b): driving while impaired on a military installation;
- G.S. 20-16.2: refusal to take a chemical test;
- G.S. 20-16.5: pretrial civil license revocation;
- G.S. 20-17(a)(2): impaired driving or impaired driving in a commercial vehicle;
- G.S. 20-138.5: habitual impaired driving;
- G.S. 20-17(a)(12): transporting an open container of alcohol;
- G.S. 20-16(a)(7): impaired driving while out of state resulting in revocation of North Carolina driver's license;
- G.S. 20-17(a)(1): manslaughter or second-degree murder involving impaired driving;
- G.S. 20-17(a)(3): felony involving use of motor vehicle involving impaired driving;
- G.S. 20-17(a)(9): felony or misdemeanor death by vehicle or felony serious injury by vehicle involving impaired driving;
- G.S. 20-17(a)(11): assault with motor vehicle involving impaired driving;
- G.S. 20-28.2(a)(3): the laws of another state and the offense for which the person's license is revoked prohibit substantially similar conduct that, if committed in North Carolina, would result in a revocation under any of the statutes listed above.

---

14. *Id.* § 20-4.01(24a). While an offense committed in another jurisdiction that prohibits substantially similar conduct to that prohibited by North Carolina's impaired driving laws is included in this definition, such an offense will never be the charged offense for purposes of a vehicle seizure under G.S. 20-28.3. Law enforcement officers may only seize a motor vehicle pursuant to a charge of an impaired driving offense that is leveled in North Carolina.

There is no requirement that the driver be charged with, or that he or she commit the offense of, driving while license revoked. If the person commits an offense involving impaired driving while subject to an impaired driving license revocation, a law enforcement officer must seize the motor vehicle the person was driving, subject to the exceptions noted in section III.B below. Suppose, for example, that a person whose license is revoked for a previous impaired driving conviction drives while impaired on a public vehicular area. Notwithstanding the revocation, this person has not committed the offense of driving while license revoked, which requires that a motor vehicle be driven on a street or highway.[15] Nevertheless, the motor vehicle the person drove is subject to seizure because the person committed an impaired driving offense while subject to a prior impaired driving revocation.

2. Driving without a Valid Driver's License

With respect to the provision for seizure of a vehicle driven by a person charged with an impaired driving offense who was driving without a license and without liability insurance, it is important to note that a person who has a complete defense pursuant to G.S. 20-35 to a charge of driving without a driver's license is considered to have had a valid driver's license at the time of the violation. Thus, a motor vehicle driven by such a person is not subject to seizure.[16] A person may *not* be convicted of the offense of driving a motor vehicle without a driver's license if the person demonstrates the following: (1) that at the time of the offense, the person had an expired license; (2) that the person renewed the license within thirty days after it expired; and (3) that the person could not have been charged with driving without a license if the person had the renewed license when charged with the offense.[17] In essence, this provision establishes a thirty-day grace period for renewing one's driver's license. Moreover, a person's simple failure to carry a license on his or her person does not satisfy the "driving without a license" prong so as to subject his or her vehicle to seizure.[18]

3. Driving While Not Covered by Automobile Liability Policy

In addition to having probable cause to believe that the driver was charged with an impaired driving offense and did not have a valid license, in order to seize a motor vehicle under G.S. 20-28.3(a)(2), a law enforcement officer must have probable cause to believe that the driver was not at the time of the violation covered by an automobile liability policy. G.S. 20-309 requires financial responsibility in the form of a liability insurance policy, financial security bond, or financial security deposit, or by qualification as a self-insurer, as a prerequisite to registration. G.S. 20-313 makes it a Class 3 misdemeanor for the owner of a motor vehicle registered or required to be registered in North Carolina to operate the motor vehicle or permit the motor vehicle to be operated in the state without having the required financial responsibility. It is important to note that G.S. 20-28.3(a)(2)b. refers to whether the driver—not the motor vehicle—is covered by an automobile liability policy. A person who drives a motor vehicle owned by someone else with the owner's permission is covered by the automobile liability policy for the motor vehicle being driven, if such a policy exists.[19] In addition, the authorized driver may be covered by an automobile liability insurance policy under which he or she is an insured driver, even if the motor vehicle itself is not listed on a policy.

---

15. *Id.* § 20-28(a).
16. *Id.* § 20-28.3(a).
17. *Id.* § 20-35(c).
18. *Cf. id.* § 20-7(a) (requiring that, to drive a motor vehicle on a highway, a person must be licensed and must carry the license while driving); *id.* § 20-35(c) (providing that a person may not be convicted of failing to carry a regular driver's license if he or she produces the license in court).
19. *Id.* § 20-279.21(b)(2).

4. Motor Vehicle Owner

Law enforcement officers must seize motor vehicles under G.S. 20-28.3 when the statutory requirements are satisfied even when a motor vehicle is driven by someone other than the owner. The definition of "motor vehicle owner" is important, however, in determining whether a person is eligible to obtain the vehicle's release. A motor vehicle owner is a person in whose name a registration card or certificate of title is issued at the time of seizure.[20]

III. Seizure and Impoundment

A. Affidavit of Impoundment

Law enforcement officers who seize or plan to seize a motor vehicle pursuant to G.S. 20-28.3 must present to a magistrate within the county where the driver was charged an affidavit of impoundment setting forth the basis upon which the motor vehicle has been or will be seized for forfeiture.[21] Upon determining that the statutory requirements for seizure are met, the magistrate to whom the affidavit is presented must order that the vehicle be held. If the motor vehicle has not yet been seized and the magistrate determines that seizure is warranted, the magistrate must issue an order of seizure.[22] If the vehicle already has been seized and the statutory conditions for seizure are satisfied, the magistrate must order that the seized vehicle be impounded and held.[23] The magistrate must provide a copy of the order to the clerk of court, who, in turn, must provide copies to the district attorney and the attorney for the county board of education.[24] If the magistrate determines that the statutory requirements for seizure and impoundment are *not* satisfied, he or she must order the vehicle released to its owner upon payment of towing and storage fees.[25] Towing and storage fees may not be waived—even when the magistrate orders the vehicle released based on a finding that the statutory requirements for seizure have not been met.[26]

B. Exceptions to Seizure

There are two instances in which a motor vehicle is not subject to seizure even if the above-described requirements are satisfied. First, if a law enforcement officer determines prior to seizure that a motor vehicle has been reported stolen, he or she may not seize the vehicle.[27] Second, if an officer determines before seizure that the motor vehicle is a rental vehicle and the driver is not listed as an authorized driver under the rental contract, the motor vehicle may not be seized.[28]

If the motor vehicle is reported stolen after it has been seized, the owner may seek to have it returned on the basis that he or she is an "innocent owner."[29] The procedures allowing non-defendant

20. *Id.* § 20-28.2(a1)(3a). Procedures for transferring title to a motor vehicle are set forth in G.S. 20-72(b).
21. *Id.* § 20-28.3(c). AOC-CR-323A is the form on which the officer may complete an affidavit in support of the seizure and/or impoundment. Available on the website of the North Carolina Court System, at www.nccourts.org/Forms/Documents/690.pdf.
22. G.S. 20-28.3(c).
23. *Id.*
24. *Id.*
25. *Id.*
26. *Id.* § 20-28.3(n).
27. *Id.* § 20-28.3(b).
28. *Id.*
29. *See id.* § 20-28.2(a1)(2) (defining "innocent owner").

owners to reclaim motor vehicles are discussed in more detail in section IV.C below. If a vehicle owner files a report of unauthorized use of a motor-propelled conveyance and agrees to support the prosecution of the unauthorized user, he or she also can obtain the motor vehicle's release after the seizure, again on the ground that he or she is an innocent owner. It is unclear whether the filing of a report of unauthorized use *before* a vehicle is seized precludes seizure of the vehicle. On the one hand, the exception applies to vehicles *reported stolen*, while the innocent owner provisions refer to filing a report of *unauthorized use*. Perhaps the use of these different terms implies that the term "reported stolen" means something different from "unauthorized use," and thus requires a report of larceny,[30] a crime that requires intent to permanently deprive another of property,[31] whereas unauthorized use of a motor-propelled conveyance[32] requires only a taking of property. On the other hand, the term "reported stolen" could reasonably be construed to encompass reports of both unauthorized use of a motor-propelled conveyance and larceny.

There is no exception in the seizure law for motor vehicles that have titles and registration in other states or countries. Although practical issues may arise in securing transfers of titles to these forfeited vehicles, the statute applies to them in the same manner as it applies to vehicles titled and registered in North Carolina.

C. Executing an Order of Seizure

Orders of seizure under G.S. 20-28.3 are valid anywhere in North Carolina and may be carried out by any law enforcement officer with territorial jurisdiction who has subject matter jurisdiction for violations of G.S. Chapter 20.[33] Such an officer may use reasonable force to seize the motor vehicle and may enter upon the property of the defendant in order to accomplish the seizure.[34] If an officer has probable cause to believe that the motor vehicle is located on the property of someone other than the defendant, the officer may obtain a search warrant to enter that property for the purpose of seizing the vehicle.[35]

D. Custody of Motor Vehicle

G.S. 20-28.9 authorizes the North Carolina Department of Public Instruction (DPI) to enter into regional or statewide contracts for the towing, storage, and sale of seized and forfeited vehicles. The department has, in fact, entered into regional contracts. Pursuant to these agreements, the contractors act as agents for the county school boards.[36] The contractors retrieve impounded vehicles from the local towing companies that initially tow vehicles at the direction of local law enforcement officials.

---

30. *Id.* § 14-72.

31. *See, e.g.*, State v. Jackson, 75 N.C. App. 294, 298 (1985) (finding sufficient evidence that the defendant intended to permanently deprive the victim of the use of her car and thus determining that the trial judge was not required to instruct the jury only on the lesser-included offense of "unauthorized use of a motor-propelled conveyance").

32. *See* G.S. 14-72.2.

33. *Id.* § 20-28.3(c1).

34. *Id.*

35. *Id.*

36. *Id.* § 20-28.3(d). Motor vehicles seized under G.S. 20-28.3 may be towed pursuant to a statewide or regional contract or under a contract with the county board of education. *Id.* Seized motor vehicles that are not towed pursuant to a statewide or regional contract or by the county board of education are towed by a commercial towing company designated by the law enforcement agency that seized the motor vehicle. Seized motor vehicles that are not towed pursuant to a statewide or regional contract or under a contract with the county board of education must be retrieved from the commercial towing company within ten days by the

The contractors then store the motor vehicles pursuant to statewide contracts at a rate of up to $10 per day.[37]

E. Retrieval of Personal Property

The entity charged with storing the motor vehicle may permit owners of personal property contained within but not affixed to the motor vehicle to retrieve those items from the motor vehicle, provided such persons provide to the storing entity satisfactory proof that they own the vehicle or the items of personal property.[38]

F. Notification of Impoundment

A law enforcement officer who seizes a motor vehicle pursuant to G.S. 20-28.3 must notify the North Carolina Division of Motor Vehicles (NC DMV) of the seizure as soon as practical and no later than twenty-four hours after the vehicle is seized.[39] NC DMV must, in turn, within forty-eight hours of receipt within regular business hours of the notice of seizure,[40] issue notice to any lienholder of record[41] and to any motor vehicle owner who was not operating the motor vehicle at the time of the offense.[42] If the motor vehicle was damaged during the offense or incident to the seizure, NC DMV must notify the owner's insurance company as well as any other insurance companies insuring other motor vehicles involved in the accident. NC DMV must place a hold on a title to the motor vehicle to prevent it from being transferred by a motor vehicle owner unless authorized by court order.[43]

G. Motor Vehicles Involved in Accidents

If the motor vehicle subject to forfeiture was damaged during the commission of the offense giving rise to seizure or was damaged in the seizure itself, NC DMV must determine the name of any insurance companies (1) that are the insurers of record with NC DMV for the motor vehicle at the time of the seizure or (2) that may otherwise be liable for repair to the motor vehicle.[44] If the seized motor vehicle was involved in an accident, NC DMV must notify the insurance companies that the claim for insurance proceeds for damage to the seized motor vehicle must be paid to the clerk of superior court of the county where the motor vehicle driver was charged.[45] The clerk must hold the proceeds for disbursement as ordered by the court.[46]

---

county board of education or its agent, who must then pay the towing and storage fees that have accrued to the commercial towing company.

37. *Id.* § 20-28.9(b).

38. *Id.* § 20-28.3(j).

39. *Id.* § 20-28.3(b).

40. A notice of seizure received outside of regular business hours is considered to have been received at the start of the next business day. *Id.* § 20-28.3(b1).

41. If a lienholder has provided NC DMV with a designated facsimile number for notification of impoundment, NC DMV must provide an additional notice via facsimile transmission within eight hours of receipt, within regular business hours, of the notice of seizure. *Id.* § 20-28.3(b2).

42. The notice must be sent by first-class mail to the most recent address contained in NC DMV records or in the records of the state where the motor vehicle is registered. The notification must state the reason for the seizure and the procedure for requesting release of the motor vehicle.

43. *Id.* § 20-28.3(b1).

44. *Id.* § 20-28.2(c1).

45. *Id.*

46. *Id.*

The county board of education or its designee is authorized to negotiate the county board of education's interest with the insurance company and to compromise and accept settlement of any claim for damages.[47] The insurance company must pay directly to the clerk of court any property insurance proceeds that accrue to the defendant or owner of the seized motor vehicle. If the insurance company declares the motor vehicle to be a total loss, the clerk, upon application of the county board of education, must order the motor vehicle released to the insurance company upon payment into the court of all insurance proceeds for damage to the motor vehicle after payment of towing and storages costs and all valid liens.[48] The clerk must provide NC DMV with a certified copy of an order releasing a motor vehicle to an insurance company in these circumstances, and NC DMV must transfer title accordingly.[49] Insurance proceeds paid to the clerk of court pursuant to G.S. 20-28.3(h) are subject to forfeiture pursuant to G.S. 20-28.5 and must be disbursed pursuant to court order.[50]

IV. Release of Vehicles Pending Trial

Vehicles that have been seized generally are impounded until an expedited sale may be conducted in light of the accrued towing and storage charges, a forfeiture hearing is held, or the underlying criminal case is disposed of without a conviction. There are some additional circumstances in which a vehicle may be released to an owner or lienholder, and those are discussed in the following section.[51]

A. Permanent Release to a Defendant-Owner

A defendant-owner may secure a motor vehicle's early release only by demonstrating that his or her license was not revoked for a prior impaired driving revocation, see G.S. 20-28.3(e2), or—presumably—by demonstrating that he or she had a valid license and/or insurance (if this condition is the basis for the seizure).[52] If the statutory requirements for seizure exist, however, the defendant-owner cannot secure the vehicle's release.

A defendant motor vehicle owner who wishes to obtain a motor vehicle's release on the basis that his or her license was not revoked for a qualifying reason or that he or she had a license and insurance may file a petition with the clerk of court seeking a pretrial determination of this issue.[53] The clerk must schedule a hearing before a judge of the division in which the underlying criminal charge is pending, to be held within ten business days or as soon thereafter as is feasible.[54] Notice of the hearing must be given to the defendant, the district attorney, and the attorney for the county board of education. The clerk must forward a copy of the petition to the district attorney. If the district

47. *Id.* § 20-28.3(h). A motor vehicle owner or lienholder who objects to any agreed upon settlement under G.S. 20-28.3(h) may file an independent claim with the insurance company for additional funds owed. *Id.*

48. *Id.*

49. *Id.*

50. *Id.*

51. A clerk must electronically report to NC DMV the entry of an order of release as defined in G.S. 20-28.3 and 20-28.4. G.S. 20-28.8.

52. When G.S. 20-28.3(a)(2) (the no license/no insurance basis for seizure) was enacted in 2006, no corresponding amendments were made to G.S. 20-28.3(e2) to allow a defendant to reclaim a seized vehicle by demonstrating that he or she in fact was licensed and/or insured. Arguably, however, affording a defendant the right to make such a showing is required by due process, and a court could construe the statute accordingly.

53. *Id.* § 20-28.3(e2).

54. *Id.*

attorney determines that the defendant's motor vehicle is not subject to forfeiture, the district attorney may note the State's consent to the release of the motor vehicle on the petition and return the petition to the clerk of court. The clerk of court must then enter an order releasing the motor vehicle to the defendant upon payment of all towing and storage charges incurred as a result of the seizure and subject to the defendant's establishing that he or she is an owner of the motor vehicle and that he or she has the financial responsibility required by law. No hearing is held in such a circumstance.

When the district attorney does not make such a determination, the court must hold a hearing solely on the issue of whether the defendant's license was revoked for a prior impaired driving revocation or whether he or she had no license or insurance. The court is not required to determine whether the defendant drove while impaired. An order finding that the defendant is not entitled to pretrial release of the motor vehicle on the basis that his or her license was not revoked for impaired driving or that he or she had a license and/or insurance may be reconsidered by the court as part of the forfeiture hearing conducted pursuant to G.S. 20-28.2(d).

B. Permanent Release to an Innocent Owner

Owners of motor vehicles driven by another person in the commission of an impaired driving offense, in contrast, may secure the permanent release of a seized motor vehicle upon satisfying certain conditions. A motor vehicle owner who is not a defendant in the case may file a petition with the clerk of court seeking a pretrial determination that the petitioner is an "innocent owner."[55] An innocent owner is a motor vehicle owner

(a) who did not know and had no reason to know
  (i) that the defendant's driver's license was revoked or
  (ii) that the defendant did not have a valid driver's license or liability insurance;
(b) who knew
  (i) that the defendant's driver's license was revoked or
  (ii) that the defendant had no valid driver's license and no liability insurance, but
  (iii) the defendant drove the vehicle without the owner's expressed or implied permission and
  (iv) the owner files a police report for unauthorized use of the motor vehicle and agrees to prosecute the unauthorized operator of the motor vehicle;
(c) whose vehicle was reported stolen;
(d) who is
  (i) in the business of renting vehicles, and the vehicle at issue was driven by a person who is not listed as an authorized driver on the rental contract or
  (ii) in the business of renting vehicles, and the vehicle was driven by a person who is listed as an authorized driver on the rental contract and who was charged with an impaired driving offense, but the rental company did not know about the revocation of the driver's license at the time of the contract; or
(e) who is in the business of leasing motor vehicles, who holds legal title to the motor vehicle as lessor at the time of seizure, and who has no actual knowledge of the revocation of the lessee's driver's license at the time the rental agreement is entered.[56]

55. *Id.* § 20-28.3(e1).
56. *Id.* § 20-28.2(a1)(2).

The form petition for an innocent owner is form AOC-CR-330A.[57]

The clerk must consider a petition filed by a non-defendant motor vehicle owner and make a determination as to whether the vehicle should be released as soon as may be feasible.[58] If the clerk determines that the petitioner is an innocent owner (see the discussion above), the clerk must release the motor vehicle to the petitioner subject to the following conditions:[59] First, the innocent owner must pay the towing and storage charges incurred as a result of the seizure and impoundment of the motor vehicle. Next, the person must prove his or her identity as the motor vehicle owner and show that he or she has the financial responsibility required by law. Finally, the person must execute an acknowledgment of the type described in G.S. 20-28.2(a1).[60] This document must acknowledge the following:

(1) That the motor vehicle was operated by a person charged with an offense involving impaired driving and (a) that person's driver's license was revoked as a result of a prior impaired driver's license revocation or (b) that person did not have a valid driver's license or liability insurance.

(2) That, if the motor vehicle is again operated by the person currently being charged, and if that person is charged with an offense involving impaired driving, then the vehicle is subject to impoundment and forfeiture if (i) the offense occurs while that person's driver's license is revoked or (ii) the offense occurs while the person has no valid driver's license and no liability insurance.

(3) That a lack of knowledge or consent to the operation of the motor vehicle will not be a defense in the future, unless the motor vehicle owner has taken all reasonable precautions to prevent the use of the motor vehicle by this particular person and immediately reports, upon discovery, any unauthorized use to the appropriate law enforcement agency.[61]

The acknowledgment may be completed on the form petition, AOC-CR-330A.

No motor vehicle may be temporarily or permanently released to a non-defendant motor vehicle owner if NC DMV records show that the owner previously signed an acknowledgment pursuant to G.S. 20-28.2 and if the same person was operating the motor vehicle while that person's license was revoked, unless the motor vehicle owner shows by the greater weight of the evidence that he or she has taken all reasonable precautions to prevent this person from using the motor vehicle.[62] The motor vehicle owner also must have immediately reported any unauthorized use of the motor vehicle to the appropriate law enforcement agency.[63]

If the clerk denies the owner's petition, the owner has no statutory right to appeal from that decision. The owner may, however, petition the trial court for reconsideration of the issue as part of the forfeiture hearing.

---

57. This form is available on the website of the North Carolina Court System, at www.nccourts.org/Forms/Documents/691.pdf.

58. G.S. 20-28.3(e1).

59. *Id.* § 20-28.3(e1) (incorporating requirements of G.S. 20-28.2(e)).

60. *Id.* § 20-28.2(e). The clerk must electronically report to NC DMV the execution of an impaired driving acknowledgment. *Id.* § 20-28.8.

61. *Id.* § 20-28.2(a1)(1a).

62. *Id.* § 20-28.2(e).

63. *Id.*

C. Temporary Release to Motor Vehicle Owner Other than Defendant

A motor vehicle owner other than the driver at the time of the underlying offense resulting in seizure may apply to the clerk of superior court in the county where the charges are pending for temporary pretrial release of the motor vehicle.[64] This type of release is available to an owner who cannot satisfy the innocent owner criteria set forth in the previous section.

The clerk must release the motor vehicle to a non-defendant motor vehicle owner after it has been seized for at least twenty-four hours, subject to the following conditions.[65] First, the owner must pay the towing and storage charges incurred as a result of the seizure and impoundment.[66] Second, the owner must execute a secured bond[67] in an amount equal to the fair market value of the motor vehicle.[68] The bond must be conditioned on return of the motor vehicle in substantially the same condition as it was in at the time of seizure and without any new or additional liens or encumbrances on the day of the forfeiture hearing, unless the motor vehicle has been permanently released.[69] The owner also must execute an acknowledgment as defined by G.S. 20-28.2(a1). This is the same acknowledgment required to obtain permanent release of a motor vehicle, and it is discussed above in connection with such releases. Finally, before a motor vehicle may be released to a non-defendant owner under G.S. 20-28.3(e), the clerk must check NC DMV records to ensure that the motor vehicle owner has not previously executed an acknowledgment naming the operator of the seized motor vehicle and must verify that a bond posted to secure the release of this motor vehicle has not previously been ordered forfeited.[70] The owner has no statutory right to appeal from a clerk's denial of an owner's petition for pretrial release of the motor vehicle.

If the owner does not return the motor vehicle on the day of the forfeiture hearing or otherwise violates a condition of the pretrial release of the motor vehicle, the bond must be ordered forfeited and the court must issue an order of seizure.[71]

If the owner posts bond in district court for release of the motor vehicle and the defendant appeals from his or her conviction in district court to superior court, the bond continues in effect in superior court.[72] An owner also may apply to the superior court for temporary pretrial release of a vehicle in a case appealed to the superior court from the district court once the case has been transferred to superior court.[73]

---

64. *Id.* § 20-28.3(e).
65. *Id.*
66. *Id.*
67. The bond may be secured by a cash deposit in the full amount of the bond, a recordable deed of trust to real property in the full amount of the bond, a bail bond, or by at least one solvent surety, and it must be payable to the county school fund. *Id.*
68. *Id.* The fair market value of a motor vehicle is determined pursuant to the schedule of values adopted by NC DMV pursuant to G.S. 105-187.3. *Id.* § 20-28.2(a1)(1).
69. *Id.* § 20-28.3(e).
70. *Id.*
71. *Id.*
72. *Id.* § 20-28.3(m).
73. *Id.*

D. Permanent Release to Lienholder

Lienholders, like innocent owners, also may obtain the permanent pretrial release of motor vehicles seized pursuant to G.S. 20-28.3.[74] A lienholder is a person who holds a perfected security interest in a motor vehicle at the time of seizure.[75] To obtain the release of a vehicle under this provision, the lienholder must file a petition with the clerk of court and must serve the petition on the registered owner, the titled owner, the district attorney, and the county board of education attorney. A judge must hold a hearing on the matter, and the lienholder must provide all interested parties with notice of the hearing at least ten days before it occurs. A judge must order a motor vehicle released to a lienholder conditioned upon payment of all towing and storage costs if the judge determines, by the greater weight of the evidence, that all of the following conditions are present/satisfied:

1. The borrower has defaulted on the obligation secured by the motor vehicle.
2. The lienholder is entitled to possession of the motor vehicle as a result of the default.
3. The lienholder agrees to sell the motor vehicle in accordance with its agreement and pursuant to the State's secured transactions laws.
4. Upon sale of the motor vehicle, the lienholder pays to the clerk of court of the county in which the driver was charged all proceeds from the sale, less the lien and any towing and storage costs paid by the lienholder.
5. The lienholder agrees not to sell, give, or otherwise transfer possession of the motor vehicle to the defendant or the motor vehicle owner.
6. The motor vehicle had not previously been released to the lienholder as a result of a prior seizure involving the same defendant or motor vehicle owner.[76]

A lienholder's violation of the conditions of release is punishable by civil or criminal contempt.[77]

If all interested parties waive in writing the right to notice and hearing and the lienholder agrees not to transfer possession of the motor vehicle to the defendant or to the motor vehicle owner, the clerk of superior court may order a seized motor vehicle released to the lienholder conditioned upon payment of all towing and storage costs.[78]

A lienholder has no statutory right to appeal from a clerk of court's determination that it is not entitled to possession of a seized motor vehicle.

V. Expedited Sale

To avoid the accumulation of towing and storage charges in an amount that exceeds the value of a motor vehicle, the law permits seized motor vehicles to be sold in certain circumstances before the underlying criminal case is resolved and without a court order.[79] A motor vehicle seized and impounded pursuant to G.S. 20-28.3 that is valued at $1,500 or less may be sold after ninety days

74. *Id.* § 20-28.3(e3).
75. *Id.* § 20-28.2(a1)(3).
76. *Id.* §§ 20-28.3(e3)(1)a.–e.
77. *Id.* § 20-28.3(e3)(2).
78. *Id.* A lienholder who refuses to transfer possession of a seized motor vehicle to the defendant, to the motor vehicle owner, or to someone acting on behalf of the defendant or owner is not liable for damages arising out of that refusal.
79. *Id.* § 20-28.3(i).

from the date it was seized.[80] In addition, a seized motor vehicle may be sold any time outstanding towing and storage costs exceed 85 percent of the vehicle's fair market value.[81] Such a vehicle also may be sold with the consent of all the motor vehicle owners.[82] The sale must be conducted in accordance with the forfeiture sale provisions of G.S. 20-28.5(a), which are discussed below in the section on sale and proceeds.[83]

The motor vehicle may not be sold, given, or otherwise transferred at the sale to the defendant, to the motor vehicle owner who owned the motor vehicle immediately prior to sale, or to any person acting on the defendant's or motor vehicle owner's behalf.[84] Proceeds of the sale, after the payment of outstanding towing and storage costs or reimbursement of towing and storage costs paid by a person other than the defendant, must be deposited with the clerk of superior court. When (as is typically the case) there are no net proceeds, this is the end of the process, and no forfeiture order is entered. When an order of forfeiture is entered by the court, the court must order the proceeds held by the clerk to be disbursed as provided in G.S. 20-28.5(b).[85] The provisions of that statute are discussed below in the section on sale and proceeds.

A. Sentencing

1. Restitution

If the driver of a motor vehicle seized pursuant to G.S. 20-28.3 is convicted of the underlying offense resulting in the seizure, the defendant must be ordered to pay as restitution the cost paid or owing for the towing, storage, and sale of the motor vehicle to the extent the costs were not covered by the proceeds from the forfeiture and sale of the motor vehicle.[86] A clerk of court must docket a civil judgment for the costs in favor of the party to whom the restitution is owed.[87] If the defendant is sentenced to an active term of imprisonment, the civil judgment becomes effective and must be docketed when the defendant's conviction becomes final.[88] If the defendant is placed on probation and does not pay the restitution, the clerk must docket a civil judgment in the amount found by the judge during a probation revocation or termination hearing.[89]

2. Registration Forfeiture

When NC DMV is notified that a person has been convicted of an offense involving impaired driving while the person's license is revoked for a prior impaired driving license revocation, NC DMV must revoke the registration of all motor vehicles registered in the convicted person's name.[90] NC DMV must not register a motor vehicle in the convicted person's name until the convicted person's license is restored, except as necessary to abide by the ignition interlock installation requirements in

80. *Id.*
81. *Id.*
82. *Id.*
83. *Id.*
84. *Id.* § 20-28.5(a).
85. *Id.* § 20-28.3(i).
86. *Id.* § 20-28.3(l).
87. *Id.*
88. *Id.*
89. *Id.*
90. *Id.* § 20-54.1(a).

G.S. 20-17.8.[91] When the defendant receives notice from NC DMV that his or her registrations are being revoked, the defendant must surrender the registrations to NC DMV within ten days.[92]

NC DMV also must revoke the registration of a vehicle seized pursuant to G.S. 20-28.3 if the defendant is convicted of an offense involving impaired driving while the person's license was revoked for a prior impaired driving license revocation.[93] The owner must not be allowed to register the seized motor vehicle until the convicted operator's license is restored.[94] NC DMV may not, however, revoke the registration of the owner of a seized motor vehicle if the owner is determined to be an innocent owner as that term is defined in G.S. 20-28.2.[95] The owner must be given an opportunity for a hearing to prove that he or she is an innocent owner (see section IV.B, above, for further discussion of this topic).[96] An owner who receives a notice of registration revocation from NC DMV must surrender the registration within ten days of the date of the notice.[97]

VI. Forfeiture

A. Trial Priority

To expedite the determination of whether a motor vehicle seized pursuant to G.S. 20-28.3 is subject to forfeiture, G.S. 20-28.3(m) requires that district court trials of impaired driving offenses involving forfeiture of motor vehicles be scheduled on the arresting officer's next court date or within thirty days of the offense, whichever comes first.

The provision goes on to state that once scheduled, the case must not be continued unless the following conditions are met: (1) a written motion for a continuance is filed with notice given to the opposing party before the motion is heard; (2) the judge makes a finding of a compelling reason for the continuance; and (3) the motion and finding are attached to the court case record.[98]

The trial priority provisions frequently are not followed in practice. Typically, this occurs because the case either is calendared for trial more than thirty days after the offense or, at the first setting, the defendant moves orally for a continuance. While no remedy for such a violation is prescribed by statute, defendants occasionally move to dismiss the underlying criminal charges on the basis that the failure to comply with the trial priority provisions in G.S. 20-28.3(m) warrants such relief. No statute or case so provides, however, and providing relief in the criminal case seems inconsistent with the purpose of this provision, which appears to have been designed to ensure that the owner of a motor vehicle subject to forfeiture receives a prompt determination of that issue and that towing and storage fees do not exceed the value of the vehicle. Moreover, when the defendant seeks a continuance and fails to comply with the statutory requirements, it seems particularly inequitable to allow the defendant to benefit from his or her own statutory violation.

---

91. *Id.*
92. *Id.*
93. *Id.* § 20-54.1(b).
94. *Id.*
95. *Id.*
96. *Id.*
97. *Id.*
98. *Id.* § 20-28.3.

B. Forfeiture Hearing

Unless a motor vehicle that has been seized pursuant to G.S. 20-28.3 has been permanently released to an innocent owner pursuant to G.S. 20-28.3(e1), to a defendant owner pursuant to G.S. 20-28.3(e2), or to a lienholder pursuant to G.S. 20-28.3(e3), the trial court presiding over the defendant's criminal case must conduct a hearing on the forfeiture of the motor vehicle.[99]

The hearing may be held at the sentencing hearing on the underlying offense involving impaired driving, at a separate hearing after the defendant's conviction, or at a separate forfeiture hearing held not less than sixty days after the defendant failed to appear at the scheduled trial for the underlying offense and the order for the defendant's arrest for failing to appear has not been set aside.[100]

Before a forfeiture determination is made by a judge, the prosecutor must notify the defendant, each motor vehicle owner, and each lienholder that the motor vehicle may be subject to forfeiture and that the defendant, the motor vehicle owner, or the lienholder may intervene to protect his or her interest.[101] The notice may be served by any means reasonably likely to provide actual notice and must be served ten days before the hearing at which an order of forfeiture may be entered.[102] If a judge determines that a motor vehicle is subject to forfeiture but adequate notice has not been given, the judge must continue the forfeiture proceeding until adequate notice is provided. The sentencing of the defendant may not, however, be delayed as a result of the prosecutor's failure to give adequate notice.[103]

A motor vehicle is subject to forfeiture if the greater weight of the evidence shows that the defendant is guilty of an offense involving impaired driving and (a) the defendant's license was revoked for an impaired driving revocation or (b) the defendant was driving without a valid driver's license and was not covered by an automobile liability policy.[104]

If at the forfeiture hearing the judge determines that the motor vehicle is subject to forfeiture pursuant to G.S. 20-28.2 and proper notice of the hearing has been given, the judge must order that the motor vehicle be forfeited unless another motor vehicle owner establishes, by the greater weight of the evidence, that such motor vehicle owner is an innocent owner as that term is defined in G.S. 20-28.2.[105] In that case, rather than ordering that the motor vehicle be forfeited, the judge must order that the motor vehicle be released to the innocent owner. If the motor vehicle is ordered forfeited, the judge must

- authorize the sale of the motor vehicle at a public sale or allow the county board of education to retain the vehicle for its own use, both pursuant to G.S. 20-28.5, or order the vehicle released to a lienholder pursuant to G.S. 20-28.2(f); and
- order any proceeds of sale or insurance proceeds held by the clerk to be disbursed to the county board of education as well as order any outstanding insurance claims to be assigned to the county board of education in the event the motor vehicle has been damaged in an accident incident to its seizure.

---

99. *Id.* § 20-28.2(d). An exception also applies when the motor vehicle already has been sold pursuant to the expedited sales provision in G.S. 20-28.3(i) and there are no proceeds deposited with the clerk.

100. *Id.* § 20-28.2(d); *see also id.* §§ 20-28.2(b), (b1).

101. *Id.* § 20-28.2(c).

102. *Id.*

103. *Id.* § 20-28.2(d).

104. *Id.* §§ 20-28.2(b), (b1). The clerk must electronically report to NC DMV the entry of an order of forfeiture. *Id.* § 20-28.8.

105. *Id.* § 20-28.2(d).

1. Release to Innocent Motor Vehicle Owner

At a forfeiture hearing, if a non-defendant motor vehicle owner establishes by the greater weight of the evidence that the motor vehicle was being driven by a person who was not the only motor vehicle owner or who had no ownership interest in the motor vehicle at the time of the underlying offense, and if the petitioner is an innocent owner as that term is defined by G.S. 20-28.2, the judge must order the motor vehicle released to that owner, conditioned upon payment of all towing and storage charges.[106]

A vehicle may be released to an innocent owner only upon satisfactory proof that the person is the motor vehicle owner and that the person has the financial responsibility required by law. The person also must execute an acknowledgment of the type set forth in G.S. 20-28.2(a1)(1a) and discussed above in the section describing pretrial release to an innocent owner.[107]

If the non-defendant owner is a lessor, the release also shall be conditioned upon the lessor agreeing not to sell, give, or otherwise transfer possession of the forfeited motor vehicle to the defendant or to any person acting on the defendant's behalf.[108]

No motor vehicle may be released to a non-defendant motor vehicle owner if NC DMV records show that the owner previously signed an acknowledgment pursuant to G.S. 20-28.2 and if the same person was operating the motor vehicle while that person's license was revoked, unless the motor vehicle owner shows by the greater weight of the evidence that he or she has taken all reasonable precautions to prevent this person from using the motor vehicle. The motor vehicle owner also must have immediately reported any unauthorized use of the motor vehicle to the appropriate law enforcement agency.[109]

A determination by the court at the forfeiture hearing that the petitioner is not an innocent owner is a final judgment and is immediately appealable to the court of appeals.[110] When a defendant appeals his or her criminal conviction in district court to superior court, the issue of forfeiture is, under statute, determined in the superior court de novo.[111] That provision apparently would entitle the owner of a motor vehicle to raise again the issue of innocence in superior court, although it is inconsistent with the provision in G.S. 20-28.2(e) allowing a determination that the owner is not entitled to release to be appealed to the court of appeals. Perhaps these statutes afford the owner a choice, in cases in which the defendant appeals his or her conviction to superior court, as to whether to contest the matter in superior court or before the court of appeals.

2. Release to Lienholder

At a forfeiture hearing, the trial judge must order a forfeited motor vehicle released to the lienholder upon payment of all towing and storage charges incurred as a result of the seizure of the motor vehicle if the judge determines, by the greater weight of the evidence, that all of the following conditions are present/satisfied:

1. The lienholder's interest has been perfected and appears on the title to the forfeited motor vehicle.

---

106. *Id.* § 20-28.2(e).

107. *Id.*; see *supra* section IV.B.

108. G.S. 20-28.2(e). A lessor who refuses to sell, give, or transfer possession of a seized motor vehicle to the defendant or to any person acting on the defendant's behalf is not liable for damages arising out of the refusal. *Id.*

109. *Id.*

110. *Id.*

111. *Id.* § 20-28.5(e).

2. The lienholder agrees not to sell, give, or otherwise transfer possession of the forfeited motor vehicle to the defendant, to the motor vehicle owner who owned the motor vehicle immediately prior to forfeiture, or to any person acting on the defendant's or owner's behalf.
3. The forfeited motor vehicle has not previously been released to the lienholder.
4. The owner is in default under the terms of the security instrument evidencing the interest of the lienholder and, as a consequence of the default, the lienholder is entitled to possession of the motor vehicle.
5. The lienholder agrees to sell the motor vehicle in accordance with the terms of its agreement and pursuant to the State's laws on secured transactions.[112]

Upon sale of the motor vehicle, the lienholder must pay to the clerk of court in the county in which the vehicle was forfeited all proceeds from the sale, less the amount of the lien in favor of the lienholder, and any towing and storage costs paid by the lienholder.[113]

A lienholder who refuses to sell, give, or transfer possession of a forfeited motor vehicle to the defendant, to the vehicle owner who owned the vehicle immediately prior to forfeiture, or to any person acting on behalf of the defendant or owner is not liable for damages arising out of that refusal. The defendant, the motor vehicle owner who owned the motor vehicle immediately prior to forfeiture, and any person acting on the defendant's or owner's behalf are prohibited from purchasing the motor vehicle at any sale conducted by the lienholder.

3. Towing and Storage Charges

Any order issued pursuant to G.S. 20-28.2 that authorizes the release of a seized motor vehicle must require the payment of towing and storage charges incurred as a result of the seizure and impoundment.[114] Indeed, G.S. 20-28.2(h) specifies that this requirement "shall not be waived." The requirement that towing and storage charges be paid before a seized motor vehicle may be released to any party is a consistent refrain throughout the entire statutory seizure scheme. Innocent owners must pay such fees,[115] as must lienholders[116] and defendants,[117] even those acquitted at a criminal trial.[118]

4. Release of Impounded Motor Vehicles

In certain circumstances, a judge must order that a seized motor vehicle or its insurance proceeds be released to the motor vehicle owner, conditioned upon payment of towing and storage charges. Such an order is required when the driver of a motor vehicle seized pursuant to G.S. 20-28.3 is acquitted of impaired driving charges or when the charges are dismissed and the motor vehicle has not previously been released to a lienholder pursuant to the provisions of G.S. 20-28.3(e3).[119] An order releasing the motor vehicle also is required if the judge at a forfeiture hearing fails to find that the person's driver's license was revoked as the result of a prior impaired driving license revocation or that the defendant was driving without a license and/or insurance, again if the vehicle has not previously been released to a lienholder pursuant to G.S. 20-28.3. As with all releases, this release too must be conditioned

---

112. *Id.* § 20-28.2(f).
113. *Id.*
114. *Id.* § 20-28.2(h).
115. *Id.* § 20-28.2(e); 20-28.3(e1).
116. *Id.* § 20-28.2(f); 20-28.3(e3)(2).
117. *Id.* § 20-28.3(e2).
118. *Id.* § 20-28.4(a).
119. *Id.*

upon payment of towing and storage charges. The court must include in any release order notice to the owner that he or she must pay the outstanding towing and storage costs within thirty days or give notice to NC DMV requesting a judicial hearing on the validity of the lien for towing and storage costs.[120]

If the owner of the motor vehicle does not obtain release of the vehicle within thirty days from the date of the court's order, the possessor of the seized motor vehicle has a mechanics' lien on the motor vehicle for the full amount of the towing and storage charges incurred since the motor vehicle was seized.[121] The possessor may dispose of the vehicle pursuant to Article 1 of G.S. Chapter 44A, which sets forth the procedures for enforcing possessory liens on personal property.

VII. Sale and Proceeds

A. Sale

A motor vehicle ordered to be forfeited and sold or a seized motor vehicle authorized to be sold pursuant to the expedited sales provisions in G.S. 20-28.3(i) must be sold at a public sale conducted by the county board of education or by someone acting on its behalf.[122] Notice of sale, including the date, time, location, and manner of sale, must be given by first-class mail to all owners of the motor vehicle to be sold at the address(es) contained in NC DMV records. Written notice of sale also must be given to all lienholders on file with NC DMV. Notice of sale must be given to NC DMV in accordance with procedures established by NC DMV. Notices must be mailed at least ten days before the date of sale. A lienholder may purchase the motor vehicle at any such sale by bidding in the amount of its lien, if that is the highest bid, without being required to tender any additional funds other than towing and storage fees. The county board of education or its agent may not sell, give, or otherwise transfer possession of the forfeited motor vehicle to the defendant, to the motor vehicle owner who owned the motor vehicle immediately prior to forfeiture, or to any person acting on the defendant's or owner's behalf.

B. Sale Proceeds

Proceeds of any sale conducted under G.S. 20-28.5, 20-28.2(f)(5), or 20-28.3(e3)(3) must first be applied to the cost of sale and then to the payment of towing and storage costs.[123] The balance of the proceeds then must be used to satisfy any other existing liens of record that were properly recorded before the date the motor vehicle was seized. Any remaining balance is paid to the county school fund in the county in which the motor vehicle was ordered forfeited. If there is more than one school board in the county, then the net proceeds of sale, after reimbursement to the county board of education of reasonable administrative costs incurred in connection with the forfeiture and sale of motor vehicles, must be distributed in the same manner as other fines and forfeitures. The sale of a motor vehicle pursuant to G.S. 20-28.5 extinguishes all existing liens on the motor vehicle.

---

120. *Id.*

121. *Id.* § 20-28.4(b).

122. *Id.* § 20-28.5(a). The sale must be conducted in accordance with the provisions of Article 12 of G.S. Chapter 160A, applicable to sales authorized pursuant to G.S. 160A-266(a)(2), (3), or (4), subject to the notice requirements of G.S. 20-28.5. *Id.*

123. *Id.* § 20-28.5(b).

A county board of education may retain a forfeited motor vehicle for its use upon payment of towing and storage costs.[124] If the motor vehicle is so retained, any valid lien of record at the time of the initial seizure must be satisfied by the county board, thus relieving the motor vehicle owner of liability for the obligation secured by the motor vehicle.[125] If there is more than one school board in the county and the motor vehicle is retained by one of them, then the fair market value of the motor vehicle, less the costs for towing, storage, reasonable administrative costs, and liens paid, shall be used to determine and pay the share due to the other school boards.[126] It is unclear what procedures should be followed if both school boards in the county wish to retain the motor vehicle.

C. Appeals

Orders of forfeiture are stayed pending appeal of a conviction for an offense that is the basis for the forfeiture order.[127] When the conviction for such an underlying offense is appealed from district court, the issue of forfeiture must be heard in superior court de novo.[128] A final order of forfeiture may be appealed to the court of appeals.[129]

A vehicle owner may apply for temporary pretrial release of a vehicle in a case appealed to the superior court from the district court once the case is in superior court. If the owner posted a bond in district court for release of the vehicle, the bond continues in effect in superior court.[130]

---

124. *Id.* § 20-28.5(c).
125. *Id.*
126. *Id.*
127. *Id.* § 20-28.5(e).
128. *Id.* When the owner is not the defendant, the owner's appeal rights from the district court appear to depend upon whether the defendant appeals the conviction.
129. *Id.*
130. *Id.* § 20-28.5(e).

Chapter 8

Collateral Estoppel and *Corpus Delicti*

Chapter 8

Collateral Estoppel and *Corpus Delicti*

I. Collateral Estoppel

The legal doctrine of collateral estoppel—or issue preclusion—precludes the relitigation of an issue decided previously in a judicial or administrative proceeding so long as the party against whom the prior decision is asserted had a full and fair opportunity to litigate the issue in the earlier proceeding.[1] The purpose of the doctrine is to prevent repetitious lawsuits over matters already decided that have "remained substantially static, factually and legally."[2] North Carolina's Supreme Court has explained that "[w]hen a fact has been agreed upon or decided in a court of record, neither of the parties shall be allowed to call it in question, and have it tried over again at any time thereafter, so long as the judgment or decree stands unreversed."[3]

For collateral estoppel to bar reconsideration of an issue, the issue must

- be the same as that involved in a previous action,
- have been raised and actually litigated in the previous action, and
- have been material and relevant to the disposition of the earlier action.

Also, the determination of the issue must have been necessary and essential to the resulting judgment.[4]

Furthermore, the parties in the earlier action must have been identical to or in privity with the parties in the instant action.[5] "Privity exists when one party is so identified in interest with another that [it] represents the same legal right [as the other]" party[6] and requires that the party against whom the bar is asserted have been "fully protected" in the earlier proceeding.[7] Finally, the doctrine does not apply when the burden of proof in the earlier action was higher than that required to prove the current case.[8]

---

1. Rymer v. Estate of Sorrells, 127 N.C. App. 266, 268 (1997).
2. State v. Summers, 351 N.C. 620, 623 (2000) (citations, internal quotation marks omitted).
3. King v. Grindstaff, 284 N.C. 348, 355 (1973) (citations, internal quotation marks omitted).
4. *Summers*, 351 N.C. at 623.
5. *Id.* at 622. Note that in *Thomas M. McInnis & Associates, Inc. v. Hall*, 318 N.C. 421, 432, 432–34 (1986), the North Carolina Supreme Court embraced the "modern trend . . . to abandon the requirement of mutuality [of parties]" in cases of defensive collateral estoppel where the party to be estopped "had a full and fair opportunity to litigate the issue in the earlier action."
6. Brower v. Killens, 122 N.C. App. 685, 687 (1996) (citations, internal quotation marks omitted).
7. *Id.*
8. Powers v. Tatum, 196 N.C. App. 639 (2009).

The bar of collateral estoppel is raised in implied consent cases when an issue necessary to the determination of a defendant's guilt also is an issue necessary to the determination of whether a defendant's license is subject to revocation, and when the issue has been decided in one of those forums. Whether a defendant refused a chemical analysis[9] is the most common of these issues. Chemical analysts make the initial judgment as to whether a person has deliberately refused testing.[10] Their determinations later may be reviewed by a magistrate at a civil revocation hearing,[11] by a hearing officer for the North Carolina Division of Motor Vehicles (NC DMV) conducting license-revocation hearings,[12] or by the superior court considering an appeal from an NC DMV revocation order.[13] Chemical analysts' conclusions also may be reviewed by trial courts at the district and superior levels to determine whether evidence of a refusal is admissible at trial[14] and, in superior court, to decide how to properly instruct a jury to consider such refusals. The issue of whether a law enforcement officer had probable cause to arrest a defendant also arises in both license revocation proceedings[15] and criminal trials.[16] In certain circumstances, the determination of these types of issues in one forum precludes its subsequent consideration in another.

A. Prior Ruling Bars Reconsideration

North Carolina's courts have determined that a prior ruling on an issue central to both the revocation of a defendant's driver's license as well as his or her prosecution on implied consent charges precludes later reconsideration of that issue in another forum. Below are some examples.

- When a superior court determines, pursuant to an appeal under Section 20-16.2(e) of the North Carolina General Statutes (hereinafter G.S.) from an NC DMV–issued refusal revocation, that a defendant did not willfully refuse a chemical analysis, the issue of refusal may not later be relitigated in the defendant's criminal trial.[17]
- When a trial court suppresses evidence for lack of probable cause to arrest, NC DMV may not reconsider, in an administrative revocation hearing conducted after final judgment in the criminal case, whether reasonable grounds existed for the impaired driving charge.[18] Because one of the requirements for a license revocation under G.S. 20-16.2(d) based on a defendant's refusal to submit to chemical testing is that the officer had reasonable grounds to charge the person, NC DMV may not issue a refusal revocation in these circumstances.

---

9. The considerations for determining whether a suspect has refused a chemical analysis are discussed in chapters 1 and 7.
10. Section 20-16.2(c1) of the North Carolina General Statutes (hereinafter G.S.).
11. G.S. 20-16.5(e).
12. *Id.* § 20-16.2(d).
13. *Id.* § 20-16.2(e).
14. *Id.* § 20-139.1(f).
15. *Id.* § 20-16.2(d).
16. U.S. CONST. amend. IV; G.S. 15A-974(a)(1).
17. State v. Summers, 351 N.C. 620 (2000) (decided under former version of G.S. 20-16.2(e), which provided for de novo review of revocation order in superior court; current G.S. 20-16.2(e) provides for more limited review).
18. *See* Brower v. Killens, 122 N.C. App. 685 (1996).

B. No Collateral Estoppel Bar

North Carolina's appellate courts have determined in the following circumstances that an earlier ruling on an issue in an implied consent case does not preclude its subsequent reconsideration in a different forum.

- When a trial court determines in a criminal proceeding that the defendant's statutory implied consent rights were violated, NC DMV may nevertheless consider in a subsequent administrative revocation hearing whether the defendant willfully refused a chemical analysis.[19]
- When NC DMV administratively determines that the defendant did not willfully refuse a chemical analysis, the trial court may reconsider that issue for purposes of the criminal trial.[20] The rationale for the court's conclusion that collateral estoppel does not apply in this circumstance is that even though NC DMV and the district attorney both represent the interests of the State, the interests of the district attorney are not adequately protected in an administrative license revocation proceeding.[21]
- A defendant's acquittal on implied consent charges does not estop NC DMV from revoking his or her license based on a willful refusal to submit to a chemical analysis.[22] The State must prove that a law enforcement officer had probable cause to believe that a person committed an implied consent offense before the person's license may be revoked for refusing to submit to a chemical analysis. The probable cause standard differs from the beyond a reasonable doubt standard necessary to convict the defendant of the implied consent offense with which he or she was charged. A verdict of not guilty indicates that the finder of fact concluded that the State did not meet the latter—and higher—burden. The criminal verdict does not, however, bar the State from demonstrating that a law enforcement officer had probable cause to believe the suspect committed an implied consent offense.
- A district court's determination as to whether a defendant refused a chemical analysis does not bar reconsideration of that issue by the superior court upon trial de novo.[23] This is so because a trial de novo in superior court "is a new trial from beginning to end, on both law and facts, disregarding completely the plea, trial, verdict and judgment below."[24]
- A superior court retrying a defendant following a mistrial in superior court is not bound by the earlier court's ruling on the refusal issue.[25]

---

19. Powers v. Tatum, 196 N.C. App. 639, 644 (2009) (finding that, having determined that the defendant's right to have a witness observe the testing had been violated, "the district court never reached the issue of willful refusal"; thus, the issue of willful refusal was not litigated by the parties or determined in the criminal proceeding).

20. *Brower*, 122 N.C. App. 685.

21. *Id.*

22. Gibson v. Faulkner, 132 N.C. App. 728 (1999).

23. State v. Petty, 212 N.C. App. 368, 371 (2011) (citation omitted).

24. *Id.* at 371 (citation, internal quotation marks omitted); *cf.* G.S. 15A-953 ("no motion in superior court is prejudiced by any ruling upon . . . the subject in district court").

25. State v. Macon, ___ N.C. App. ___, ___, 741 S.E.2d 688, 692 (2013). In *Macon*, the superior court in the defendant's first trial refused to instruct the jury that the defendant's refusal could be considered as evidence of her guilt, based upon the judge's determination that the instruction was not supported by the evidence. A mistrial was declared when the jury could not reach a verdict. The defendant was retried before a different superior court judge. The judge in the later trial determined that the refusal instruction was warranted and delivered it to the jury, which found the defendant guilty of impaired driving. The court of appeals held that on retrial de novo, the judge was not bound by jury instruction rulings made during the first trial.

C. Open Questions

One issue not clearly addressed by North Carolina's appellate courts is whether a superior court's ruling pursuant to G.S. 20-16.2(e) that the NC DMV did not err in revoking the person's license for a willful refusal precludes a defendant from litigating the issue of refus
al in his or her subsequent criminal trial.[26]

The effect on a defendant's subsequent criminal trial of a ruling by NC DMV that a person willfully refused that is not appealed to superior court also is unclear. While the parties arguably are the same, and the issue appears to be the same, it is unclear whether collateral estoppel would bar a defendant from relitigating in a criminal trial an issue finally resolved by an administrative agency.[27]

II. *Corpus Delicti*

The rule requiring proof of the *corpus delicti*, literally translated as "body of the crime,"[28] to establish a defendant's guilt essentially is a rule of corroboration. In its traditional formulation, the rule requires that there be some evidence other than a defendant's out-of-court confession that tends to establish that a crime occurred.[29] Proof of the body of the crime is evidence both that the injury or harm constituting the crime occurred and that the injury or harm was caused by someone's criminal activity.[30] Thus, to prove homicide, the State must prove both that a person died and that the death was caused by criminal activity.[31] The principal purpose of the rule is to ensure that a defendant will not "be convicted of a crime that has not been committed."[32] The extent of the corroboration and proof required varies among jurisdictions.

The North Carolina Supreme Court held in *State v. Parker*[33] that, in non-capital cases, when the State relies upon a defendant's confession to obtain a conviction, there is no requirement that there be independent proof tending to establish the *corpus delicti* of the crime charged if the confession is supported by substantial independent evidence to establish its trustworthiness, "including facts that

---

26. The parties are the same, and the issues and standards appear to be the same, so arguably the collateral estoppel bar would apply. *But see* Powers v. Tatum, 196 N.C. App. 639, 644–45 (2009) (suggesting in dicta that the State was required to prove a refusal in a criminal trial beyond a reasonable doubt, a standard that, if applied, obviously differs from the preponderance of the evidence standard applicable in the civil context). There is some question, however, about the State's ability to bar a defendant from presenting evidence in his or her defense based upon a finding in a civil or administrative proceeding. *Cf.* State v. Cornelius, 219 N.C. App. 329 (2012) (concluding that collateral estoppel applied to bar defendant from retrying in second felony murder trial the issue of whether the defendant committed the underlying felony when a jury previously had found the defendant guilty of that felony).

27. *Cf.* Rymer v. Estate of Sorrells, 127 N.C. App. 266, 270–71 (1997) (noting that two considerations in determining whether to allow offensive use of collateral estoppel by a plaintiff in a civil action are whether the defendant had an incentive to vigorously defend in the earlier action and whether the second action affords the defendant procedural opportunities that were not available in the first action that could readily cause a different result; concluding that the trial court abused its discretion by allowing the plaintiff to offensively use collateral estoppel in the instant case).

28. 1 Kenneth S. Broun et al., McCormick on Evidence 809 (7th ed. 2013) (hereinafter McCormick).

29. *Id.*

30. State v. Parker, 315 N.C. 222, 231 (1985).

31. McCormick at 810.

32. *Parker*, 315 N.C. at 235.

33. *Id.*

tend to show the defendant had the opportunity to commit the crime."[34] "[W]hen independent proof of loss or injury is lacking, there must be *strong* corroboration of *essential* facts and circumstances" in the confession to support a defendant's conviction.[35] Corroboration of insignificant facts or of facts unrelated to the commission of the crime is insufficient.[36]

The rule of *corpus delicti* arises in connection with implied consent offenses most frequently when the alleged offense results in a single vehicle crash to which there are no witnesses other than the driver. When the State seeks to prove a defendant's guilt based in part on the defendant's admission that he or she was driving at the time of the crash, it sometimes encounters an argument from the defendant that the rule of *corpus delicti* renders the State's evidence insufficient to convict. Typically, the State does not seek to rely solely on the defendant's confession to prove the implied consent offense. Instead, it relies on the confession to prove some element of the alleged crime (for example, driving) and produces independent evidence of the *corpus delicti*—as well as the remaining statutory elements.

North Carolina's appellate courts have applied the *corpus delicti* rule in the following cases involving violations of the motor vehicle laws since *Parker* was decided, concluding in each that the State's evidence was sufficient to survive the defendant's motion to dismiss.

State v. Trexler, 316 N.C. 528 (1986)

The trial court did not err by denying the defendant's motion to dismiss on the basis that the State had failed to prove the *corpus delicti* of impaired driving. The defendant admitted that he wrecked his car a short time after drinking, that he left the scene, and that he returned a short time later. The following independent evidence established the *corpus delicti*: (1) an overturned automobile was lying in the middle of the road and a single person was seen leaving the automobile; (2) when the defendant returned to the scene, he appeared to be impaired as a result of using alcohol; (3) the defendant later blew 0.14 on a breathalyzer; and (4) the wreck was otherwise unexplained.

State v. Brown, 87 N.C. App. 13 (1987)

The defendant's admission in an involuntary manslaughter case that on the night of the accident at the heart of the case he was intoxicated and had consumed too much beer was supported by substantial independent evidence tending to show its trustworthiness. Other evidence established that the defendant was an experienced drinker, and the defendant himself "acknowledged that he drank often, and that he generally did not drink more than eight beers in an evening."[37] Thus, the court concluded that his "admission of intoxication [was] trustworthy and was sufficient evidence" of his impairment to permit the jury to conclude that he was impaired at the time of the crash.[38]

State v. Highsmith, 173 N.C. App. 600 (2005)

The *corpus delicti* rule was not violated where the defendant's admission that he had taken a pain medication called Floricet was corroborated by expert testimony about the effects of this medication and by testimony from a law enforcement officer about the defendant's behavior.

---

34. *Id.* at 236.
35. *Id.* (emphasis in original).
36. *Id.*
37. 87 N.C. App. at 22.
38. *Id.*

State v. Cruz, 173 N.C. App. 689 (2005)

The State sufficiently corroborated the essential facts of the defendant's confession that he was driving in a case in which, "[a]bsent defendant's confession, the circumstantial evidence of defendant's driving would likely not be enough to support a conviction."[39] Several officers and witnesses testified as to the defendant's drinking and impairment. A car similar to the defendant's was seen traveling down the road near an accident involving another car and turning down a side street, just as the defendant confessed to doing. The State also corroborated other aspects of the defendant's confession. The court concluded that under either the traditional or trustworthiness approach to the *corpus delicti* rule, the State offered corroborating evidence that, when considered with the defendant's statements, was sufficient to survive the defendant's motion to dismiss.

State v. Foye, ___ N.C. App. ___, 725 S.E.2d 73 (2012)

The State presented sufficient evidence that the defendant drove while impaired, and the State's reliance on the defendant's admission that he had been driving after leaving a club did not violate the rule of *corpus delicti*. In addition to the defendant's admission that he drove the vehicle that an officer discovered in a ditch, the State introduced evidence that the vehicle was registered to the defendant, the defendant was found walking on a road near the scene of the accident, the defendant had injuries consistent with someone who had been in a wreck, and the defendant was impaired based on the results of a blood test administered approximately two and a half hours after the accident.

State v. Morvay, ___ N.C. App. ___, 731 S.E.2d 276, No. COA12-118, 2012 WL 3573707 (Aug. 21, 2012) (unpublished, not paginated for S.E.2d)

The State presented sufficient evidence that the defendant was the driver of the vehicle at issue in the case. Strong corroboration of the defendant's confession was not required by the *corpus delicti* rule where the State "presented substantial independent evidence" that the defendant was the driver.[40] The State's evidence showed that (1) the defendant was at the scene of the accident and was the only person located near the vehicle and (2) the driver's side door was open and the defendant was placed on a gurney touching the driver's side of the vehicle.

***In re* A.N.C., Jr., ___ N.C. App. ___, 750 S.E.2d 835 (2013)**

The State presented sufficient evidence in this juvenile delinquency case to support a determination that the juvenile operated a motor vehicle without being properly licensed to do so. In addition to the juvenile's admission that he drove the wrecked vehicle, the law enforcement officer who arrived at the scene testified that the motor vehicle was still warm. Moreover, the juvenile and his friends were the only people in the vicinity of the accident scene when the officer arrived, and the vehicle was registered to the juvenile's mother.

---

39. 173 N.C. App. at 696–97.
40. 2012 WL 3573707, at *4.

Subject Index

B

C

I

J

L

M

W

Z

Case Index

K

L

M

N

O

P

R

S

T

U

V

W

Y

Table of Statutes

North Carolina General Statutes

North Carolina Session Laws

North Carolina Administrative Code

Federal Statutes

United States Code

www.ingramcontent.com/pod-product-compliance
Lightning Source LLC
Chambersburg PA
CBHW082102270226
40386CB00024B/394